ANTICLERICALISM IN BRITAIN

c. 1500–1914

ANTICLERICALISM IN BRITAIN

c. 1500–1914

EDITED BY
NIGEL ASTON & MATTHEW CRAGOE

SUTTON PUBLISHING

First published in the United Kingdom in 2000 by
Sutton Publishing Limited · Phoenix Mill
Thrupp · Stroud · Gloucestershire · GL5 2BU

This paperback edition first published in 2001.

British Library Cataloguing in Publication Data
A catalogue record for this book is available from the British Library

ISBN 0-7509-2205-2 (HB)
    0-7509-2206-0 (PB)

Typeset in 10/12pt Baskerville MT.
Typesetting and origination by
Sutton Publishing Limited.
Printed and bound in England by
J.H. Haynes & Co. Ltd, Sparkford.

CONTENTS

LIST OF CONTRIBUTORS   vii

ACKNOWLEDGEMENTS   ix

FOREWORD by *Professor Keith Robbins*   xi

INTRODUCTION by *Nigel Aston and Matthew Cragoe*   xiii

1. *David Loades*
ANTICLERICALISM IN THE CHURCH OF ENGLAND BEFORE 1558:
AN 'EATING CANKER'?   1

2. *Christopher Haigh*
ANTICLERICALISM AND CLERICALISM, 1580–1640   18

3. *J.A.I. Champion*
'TO GOVERN IS TO MAKE SUBJECTS BELIEVE': ANTICLERICALISM,
POLITICS AND POWER, *c.* 1680–1717   42

4. *James E. Bradley*
ANTI-CATHOLICISM AS ANGLICAN ANTICLERICALISM:
NONCONFORMITY AND THE IDEOLOGICAL ORIGINS OF RADICAL
DISAFFECTION   67

5. *G.M. Ditchfield*
THE CHANGING NATURE OF ENGLISH ANTICLERICALISM,
c. 1750–*c.* 1800   93

6. *Nigel Aston*
ANGLICAN RESPONSES TO ANTICLERICALISM IN THE 'LONG'
EIGHTEENTH CENTURY, *c.* 1689–1830   115

7. *Callum G. Brown*
ROTAVATING THE KAILYARD: RE-IMAGINING THE SCOTTISH
'MEENISTER' IN DISCOURSE AND THE PARISH STATE SINCE 1707   138

8. *Frances Knight*
DID ANTICLERICALISM EXIST IN THE ENGLISH COUNTRYSIDE IN
THE EARLY NINETEENTH CENTURY? 159

9. *Matthew Cragoe*
ANTICLERICALISM AND POLITICS IN MID-VICTORIAN WALES 179

10. *Hugh McLeod*
VARIETIES OF ANTICLERICALISM IN LATER VICTORIAN AND
EDWARDIAN ENGLAND 198

INDEX 221

LIST OF CONTRIBUTORS

NIGEL ASTON is Senior Lecturer in History at the University of Luton. His latest publication is *Religion and Revolution in France, 1780–1804* (Macmillan, 2000).

MATTHEW CRAGOE is Senior Lecturer in British History at the University of Hertfordshire. He is the author of *An Anglican Aristocracy. The Moral Economy of the Landed Estate in Carmarthenshire, 1832–95* (Oxford University Press, 1996). He is currently engaged in writing *Culture, Politics and the Rise of National Identity in Wales, 1832–95*.

DAVID LOADES is Professor Emeritus of History at University of Wales, Bangor. He is Honorary Research Professor at the University of Sheffield and Director of the British Academy John Foxe Project. He has published extensively on sixteenth-century topics. Among his most recent books are *John Dudley, Duke of Northumberland, 1504–1553* (Clarendon Press, 1997) and (as editor), *John Foxe and the English Reformation* (Scolar Press, 1997).

CHRISTOPHER HAIGH teaches at Christ Church, University of Oxford, and has research interests in religion and politics in early modern England. His books include *English Reformations: Religion, Politics and Society under the Tudors* (Oxford University Press, 1993) and *Elizabeth I* (Longman, 2nd edn, 1998). He is now writing *The Church of England and its People, 1559–1642*.

J.A.I. CHAMPION teaches at Royal Holloway, University of London. He published an edition of John Toland's *Nazarenus* in 1999 (Voltaire Foundation, Oxford).

JAMES E. BRADLEY is the Geoffrey W. Bromiley Professor of Church History at Fuller Seminary in Pasadena, California, where he has taught for the past twenty-four years. He is the author of *Religion, Revolution, and English Radicalism: Nonconformity in Eighteenth-Century England* (Cambridge University Press, 1990), and he has recently co-edited a book of essays on religion and politics in enlightenment Europe with Dale K. Van Kley (forthcoming).

GRAYSON DITCHFIELD is Reader in Eighteenth-Century History, University of Kent at Canterbury. He is co-editor of *British Parliamentary Lists 1660–1800: A Register* (1995) and author of *The Evangelical Revival* (1998) and many articles on eighteenth-century British history.

CALLUM G. BROWN teaches in the Department of History at the University of Strathclyde. His research interests centre on the social history of religion and his most recent book is *Up-Helly-Aa. Custom, Culture and Community in Scotland* (Mandolin, 1998).

FRANCES KNIGHT is Senior Lecturer in Christian Theology, University of Wales, Lampeter, where she is director of the Master of Theology programme. She has published *The Nineteenth-century Church and English Society* (Cambridge, 1995).

HUGH McLEOD is Professor of Church History, University of Birmingham, and author of *Religion and the People of Western Europe, 1789–1989* (Oxford University Press, 2nd edn, 1997), and *Religion and Society in England, 1850–1914* (Macmillan, 1996).

ACKNOWLEDGEMENTS

Any collection of this sort imposes a variety of obligations upon its editors. Most of the papers were first delivered at the Anglo-American Historians' Conference held at the Institute of Historical Research in July 1996, and we are very grateful both to all those who gave papers, and to Professor Patrick O'Brien and Dr Debra Birch for all their hard work in organising that event. The topic was revisited at a one-day Colloquium, again in London, in the summer of 1999, and the editors would like to express their gratitude both to those contributors who attended, and to Dr Arthur Burns, whose stimulating presence added greatly to the success of the day's proceedings. We are very grateful to Richard Sharp of Worcester College, Oxford, for his advice on the dust-jacket illustration.

The task of collecting the papers for publication was greatly expedited by the care with which all the contributors presented their texts and the alacrity with which they responded to our numerous deadlines! We thank them all. For the publishers, Christopher Feeney was constantly resourceful and helpful, and his skill eased our own editorial duties considerably. Finally, we would like to say a big thank you to our respective spouses, Caroline and Carol, whose support and patience were crucial in seeing us and the volume through to completion.

Nigel Aston and Matthew Cragoe
July 2000

FOREWORD

by

Professor Keith Robbins

In 1839 a considerable crowd assembled at a public meeting in Rochdale to congratulate Queen Victoria on her marriage. The gentleman who had called the meeting proposed that the vicar should take the chair. He was opposed from the floor by a 28-year-old Quaker who strenuously took the view that the meeting should elect its own chairman. It was no longer appropriate to assume that a clergyman should have such a role. Eventually, after much argument, the meeting dissolved in uproar and the dissentients organised their own gathering which concluded with three hearty cheers for the Queen. The young Quaker's name – subsequently to become one of the most well-known in Victorian Britain – was John Bright. A little after this particular episode, he and a colleague 'occupied' the pulpit in the parish church in protest against church rates and then adjourned to the churchyard for a further demonstration. The men of Rochdale, Bright there declared, had to choose between civil and religious liberty on the one hand and the mental thraldom of a hireling state priesthood on the other. He restricted his anticlericalism, however, to verbal onslaughts. It would have been against his principles to do otherwise.

Historians have long been aware, however, that physical violence directed specifically and deliberately against men of the cloth has not been absent from European history. 'Anticlericalism' as a phenomenon has been regularly identified, to a greater or lesser degree, as an important aspect of the cultural politics of modern Europe. Britain, by comparison, has often been supposed to lack such an ingredient and its absence has been seen as a defining element in a British *Sonderweg*. It is this issue which this valuable collection of essays seeks to address. The authors make it plain that 'anticlericalism' has not in fact been absent from the communities of Britain. Spanning both time and space, their contributions come together to make this volume a pioneering exploration of a complex, neglected and important topic. Its publication constitutes a defining moment in the historiography of the subject, though it is not in itself definitive because, for that to be the case, there would need to be certainty of definition. In fact, the editors and authors, from their several standpoints, have all been grappling with what 'anticlericalism' should be taken to be. It becomes clear that it is a shorthand term which embraces a considerable variety of attitudes and opinions. Are clergy the objects of hostility/ridicule because, irrespective of their personal qualities, they are the conspicuous representatives of 'the Church' and as such, in certain contexts, part of an oppressive 'Establishment'? Or, considered personally, are they stigmatised because they are fat, jolly and 'worldly' or because they are emaciated, 'feminine' and ascetic? Is the conflict around 'clericalism' an aspect of an Enlightenment battle to dislodge Christianity from the modern world or is it a struggle within Christianity itself, sometimes between 'laity' and 'clergy', concerning the nature and necessity of 'priesthood'. And these are only some of the issues which are explored in this volume.

It would be misleading to suppose that clear-cut answers emerge. The contributors, however, do take us collectively beyond simplicities. We can no longer say, if we were ever inclined to do so, that Britain is the land without anticlericalism. Nor, however, should we now say that the anticlericalism discerned in these essays means that Britain is 'just like' France after all. Clearly, it was not and is not. Britain did not have that powerful, coherent, politically articulated anti-Christian anticlericalism on the same scale. Although this is an issue which the authors do not directly address, this volume helps to explain why. Context is all and we need to hold together, in any enquiry, the personal and the institutional, and the 'national' and the 'local'. What holds true of attitudes in the case of nineteenth-century Cardiganshire may not even apply in nineteenth-century Pembrokeshire. And there was no one quite like John Bright in the history of nineteenth-century France.

INTRODUCTION

Nigel Aston and Matthew Cragoe

The theme of anticlericalism has long been recognised as being of central importance in European history. No examination of the sixteenth-century French Religious Wars, for example, or the Thirty Years War in Central Europe could ignore the acts of random violence inflicted on individuals simply because they were wearing a cassock or ministerial bands. It has remained important as part of the republican inheritance in both France and Spain, fuelling the periodic drives towards laicisation witnessed from the revolution of 1789 up to the Second World War, and encapsulated in events such as Briand's 1905 law expelling the Religious Orders or, in Spain, the Civil War of 1936–9.[1]

In English history, however, anticlericalism seems to have attracted far less scholarly attention. This is partly because at no point in this period did English anticlericalism exhibit anything like the venom and the resort to violence found on the continent. Even during the Reformation and its aftermath – when, as Christopher Haigh shows, anticlerical comment could be uncompromisingly salty – lay intimidation of the minister, let alone physical assaults on his person, was extremely rare. That may have been because, compared to late Valois France or Germany before the Peace of Westphalia, early modern England (prior to the first Civil War of 1642–6) had no confessional imbalance, and Nonconformist minorities were tiny. In other parts of the British Isles, notably Ireland, violence against one's confessional enemies was more common, and the year 1641 held a place in Protestant commemorations equivalent to 1572 for the French Huguenots. But the Ulster Massacres of 1641 were as much directed against the laity as against Protestant ministers, and thereafter, ascendancy Anglican clergy had little to fear personally from the Catholic majorities in most parishes outside Ulster. They felt more pain from attacks on their tithes, on the one side from rural Catholic malcontents like the Whiteboys, on the other from covetous ascendancy MPs in the Dublin Parliament.

The papers gathered in this volume represent an attempt to rectify this perceived deficiency in British historiography. Its ten chapters are the fruit of a very successful session at the 1996 Anglo-American Historians' Conference held at the Institute of Historical Research in London. The essays focus on the theme of anticlericalism in Great Britain from the Reformation to the First World War, and represent the first attempt to bring sustained scholarly attention within Britain to bear on a topic that has long proved fruitful territory for European historians. The lack of any previous literature on the subject naturally shapes the agenda of this book. The editors and contributors have striven to offer an introduction to anticlericalism across four hundred years of history that will be of interest to both scholars and students alike. The volume is not intended to be a definitive history of anticlericalism in Britain across these four centuries; rather, it is hoped that the essays included here will stimulate further research on a topic that is no less important than it is elusive.

Offering a close definition of anticlericalism is an almost impossible task. The term itself, as Grayson Ditchfield points out, is an early nineteenth-century invention used first on the continent and only subsequently domesticated in British argumentation. Yet the range of circumstances to which it might apply is great, as all the contributions, from David Loades's study of anticlericalism in the Reformation onwards, make clear. The factors fuelling displays of anticlericalism might be theological, political, social, cultural, economic, or any of these in combination, depending on the time or the place. Its spokesmen could be rich or poor, or drawn from some group in between. They might hail from the towns, or acknowledge roots in the countryside, and be English, Welsh, Scottish or Irish – as could those accused of anticlericalism. Nor was anticlericalism confined to conflicts between laymen and clergymen: it often took the form of disputes between two groups of clergymen, sometimes drawn from the same religious body, at other times not. In all these ways, and in many others, anticlericalism defies a simple, one-line definition. Nevertheless the essays contained in this volume do allow us to begin constructing some general overview of the parameters within which anticlericalism might be manifested, and several prevailing features can be noted.

The first point that seems clear is that English anticlericalism, whatever its precise manifestation in any particular circumstance, was essentially moderate. There is certainly nothing in these islands to compare with the state sponsorship of dechristianisation by republican France in the 1790s, or even the Bismarckian *Kulturkampf* of the 1870s, when the new Reich sought to undermine the ministry of Roman Catholic clergy in imperial Germany. Similarly, examples of concerted opposition to a state-supported clergy on grounds of theological principle have been rare in Britain, although as James Bradley makes clear it is unwise to underestimate the importance which, as in the early eighteenth century, this might assume. In a provocative essay focusing on Dissenting writers of that era, he shows clearly how Dissenting polemic, ostensibly aimed at the Catholic Church, was recognised by contemporary Anglicans (as it was fully intended it should be) as a veiled attack on the Established Church. Bradley goes so far as to suggest that the 'backward-looking prejudice common to all Dissenters . . . grounded in an age-old anti-Catholicism', combined with a repeated emphasis on Christ as the sole head of the Church, offers a much more convincing explanation for the civil disaffection of the Dissenters in the reign of George III than that promoted by J.C.D. Clark in his influential *English Society, 1689–1832*, where heterodoxy (described by Bradley as inherently 'modern' and 'forward-looking') plays the leading role.

Nevertheless the extent to which such theoretical denunciations of the clergy made it off the printed page and into the parishes, there to inflame grassroots opinion, is difficult to gauge. While the Dissenters' critiques cited by Bradley may have spurred men to revolutionary action in the American colonies, in England the most their writings seem to have produced is a solid Whig vote among Dissenters. Something similar may be true of mid-Victorian Wales. Here again, print provided an important medium for the dissemination of explicitly anticlerical views. Yet the Church they attacked remained not only physically unmolested (even at times of considerable strife), but its clergymen were generally respected, and parishioners continued, by and large, to pay the taxes demanded by the Establishment, with scant opposition.

Indeed, the essays in this collection suggest that, in general, the Anglican clergyman's status in society was accepted with little argument by most British people, most of the time. While the clergyman was acknowledged to possess an authority derived both from his cloth and from the sanction of the state, the relationship between him and the laity was, as David Loades remarks, 'many-layered', and thus generated a variety of responses, of which overt anticlericalism was only one among many. The lesson of the anticlericalism displayed towards individual clergymen, as Nigel Aston points out, is that when an individual cleric failed to identify himself sufficiently with his flock, he ceased to be an effective pastor, and this was the main source of enmity towards him. But it is important to recognise that the anticlericalism which ensued was focused on the individual, and not on the order of clergymen *per se*.

Many of the characteristic features of the relationship between priests and people in England can be identified from an examination of the British countryside, where the presence of the clergyman seemed part of the necessary (and divinely ordained) ordering of society. Not all rural dwellers might choose to attend his services, but the right of the Anglican clergyman to hold them was denied by none save the most radical and the most eccentric. This is not to imply that there were no tensions in the relationship between many clerics and their parishioners: in the countryside anticlericalism was always a possibility. Smallholders and labourers were acutely vulnerable to harvest yields: a poor year and a hungry family might well intensify resentment over tithe payments, especially the 'small tithe'. Examples of popular hostility to priests who had apparently enriched themselves at the expense of their parishioners by means of enclosure, or who adopted airs and graces and identified themselves strongly with the ruling classes, underlining their pretensions by joining the hunt and assuming a place on the magistrates' bench, were as commonly encountered in the nineteenth as in the seventeenth century.

Yet the way in which clergy and laity rubbed along together, in spite of everything, is well illustrated by Frances Knight's consideration of rural anticlericalism in the first half of the nineteenth century. She contends that too much can be made of the rural anticlericalism manifested in such historiographically celebrated incidents as the Littleport demonstration of 1816 or the Swing Riots of 1830–1. She suggests that Eric Evans, in his seminal essay in *Past & Present* on the subject of English rural anticlericalism, was too ready to construe such incidents as indicating a pervasive feeling of hostility towards the clergy in the countryside.[2] Knight, on the contrary, argues that such incidents were exceptional, and that their real importance lies in the participants' sense of their clergymen's failure to adhere to the high pastoral standards expected of them. Ultimately, the riots underline the fundamental quiescence of the average rural Englishman and the difficulty of breaking the bonds of deference in the countryside; even in times of hardship and distress, it seems, the average person rarely went beyond grumbling in the privacy of his or her own cottage. Something similar would seem to be true in the Welsh countryside, where, as Matthew Cragoe demonstrates, relations between the Nonconformist majority and their Anglican clergymen were, for the most part, remarkably good. Even during social upheavals such as the Rebecca Riots of 1842–3, when many personal scores were settled under the cloak provided by the larger grievance, Anglican clergymen were rarely the targets of popular vengeance.

On the contrary, it was the expanding cities that seem to have offered the more congenial home to anticlericals in nineteenth-century England. The great majority of those thousands of people who supported Richard Carlile, that most extreme critic of the Church and all its doings, were, according to Knight, town dwellers. The theme of urban anticlericalism is pursued by Hugh McLeod. He, too, challenges the orthodoxy set up in the 1970s by Eric Evans, in this case the claim that anticlericalism was in sharp decline after 1840. Not so, argues McLeod, in a ground-breaking essay that lays down a new typology of anticlericalism which will surely have wide application for other students. It may have faltered as a rural phenomenon, but in the metropolis and the great provincial centres of Victorian Britain a whole series of fresh objections to clerical power – whether wielded by Anglican clergymen or Dissenting ministers – were being refined. Conservatives and Liberals alike could feel aggrieved at the way the clergy deployed its moral authority, and were not afraid to say so; newspapers and magazines were also ready to mock clerical lifestyles, and in particular used the perceived effeminacy of young Puseyite clergymen as a scourge against the growth of ritualism in the cities. As McLeod argues, however, urban anticlericalism had more diverse roots than anti-ritualism alone, and remained an important element hindering the relationship of the Church and its parishioners until the First World War.

If, as this implies, the triggers for displays of anticlericalism were often highly localised, it becomes important to recognise the regional variations in its manifestation. Anticlericalism does not appear to have affected all parts of Britain equally. Callum Brown's essay, 'Rotavating the Kailyard', emphasises the extent to which Church of Scotland ministers almost universally retained the trust and affection of their parishioners to a degree which Anglicans south of the border would have envied. The key, as Brown observes, was the way in which the Scottish clergy suffered from the vicissitudes of industrial capitalism to the same extent as did their poorer parishioners:

> In theology, the civil constitution, economics and the discourses of popular culture, the Scottish minister had a significantly less privileged, less segregated and less elevated place in Scottish society than [in] most other countries of Western Europe.

As a consequence, Brown concludes: 'The minister was democratised with his people, his popularity assured.' Much the same, as Frances Knight records, has been suggested elsewhere by Mark Smith as a primary cause of the low levels of anticlericalism discernible in the rapidly industrialising region of Oldham between 1750 and 1850.[3]

Wales, on the face of it, would seem to possess all the right ingredients for the growth of a vigorous native anticlericalism. In the nineteenth-century principality a vigorous Nonconformity (80 per cent of those recorded as attending a place of worship in 1851 were to be found in the chapels) thrived at the expense of the established Anglican Church; the disestablishment of the Church in 1920 seems an almost inevitable conclusion to the unhappy experience of Anglicanism in Wales. Yet was there a genuine populist anticlericalism directed towards the established Church? Matthew Cragoe queries the extent to which one can be found. He finds it a largely rhetorical phenomenon, conjured up by radical propagandists and activists, in the last analysis part of a distinctively Welsh political vocabulary articulated by Liberals coming to prominence in the years around the Second Reform Act of 1867.

Ireland is not treated directly in this book, but again it might be expected that the overwhelming numerical predominance of Catholicism would have called forth a pan-Protestant front, with members of the Church of Ireland and the free Protestant Churches banding together to denounce the activities of the Catholic clergy. Yet, as Nigel Aston's essay demonstrates, the lines of division in eighteenth-century Ireland ran along a different course. The Anglican clergy felt acutely vulnerable to lay elite attempts to hive off tithe, while Protestant Dissenters were so vexed by tithe payments and other establishment privileges that in the revolutionary era many of their leaders made common cause with Catholic radicals in the United Irishmen. It would only be in the nineteenth century, after the 'Second Reformation' of the 1820s, that inter-Protestant sympathies readily crossed denominational lines: the increasingly strident nationalism of the Catholics and the slow surrender of its privileges by the Irish Church between 1833 and 1869 saw anticlericalism within Irish Protestantism apparently tail off.

In the Celtic heartland, therefore, the extent to which anticlericalism was an important factor is played down by the contributors to this volume. National identity or race did, however, have a place in the vocabulary of anticlericalism in England, if nowhere else. As Christopher Haigh demonstrates, those who sought to defame clergymen in English parishes frequently made the obnoxious minister's country of origin part of the 'rhetoric of reproach', making it synonymous with low status and breeding. Thus the incumbent of Towersey in Oxfordshire was damned by one of his parishioners in 1608 as 'jacksauce and Welsh rogue', while a brother clergyman from Ovingham in Northumberland was denounced as a 'false cullion carl and Scottish rogue'. If the Celtic nations were remarkably free of sustained demonstrations of anticlericalism, the distinctive identity they bequeathed their sons might be held against them when they moved across the border to England.

Anticlericalism was therefore a phenomenon that could be found to a greater or lesser extent across all four of Britain's home nations, and in both urban and rural areas. Yet within this general picture, specific triggers are identifiable which explain the incidence of overt displays of anticlericalism. The demands of the clergy for tithe, for example, remained contentious throughout the period under discussion in this volume, especially when, as Dr Haigh shows, they sought to extend that right to cover produce not previously deemed liable to the charge. Even at times when Anglican priests were giving as good as they got in the paper exchanges surrounding their position in society – as, for example, in the 1730s – the very material issue of tithe remained a recurrent source of strained relations between beneficed priest and the average layman in a typically rural parish. Both Haigh and Aston indicate that while the clergy never ceased to defend its right in principle to tithe, in practice it would bend and trim depending on an incumbent's own character and the intensity of pressure coming from his parishioners. That pressure could be quite personal and vitriolic, as one clerical poet, the Revd William Dodd, noted of an imagined complainant in his 'The Parsons. An Eclogue', dating from the early 1760s:

> Yet when the small, the half-demand I made,
> He bullied, swore, and damned the preaching trade;
> All God's good household with irreverence curs'd,
> And me with foul abuse as far the worst![4]

The conscientious among the clergy – and that was probably the majority – appreciated that sensitive pastoral handling might usually prevent grumbling about the priest turning into more intransigent objections in principle to his tithing rights. The relatively small number of major tithe disputes in eighteenth-century England (and those there were tended to be between parson and squire, rather than parson and people) is a testimony to the clergy's success in disarming opposition at grassroots level. Only at times of extreme economic pressure and rapid social change, as in late nineteenth-century Wales, do tithes seem to have had the power to mobilise sustained popular hostility to the clergy.[5]

The involvement of the clergy in politics was another enduring cause of anticlerical feeling. Justin Champion argues that 'the correct ideological behaviour of the priesthood' was an issue that remained 'at the epicentre of national and local politics' in the Glorious Revolution period, when opposition to the pretensions of the clergy was widespread. He shows that there were even many Whiggish lower clergy anxious to define priestly power in a minimalist way, and that it was from this context that the notorious figure of Benjamin Hoadly emerged at the start of George I's reign, arguing for a Church stripped of its sacrality. Since Hoadly was to hold some of the most lucrative bishoprics in England during his long career, he had a pronounced influence on diminishing sacerdotalist tendencies in the Church of England over several decades. The anticlericalism embodied by such figures lay at the root of a number of notable victories for opponents of the Church party, notably the suspension of Convocation, 'the most effective alternative forum for political opposition to the successive Whig ministries of the 1700s'. The current of anticlerical feeling would appear to have still been running strongly a century later, when, as Francis Knight and Hugh McLeod remark, the votes of the bishops in the House of Lords provoked a new and very public wave of anticlerical feeling. The role of the clergy in countries like Wales, where Dissenting ministers were particularly active politicians, remained very controversial right up to the end of the century.

Yet if these examples indicate that flashpoints of anticlerical feeling could occur, the general tenor of public opinion was more generally on the side of the Church, and helped make the political climate unfavourable to its anticlerical opponents. Grayson Ditchfield's contribution indicates the extent to which anticlericalism might be encouraged or retarded by the wider political context. He reveals how those who might be considered part of a loose, Hoadlyan tradition were confronted by the forces making for change towards the close of the century, during the French revolutionary wars. The wars, he suggests, gave the Church of England a last taste of confessional supremacy; anticlericalism was made to appear as just another manifestation of unpatriotic radicalism at a time when national survival against the threat from France could not be assured. Where anticlericalism had been acceptable in 1689 as a central plank of Whig political culture, such was decidedly not the case a century later.

The picture presented by Ditchfield seems to be typical of the general pattern of lay–clerical relations revealed by this book. With some notable exceptions, the relative absence of sustained hostility to the clerical order at the grassroots level, where the interaction between Church and people was at its most intimate, marked the four hundred years covered here. And this was as true at the beginning of the period as at its end. David Loades returns to the clichés of the pre-Reformation era to show beyond contradiction that the average priest was neither 'an evil hypocrite, nor a lascivious bully'. In this, of course, he confirms the picture given most extended recent treatment by Eamon Duffy in his *Stripping of the Altars*.[6] Some individuals might provoke anger by their lax attitudes, as noted earlier, but the Protestant zealots who were quickest to find fault with such clergymen were relatively few in number, and in any case, as Dr Haigh reveals, the conscientious minister might cause as many problems within the parish community as the lax incumbent. As one 'godly preacher' grumbled, parishioners preferred a sociable 'Sir John', who would 'use them kindly for their tithes', 'sit neighbourly with them . . . in the alehouse', 'trouble them not with preaching too often' and, on the regrettable occasions when he did feel the need to sermonise them, 'meddle not too much with their sins'! There was in the end, perhaps, no way out: in Haigh's words, 'The working life of a minister brought unavoidable dispute'; and yet, as Frances Knight remarks, had the 'clerical class' opted for withdrawal from the world around them, they would have been 'severely censured by people of all classes'. Parish-level opinion might be nettled whatever an individual clergyman did, or did not, do.

That some level of anticlericalism would recur repeatedly in the history of the Anglican Church in the British Isles was perhaps inevitable. The Reformation had brought with it the Lutheran doctrine of the priesthood of all believers, something that was not, on the face of it, easy to reconcile with Anglicanism's retention of the Catholic order of bishops, priests and deacons, or the reduced claims to ministerial authority espoused by some of its kindred Churches more centrally within the Reformation tradition. Anglicans who later embraced the Reformation unreservedly always felt that cutting the clergy down to size was part of a Protestant heritage, but their efforts invariably had the effect of disquieting other, more conservative, Catholic elements inside the Church. This basic problem was aggravated by the fact that the clergy were not, as a group, socially static. They experienced slumps and booms in their secular status and wealth, which might profoundly alter their relationship with their parishioners. The increase in clerical magistracy from the early sixteenth century, as Haigh's essay demonstrates, or the thorny issue of enclosure, of which Knight writes, might have a profound impact on both the parishioner's expectations of his or her clergyman, and the clergyman's willingness to gratify them.

If, as a consequence of these two basic variables, anticlericalism as a presence in British history since the Reformation remains frustratingly elusive, some tentative conclusions can be suggested. Perhaps the most important is that British anticlericalism has been as much a secular response as a theological one, and has more to do with one group's hostility towards another group's perceived rapacity and cupidity than with any clearly defined notion of how the world under heaven should be ordered, and what mediation between God and Man it was necessary for the state to provide. Similarly, in the absence of any large-scale and well-organised hostility to the Church of England clergy, it appears that outright opposition remained the preserve of relatively small, vocal groups. David Loades has remarked that the Reformation witnessed 'the strident and genuine anticlericalism of a few Protestant writers and preachers', while Ditchfield's late eighteenth-century writers 'belonged to small coteries of the educated', divorced from any involvement with a 'world of mass political activity'. Matthew Cragoe argues a similar case in respect of mid-Victorian Wales: although there were some among the Nonconformist majority who were genuinely committed to disestablishment and opposed to a state-supported clerical order, their vocal campaigning must not obscure the fact that most people in the principality seem to have been happy enough to give the clergy their due, and to contribute to the funds of the Church through, for example, the payment of church rates.

These tentative conclusions will, it is hoped, inspire fresh research into the topic discussed in these pages. That research might take many different directions. Anticlericalism itself, for example, is likely to retain a degree of blurredness until the culture of clericalism is much more fully reconstructed over time. A key area for investigation would appear to be the relationship between the clergy and their parishioners, of both genders. On the evidence given here, anticlericalism appears as an essentially masculine activity, but could clergy rely on general support from women? If they did so, did this in itself increase the 'anticlerical' reaction of other parishioners? Or were women, as some of Haigh's examples of anticlerical comment suggest, equally liable to malign their clergymen? How did relationships between clergymen and parishioners compare between those involving the laity and unbeneficed clergymen such as curates? And what of the relationship within the ranks of the clergy themselves? How anticlerical were the curates, doomed, as so many were until well into the nineteenth century, to a life on the margins, and on the breadline? This last is among several themes touched on by the authors in this collection but which would benefit from much more detailed exploration.

It is, perhaps, appropriate that this book should appear at a juncture when the clergy appear to have been relegated to the margins of contemporary life, and expectations of them and their role are under review. As Callum Brown notes, the Kirk minister's status has 'withered with the dwindling of his Sabbath congregations to be replaced by the kilt, the football team and Scottish nationalism'. And that is much the case in England, Wales and Ireland. It was not ever thus. These essays give readers the chance to explore the four centuries after the Reformation, when no layman could ignore the status and work of his parish minister, and when an anticlericalist response was always risky because it challenged the authority of one of the central figures in British history.

Notes

1   There are important collections of essays in E. Badone, *Religion, Orthodoxy and Popular Faith in European Society* (Princeton, 1996), and P.A. Dykema and Heiko A. Oberman (eds), *Anticlericalism in Late Medieval and Early Modern Europe* (Leiden, 1993). For Spanish anticlericalism, see Julio de la Cueva, 'The Stick and the Candle: Clericals and Anticlericals in Northern Spain, 1898–1913', *European History Quarterly*, 26 (1996), pp. 241–66. For France, see Alec Mellor, *Histoire de l'anticlericalisme Français* (Paris, 1966), p. 164; René Remond, *L'anti-clericalisme en France de 1815 à nos jours* (Paris, 1976); and G. Cubbitt, *The Jesuit Myth: Conspiracy Theory and Politics in Nineteenth Century France* (Oxford, 1993).

2   Eric J. Evans, 'Some reasons for the growth of English anti-clericalism', *Past & Present*, 66 (1975), pp. 84–109.

3   Mark Smith, *Religion in Industrial Society: Oldham and Saddleworth, 1740–1865* (Oxford, 1994).

4   Revd William Dodd LLD, *Moral Pastorals, and other Poems* (Edinburgh, 1824), p. 106.

5   J.P.D. Dunbabin, *Rural Discontent in Nineteenth Century Britain* (New York, 1974), pp. 211–31, 282–96; M. Cragoe, *An Anglican Aristocracy: the Moral Economy of the Landed Estate in Carmarthenshire, 1832–95* (Oxford, 1996), pp. 236–40.

6   E. Duffy, *The Stripping of the Altars: Traditional Religion in England* c. *1400–1580* (New Haven, CT, 1992).

ANTICLERICALISM IN THE CHURCH OF ENGLAND BEFORE 1558: AN 'EATING CANKER'?

David Loades

In a well-known article on this subject, published originally in 1983, Christopher Haigh robustly declared that anticlericalism in this period was a fiction.[1] It was, he argued, a 'convenience concept', used by those with too many traditional prejudices and too little intellectual curiosity to explain the success of the English Reformation. Drawing on detailed statistical research in a number of diocesan archives, Dr Haigh demonstrated that in the first thirty years of the sixteenth century the number of cases of laymen suing priests or complaining against them in the ecclesiastical courts was remarkably small.[2] The so-called anticlericalism of the City of London, or of the House of Commons in the early sessions of the Reformation Parliament, were manifestations of particular political circumstances, exaggerated out of all proportion by the polemical reporting of John Foxe and Edward Hall.[3] Ordination to the clerical estate was buoyant until at least 1530, and the only consistent animus was directed against Cardinal Wolsey. Neither Lollardy (which had strong anticlerical overtones) nor early Protestantism (which objected to priesthood, if not to ministry) had any widespread influence or power base. The apparent increase in Lollardy after 1500 was largely an optical illusion created by greater episcopal vigilance, and it had been virtually wiped out in one of its strongholds, Buckinghamshire, by 1540. At the same time Protestantism attracted the allegiance of no more than a tiny minority until it finally secured the reins of power in 1559.

Dr Haigh's purpose was polemical. He was principally concerned to discredit that school of traditional Reformation historiography which had used anticlericalism and the evidence of early Protestant sympathies to postulate a reformation carried out upon a broad swell of popular support – what might be described as a 'manifest destiny' view.[4] He was remarkably successful, and most Reformation scholars would now follow his lead, at least to the point of abandoning simple populist interpretations and portraying instead a prolonged, complex and highly politicised conflict.[5] However, as Dr Haigh himself recognised (but some of his subsequent followers have forgotten), to go too far in the other direction also creates problems. If everyone was so happy with the

Church and its clergy, why was there a Reformation at all? Was the Crown far more powerful than anyone had hitherto suspected? Was there an 'elite conspiracy' to rob the Church of its property, and the mass of the population of its spiritual solace? If the latter, how can the sharp distinction between the elite and the rest be explained? Amid all this tangle of questions, some things have emerged clearly. Anticlericalism was indeed a fiction, not because the clergy were overwhelmingly popular but because it is a misleadingly simplistic term to use to described the many-layered relationship between clergy and laity. At the same time it did not really matter what the majority of people thought or felt between 1500 and 1530. Modern historians tend to be victims of the 'democratic myth', and to assume that in order to succeed major changes need to have majority support. As Dr Haigh quite rightly observed, anticlericalism as that term is normally understood was much more prevalent in the Elizabethan Church than it had been earlier: in other words it was a product of the Reformation, rather than a cause of it.[6] The same could be said of other factors, and the conclusion must be that where lawful authority led, the community, reluctantly or otherwise, followed.[7] The Reformation was accepted by English society as a whole, not created by it.

Anticlericalism as a device for explaining the Reformation is therefore useless, but that does not mean that relations between clergy and laity in the early sixteenth century are either meaningless or uninteresting. Fashions in piety change, not because of heresies or schisms but simply because priorities shift between generations. Before the twelfth century, it had been normal for great men (and women) to secure their spiritual futures by founding monasteries and nunneries. In return, they usually required specific prayers, often in the form of masses of special intention, for their own souls and those of their families.[8] However, the purpose of such foundations was much wider. They were established to maintain the *opus dei*, that constant fountain of prayer and praise which kept the human race in touch with its God. The value of such prayer, and its place in the scheme of things, had been unquestioned for centuries. It was equally unquestioned that those whose vocation it was to maintain the *opus dei* should withdraw from the world, and be supported by resources managed by others on their behalf. Such withdrawal was seen as the highest form of Christian life, and the purity of the communities enhanced the value of their prayers. Unfortunately, human nature being what it is, these ideals were very seldom achieved. The monastic life may have been austere, but it was predictable and offered security, both physical and spiritual, in a turbulent world. The piety of benefactors also turned rigorous cells into rich and stately houses, owning wide estates. In short, the monasteries were undermined by their own success, and the efforts of reformers such as Bernard of Clairvaux only ended by making matters worse.[9] There was no sudden collapse of the monastic orders, but during the thirteenth century new foundations petered out and major benefactions to existing houses became rare. This was partly for the very practical reason that kings and nobles were becoming concerned at the amount of land which was passing into mortmain, and thus being withdrawn from the available stock,[10] but it was also partly because the *opus dei* was losing its credibility. Withdrawal from the world gradually lost its prestige as a method of confronting the evils and follies of daily life. Like the rest of the population, the monasteries suffered heavily from the Black Death after 1349, and their recovery was patchy and incomplete. By the early sixteenth century monks were no longer in the spiritual front line. Most English houses were seriously under strength, and some were barely surviving.[11] The educated laity, even the most pious, were unimpressed by the *opus dei*, and did not regard those who devoted themselves to it with much respect. Individual communities were valued (or not) for the social contribution which they made to their neighbourhoods, rather than as essential channels of communication with God.[12] Monks were not actively hated, but they were frequently the butts of coarse humour and amused contempt. If this was anticlericalism, it was very low-key – but it was of crucial importance. In effect, the monasteries were redundant, and although custom and nostalgia supported them, when the King moved against them between 1535 and 1540, there was no powerful or coherent religious lobby to come to their assistance.[13]

When fashion first deserted the monks, the original beneficiaries were the mendicant orders. Their whole spiritual strategy was different. Like the monks, they were not averse to offering intercessory prayers for their benefactors and patrons, but the *opus dei* played no part in their lives. They were trained to confront evil and misfortune in the world where it flourished. The Dominicans were particularly educated as preachers, while the Franciscans specialised in the care of the sick and destitute. There were a number of other orders which also conformed to this broad pattern, notably the canons regular, but the Dominicans and Franciscans were the most numerous. Unlike the monks, they concentrated in towns and cities, and they were not supposed to receive endowments or collect large estates. From the point of view of their patrons, they were focused, efficient and relevant. Partly for this reason, they were also a nuisance to the hierarchy. Their particular sense of vocation called upon them to meddle constantly in what were, in theory, other men's cures, preaching in parishes where the incumbent was unable to do so (and not always asking permission), carrying out missions in neglected areas and frequently becoming chaplains and confessors to the great. The Franciscans also showed an embarrassing devotion to the doctrine of apostolic poverty, which caused some of them to be condemned as heretics.[14] Unlike the monks, the friars recovered strongly from the Black Death, and could be described as flourishing both in England and in Ireland in the early sixteenth century.[15] However, their superior education and sharp engagement with the world also gave them a livelier curiosity about spiritual truth than was convenient to their ecclesiastical masters. Girolamo Savonarola was a Franciscan, Martin

Luther was an Augustinian, John Bale, the author of the *Actes of the English Votaryes*, was a Carmelite, and Bernardino Ochino was a Capuchin. The friars were more accessible to Reforming ideas in general, and to Protestant ideas in particular, than were either monks or secular clergy. Moreover, as in the case of Bale, the converts were often the bitterest critics of those whom they had left behind.[16] Orthodox friars were similarly the fiercest enemies of those who had become heretics, so what appears at first sight like an outburst of anticlericalism was actually produced by a deadly feud among the friars themselves. The fact that orthodox friars continued to work in the world, and indeed increased their endeavours as the Reformation gained pace, also made them vulnerable to charges of fornication, conspiracy and fraud. By the time John Foxe was writing in the 1560s, it was a commonplace of Protestant polemic to represent the friars as particularly obnoxious hypocrites, whereas in fact they were unusually tenacious opponents.[17]

The secular clergy were a very different matter, and indeed it is not realistic to speak of them as a single order. Priests and bishops were in a different situation from those in minor orders, and the educated were in a different situation from the uneducated. Apart from students, those who stayed in minor orders for more than a short period constituted a clerical proletariat, often very difficult to distinguish from the laity. There was no worthwhile career open to such men, except to proceed to major orders. They might be menial servants in an ecclesiastical household, or they might marry and fade into the artisan community. Those who remained theoretically celibate and hovered on the fringes of ecclesiastical institutions were a generally acknowledged embarrassment. There were too many of them, and they too often escaped punishment for their crimes and misdemeanours by claiming benefit of clergy, which was the ancient privilege of a man in holy orders to be tried by an ecclesiastical rather than a secular court.[18] Sir Thomas More was one of their sternest critics. Benefit of clergy had not been designed for them, and the fact that they used it increasingly enabled the Crown to whittle it away with comparatively little protest from the Church. Kings had choked on this jurisdictional privilege for centuries, and in theory it should have been one of the main causes of anticlericalism, because clerks could escape punishment for offences that would have brought a layman to the gallows. However, the literate, who might have articulated such resentment, did not feel it because they could claim the benefit themselves. Such emotions had in the past occasionally erupted into acts of violence, but not in the early sixteenth century, when the issue was well on the way to a solution.

Setting aside the highly educated for the moment, ordinary priests occupied a unique position. By virtue of their orders they administered the sacraments of the Church which were the essential gateway to salvation, they heard confessions, and they were able to offer intercession of a quality to which no mere layman could aspire. At the same time, they were humble men, often born and brought up in the communities which they served, minimally educated and without any formal training.[19] What this usually meant was that their parishes accepted them for what they were, essential to an established way of life, and did not expect too much of them as individuals. Canon law forbade them to marry, but only a minority of them were celibate. Their communities normally accepted that a man needed a woman, and as long as he treated her decently and provided for his children, they were not disposed to be critical. Such an arrangement was not logical but it worked, and usually guaranteed that the priest did not take out his sexual frustrations on the wives and daughters of his parishioners. Anxiety on that score is impossible to quantify, but formal complaints (as opposed to general grumbling) were few and far between. The Reformers were technically justified in denouncing a Church that forbade lawful marriage while treating fornication as a mere peccadillo, but there is not much evidence from the early sixteenth century that sexual irregularities by the clergy were frequently identified, or that the clergy were more likely to offend in that respect than laymen. Such priests were poorly equipped to instruct their flocks, as opposed to ministering to them, but that did not matter as long as the laity were predominantly illiterate. They were often good mediators and arbitrators because they empathised with the people they were dealing with, and attracted grateful bequests for that reason.[20] Sometimes they were leaders, sometimes not, depending on circumstances and individual character. The authority derived from their office might, or might not, influence the laymen whose wealth or status conferred a similar role. A priest was also entitled to a decent remuneration for his efforts. There was little chance that the vicars and curates who served the majority of parishes and received the 'small tithes' (the dues paid on minor produce such as fruit or eggs, often in kind) would become bloated or pretentious on what they received.[21] When there were tithe disputes in this period, they were more likely to involve the rector, who might also be the resident incumbent, but was usually an absentee pluralist or an ecclesiastical institution. More relevant were disputes over fees, particularly fees for indispensable services like conducting weddings and funerals. Here, a hard-up or avaricious curate might take advantage of his position, or be perceived as doing so, and such cases occasionally surface in litigation. However, they do not constitute evidence for any perception of widespread or systematic abuse. Where the evidence can be recovered from parish level, it supports the conclusion which Peter Heath reached many years ago, that the great majority of parochial clergy were doing a decent job according to their lights, and were on good terms with most of their neighbours most of the time.[22]

However, this rather unexciting confirmation of Dr Haigh's thesis is not the whole story. In the first place, the Church was an immensely wealthy and powerful institution, and you did not have to be a heretic to be uneasily aware that this was not quite what the fishermen of Galilee had intended. Secondly, because of its wealth and power, it attracted a class of educated professional men who were anxious to control it. Because of its nature, these men had to enter priests' orders and to become theoretically celibate, without necessarily having the slightest vocation or any real desire to discharge a priestly function. So strong a grip had the Church obtained over higher education by the twelfth century that it was virtually impossible, in England at any rate, for anyone to pursue a non-military professional career without being forced into holy orders.[23] Bishops and abbots were temporal lords, deans and archdeacons the equivalent of substantial gentlemen, and the Church was the only 'career open to talent'. Such a situation bred resentment, not among the rural rank and file, whom it scarcely affected, but among such educated laymen as there were, and within the ranks of conscientious and reforming clergy. The kind of anticlericalism expressed by the court poet Geoffrey Chaucer at the end of the fourteenth century was not directed against priests as such, but against the Church as an institution, which neglected its missionary function and bred a swarm of greedy parasites to take advantage of its unassailable position.[24] Given the nature of ecclesiastical power, it is more surprising that so many senior clergy took their spiritual responsibilities seriously, and tried to live up to their status, than that there should have been numerous conspicuous backsliders. The King encouraged resentment when it suited his purpose, because tension between secular and ecclesiastical power was endemic, and it was always useful to have a few cards in your sleeve.[25]

The Church also held a massive amount of land – as much as one-third of the kingdom by 1500 – and this created an interface with secular landholders which ran from the top to the bottom of society. It was not only great monasteries which held broad acres. The revenues of the sees of England equalled those of the greatest peers; cathedrals and colleges also held large estates; and every parish had its glebe land.[26] This meant that litigation was constant. Cathedral chapters were in dispute with the corporations of their proximate towns; bishops tussled with neighbouring lords; yeomen and gentlemen disputed titles with rectors. Because it involved property, the common lawyers kept a firm grip on this litigation, and the clergy not infrequently sought to redress the balance by citing their opponents before their own courts on some charge real or imaginary, with a view to forcing a trade-off. Such tactics were much resented, and did result in anticlerical outbursts. Although only a few people were involved, it was precisely this type of dispute which created among the lay aristocracy that ambivalence towards the Church which Henry VIII was able to turn to his advantage.[27]

At the same time cultural changes were also taking place which undermined the ecclesiastical Establishment. We have seen that shifts of fashion had left the monasteries high and dry by the early sixteenth century and enhanced the importance of the friars. In the fourteenth century, partly because the friars did not welcome large gifts and partly because they did not see intercessory prayer as one of their main functions, anxious benefactors were protecting their futures by endowing perpetual chantries.[28] Sometimes these were free-standing, sometimes in connection with hospitals, schools or university colleges. By the middle of the fifteenth century charitable or educational foundations were the norm. These created a whole new area of clerical employment, but because the duties were often light they also attracted entrepreneurs. Individuals might hold a number of such preferments, often miles apart; they kept small schools for which they charged fees, and sometimes they brewed ale or kept public houses.[29] If judgements have to be made on clerical conduct, the cantarists were a bit of a liability. At the same time the enthusiasm for education was born of a desire to bring up more boys in Godliness and Good Learning, and to enhance the quality of the clergy. By 1500 two related but distinct things were happening. On the one hand there was a slow but accelerating expansion of lay education and literacy, of which the development of printing was as much a symptom as a cause. On the other hand was a growing conviction that the Church was failing to address a widespread condition of acute spiritual anxiety.[30] The results were some localised but important changes of expectation, most notable in cities where the literacy rate was highest. This can be seen in places like Strasburg, Augsburg and Nuremburg; in England it is most obvious in London.[31] Such anxieties had arisen before, and produced demands for reform to which the Church had usually responded. This time, perhaps because of the printing press, the tide rose more rapidly, and the Church did not respond quickly enough. By 1510 sharp criticism (usually called 'humanist') was audible, not only from educated laymen but also from sections of the educated clergy, including a number of friars.

Before assessing the consequences of this, it is necessary to remember that there had been exceptions to the general complacency of the fifteenth century. The intellectual turbulence of the fourteenth century had thrown up in England a radical anticlerical called John Wycliffe, who had challenged the whole basis of the *potestas ordinis* (literally, 'the power of the order') by declaring that a sacrament was only valid if the celebrant was in a state of grace.[32] Since no man can know certainly whether another is in a state of grace or not, what this meant in practice was that he should be seen to behave himself properly. Wycliffe's followers, loosely known as Lollards, had at first included men who were both educated and influential, but Henry IV's need for ecclesiastical support had resulted in prolonged and successful persecution. By 1450 the Lollards had neither leadership nor a coherent creed. They were scattered, and no one can now tell how numerous they were.[33] It used to be fashionable to regard them as important trail-blazers for protestantism, and although that was an exaggeration the present tendency to dismiss them altogether is also a mistake. It was the Lollards who asserted that there must be a functional connection between a priest's office and his lifestyle, and it was a poor defence against charges of drunkenness or incontinence to claim that the accuser must be a heretic to have brought them. Lollards were often unpopular because their tendency to be hypercritical of clerical conduct disrupted relationships which worked perfectly well for their more relaxed neighbours. However, some better-educated congregations were beginning to come to the same position from a different angle, and to look to their parish priest for instruction and example as well as the traditional offices. This was hard on men brought up in the old way, and sometimes they could not cope. They complained vociferously against the 'new learning', and hinted darkly about heretical ideas when there was no justification to do so. Parishioners who wanted a better quality of ministry were not anticlerical, but they might become so if they found themselves accused of heresy, which could have serious legal and social consequences.

Laymen at all social levels were worried by accusations of heresy. Not only could they be ruined by a successful prosecution, but the charges could be very hard to refute – especially if you did not know what your heresy was supposed to have consisted of. The feeling in London in 1511 that Richard Hun had been charged with heresy 'for suing *a praemunire*' disclosed a sensitive spot.[34] Praemunire was a late fourteenth-century statute law against exercising ecclesiastical jurisdiction without the King's consent – a relic of an old dispute between King and Pope.[35] How it could have been applied to the dispute between Hun and his curate over a mortuary fee is not clear. When Hun took out these writs, it was probably as a precaution – or a threat. The real significance of the incident is that the authorities of the London diocese were perceived to be using a charge of heresy (of which the Church was sole judge) to put down a layman who was making a nuisance of himself. In fact, the charge seems to have been justified, and may have been unconnected with the other dispute, but that is hardly relevant. Foxe did not invent the indignation, for which there is contemporary evidence, and Hun's subsequent death added fuel to the flames.[36] The fact that heresy charges were very rare, and even rarer against men of Hun's education and substance, does not affect the issue. Those who wanted to attack the Church, for whatever reason, could accuse it of using heresy charges in order to be both accuser and judge in its own cause.

There was therefore a certain amount of anti-ecclesiasticism before the Reformation; a feeling that the Church was too rich, too self-satisfied and not capable of responding to new challenges. Of anticlericalism, however, in the sense of feeling that the clergy were frequently abusing their status for gain or power, there is very little evidence. A few individual charges against inadequate priests do not make a case. The roots of anticlericalism were not institutional or behavioural, but *doctrinal*. We have seen this in the case of the Lollards, but they were too scattered, and latterly too incoherent, to pose a serious threat. Real anticlericalism comes with the first committed Protestants, and that is why Dr Haigh was right to identify it as a product of the Reformation, rather than as a precursor. To Bale or Tyndale, no less than to John Foxe, the mass priest was the purveyor of an evil superstition. Transubstantiation was the epitome of false doctrine.[37] By claiming to convert material substances into the body and blood of Christ, it elevated the host into an object of idolatrous worship, and turned the priest into a magician. In the eyes of the Protestants, there could be only one reason for this gross perversion of Christianity: a desire to deceive ignorant laymen into accepting the oppressive authority of the servants of Antichrist – the Pope and his henchmen. In this situation the quality of the individual priest's life or ministry was almost irrelevant. If he was loose-living and negligent, that was only to be expected; if he appeared to be virtuous and conscientious, then the Devil was full of cunning deceptions. The man did not matter; it was the priestly office itself which was evil.

Early Protestant polemic focused remorselessly on the mass. Many popular writers, like Luke Shepherd, mocked the apparent absurdity of converting bread into God 'with five words'.[38] The Church was also vulnerable to such attacks because of the near-impossibility of explaining the doctrine in terms which the ordinary man could understand. The only defence was to invoke the faith of the believer, and to denounce the 'carnal imaginings' of those who did not share it. The war was already fierce on both sides before Henry VIII's death. Each regarded the other's position as blasphemous, and the defenders of orthodoxy were also keenly aware that in a sense, the whole validity of the Church as an institution hung on this point. Without the miracle of the mass, the *potestas ordinis* would lose its credibility, and without that power, the Church became merely a service organisation. It was its coercive jurisdiction, at least as much as its spiritual monopoly, which gave the Church its unique role in medieval society. As the subsequent histories of both England and Scotland were to show, a Church did not necessarily lose its authority when the priestly role was diminished, but it did lose its autonomy. So the Protestants believed not only that the orthodox were defending their absurd superstition out of ulterior motives, but that such defence also demonstrated their crass ignorance, particularly of the scriptures. In fact, the doctrine of transubstantiation as it was usually held in the sixteenth century was a medieval construct, and there was some room to argue about it before the Council of Trent produced its authoritative definition.[39] It was unknown to the writers of Scripture, and to the practices of the early Church. The early reformers, who were nearly all themselves educated clergy, consequently dubbed it a 'human invention'. To them, the Bible contained everything necessary to salvation, and the early Church was the model. To defend the 'traditions of the Church' as an alternative source of authority was therefore, like the defence of the mass, a self-interested justification of priestcraft.

A traditional priest was therefore (almost by definition) ignorant. He did not have a proper understanding of the Bible, nor appreciate its unique authority. It was also inevitable that the vast majority of the existing priests in 1530 would be soft targets for such attacks. They were not educated, because their function, as that had been understood for generations, did not require them to be; nor had most of them either the means or the opportunity to acquire such training. They needed enough Latin to be able to recite the offices and to find the required prayers and readings; anything more was a work of supererogation. It is not surprising, therefore, that most of them wilted when assailed by the scriptural barrages which were directed against them by Protestant clergy and laymen alike. Accusations of clerical ignorance are very rare before the Reformation, but during and after it they become commonplace. 'Sir John Lack Latin', a 'bouncing priest', a 'fat headed priest' – the abuse from Protestant pens is unstinting.[40] So a lot of Reformation anticlericalism was the result of radical changes in the perception of the clerical function. To the Protestant, a priest was primarily a minister of the word, a teacher and instructor. For this, he needed to be literate in both English and Latin, and familiar with the main outlines of Christian theology. His functions as a distributor of communion and a baptiser of infants, although necessary, were strictly ancillary.

Those who argue that English Protestants were a tiny minority before 1559 are correct, but miss the point. The English Reformation was not prompted by mass discontent with the Church as it was, or the clergy as they were. However, there were malcontents, for a variety of reasons:

[I] exhort you, reverend fathers, to the endeavour of reformation of the church's estate (because that nothing hath so disfigured the face of the church as hath the fashion of secular and worldly living in clerks and priests). I know not where more conveniently to take the beginning of my tale than of the apostle Paul, in whose temple ye are gathered together . . .[41]

The speaker was not a Protestant or a Lollard, but Dean Colet of St Pauls, addressing Convocation in 1511. Like many alert and educated clergy, Colet was aware that the Church was not responding adequately to the challenges presented by the rise of lay literacy. He was certainly not anticlerical, and would have been horrified by Protestant attacks on the mass, but he was aware that expectations were changing, and that the rank-and-file clergy were poorly equipped to respond. It was because he valued their office, and wished to see them more worthy of it, that he went on to be severely critical of contemporary standards and mores. Colet was not an isolated voice. More than twenty years earlier Parliament had urged ecclesiastical ordinaries to be more severe in the punishment of 'avowtry [adultery], fornication, incest or any other fleshly incontinency' among their clergy, extending to them protection against counter-charges of false imprisonment.[42] So, although we may look in vain for evidence of widespread disillusionment with the clergy, that was more because of the complacency of their congregations than because nothing was amiss. When the seeds of Protestant polemic began to spread, mainly after 1530, they lodged here and there, with individuals and small groups, and we usually have no idea why. The new literate laity were pious – and zealous, if the number of religious books printed before 1520 is anything to go by – but they were also more prone to ask questions, and to expect answers.

In this connection it is not at all helpful to play the numbers game, or to suppose that by 1547 the country was divided into 'Catholics' and 'Protestants' – however they are counted. Protestant ideas were picked up piecemeal, and not usually by 'conversion' in the full sense. Even Thomas Cranmer, who followed Luther on justification (and on clerical celibacy), remained orthodox on the mass until 1548.[43] William Tyndale may have been a Lutheran in the full sense, and John Lambert a Zwinglian, but important figures like Robert Barnes and John Frith cannot be pigeonholed so easily. The King himself set an example of ambivalence, remaining orthodox on most doctrinal issues but rejecting the Papacy, dissolving the intercessory foundations and encouraging the vernacular Bible. Orthodox writers made the most of Protestant divisions, particularly on the eucharist, but in fact were almost equally divided themselves. Some, like Stephen Gardiner or Cuthbert Tunstall, saw ecclesiastical jurisdiction as a matter indifferent to the faith; others, like John Fisher and the Abbot of Winchcombe, thought that it was essential.[44] Reginald Pole, fiercely orthodox on the sacraments and on papal jurisdiction, was ambivalent about justification.[45] Richard Whitford, that soul of orthodox piety, saw no reason to reject vernacular scripture. To the orthodox, holy orders were a sacrament administered by the Church, and in theory it made no difference to their validity whether the recipient was worthy or not. However, too much obvious inadequacy called the whole sacrament into question, and that was why people like Colet worried so much about it. This was an Achilles heel as and where expectations began to rise. What should one think of a Church which appeared to ordain indiscriminately such large numbers of very ordinary men to such an important function?

The fact that such a doubt did not occur to the even larger numbers of equally ordinary men and women to whom they ministered does not invalidate the question. We must not be misled into thinking that mass opinion was of critical importance in the sixteenth century. Changes were brought about by a small elite of noblemen, gentry, literate citizens and educated clergy. These were people who might influence the Crown, and whose support or acquiescence was essential to the success of any policy. Only when driven to desperation by genuine hardship or alarming rumours did large numbers of people attempt to reject such leadership and participate in protest demonstrations like the Pilgrimage of Grace or the 'Prayer Book' rising of 1549:[46]

'. . . towchinge the people alone' (Sir Thomas Wyatt wrote in that same year) 'of themselves either they stirr not, or yf theie do there fury falethe with a lytle delaie of tyme, and a while endured doth calme of itself. Without ordre they rise, without ordre they are quieted, and all theyr blase ys soone up soone downe . . .'[47]

The traditional Church in England was not swept away by mass dissatisfaction with either its teaching, its jurisdiction or its clergy. However, in the early sixteenth century it was an institution riddled with self-doubt, particularly among its most thoughtful and conscientious members. Could the huge endowments of the ancient monasteries any longer be justified? Could the spiritual anxieties of educated laymen continue to be met with sacramental formulae? Should privileges like the benefit of clergy be defended? Was it not time that a grip was taken on standards of clerical training and behaviour? Were too many men being ordained without adequate scrutiny of their credentials? If the King's Great Matter had not intervened to put the Church in the political firing line, it is difficult to judge what might have happened. However, it is unlikely that the sheer weight of orthodox complacency would have stifled such questions. Reform was in the air, certainly by 1511, when Colet delivered his blast. More, Erasmus and even Wolsey wanted change, and Henry was open to persuasion.

Unfortunately, a number of things derailed the hopeful initiatives which were beginning to appear. Firstly, Reforming ideas began to be imported from Germany, which looked encouraging at first sight, but soon turned out to be heretical, enabling opponents of change to dub the Reformers Lutherans. Secondly, Henry's quarrel with the Pope changed the agenda, confusing issues of reform with jurisdictional issues from which they should have been kept separate. Thirdly (and most important in this context), with a few exceptions the rank-and-file clergy rejected any moves which threatened their established and relatively comfortable position. They did not want to confront new ideas, even in defence of orthodoxy; they did not want English Bibles giving their flocks inconvenient ideas, or prompting questions which they could not answer. Above all, they did not want to think through what they were supposed to be doing. In their own way, they were mostly conscientious and hard-working men, but they were running on tracks which had been laid down centuries before and had become sanctified by custom. To the Reformers, whether Catholic or Protestant, they thus became a major obstacle, and it is this which we rather loosely call anticlericalism.[48] Without the King's intervention, English Protestants might have remained a troublesome minority, but the issue of what to do about the clergy would still have had to be faced. Cardinal Pole placed his trust in the long-term solution of radically improved education and professional training, and that might well have worked.[49] Some Catholic countries leavened the lump with new religious orders, and that also worked, up to a point. However, because of the eventual Protestant triumph in England, English Reformation historiography has tended to embrace a doctrinally motivated exaggeration in its representation of the pre-Reformation clergy. The mass priest was not an evil hypocrite, nor a lascivious bully, but he did stand firmly in the way of anything which could be called a Godly ministry. And the more he outwardly conformed, the bigger a nuisance he became, because you could not get rid of him. Eventually, in the lengthy reign of Elizabeth, this problem was to solve itself, but it was to be a long time before the rank-and-file clergy began to measure up to the professional standards that Grindal or Parker were looking for. Post-Reformation anticlericalism was mostly fuelled by disappointment. Moreover, if you did have a grievance, you were more likely to articulate it if you no longer believed that your vicar held your eternal destiny in the hollow of his hand.

Anticlericalism was therefore not a prime motivating force driving the English Reformation, but rather a consequence of the dwindling role and collapsing prestige of the Church. It featured in the rhetoric of the royal assault on ecclesiastical autonomy because it was a convenient weapon, rather than because it evoked a powerful response. Henry VIII's immediate concern was to secure the succession by begetting the legitimate son that contemporary ecclesiastical law would have denied him, but that was not the whole story. Long before the crisis arose, he had complained that the clergy were 'scarse his subjects', and were evading his laws. Whether he would have confronted this issue if it had not been for his matrimonial suit, we cannot tell. What we do know is that after he had taken the plunge, he swiftly convinced himself that by the will of God, all Christian princes should be heads of the Church (under Christ) within their dominions. There was no logical reason why he should not have renegotiated his position in the summer of 1536, when both his wives were dead and both his daughters illegitimate, but he declined to do so. He was the Defender of the Faith, *ex officio*, and he would make a better job of it than some meddlesome Italian at the other end of Europe. It was this position which his subjects (for the most part) accepted, even at the price of his tinkering with the calendar and promoting vernacular scripture. In their eyes, Henry was not a heretic, but a king who stood up for himself, and if that involved taking the clergy down a peg or two – well, nobody minded very much. But he would have roused faint cheers on that score alone. The Parliament which facilitated these changes was not so much anticlerical (let alone heretical) as sympathetic to the King's desire to be master in his own house.

Similarly, the monasteries were dissolved not because monks were universally disliked or despised, but because they were no longer seen as performing the vital spiritual function that had once justified their huge resources. Henry may have feared them as adherents of the Pope, and some were, but most accepted his supremacy readily enough. Those who claim that the King coveted their wealth are correct, but his move would never have succeeded if many others had not shared his covetousness, or if the prestige of all the orders had been as high as that of the Carthusians. Henry's propaganda against the monks did not extend beyond the ambiguous wording of one statute. His agents made no attempt to facilitate their work by stirring up anticlerical passions, and there would have been little response if they had tried. In assessing the crucial actions of Henry VIII, we must not assume that he was motivated, or even influenced, by the strident and genuine anticlericalism of a few Protestant writers and preachers. They may have represented the direction in which the Church would eventually move, but hindsight makes them appear much more important than they really were in the 1530s. Henry established a new Church order to satisfy his own agenda. He did not see himself as attacking the Church or the clergy, but as imposing a salutary and needed discipline to make it function more efficiently. Only after his death did the mass become a superstition, and the mass priest, in consequence, a confidence trickster.

Notes

1   'Anticlericalism and the English Reformation', *History*, 68 (1983); reprinted in C. Haigh (ed.), *The English Reformation Revised* (Cambridge, 1987).

2   Ibid., citing M. Bowker, *The Secular Clergy in the Diocese of Lincoln, 1495–1520* (Cambridge, 1968), pp. 3, 114 and 116; R.A. Houlbrooke, *Church Courts and the People during the English Reformation* (Oxford, 1979), pp. 178–9, and R.A. Merchant, *The Church under the Law* (Cambridge, 1969), p. 219.

3   J. Foxe, *Actes and Monuments of matters most speciall and memorable* (1583), pp. 805–14; Edward Hall, *The Union of the Two Noble and Illustre Femelies of York and Lancaster*, ed. H. Ellis (London, 1809), pp. 766–71. On the politics of the early Reformation parliament, see particularly G.R. Elton, *The Tudor Constitution* (Cambridge, 1982), pp. 327–33, and S.E. Lehmberg, *The Reformation Parliament* (Cambridge, 1970), pp. 76–104. It is also worth remembering that when Richard Fitzjames, the Bishop of London, told Wolsey that a London jury would hang his chancellor 'though he were as innocent as Abel', it was on account of their malicious heresy.

4   Dr Haigh traces this view back to John Foxe, but it really originated in Timothy Bright's abridgement of 1589. In 1583, Foxe had written: '. . . therefore in this history, standing upon such a general arguement, I shall not be bound to any one certain nation, more than another . . .'. Haigh's main target was A.G. Dickens, *The English Reformation* (London, 1964).

5   See, for example: Beat Kumin, *The Shaping of a Community: The Rise and Reformation of the English Parish, 1400–1560* (Aldershot, 1996); M.C. Skeeters, *Community and Clergy: Bristol and the Reformation, c. 1530–1570* (Oxford, 1993); and Caroline Litzenberger, *The English Reformation and the Laity: Gloucestershire, 1540–1580* (Cambridge, 1997).

6   Haigh, 'Anticlericalism'; and *English Reformations. Religion, Politics and Society under the Tudors* (Oxford, 1993), pp. 279–80.

7   For a strong case along these lines, relating to a conservative part of the country, see R. Whiting, *The Blind Devotion of the People* (Cambridge, 1989).

8   J. Burton, *Monastic and Religious Orders in Britain, 1000–1300* (Cambridge, 1994), pp. 215–17.

9   Bernard set out to correct what he saw as an overemphasis upon elaborate ritual, particularly among the Cluniacs, by introducing a strict regime of manual work. As a result, the Cistercian houses became richer than ever. M.C. Knowles, *The Monastic Order in England* (Cambridge, 1963), pp. 246–67.

10   Land granted to the Church was said to be in mortmain because the Church did not die, and was not subject to forfeiture. The practice was forbidden by statute in 1279, although loopholes in the law could be found, and special licences could be obtained – at a price.

11   Philip Hughes, *The Reformation in England; The King's Proceedings* (London, 1956), pp. 60–1.

12   M.C. Knowles, *The Religious Orders in England*, III (Cambridge, 1959), pp. 291–303. See the contrasting fortunes of Hexham and Tynemouth, both in Northumberland, ibid., pp. 324 and 341.

13   Theoretically, there was no attack upon the monastic way of life. The smaller houses were dissolved for their 'manifest sin, vicious, carnal and abominable living' (27 Henry VIII, c.28), but the same statute went on to praise the greater houses, 'where, thanks be to God, religion is right well kept and observed'. These houses were not dissolved, but surrendered to the King, who then appropriated their property by statute (31 Henry VIII, c.13). These houses were not canonically extinguished until 1555. It is necessary, in connection with all this Reformation legislation, to remember that in the English Parliament (unlike most representative estates) there was no House of Clergy. Only the bishops in the House of Lords could present an ecclesiastical point of view, and they were appointed by the Crown.

14   J. Moorman, *A History of the Franciscan Order from its Origins to the Year 1517* (Oxford, 1968); D. Nimmo, *Reform and Division in the Franciscan Order, 1226–1538* (Rome, 1987).

15   Hughes, *The King's Proceedings*, pp. 68–9; B. Bradshaw, *The Dissolution of the Religious Orders in Ireland* (Cambridge, 1974).

16   J.P. Fairfield, *John Bale* (West Lafayette, Indiana, 1976), pp. 31–49.

17   Foxe, *Actes and Monuments*, pp. 259, 261, 264, 409, 411, 506.

18   Ecclesiastical courts did not have the power of life and death, and therefore administered lesser penalties, even for capital offences. Access to such benefit was claimed not by displaying letters of ordination, but by an ability to read. In theory, it could be claimed only once, but this was often evaded. J.G. Bellamy, *Criminal Law and Society in Late Medieval and Tudor England* (Gloucester, 1984), pp. 115–32.

19   Peter Heath, *The English Parish Clergy on the Eve of the Reformation* (London, 1969).

20   P. Marshall, 'Attitudes of the English people to Priests and Priesthood, 1500–1553' (Oxford University, DPhil, 1990), pp. 194–235, confesses to a certain puzzlement that clerical celibacy was such a well-known 'Irish joke', but that recorded instances of complaint were so few. Complacency seems the most likely explanation. The ideal that 'men of Holy Church may better withstand the fleshly temptation than wedded men for they ought to pass the people in virtue' may not have been treated very seriously, except by a small minority. On arbitration and other pastoral functions, see ibid., pp. 236–42.

21   The great majority of curates and vicars enjoyed stipends of between £5 and £10 a year. F. Heal and R. O'Day (eds), *Princes and Paupers in the English Church, 1500–1800* (Leicester, 1981).

22   Heath, *Parish Clergy*; Marshall, 'Attitudes of English people', pp. 264–83; E. Duffy, *The Stripping of the Altars* (London, 1992), pp. 209–33.

23   Many forms of employment requiring literacy, such as estate administration, were in the hands of clerks. The main exceptions were trade and the common law.

24   Most of the clerical officers portrayed in *The Canterbury Tales* are heavily satirised: the monk, the summoner, the pardoner, the nun's priest. The notable exception is the 'poor parson of a town'. The same could be said of Langland, and some other contemporaries.

25   A. Tuck, *Richard II and the English Nobility* (London, 1973); J.H. Dahmus, *The Prosecution of John Wycliffe* (New Haven, CT, 1952); K.B. MacFarlane, *Lancastrian Kings and Lollard Knights* (Oxford, 1972). The position of the English Church was in any case relatively weak as there were no major ecclesiastical liberties, except the Palatinate of Durham, which was firmly under royal control.

26   Winchester, at about £3,800 p.a., was the richest see; Rochester, at about £450, the poorest. Durham and Canterbury priories were both valued at over £2,000 (*Valor Ecclesiasticus* II, 2; V, 301). Peerage incomes are much harder to determine, but the rental income of the 5th Earl of Shrewsbury in 1538–9 was put at £1,735, and the 'current charge' of the Duke of Buckingham in 1518–19 was £3,674. G.W. Bernard, *The Power of the Early Tudor Nobility* (Brighton, 1986), p. 143; C. Rawcliffe, *The Staffords, Earls of Stafford and Dukes of Buckingham* (Cambridge, 1978), p. 134.

27   E.W. Ives, *The Common Lawyers in Pre-Reformation England* (Cambridge, 1983); J.A. Guy, 'Law, Lawyers and the English Reformation', *History Today* (November 1985).

28   K. Wood Legh, *Perpetual Chantries in Britain* (Cambridge, 1965).

29   A. Kreider, *English Chantries: The Road to Dissolution* (Cambridge, MA, 1979). The keeping of taverns was repeatedly (and vainly) forbidden. W.H. Frere, *Visitation Articles and Injunctions of the Period of the Reformation* (London, 1910), pp. iii, 263 and 280.

30   *The Reformation and the Book*, ed. F. Gilmont, trans. K. Maag (Aldershot, 1998). Luther was the most forceful expresser of this angst, but he was not the first. See particularly Euan Cameron, *The European Reformation* (Oxford, 1991), pp. 79–99.

31   L.J. Abray, *The People's Reformation: Magistrates, Clergy and Commons in Strasburg, 1500–1598* (Oxford, 1985); F. Roth, *Augsburgs Reformationsgeschichte* (4 vols, Munich, 1901–11); G. Strauss, *Nuremburg in the Sixteenth Century* (New York, 1966); S.E. Ozment, *The Reformation in the Cities* (New Haven, CT, 1975); S.E. Brigden, *London and the Reformation* (Oxford, 1989).

32   A. Hudson, *The Premature Reformation: Wycliffite Texts and Lollard History* (Oxford, 1988).

33   J.A.F. Thompson, *The Later Lollards, 1414–1520* (Oxford, 1965).

34   R. Wunderli, 'Pre-reformation London summoners and the murder of Richard Hunne', *Journal of Ecclesiastical History*, 33 (1982), pp. 218–24.

35   1393 (16 Richard II, c.5); S.M. Jack, 'The conflict of common law and canon law in sixteenth century England: Richard Hunne revisited', *Parergon*, n.s. 3 (1985), pp. 135–8.

36   Haigh, *English Reformations*, pp. 78–9.

37   For a full discussion of the doctrine, its significance and the reasons for its repudiation, see Paul N. Jones, *Eucharistic Presence: A History of the Doctrine* (New York, 1994).

38   'After that we consecrate Very God and Man;/And turn the bread to flesh with five words we can.' *John Bon and Mast[er] Parson* (London, 1548), in E. Arber, *Tudor Tracts* (London, 1903), p. 166.

39   In the fourth chapter of the *Decretum de sanctissimo eucharistiae sacramento*: '. . . through the consecration of bread and wine there takes place a conversion of the whole substance of the bread into the substance of the body of Christ our Lord and of the whole substance of the wine into the substance of his blood. This change is suitably and properly called Trans-substantiation by the Holy Catholic Church.'

40   Bale, as usual, was the most vociferous, writing in *An Epistle exhortatorye* (f. 11): 'By these your fylthye fore fathers and soche other hath the realme bene in most myserable captivite . . . and now last of all under the most blasphemous Behemoth your Romishe Pope.' The pre-Reformation parish

clergy were supposed to preach, and some did so, but their efforts often seem not to have been appreciated. Protestant denunciations of 'dumb dogs' need not be taken too literally. P. Marshall, 'Attitudes of the English', pp. 119–50.

41   John Colet, *Oratio habita ad Clerum in Convocatione* (1511); J.H. Lupton, *Life of John Colet* (London, 1887), Appendix C, pp. 293–304.

42   4 Henry VII, c.13 (1489); *Statutes of the Realm*, II, p. 538.

43   D. MacCulloch, *Thomas Cranmer* (London, 1996), pp. 399–403. According to Cranmer himself, it was Ridley who converted him to 'sound' views. Foxe, *Actes and Monuments*.

44   Richard Kidderminster, who preached at Paul's Cross in February 1515 against the punishment of clergy in secular courts.

45   Dermot Fenlon, *Heresy and Obedience in Tridentine Italy* (Cambridge, 1972), pp. 107–14 and 200–8.

46   M.L. Bush, *The Pilgrimage of Grace* (Manchester, 1996); Whiting, *The Blind Devotion of the People*.

47   D. Loades (ed.), 'A Treatise on the militia by Sir Thomas Wyatt the younger', *The Papers of George Wyatt* (Camden Society, 4th series, 5, 1968), p. 169.

48   Most of the sentiments described as 'anticlerical' actually arose from the desire to make the clergy more effective (in one way or another), rather than from hostility or jealousy. Haigh, *English Reformations*, pp. 44–51.

49   J. Strype, *Ecclesiastical Memorials* (Oxford, 1820), III, pp. ii and 484–5; J.P. Marmion, 'The London Synod of Cardinal Pole' (Keele University, MA, 1974).

FURTHER READING

Dickens, A.G., *The English Reformation* (2nd edn, London, 1989).

Duffy, E., *The Stripping of the Altars* (London, 1992).

Haigh, C., *English Reformations* (Oxford, 1993).

——, *The English Reformation Revised* (Cambridge, 1987).

Heath, P., *The English Parish Clergy on the Eve of the Reformation* (London, 1969).

Kumin, B., *The Shaping of a Community: The Rise and Reformation of the English Parish, 1400–1560* (Aldershot, 1996).

Thompson, J.A.F., *The Later Lollards, 1414–1520* (Oxford, 1965).

2

ANTICLERICALISM AND CLERICALISM, 1580–1640

Christopher Haigh

For our times have received all the pollutions and abominations which the course and current of former ages have carried into the sink of sin, which is now a thousand times more full and filthy than ever it was before. There was never more and more cruel enclosing, never more and more hateful carousing, never more and more abominable pride, oppression, corruption in all estates, usury, drunkenness, uncleanness, mercilessness to the poor, ignorance in the common people, contempt of the ministry; in a word, there was never more hell upon earth.[1]

Robert Bolton could see the black side of everything, and was clearly a pessimist. But many of his fellow clergy agreed with him on one thing: 'there was never more . . . contempt of the ministry'. William Harrison thought there was 'general contempt of the ministry, and small consideration of their former pains taken'. Arthur Dent's Philogathus complained in 1601 that 'now every rascal dares scoff and scorn at the most grave and ancient fathers and pastors of the Church, and dares flout them as they walk in the streets and as they ride by the highways'. In 1602 Josias Nichols railed against the people who picked quarrels with their ministers, were reluctant to pay them and held them in no respect or reverence. George Downame regretted in 1608 that 'the ministry above all callings is most subject to the contempt and disgrace of profane and godless men', and in 1609 Richard Bernard had to argue that there was no reason why the ministry 'should be esteemed so contemptible a calling'. The status of ministers was low, and there was always the embarrassing risk that laymen would 'instead of "Sir" give them the "Sirrah!"'[2]

William Perkins thought that 'the contempt and reproach and dangers' ministers encountered deterred recruits, and Bernard declared that for the upper ranks, any career – even crime – was better than the ministry, some wishing:

their children anything, worldly lawyers, fraudulent merchants, killing physicians, bloody captains, idle loose livers, swearing ruffians, walkers on Shooters' Hill, and coursers on Salisbury Plain, to maintain their riot, rather than to be (as they call them) priests.

For men of education or standing, entry to the ministry would be 'derogatory to their dignity'. Downame objected that 'every mean man' thought himself better than a minister, 'disdaining to bestow either his son on the ministry or his daughter on a minister', and Peter Barker in 1624 resented 'such proud and arrogant squires, which think so basely of their minister that he is not worthy so much as to wait upon their trencher'. George Herbert noted 'the general ignominy which is cast upon the profession', and prescribed five rules for the country parson to cope with contempt from parishioners.[3]

Perkins and Downame and Herbert knew that contempt of the clergy was nothing new: 'Indeed it is and always hath been the lot and condition of God's ministers in this world to be contemned, scorned and abused,' acknowledged Downame. Sinners hated their minister's corrections, and sought revenge by seizing on his failings and exaggerating them. As Charles Richardson remarked in 1616:

> It is strange to see how curiously many men with gazing eyes do pry into the lives and conversations of ministers, and if they find anything never so little amiss they stretch it on the tenterhooks and make a mountain out of every molehill, crying out with open mouths against the ill lives of all ministers, though their own be a great deal worse.[4]

William Crashaw gave an economic rather than moral explanation for the low estate of the English clergy, and argued in 1605 that it was the result of the 'poverty and base maintenance of our ministry': he blamed monastic impropriators and (by implication) Henry VIII. Perkins noted that the law attracted bright young men 'because they have all the means to rise, whereas the ministry for the most part yieldeth nothing but a plain way to beggary'. But the clergy should stick together: 'let all good and godly ministers give the right hand of fellowship one to another, and join together in love, and by that means arm themselves against the scorn and contempt of the world'.[5]

The authors of the 1559 royal injunctions thought it would be the former popish priests who faced abuse, but the papists died out, abuse continued and Church leaders remained nervous. In 1607 Bishop Chaderton of Lincoln asked at visitation, 'Whether any of your parish unreverently used your minister, or have laid violent hands upon him, or disgraced his office or calling by word or deed?', and several other bishops used his formulation. In 1613 the Archdeacon of Leicester wanted to know if there were 'any scoffers, rhymers or deriders of ministers', and in 1619 the bishop of Oxford was on the look-out for 'railers against ministers and against their marriage'. In another much-copied set of articles, Bishop Overall of Norwich inquired in 1619: 'Hath any of your parish spoken slanderous and reproachful words against your minister, to the scandal of his vocation, or against their marriage or wives?' Towers of

Peterborough had a long list of possible misconduct towards ministers in 1639, and asked if there were:

> any man or woman that hath abused their parson, vicar or curate, or any other that is in holy orders, with contumelious words or uncivil gestures or deeds, or behaved themselves rudely towards them? Or that have reproached either the marriage or the single life of priests, or have said or done anything else that did redound to the scorn or dishonour of their persons or of their holy function and calling?[6]

The honest answer to these questions was often 'yes', and laypeople were reported in large numbers for insulting their clergy. There were accusations of abuse, contempt, scoffing, slandering, railing, irreverence and depraving from many parishes – from Danbury (Essex) in 1583, Tiltington (Sussex) and Wighton (Yorkshire) in 1584, Wendover (Buckinghamshire) and East Hanningfield (Essex) in 1585, Goldhanger (Essex) in 1591, Sydenham (Oxfordshire) in 1605, Hutton (Essex) in 1611, Bosham (Sussex) in 1621, Stratford (Warwickshire) in 1624 and Hermitage (Wiltshire) in 1635, for example.[7] When an individual was presented by churchwardens for disrespect, the fault perhaps lay with the abuser rather than the abused; when the minister made the report, the truth is more obscure. But the insults were often formulaic, reflecting stereotypes of errant clergy, the laity's likes and dislikes, and the irritations ministers might cause. Parishioners seem to have employed a limited vocabulary of abuse, and where we know the precise terms used they were usually attacks on a minister's social status, or his learning, his skills or his morals.

Ministers demanded to be treated with respect, but their pretensions were mocked. A minister could be derided as a servant 'knave' (Howden, Yorkshire, 1584), 'knave and plaguey knave' (Bicester, Oxfordshire, 1584), 'black, sooty-mouthed knave' (New Buckenham, Norfolk, 1597), 'snotty-nose knave' (Colchester, 1608), 'blockhead knave' and 'horneyheaded knave' (Little Lavor, Essex, 1611) or 'great base rascal and base knave' (Lyme Regis, 1635).[8] He might be a nobody, 'jackanapes' (Hermitage, Wiltshire, 1606), 'jacksauce and Welsh rogue' (Towersey, Oxfordshire, 1608), 'scurvy jack and scurvy companion' (Little Lavor, 1611) or 'cowardly jackanapes' (Burton Dassett, Warwickshire, 1626).[9] Mr Harris of Messing (Essex) was called 'damned idle dog' in 1587, and in 1622 John Gawler of Winterborne Kingston (Dorset) mocked ministers as 'black dogs'.[10] Clergy were sometimes treated with contempt. In 1610 Hugo Holland of King's Sutton (Northamptonshire) told his minister to 'kiss his horse under the tail, and saith the world was never merry since priests were married'. When Robert Shore was rebuked in 1619 for leaving Knook Church (Wiltshire) before the sermon was over, he told the preacher: 'Well, we may give you leave to speak, but what remedy you will have for it I know not!' The curate of Ford (Sussex) reported in 1621 that a churchwarden 'hath required me to put my nose in his tail, and in a maid's bum standing by'.[11]

When laymen quarrelled with their ministers, they often sought to undermine their status. Some were called vagabonds, 'rascal and drunken rascal' (Hermitage, Wiltshire, 1606), 'false cullion carl and Scottish rogue' (Ovingham, Northumberland, 1607) or just 'rogue' (Stowe, Buckinghamshire, 1633).[12] Ministers were dismissed as low company, 'lousy rogue, cogging companion and scurvy rascal' (Market Harborough, Leicestershire, 1607) or 'base companion' (North Crawley, Buckinghamshire, 1633);[13] or as contemptible, no better than the mass priests of the old Church – 'scurvy priest' (Cold Norton, Essex, 1605), 'scurvy vicar' (Newport, Buckinghamshire, 1633), 'poll priest and base priest' (Charminster, Dorset, 1635). In 1609 Sir William Clifton was brought before the High Commission 'for beating a reverend minister in very violent manner, bragging that he had beaten forty ministers and that was the forty-first, and reproaching the minister in very scandalous terms'. When Mr Austen of Aveley, Essex, went to discuss tithes with Sir Ferdinand Wenham in 1609, he was called 'proud prelate' and thrown out of the house by the collar: 'thou art a base priest; doth it become a man of your fashion to speak thus unto me?'[14]

The learning of the clergy was derided – as was the lack of it. In 1586 Henry Page of Westbourne in Sussex said that all non-preaching ministers were 'blind shepherds and guides', and Thomas Staker of Barnham claimed that the bishop ordained 'very blind and unskilful ministers'. In 1599 John Cheney of Everley (Wiltshire) called the curate 'dumb dog' to his face.[15] A preaching minister could be called 'prattling fool' (Sandon, Essex, 1592) or simply 'fool' (Prittlewell, Essex, 1605), or 'you saucey prattler' (Towersey, Oxfordshire, 1608), and in 1634 the Vicar of Thornborough in Buckinghamshire was told to 'go prate in his pulpit'.[16] Some clergy were derided as inadequate pastors. The minister of Stanton St John (Oxfordshire) 'was not a man of God but more like a man of the devil' in 1598, and at Barford St Martin (Wiltshire) in 1606, the rector 'yieldeth very sour and bitter fruit to his parishioners'. In 1631 the Rector of Bourton-on-the-Water (Gloucestershire) was 'not fit to feed a flock of Christians, but rather a flock of pigs' – 'Well if he were rooted out and they had a better in his place.' At Worth in Sussex Bridget Weekes called out during a service in 1637 that 'the minister was too busy, and busied himself too much'. 'God deliver us from such a malicious priest!', cried Anne Farmer of Hooe (Sussex) in 1637, 'but if none cared any more for him than herself they would deal well enough with him.'[17]

Ministers were damned as liars, cheats, drunkards and adulterers. Christopher Bayly, curate of Honley, was 'but a lying lad, a double-tongued rascal, unfit for the ministry, and careth not for the best friend that he hath in Yorkshire', according to two parishioners in 1586. Others were called 'usurer' (Bisham, Berkshire, 1592), 'cozener and liar' (Slaughterford, Wiltshire, 1606), 'Judas' (Uffcombe, Devon, 1606), 'liar and common brawler' (Hermitage, 1607), 'thief and naughty person' (Haydon, Northumberland, 1610), 'reprobate and bloodsucker' (King's Sutton, Northamptonshire, 1610) and 'a cozener and a cheat' (Iver, Buckinghamshire, 1634).[18] The Vicar of St Mary's, Beverley, was termed 'common drunkard' in 1586, and his wife 'curtall', or drab. In 1603 the Vicar of Box (Wiltshire) was 'a common drunklord', and in 1622 Thomas Gubbin declared that the ministers of Wardington (Oxfordshire) had been 'both drunkards and whoremasters'.[19] In 1584 the Vicar of Great Tey (Essex) was denounced as 'an evil person and a naughty pack', and the Rector of Halsall (Lancashire) as 'he (meaning the said George Hesketh, clerk, and pointing at him with his finger) that corrupteth all the women in the country'. The curate of Blackmore (Essex) was called 'whoremaster knave' in 1585, and the minister of Folke (Dorset) was told in 1607 that 'there was never a whore or thief in the parish but I took their part'. In 1608 John Everett of Aveley, Essex, was presented 'for saying to Mr Austen that when he were hanged his arse would be colder'.[20]

Ministers were mocked and made fun of, but perhaps sometimes they deserved it. James Dalby, curate of Howden in Yorkshire, had a reputation as an adulterer and brought discredit on other clergy. Richard Gaythorne offered a shoulder of mutton to know if one Dowson 'had made a cap-ease (meaning a thing to keep a man's privy members)' for the curate. There were rhymes against Dalby circulating in the parish in 1583, and a song against all men of the cloth – which Thomas Crozier wanted to sing at a wedding to deride the archbishop. Seven men were called before the High Commission at York for their treatment of Dalby – and he had to purge himself.[21] In 1605 Anne Vincent mimicked the godly vicar of Haydon in Dorset, dressing up in a surplice and spectacles, carrying a book in her hands and crying: 'I cannot endure this papistical book!' James Westwood disturbed a sermon at Shelley in Essex in 1612, calling out from the churchyard in pretence that the minister's roast meat was burning.[22] At Christmas 1636 Thomas Thorne of Barrington, Somerset, preached a mock sermon standing in a barrel, 'to the great laughter of those present and the disgrace of the clergy'. The curate had the good sense not to report the incident, but then was in trouble himself. In 1637 John Fuller of Wilmington, Sussex, tried to make a fool of the minister, 'to put a trick upon him, whereby he might lose his living'. Fuller persuaded 'certain simple women' to take his child up to the font to be christened without notice, 'to try what our minister would do'; 'he should have sent back the child unchristened, if he durst, that I looked for, and thereof would have been glad, for I would go forty miles and further to do him a shrewd turn'.[23]

Married ministers, their wives and children were subjected to frequent abuse; such cases were most common in the obviously conservative parts of England, but were not confined to those regions. In Yorkshire in 1580 a libel against ministers and their wives was circulating at New Malton, five women of Hatfield were given penance for beating the curate and declaring his marriage unlawful, and the wife of a vicar-choral of York Minster slandered married ministers and their wives and children. In 1584 Richard Fox of Gringley (Nottinghamshire) declared 'it was never a good world since priests were married', called the vicar's wife 'painted stock', and predicted that 'priests' calves and bishops' calves would overrun the realm'.[24] John Mous of Little Stambridge in Essex said in 1592 'that all priests wives are whores and their children bastards, and that it is no fame to abuse their bodies for that they are whores'. At Stewton (Lincolnshire) in 1604 Isabel Huddleton talked of 'priests' calves in despiteful manner', and at Thornford in Dorset in 1610 Christian Barnes called the parson's children 'bastards and priest's chits'.[25]

Many slights and attacks arose from the ambiguity of a minister's position, and the difficulty of fitting him and his family into the hierarchies of parish and county. The laity's vocabulary of contempt is illuminating. The insults alleging low status – knave, jackanapes, rascal, rogue, and so on – may suggest that some ministers were claiming a higher rank and were resented, or that others had failed to achieve such a new respectability and were scorned. The assaults on learning and preaching may reflect the higher education and new tasks of the clergy, or again, the inability of some – dumb dogs, for example – to fulfil new roles. The attacks on ministers' morals may result from the grave, aloof, scholarly style adopted by godly clergy, or from the failure of the sociable alebench-curates to adjust to new expectations. Since the social composition, education, wealth and role of the clerical corps were changing rapidly, both social arrangements and social perceptions had to be renegotiated.

The formal complaints which parishioners made against their clergy are also suggestive of lay attitudes and expectations. At each visitation, churchwardens were asked whether their minister had offended against ever-longer lists of ecclesiastical rules – moral, sartorial, social, pastoral, charitable, liturgical and theological. This regular invitation to whinge might have created a culture of complaint – but it did not. Given the range of obligations and the fallibility of men, it is surprising how rarely the wardens complained. Of course, when a minister fell out with his parishioners, they might throw the whole book of articles at him. In October 1617 the people of Upminster in Essex denounced Michael Halke, the rector, as 'a frequenter of taverns, a striker, a fighter, and at contention with his parishioners'; he did not wear a surplice, or catechise or say service on Wednesdays or Fridays – and in the following March they accused him of getting a servant pregnant. In 1634 the Vicar of Thornborough in Buckinghamshire, James Carey, was presented at visitation for contention with his people: he had struck the parish clerk, 'railed upon him in the church', 'called one Nelson, a husbandman, cur dog' in church, and got into squabbles with various others. The parishioners then petitioned the Bishop of Lincoln against Carey, claiming that he was 'very troublesome to his neighbours, little hospitable to strangers, scandalous in his life and his profession'.[26]

When parishioners were angry, any charge would do. By 1636 some of the villagers of Burton Dassett in Warwickshire were gunning for Robert Kenrick, their vicar. In a Laudian world it was convenient to denounce him as a puritan: he did not wear the surplice or his academic hood; he cut out parts of the Prayer Book liturgy; neither he nor his family stood for the Creed and Gospel, or bowed at the name of Jesus; he did not say services on Wednesdays, Fridays, Saturdays or holy days; he churched women in their own seats, without requiring them to be veiled; he shielded Nonconformists from presentment – and he was 'a common haunter of alehouses and reputed to be a common drunkard', or so William Tooley and his friends claimed. But by 1641 things had changed, and Kenrick was now fitted up as a Laudian, 'an innovator of new fashions in his church': he had set the communion table like an altar and railed it in; he insisted that parishioners take communion, women be churched, and newly married couples give thanks at the rail; he did not preach himself, and presented those who went to sermons elsewhere; he reported godly Nonconformists, but protected sinners – and he was still a drunkard, and a 'turbulent and vexatious man', or so William Tooley and his friends claimed.[27] Many laymen showed a sophisticated understanding of how best to make trouble for an unpopular minister.

Such wholesale indictments were rare, and parishioners were usually quite selective in their accusations. Doubtless, complaints were sometimes tailored to meet the concerns of Church authorities, but the rhetoric of reproach reflects laymen's priorities. Unclerkly conduct and neglect of duties seem to have been the most provocative failings of clergy. Visitations of the dioceses of Chichester and Salisbury in 1584 and the archdeaconry of Buckingham in 1584–5 revealed many complaints of negligence, some of them strongly worded. At Compton Shrimsley in Wiltshire in 1584, the churchwardens presented that:

> we have a very bad curate, and that our vicar is able to maintain a sufficient curate that we may have our children better instructed and ourselves better served in the church, and therefore we desire to have such a one as can well serve the cure and instruct our children as he ought to do.

'We demand what order was taken for our last complaint against Henry Ince our parson for being not resident with us, making not his quarter sermons, nor distributing the fourth [sic] part of his benefice among the poor of the parish' protested the wardens of Chalfont St Giles (Buckinghamshire) in 1584, and at Walton in 1585 they reported that:

> we have had no service upon the weekdays this half year, neither have we any service upon the sabbath day but by such a one as is not licensed that we know, neither doth our parson catechise, neither have we had any communion this half year.[28]

Formal complaints of neglect were much less common thereafter, as the supply, and perhaps the quality and discipline, of clergy improved; perhaps lay expectations were being met.

It was a common chorus of godly preachers that their efforts were unappreciated and parishes preferred a sociable 'Sir John':

> If their minister be a quiet man and will use them kindly for their tithes; if he be a good fellow and will sit neighbourly with them and spend his penny as they do theirs in the alehouse; if he read them fair service, as they call it, and trouble them not with preaching too often; or, if he do step now and then into the pulpit, if he meddle not too much with their sins . . . and so please their humours, they care for no more, he is the best minister for them that can be.

Charles Richardson was probably right, and clerical conviviality was expected. It had been the custom for the Vicar of Bere Regis in Dorset to provide bread, cheese and beer at Christmas for the people of Bere Regis and Winterborne Kingston, and when he refused to do so in 1596 both parishes protested – as did the people of Houghton in Sussex against James Pellett in 1604, 'for not paying a customary drinking on the Ascension Day this two years, which have been used'.[29]

It is noticeable that when a minister was reported for tippling, it was usually because his habits interfered with his duties or made him a nuisance. Companionable drinking with parishioners offended only the godly. The curate of Heywood in Lancashire was 'a drunkard and a brawler' in 1595, and the curate of Towersey (Oxfordshire) was 'a quarreler, a fighter and a drunkard' in 1608. John Woodcock of Littlehampton (Sussex) had been too drunk to bury a child in 1622, and Robert Evans was too drunk to read the evening service at West Wycombe (Buckinghamshire) in 1634. Wulfstan Miller, curate of Berwick Bassett (Wiltshire), was presented in 1635 'for debauched living and for being oftentimes drunk', and it was claimed that he had missed the Easter services because of drink. Miller appeared at court and admitted 'that sometimes through weakness he hath been overtaken with drink', but claimed he had been genuinely ill at Easter. A neighbouring minister confirmed the illness, and another wrote that Miller had been 'a painful minister among them these five or six years, ready to do his full endeavour to bring them to the knowledge of the truth' – but now the stipend was about to be augmented, and there was a conspiracy to get rid of the curate.[30]

A contentious minister was the worst of all: the clergy were supposed to reconcile disputes, not cause them. In 1584 the Vicar of Rodbourne Cheney (Wiltshire) was 'a brawler with his neighbours on the sabbath day', and at Barwick St John, 'our minister doth use hunting and bowling now and then, and affirming untrue tales doth set men together by the ears, and is a fighter himself'. The wardens of Ashendon (Buckinghamshire) protested in 1585 that 'our curate is so contentious that he is not to serve any cure', and in 1589 the Rector of

Latchingdon (Essex) was reported as 'a quarreler, a fighter, a brabbler, a common player and gamester, not only on working days but also on holidays, as on Midsummer Day he played at cards the most part of the day and said no divine service'.[31] (Card-playing was acceptable as long as it did not bring inconvenience: in 1595 the Rector of Claughton in Lancashire was presented as 'a dicer and carder at such times as he should edify the flock, and draweth men's servants' to play with him.) In 1597 the two rectors of Pakefield were named at visitation: Thomas Yowle as 'a fighter, a brawler and given to contentions', and Mr Wincoppe because 'he brawled with Mr Yowle in the church'. And in the same year, the curate of Blunsdon (Wiltshire) was presented 'for brawling with his neighbours in church', and because he was 'very negligent in visiting the sick'.[32] But, once again, there were few such reports thereafter.

Formal presentments of negligence and misconduct were numerous in the 1580s, but then they dwindled, and after about 1600 they were uncommon. This does not mean that every later presentment was *omnia bene*, still less that the *omnia bene* was true. Churchwardens on oath might report Nonconformity and technical defects, and it was not unusual for a minister's doctrine to be queried. There were some extreme cases of breakdown in pastoral relations, when villagers laid every charge they thought might stick. But formal presentments of ministers by churchwardens for negligence and misbehaviour became infrequent – more common against curates than incumbents, but rare in any case. It is just possible that parishioners became more careless and more tolerant, but that is most unlikely. When in the 1640s county committees solicited depositions against 'scandalous' clergy, the spontaneous (as opposed to the contrived) responses were in terms of the old grievances – neglect, unseemly conduct and trouble-making. But the charges seem often to have been laid by groups with grudges, scraping the barrel for mud to sling.[33] Parishes still cared about neglect and impropriety, but there was little of it about. Ministers may not have satisfied godly cliques or county committees, but they seem to have satisfied their people – on the whole, by and large, more or less.

There is an interesting paradox, therefore: the number of formal accusations fell, but the number of recorded insults did not. The ministry was reformed, but its members were still scorned. Individuals got into quarrels with their clergy and insulted them; the volume of personal abuse apparently did not decline, and the vocabulary did not much change. The working life of a minister brought unavoidable dispute. When the Vicar of Aveley (Essex) rebuked Margaret Jones in 1606 for swearing:

> she replied saying God's heart, she would swear in spite of his teeth, as she used much swearing, and so she laid violent hands and smote the vicar of the said parish, reproving her for swearing, and followed him swearing most devilishly from the one end of the town to the other.

At communion at Aveley Church in 1608 Elizabeth Wilson cried out that the vicar 'ever was and still is a troublesome man, and that he makes the rest to say unto him the Lord's Prayer and the Belief for very fear, but he should never make her say them whilst he lived'. When in 1610 the Rector of Arborfield (Berkshire) reproached Edward Barber 'for his lewd behaviour and misdemeanour, he avouched he was as good a man as myself, and that he was no more drunkard than myself'. The minister of West Wittering (Sussex) asked Richard Taylor for his tithe wood in 1622, and was called 'shitbreech, and divers other most unseemly names'. At Worth (Sussex) in 1637 the minister reprimanded Sarah Butler for scolding in the churchyard; she responded: '"I care not for our minister, what care I for Mr Whiston?", and so continued in her scolding terms.' Some of the women of Blatchingdon (Sussex) were mocking the minister's sermons in 1638. When he preached on 1 Corinthians 5:7, for example, Joan Wickersham said she would wash some of the parish in the sea, 'and so purge out the old leaven, that they might be a new lump', and Elizabeth Clifford said 'she should purge her ragged cat'.[34]

There was nothing much the ministers could do to escape such abuse and taunting – unless they abandoned the reproof of sin, the examination of communicants, the preaching of sermons and the collection of tithe. The occasions of conflict could not be avoided. The tithe had to be collected, and the minister had to do his job: clergy who condoned wickedness, admitted the unworthy to communion and did not preach were themselves reported to the authorities.[35] The clergy were caught uncomfortably between the demands of their office and the realities of workaday life – and between the standards of the vestry and those of the alehouse. In the 1580s ministers were criticised for not doing their duty; by the 1610s they were more likely to be damned for doing it. The reformation of the ministry brought troubles of its own, and the clergy paid the price of success – with changes in social profile, in education, in marital status, in corporate pride and in wealth.

Although William Harrison, William Perkins, George Downame and Richard Bernard all claimed that scholars and gentlemen would not enter the ministry, they did – and in rising numbers. Slowly the clergy was being gentrified. The percentage of deacons ordained in the Peterborough diocese who were sons of gentlemen rose from only two in the 1570s to six in the 1620s and 1630s. Among incumbents the proportions were much higher. In the dioceses of Oxford and Worcester ten of the graduate beneficed clergy of 1600 were sons of the gentry, but the figure was thirty-three by 1640. In these two dioceses incumbents drawn from the gentry were more likely than others to build themselves imposing new rectories.[36] Among the parish clergy of Bath and Wells between 1600 and 1643, 17 per cent were sons of gentry and 30 per cent sons of ministers; in the diocese of Exeter more than a fifth of incumbents instituted between 1598 and 1621 were sons of clergy.[37] As is well known the early Stuart clergy became a predominantly graduate profession. In Lincolnshire 33 per cent of the clergy were graduates in 1603, but 82 per cent of those presented to their first living between 1600 and 1610 were graduates, and 93 per cent of those presented in the 1630s. Even among Lincolnshire curates, half were graduates by the 1630s. In the diocese of Peterborough half of the incumbents were graduates in 1604, three-quarters by 1622 and 93 per cent by 1640. In the north the figures were lower but still increasing: 11 per cent of Durham clergy were graduates in 1578, 28 per cent in 1604, and 56 per cent in 1634.[38] These scholars and gentlemen had pretensions and expectations – and, like the clergy as a whole, most of them had wives.

What was the place of the minister's wife, and how was this novelty to be fitted into parish life? The wife of the Vicar of Graveney in Kent was unhappy with her seat in church, which was 'not thought fit for any the meanest of the parishioners there to sit, much less for the minister's wife'; instead, and provocatively, she claimed the 'chiefest pew in all the church'. Mrs Austen assumed that her position as the vicar's wife gave her authority in Aveley (Essex): she criticised the parishioners and in 1609 called Miles Shepherd 'rogue and rascal' when he went up to receive the communion. In 1631 the Rector of Bourton-on-the-Water sought permission to erect a new pew for his family in the chancel. Thomas Temple was an Oxford-educated civil lawyer, and soon to take his doctorate; he was the son of a knight, and he had just married well. The Bishop of Gloucester agreed to the pew, partly because the rector's family now included 'persons of good descent and quality'. Temple then built a pew which would reflect his dignity – but one of the gentry families was outraged, and Lucy Aylesworth declared it was 'not fit for a parson's wife to sit above the landlord'.[39]

An educated Protestant preacher demanded a social position higher than that of the massing priests of the old clerical proletariat, and expected easy familiarity with the gentry and deference from their inferiors. A minister might be the son of a gentleman or of a clergyman: he had mixed with their sons at university, and might have married one of their daughters. His education had given him the intellectual and cultural interests of a gentleman, and his university degree gave him a badge of rank. After Robert Jenison, lecturer at All Saints' in Newcastle, had taken his Cambridge doctorate, he inquired of his old tutor in 1630:

> what place, whether by university statute or by heraldry, if by occasion (more than search) you have heard, a doctor of divinity hath, not so much with respect to other degrees of learning, in law or physic, as to *the laity*, as suppose to a justice of the peace (out of his proper place), and whether their wives (by custom at least) take not place answerably. I ask not this with any intent to make other use of it than, as occasion serves, to stop their mouths that are ready too far to debase our calling and degree.[40]

Jenison and his wife wanted their proper position in society.

The Protestant ministry certainly asserted a high view of its status, role and responsibility. William Perkins taught his students at Cambridge that 'every true minister is a double interpreter, God's to the people and the people's to God . . . In which respects he is properly called God's mouth to the people, by preaching to them from God, and the people's mouth to God, by praying for them to God.' George Downame presented the minister as God's instrument for the saving of souls: 'the ministers, having the keys of the kingdom of heaven, have power to bind and loose the souls of men and to deliver the obstinate to Satan'. Downame's 1608 sermon dealt with 'the dignity and duty of the ministry', and the dignity was high: 'those whom the Lord calleth to the ministry he advanceth above the condition of other men, calling them as to a charge, so also to an honour, which might seem to become angels rather than men'. George Herbert's country parson was 'the deputy of Christ', who stood 'in God's stead to his parish'. In a visitation sermon preached at Cerne in Dorset in July 1640, ministers were exhorted to 'Uphold the dignity of your calling, who are ordained rulers of that kingly priesthood of the Church of God . . . Consider well the eminence of your ordination: you are amongst this peculiar people peculiarly consecrated to the service of your God.'[41]

Students and ordinands were told to take pride in the ministerial calling, and as serving clergy they did – but not always with sensitivity. The Vicar of Bremhill in Wiltshire seems to have been an arrogant and ill-tempered man: when reported in 1605 for mistreating his parishioners, he admitted that when provoked he had used 'some angry speeches against such of his neighbours, but not the better sort of them'. A temporary curate at Sandhurst was bragging in 1607 'that he is nothing inferior to the most preachers at the time' – but he was in the alehouse at the time. In the same year the Vicar of Yetminster (Dorset) complained that there was no parish clerk at Chetnole chapel, so he had to get things ready for services himself:

by means whereof the minister (in seeking from house to house for the chapel door key, in ringing, chiming, tolling, bringing the books in place and putting on his surplice by himself alone) is made as it were a slave, to the great reproach of his calling and slander of the Gospel.[42]

Ministers were anxious that disobedient parishioners be punished and made to obey them. The Vicar of Ogbourne St George (Wiltshire) complained in 1607 of misconduct in the church, which he was unable to control: 'I think verily that amongst the wild Irish at this day there is not a more disordered behaviour amongst them in time of divine service than in this church.' In 1620 the Rector of Charminster (Dorset) asked for a process against Alice Adams for disturbing his catechism class, or others might follow her example 'and be the ruinating of all godly order in the church at Charminster'. When a couple from Olney (Buckinghamshire) protested about the vicar's sermon on confession in 1633, he made them give a public acknowledgement of their fault in the church.[43]

Ministers had a dignity, and they stood on it. When a churchwarden at Highworth (Wiltshire) asked to see Mr Fanne's preaching licence in 1627, the minister 'called him slave and base fellow, and said before he had done of him he would make him repent it and make a poor fellow of him'. When Sir Thomas Temple suggested in 1629 that John Reignoldes, Vicar of Burton Dassett (Warwickshire), should repay rents he had charged parishioners, Reignoldes responded with righteous clerical indignation: 'you say I must remember what I owe to God and the Church; would God men of your rank would remember what they owe to God and the Church, and restore it'. The vicar was not happy with his cure, and was soon seeking to escape. He complained to Lady Hester Temple that although:

> my labour in preaching (I speak not to boast myself) is not inferior to any of my fellow-ministers in these parts, my people here are peevish, perverse, peremptory, froward, fantastical, false-hearted, in their censures void of Christianity, in their lives of charity, in their common conversation of humanity, a people that affect me not neither any way deserve to be affected by me.

The curate of Heathfield (Somerset) had no better opinion of his flock, saying in 1637: 'he would baptise or christen a sow, and make as good a Christian as any is in our parish'.[44]

Ministers had an elevated view of what their status and rights ought to be. Increasingly they based their claims to tithes not just on law and custom, but on the will of God. Just as God had set the clergy apart from (and above) the laity, so he had set aside one-tenth of his gifts for them. George Carleton laid out the terms of the debate about tithe in 1606, and said that there were three opinions on clerical incomes: that clergy should live from free offerings, that they were entitled only to 'a reasonable and competent maintenance', and that 'tithes are due to the ministers of the Church by the express word of God'. It was hoped that his book would persuade readers:

> that tithes are the Lord's portion, holy to himself; that this portion he hath given to his ministers that serve at the altar; and so consequently that they may not safely detain that from the clergy which belongs unto them, but rather make a restitution with all humility.

Thereafter, a clutch of writers asserted this third opinion. Some grounded the payment of tithe on the Fifth Commandment, arguing that honour to parents included honour to ministers, and honouring required adequate maintenance.[45] Others contended that the practice of the Old and New Testaments and of the early Church showed that God had commanded the payment of tithe to his priests.

This divine right to tithe was affirmed by Carleton in 1606, George Downame in 1608, Richard Eburne in 1609, William Sclater in 1612, Fulke Robartes in 1613 and Samuel Crooke in 1615 – and several claimed that any infringement of the clergy's strict tenth by composition or impropriation was sacrilege. Eburne argued that inflation had eroded cash incomes, and demanded a wholesale restitution of a full tithe in kind and of personal tithes from wage-earners. Significantly, one of his reasons was the rising status of ministers: a generation earlier 'the ministry was filled up with rag, tag, such as the time would yield, tailors, weavers, etc. and whosoever else but was made a priest' – now the ministry was 'stored with able and learned men', and should be paid accordingly.[46]

The implications of such assertions were shattering: statute, common law and local custom on tithe were in conflict with the law of God. By the moral law at least, impropriations of rectories should be restored, leases of tithes surrendered, compositions and exemptions abandoned, and the laity should pay more to their ministers. The common lawyer John Selden's response, in *The Historie of Tithes* (1618), was to challenge the claim that tithe had been a compulsory payment among Christians since the time of the Apostles, and to argue that in practice tithe was subject to local custom and positive human law. He insisted that the history:

> is not written to prove that tithes are not due by the law of God; not written to prove that the laity may detain them; not to prove that lay hands may still enjoy appropriations; in sum, not at all against the maintenance of the clergy.

But the clergy did not believe him. Selden had caused a stir, and had to be refuted. Richard Tillesley, Archdeacon of Rochester, replied with *Animadversions upon M. Selden's History of Tythes* in 1619, and an extended edition in 1621 – 'maintaining the *ius divinum* of tithes, or more, to be paid to the priesthood under the Gospel'. Tillesley said some readers thought Selden had demolished the clergy's claims, but pointed out that he had apologised before the High Commission in 1619 for publishing the book – though Selden retorted that the apology was for any offence caused, not for any untruth.[47]

Richard Montagu's substantial *Diatribae* appeared in 1621, and denounced Selden as:

> the most capital enemy, of a man of your rank and ability, unto the Church, and most pernicious underminer of the Church and of religion in the Church, that the prince of darkness hath set on work to do mischief many years.

For Montagu, Selden really was an anticlerical – a writer who had quite deliberately set out to attack the clergy and weaken their position. The pernicious *Historie* was being discussed in the streets, and men who had not read it were saying that 'Master Selden was unanswerable, and had given the clergy such a blow in their claim for tithes as was irrecoverable.' But Montagu claimed that only 'the violentest Puritans and arrantest Papists' among the clergy disagreed with the divine origin of tithing: 'Have any withstood or stood against the *ius divinum*? Divers have declared themselves for it, and those otherwise of a preciser cut' – and he was right. Calvinists and Arminians, puritans and conformists, all wanted the clergy's rights. But Montagu now made explicit what others had only implied, that 'no state hath power to dispense with or dispose against the natural, moral and positive law of God'.[48] This was high clericalism indeed: the clergy had a divine right to a full tithe, and there was nothing that common law or statute could properly do to limit it.

All this was much more than a theoretical debate – which is why Tillesley and Montagu took Selden so seriously, and obtained the King's support for their literary efforts. Eburne, Sclater, Robartes and the rest were advancing views that many ministers shared – that the Church's revenues should be returned, that they should have their full tithe, and that the laity should be made to pay. John Reignoldes, Vicar of Burton Dassett, got into a row with his patron in 1629 and blew his top. Sir Thomas Temple was one of the impropriators, and Reignoldes was furious with them. They held the rectory and the vicarage glebe:

> which both are my right, which your souls shall one day rue; ye have got away our tithes, ye have got away our land, and then ye bind us to discharge heavy burdens which we are not able to undergo. Your oppression is like Pharaoh's, you take away the straw and yet require the bricks. O repent, repent, before the curse wax ripe, and put an end to these disasters by yielding to God and the Church in what is meet.

Sadly, Reignoldes could not afford such righteous fury. Three months later he wrote again to Temple: he had just got married, he was off to visit his wife's family and he needed a loan – 'I confess myself to be a little hasty; my urgent occasions press me to it.'[49]

There is some evidence that the parish clergy were now more determined to assert their supposed rights – and more willing to go to court to enforce them. From 1591 they had William Clerk's *A Tithing-Table* to help them, a handy compendium of the laws of tithe, in its ninth edition by 1629. We cannot be sure whether tithe-owners were asking for more or whether tithe-payers were trying to give less, but there was a big increase in numbers of tithe cases before the courts. In the consistory court at York the number of tithe suits in a year increased from 72 in 1581–2 to 143 in 1611–12, falling back to 101 in 1634–5. In Lincolnshire there were 139 tithe suits in 1601–10, and 225 in 1631–40. In the Durham consistory the number of tithe cases rose from 287 in 1577–82 to 411 in 1595–1600 and 633 in 1629–34.[50] But in each area, lay impropriators and tithe-lessees were at least as likely as incumbents to sue parishioners for tithe, which suggests that economic pressures may have been more significant than clerical assertiveness.

There is, however, an interesting hint that lay and clerical motives may have differed. Litigation often arose from attempts by tithe-owners and lessees to overturn commutation agreements, in which cash payments had been substituted for tithe in kind, because inflation had now eroded the value of fixed payments. Lay owners and farmers of rectories tried to re-establish the payment of great tithes in kind, demanding a tithe of grain and hay to increase their profits. But from about 1600 clergy were seeking to overthrow customary commutation agreements on small tithes to achieve a full tithe in kind, and this was true in York and Lincolnshire, and the dioceses of Oxford and Worcester. Small tithes – especially the less valuable ones such as eggs, milk, chickens and rabbits – were worth comparatively little, and earlier commutations had not seriously diminished clerical incomes. From a strictly economic point of view, it was barely worth the cost of litigation to try to increase income from some small tithes – and it was not worth the ill-feeling engendered in parishes.[51] But rectors and vicars were challenging old agreements, apparently in pursuit of their 'rights', rather than profits.

It was not poverty which explains the growth in tithe-litigation, for the poorest ministers had no tithe to pursue and it was often the richer rectors who went to court. Although ministers complained about beggarly incomes, and argued that poor financial prospects deterred recruits, most of them were decently paid. In the diocese of Worcester between 1535 and 1650 rectories increased in value by six times on average, and vicarages by three-and-a-half times; in the diocese of Durham livings increased by between four-and-a-half and five-and-a-half times, and the poorest livings improved most. With the exception of curates and vicars on stipends (especially those with no glebe lands), it seems that ministers' incomes had more than kept pace with inflation and many rectors had prospered.[52] In most cases it was not necessary for incumbents to chase low-value small tithes – but they did so. Of course, ministers now had wives and children to support, but for an incumbent with glebe to farm a family could be an economic asset. Of course, an educated clergy expected a higher standard of living and had to buy the books of their trade – but this did not necessarily make them rapacious.

Although incumbents were anxious to have their rights established, they did not always enforce them in full. The rectors of Bolton Percy and of Guiseley in Yorkshire were both willing to allow tithe-payers to fall into arrears or to pay what they could afford, provided the incumbent's rights were recognised. Ministers had a high view of their calling and thought God had given them the tithe, but they lived in real pastoral situations, they had to get along with their parishioners and some of them were charitable men. That was not always how the laity saw it. A minister who counted out his tithe-eggs, or tracked beasts as they moved in and out of his parish, perhaps meant to safeguard the rights of the Church, but his parishioners may have thought him grasping and self-seeking. And changes to tithing customs could affect the whole parish, so it is not surprising that parishioners sometimes banded together to meet the cost of what was, in effect, a test-case. In 1605 the Vicar of Steeple Barton in Oxfordshire sued Paul Hurst for tithe in kind on sheep sold before tithing time: the villagers agreed to share Hurst's costs in defending what they claimed was the custom of the parish.[53]

Some ministers were more charitable than others; some were more tactful than their fellows, and no doubt some preferred a quiet life to a pursuit of rights. But it certainly seemed that under the Stuarts, the clergy were more assertive – and with royal backing. The answers to Selden's *Historie* were dedicated to James I: Sir James Sempill was a Scottish courtier and friend of the King; Richard Tillesley was a royal chaplain; and Richard Montagu was specifically recruited by James to refute Selden.[54] The clergy were asking for more – more tithe, more respect, more recognition of their dignities, and, it seemed, more power. The King, who backed their demand for a strict tithe, also promoted their authority in the state, and warned the laity – 'great men, lords, and people of all degrees from the highest to the lowest' – to treat them with respect. James appointed successive Archbishops of Canterbury, Bancroft and Abbot, to the privy council, and in 1615 he began to appoint diocesans too: Bishops Bilson, Andrewes, Montagu and Williams. Charles I appointed Bishops Laud, Neile and Juxon, and Archbishop Harsnett of York.[55] It seemed that certain bishoprics brought *ex officio* seats on the council – Canterbury and Winchester under James, and Canterbury, York and Durham under Charles. In 1621 the Bishop of Lincoln was Lord Keeper, in effect the first clerical chancellor since Wolsey; in 1636 the Bishop of London became the first clerical treasurer since Bishop Grey in 1470.

There was also a clerical invasion of the county commissions of the peace. Clergy-JPs had been unusual under Elizabeth I: in some jurisdictions the bishop, and perhaps the dean, was appointed, but parish incumbents had been rare among the justices. The rise of the clergy began about 1617: certainly in Hampshire, Somerset, Wiltshire, Northumberland and Durham it then became usual to appoint deans and often canons, and parish clergy became much more prominent on county benches. In 1604 there had been only ten clerical justices below the rank of dean in England and Wales, but by 1625 there were ninety-one; in the 1630s roughly one in ten of working JPs was a minister. The early clergy-JPs had not been very active but by the 1630s the ministers were among the most assiduous of justices, attending quarter sessions regularly and busy with out-of-sessions work, so perhaps they seemed more numerous than they really were.[56] Ministers now sat alongside the senior gentry of a county, and took places that many gentlemen would themselves have wished for. The clergy were being hauled up the social hierarchy.

There were protests in Parliament, with bills against clergymen serving as justices promoted in the Commons in 1614, 1621, 1626, 1628 (reintroduced in 1629) and 1640. The 1614 bill failed at its first reading, and the King blocked the 1621 bill, but in 1626 and 1628 the bills passed through the Commons and were lost in the Lords. There were usually exceptions for bishops and sometimes for deans, but this was anticlericalism indeed – a protest not against individual ministers or the failings of some, but against the power of the clerical order. MPs argued that judicial work distracted ministers from their pastoral responsibilities, or that clergy should not try cases of blood, or that ministers should not interfere in laymen's business, or that clergymen might not meet the property qualifications of justices.[57] In fact, a deliberate clerical invasion of the bench was probably an illusion, and the appointment of clergy-JPs owed more to the education and gentrification of the ministry. Clerical justices were often doctors of divinity, holding the best benefices in a county, and many of them came from gentry families or had important patrons. They were appointed by the same processes of patronage and lobbying as were other justices, and were the sort of men who might have joined the commissions even without the benefit of priesthood.[58] Clerical justices reflected the rising status of the ministry, not a clerical conspiracy.

If there was significant anticlericalism between 1580 and 1640, there are some arguments for thinking it was a lay reaction to clericalism – both Calvinist clericalism and Arminian clericalism. MPs' complaints against parish incumbents serving as justices were a reaction to the novelty of their presence on county benches. Selden's *Historie of Tithes* was a defensive reply to the new doctrine of the divine right to tithe. The common lawyers' resort to prohibitions against Church courts was a response to the energy of the High Commission and to the argument that secular courts should have no jurisdiction over tithe. If tithe-payers banded together against their minister, it was usually because he was seeking to overthrow long-established tithing customs and achieve a full tenth – and if they called him a thief or a cheat, it might be because his prosperity was all too obvious. If ministers were scorned as knaves or fools, it was sometimes because they were not, because some were gentlemen and others wished to be, because many had education, and all had books. If women of a parish (and it usually was the women) mocked a minister's wife, it was often because a social pre-eminence was claimed for her. And if a whole parish turned against their priest, it could be the fault of his authoritarian manner, his standing on his clerical dignity. The Root and Branch petition of 1640 claimed that the bishops had encouraged 'ministers to

despise the temporal magistracy, the nobles and gentry of the land, to abuse the
subjects and live contentiously with their neighbours, knowing that they, being
the bishops' creatures, will be supported'. Clarendon thought it was clerical
pride which alienated laymen:

> they did observe the inferior clergy took more upon them than they had used
> to do, and did not live towards their neighbours of quality or their patrons
> themselves with that civility and condescension they had used to do; which
> disposed them likewise to a withdrawing their good countenance and good
> neighbourhood from them.[59]

The clergy thought they were gentry's equals, and neither the gentry nor the
commoners liked that.

Thomas Pestell was an embittered careerist. He was the son of a Leicester
tailor but he had a Cambridge degree and a couple of benefices in Leicestershire,
and was the Earl of Essex's chaplain for a time. He was a poet, a preacher and a
royal chaplain – and then advancement stopped: he was stuck at Packington, and
his poems contrasted the success of his friends with his own obscurity. He had a
short temper and a sharp tongue: as a neighbouring minister remarked, 'Mr
Pestell would abuse any man, from prince to the peasant.' He fell out with some
of his leading parishioners, who laughed at his poems and his published sermons:
he was mocked as 'T.P., Thomas Pluralities, bodkinadoes and Spanish needles'.
There were disagreements and fisticuffs over tithe – and, worst of all, in May
1630 he had a row with his patron, the Earl of Huntingdon, in the Earl's own
house. Pestell had boarded and taught the Earl's children, and asked for his fee
with a jeer – 'Begone poor scab!', cried the Earl, and he complained to the
Bishop of Lincoln about Pestell's impudence.[60]

Pestell preached a visitation sermon at Leicester in 1630, and spoke with
feeling. It was a calamity for ministers:

> when we find ourselves disgraced, counted the scum of those that are indeed
> the scum of the world. When all we can say or do, which way soever we frame
> our doctrine or conversation, it is water spilt on the ground. For though we
> pipe unto them, they will not dance; though we mourn, they will not weep . . .
> So that the ground of the quarrel rests not in being thus or thus affected or
> qualified or endowed, but they hate us for our very calling.

Pestell was not a tactful man. He went on to criticise those who mistreated their
inferiors: 'Is a lord's flesh and blood of a purer composition than his groom's or
his footman's? Did not He that made me in the womb make him?' And he
demanded that ecclesiastical authority should uphold the dignity of the
priesthood, not just the 'pomp of some superior prelates'. He was soon in a lot

of trouble. He tried to apologise to Huntingdon, and offered to 'make him any submission that should be thought fitting for a man of his cloth, adding withal that he would lay his hands under his lordship's foot' – but it did no good. The Bishop of Lincoln held an inquiry into his conduct towards the Earl, Pestell's enemies lodged an array of charges and he was hauled before the High Commission in 1633. Thomas Pestell, like John Reignoldes of Burton Dassett, found that clerical pride was not enough, and later had to grovel: 'he confesses himself the chief of sinners, a man under infirmities and subject to passion'.[61]

Thomas Pestell, like many, many others, had tried to be a model minister: studious, dutiful, charitable to poor parishioners, stern to sinners, proud of his order – and it had led to criticism, conspiracy and contempt. He was an awkward character, it is true, but he had stood up for the dignity of a minister – and had been slapped down. But was he right? Did the laity 'hate us for our very calling'? Perhaps the clergy were too touchy, too concerned with reputation, too watchful for slights. They claimed a new status, and were only too aware that it might be refused – and Pestell could not take a joke. The anticlericalism was in the eye of the clericalist beholder: he watched for it and, in a sense, he manufactured it. In the diocese of Durham the ecclesiastical commission dealt with only one case of disrespect towards a minister between 1614 and 1617, but such cases were common from 1626. Did relations between clergy and laity really deteriorate so rapidly, or was the court being used to enforce unaccustomed deference towards ministers? With a sympathetic commission to back them, it seems that the Durham clergy were less tolerant of irreverence and more determined to have respect. Whether the court could achieve it for them is another matter. George Herbert regarded the law in such cases as a last and undesirable resort: better to treat contempt with humility, disdain, grief, pity or joy at a share in the sufferings of Christ.[62] But Herbert really was a gentleman, and he had nothing to prove.

Notes

1   R. Bolton, 'The Saints' Self-enriching Examination', in *A Three-Fold Treatise* (London, 1634), p. 279.

2   W. Harrison, *The Description of England*, ed. G. Edelen (1968), p. 40; A. Dent, *The Plaine-Man's Pathway to Heaven* (London, 1631 edn), p. 127; J. Nichols, *The Plea of the Innocent* ([Middelburg], 1602), p. 225; G. Downame, 'A Sermon of the Dignity and Duty of the Ministry', in *Two Sermons* (London, 1608), p. 90; R. Bernard, *The Faithfull Shepheard, amended and enlarged* (London, 1609), p. 5; P. Barker, *A Judicious and Paineful Exposition upon the Ten Commandments* (London, 1624), p. 216.

3   W. Perkins, *The Workes*, iii (Cambridge, 1608), p. 460; Bernard, *Faithfull Shepheard*, pp. 3 and 5; Downame, *Two Sermons*, p. 67; Barker, *Judicious and Paineful Exposition*, p. 215; G. Herbert, 'A Priest to the Temple', in *George Herbert and Henry Vaughan*, ed. L.L. Martz (Oxford, 1986), p. 226.

4   Perkins, *Workes*, iii, p. 432; Downame, *Two Sermons*, p. 4; Herbert, 'Priest to the Temple', p. 226; C. Richardson, *A Workeman that Needeth not to be Ashamed* (London, 1616), p. 57.

5   Perkins, *Workes*, iii, Crashaw's epistle dedicatory to Perkins's second sermon 'Of the Calling of the Ministry', unpaginated; Perkins, *Workes*, iii, p. 433.

6   E. Cardwell, *Documentary Annals* (Oxford, 1844), i, p. 224; *Visitation Articles and Injunctions of the Early Stuart Church*, ed. K. Fincham (Church of England Record Society, Woodbridge): i (1994), pp. 78, 129, 195 and 166; ii (1998), pp. 154–5.

7   Essex Record Office, Chelmsford (hereafter ERO), D/AE/A12, ff. 17v, 266; D/AC/A20, f. 65; D/AE/A26, f. 20v; West Sussex Record Office (hereafter WSRO), Ep.I/23/6, f. 11; Borthwick Institute, York (hereafter BIY), HC.AB10, ff. 284v–5; Buckinghamshire Record Office (hereafter BRO), D/A/V/1, f. 51v; *The Churchwardens' Presentments in the Oxfordshire Peculiars of Dorchester, Thame and Banbury*, ed. S.A. Peyton (Oxfordshire Record Society, 1928), pp. 161–2; E.R.C. Brinkworth, *Shakespeare and the Bawdy Court of Stratford* (1972), p. 164; *Churchwardens' Presentments (17th century): Archdeaconry of Chichester*, ed. H. Johnstone (Sussex Record Society, 1948), p. 11; Wiltshire Record Office (hereafter WRO), D5/28/35, no. 51.

8   BIY, HC.AB10, f. 260; *The Archdeacon's Court: Liber Actorum, 1584*, ed. E.R. Brinkworth (Oxfordshire Record Society, 1942), p. 9; *Bishop Redman's Visitation, 1597*, ed. J.F. Williams (Norfolk Record Society, 1946), p. 95; ERO, D/AC/A31, f. 17; D/AE/A26, f. 29; WRO, D5/28/35, no. 73, f. 6.

9   WRO, D5/28/9, no. 26; *Oxfordshire Peculiars*, 194; ERO, D/AE/A26, f. 29; Henry E. Huntington Library, San Marino, California (hereafter HEHL), STT Legal Ms 171.

10   F.G. Emmison, *Elizabethan Life: Morals and the Church Courts, mainly from Essex Archidiaconal records* (Chelmsford, 1973), p. 209; WRO, D5/28/22, no. 52.

11   *Oxfordshire Peculiars*, p. 286; WRO, D5/28/20, no. 25; *Chichester Presentments*, p. 6.

12   WRO, D5/28/9, no. 62; Durham University, Department of Palaeography and Diplomatic (hereafter DUDPD), D.R.II.6, f. 9v; BRO, D/A/V/2, f. 55v.

13   *The State of the Church*, ed. C.W. Foster (Lincoln Record Society, 1926), p. lxxx; BRO, D/A/V/2, f. 104.

14   ERO, D/AE/A23, f. 166v; D/AE/A25, f. 90; BRO, D/A/V/2, f. 96v; WRO, D5/28/35, no. 69; HEHL, Ms. EL2014, f. 1v.

15   WSRO, Ep.I/23/7, ff. 23, 30v; WRO, D3/7/1, f. 170v.

16   W.H. Hale, *A Series of Precedents and Proceedings* (London, 1847), p. 208; ERO, D/AE/A23, f. 218v; *Oxfordshire Peculiars*, p. 194; BRO, D/A/V/2, ff. 141–v.

17   Oxfordshire Record Office, Ms Oxf. Dioc. d.6, f. 13v; WRO, D1/39/2/6, f. 25v; HEHL, Ms EL7895, p. 2; WSRO, Ep.II/15/1, ff. 27, 33.

18   BIY, HC.AB11, f. 64v; WRO, D1/39/2/2, f. 42; D1/39/2/6, f. 11; D5/28/10, no. 92; D5/28/9, no. 32; DUDPD, D.R.II.7, f. 134; *Oxfordshire Peculiars*, p. 286; BRO, D/A/V/2, f. 168v.

19   BIY, HC.AB11, f. 83; WRO, D3/4/1, f. 194; *Oxfordshire Peculiars*, p. 315.

20   ERO, D/AC/A12, f. 142v; D/AE/A12, f. 319; D/AE/A25, f. 85; Cheshire Record Office, EDC5/1584; WRO, D5/28/9, no. 43.

21   BIY, HC.AB10, ff. 240, 243, 247–8v.

22   WRO, D5/28/10, nos 30 and 62; ERO, D/AE/A26, f. 293.

23   Somerset Record Office (hereafter SRO), D/D/Ca.313, ff. 71v–2; WSRO, Ep.II/15/1, f. 20.

24   BIY, HC.AB10, ff. 16, 54 and 59v; R.F.B. Hodgkinson, 'Extracts from the Act Books of the Archdeacons of Nottingham', *Transactions of the Thoroton Society*, xxix (1925), p. 42.

25   Emmison, *Elizabethan Life: Morals*, p. 215; *State of the Church*, p. lxvii; WRO, D5/28/13, no. 53.

26   ERO, D/AE/A30, ff. 140, 201v; BRO, D/A/V/2, ff. 141–5; HEHL, STT Manorial, Box 3(4).

27   HEHL, STT Legal, Mss 70A, 70B; STT Manorial, Box 20(25).

28   WRO, D1/43/5, ff. 33v–4; BRO, D/A/V/1, ff. 37v and 42.

29   Richardson, *Workeman*, pp. 40–1; WRO, D5/28/7, nos 116 and 124; WSRO, Ep.I/17/11, f. 103.

30   BIY, V.1595/CB1, f. 23v; *Oxfordshire Peculiars*, pp. 194–5; *Chichester Presentments*, p. 36; BRO, D/A/V/2, f. 164v; WRO, D5/28/35, nos 17, 18 and 22.

31   WRO, D1/43/5, ff. 23 and 35; BRO, D/A/V/1, f. 50v; F.G. Emmison, *Elizabethan Life: Disorder. Mainly from Essex Sessions and Assize records* (Chelmsford, 1970), p. 219.

32   BIY, V.1595/CB1, f. 61v; *Bishop Redman's Visitation*, p. 126; WRO, D5/28/7, no. 55.

33   I.M. Green, 'The persecution of "scandalous" and "malignant" parish clergy during the English Civil War', *English Historical Review*, xciv (1979), pp. 519–22.

34   ERO, D/AE/A23, f. 351; D/AE/A25, f. 11v; WRO, D5/28/10, no. 2; *Chichester Presentments*, p. 53; WSRO, Ep.II/15/1, ff. 5 and 38.

35   The troubles which arose over examination for and exclusion from communion (and from failure to examine and exclude) are discussed in C. Haigh, 'Communion and community: exclusion from communion in post-Reformation England', *Journal of Ecclesiastical History*, li (2000).

36   M. Hawkins, 'Ambiguity and contradiction in "the rise of professionalism": the English clergy, 1570–1730', in A.L. Beier, D. Cannadine and J.M. Rosenheim (eds), *The First Modern Society: Essays in English History in Honour of Lawrence Stone* (Cambridge, 1989), p. 267; D.M. Barratt, 'The condition of the parish clergy between the Reformation and 1660, with special reference to the dioceses of Oxford, Worcester and Gloucester' (University of Oxford, DPhil thesis, 1949), pp. 18–19 and 332–4.

37   M. Stieg, *Laud's laboratory: The Diocese of Bath and Wells in the early seventeenth century* (Lewisburg, PA, 1982), p. 69; I. Cassidy, 'The episcopate of William Cotton, bishop of Exeter, 1598–1621' (University of Oxford, BLitt thesis, 1963), p. 54.

38   H. Hajzyk, 'The Church in Lincolnshire, c. 1595–c. 1640' (University of Cambridge PhD thesis, 1980), pp. 174–5; E.J.I. Allen, 'The state of the Church in the diocese of Peterborough, 1601–42' (University of Oxford, BLitt thesis, 1972), p. 23; J. Freeman, 'The parish ministry in the diocese of Durham, c. 1570–1640' (University of Durham, PhD thesis, 1979), p. 28.

39   P. Collinson, 'Shepherds, sheepdogs, and hirelings: The pastoral ministry in post-Reformation England', in W.J. Shiels and D. Wood (eds), *The Ministry*; Studies in Church History xxvi (Oxford, 1989), p. 215; ERO, D/AE/A25, f. 97; HEHL, STT Manorial, Box 18 (3, 9); Ms EL7895, p. 2.

40   Bodleian Library, Oxford (hereafter BLO), Tanner Ms. 71, f. 30.

41   Perkins, *Workes*, iii, p. 431; Downame, *Two Sermons*, pp. 30–1, 39 and 56; Herbert, 'Priest to the Temple', pp. 191 and 214; BLO, Rawlinson Ms C764, f. 59. For other claims that ministers had God-given authority over laymen, see B. Donagan, 'Puritan ministers and laymen: Professional

claims and constraints in seventeenth-century England', *Huntington Library Quarterly*, xlvii (1984), pp. 84–5.

42   WRO, D3/4/1, f. 259; D5/28/10, no. 41; D5/28/9, no. 13.

43   WRO, D5/28/10, no. 68; D5/28/21, no. 8; BRO, D/A/V/2, f. 105v.

44   WRO, D10/4/1, 12 April 1627; HEHL, STT Mss 1665, 1664; SRO, D/D/Ca.313, f. 96v.

45   G. Carleton, *Tithes Examined and proved to bee due to the Clergie by a divine right* (London, 1606), f. 1, sig. Aiii; J. Dod, *A Plaine and Familiar Exposition of the Ten Commandments* (London, 1612), pp. 237–8; J. Mayer, *The English Catechisme* (London, 1621), pp. 318 and 383–7; Barker, *Judicious and Paineful Exposition*, pp. 213 and 218–19.

46   Downame, *Two Sermons*, p. 72; R. Eburne, *The Maintenance of the Ministerie* (London, 1609), pp. 82–3, 87–90, 130–9 and 175; W. Sclater, *The Minister's Portion* (Oxford, 1612), pp. 9 and 42–9; F. Robartes, *The Revenue of the Gospel is Tythes, Due to the Ministerie of the word by that word* (Cambridge, 1613), p. 25; S. Crooke, *The ministeriall husbandry and building*, in *Three Sermons* (London, 1615), p. 121.

47   J. Selden, *The Historie of Tithes* (1618), preface, sig. a2; R. Tillesley, *Animadversions upon M. Selden's History of Tythes and his Review thereof* (London, 1621), sigs A4, B4; second pagination, p. 27.

48   R. Montagu, *Diatribae upon the First Part of the late History of Tithes* (London, 1621), pp. 20–1, 86, 88 and 107.

49   HEHL, STT Mss 1665, 1666.

50   W.J. Sheils, '"The right of the Church": the clergy, tithe, and the courts at York, 1540–1640', in W.J. Sheils (ed.), *The Church and Wealth*; Studies in Church History xxiv (Oxford, 1987), pp. 235–6; Hajzyk, 'Church in Lincolnshire', pp. 211–12; Freeman, 'Parish ministry', p. 160.

51   D.M. Gransby, 'Tithe disputes in the diocese of York, 1540–1639' (University of York M.Phil. thesis, 1966), pp. 76, 100 and 233; Sheils, 'The right of the Church', pp. 244–6; Hajzyk, 'Church in Lincolnshire', pp. 214–15; Barratt, 'Condition of the parish clergy', pp. 260 and 272.

52   Ibid., pp. 195–203; Freeman, 'Parish ministry', pp. 137–8.

53   Sheils, 'The right of the Church', pp. 246–52; Barratt, 'Condition of the parish clergy', pp. 216 and 272.

54   J. Sempill, *Sacrilege Sacredly Handled* (London, 1619); Tillesley, *Animadversions*, sig. A4; D.R. Woolf, *The Idea of History in Early Stuart England* (Toronto, 1990), p. 233.

55   *The Workes of the Most High and Mighty Prince James* (London, 1616), p. 554; A. Foster, 'The clerical estate revitalised', in K. Fincham (ed.), *The Early Stuart Church, 1603–1642* (Basingstoke, 1993), p. 141.

56   Ibid., pp. 148–9; T.G. Barnes, *Somerset 1625–1640: A county's government during the 'personal rule'* (Oxford, 1961), pp. 45–6; A.D. Wall, 'The Wiltshire commission of the peace, 1590–1620' (University of Melbourne MA thesis, 1966), pp. 137–45; Freeman, 'Parish ministry', pp. 337–42; J.H. Gleason, *The Justices of the Peace in England, 1558–1640* (Oxford, 1969), p. 49.

57   Foster, 'Clerical estate revitalised', pp. 156–8; C. Russell, *Parliaments and English Politics, 1621–1629* (Oxford, 1979), pp. 43, 277 and 406.

58   Barnes, *Somerset*, p. 45; Freeman, 'Parish ministry', pp. 338–9; Wall, 'Wiltshire', pp. 139–45.

59   J.P. Kenyon, *The Stuart Constitution* (Cambridge, 1966), p. 172; Edward, Earl of Clarendon, *The History of the Rebellion and Civil Wars in England* (Oxford, 1888), i, p. 130.

60   HEHL, HA Legal, Box 5(9), ff. 9v–10, 11, 15v, 55v–6, 72v, 104–5, 112 and 119v; HA Legal, Box 5(8); HA Ms. 13329.

61   T[homas] P[estell], *God's Visitation* (London, 1630), pp. 12, 28, 33 and 166; HEHL, HA Legal, Box 5(9), ff. 94v–5; HA Legal, Box 5(8); HA Ms 13329; *The Poems of Thomas Pestell*, ed. H. Buchan (Oxford, 1940), pp. 124–8 and 141.

62   Freeman, 'Parish ministry', pp. 364 and 438; Herbert, 'Priest to the Temple', p. 226.

FURTHER READING

Collinson, P., 'Shepherds, sheepdogs, and hirelings: The pastoral ministry in post-Reformation England', Studies in Church History xxvi (1989).

Foster, A., 'The clerical estate revitalised', in K. Fincham (ed.), *The Early Stuart Church, 1603–1642* (1993).

Green, I.M., 'The persecution of "scandalous" and "malignant" parish clergy during the English Civil War', *English Historical Review*, xciv (1979).

Hill, C., *Economic Problems of the Church* (1956).

O'Day, R., *The English Clergy: The Emergence and Consolidation of a Profession, 1558–1642* (1979).

Sheils, W.J., '"The right of the Church": the clergy, tithe, and the courts at York, 1540–1640', Studies in Church History xxiv (1987).

3

'TO GOVERN IS TO MAKE SUBJECTS BELIEVE'[1]: ANTICLERICALISM, POLITICS AND POWER, *c.* 1680–1717

J.A.I. Champion

Samuel Johnson (1649–1703), educated at Trinity College, Cambridge, 'after regular Study', took Holy Orders and was made Rector of the parish of Corringham in Essex in 1670 by the generosity of his patron, Mr Bidolph. The latter, 'observing Mr Johnson's inclination to the study of politicks, advis'd him to read *Bracton* and *Fortescue de Laudibus Legum Anglia*, &c. that he might be acquainted with the old *English* Constitution'. Bidolph, far from encouraging Johnson to mix politics and religion in the pulpit, insisted that he should by no means 'make Politicks the subject of his Sermons; because he had taken notice that many Clergymen had given their hearers bad impressions, and fill'd their heads with false notions of those things which they had a very imperfect knowledge of themselves'. Although Johnson took his patron's advice and 'never meddled with Politicks in the Pulpit', he used his knowledge of the 'English Constitution' to great effect in his printed writings, 'for no man wrote with more Boldness and Zeal for the legal Polity of his Country'.[2] He became one of the central publicists for the radical Whig cause of the 1690s.[3] His reputation as a patriot and defender of English liberty against 'Popery and Slavery' brought him to the position of domestic chaplain to William, Lord Russell (d. 1683). Johnson, fiercely committed to opposing tyranny in both political and theological forms, persuaded Russell to stand firm in his advocacy of the principles of political resistance (for which he was executed in 1683), and himself suffered prosecution and imprisonment for his writings comparing James, Duke of York, to Julian the Apostate. In particular, Johnson had exposed the false doctrine of passive obedience and 'the Divine, Indefeasible and Hereditary Right of the Lineal Sucession [sic]' which had been advanced by churchmen inclined to 'Popery and Slavery'. Committed to a belief that 'Resistance may be us'd in case our religion and rights be invaded', coupled with an assertion that 'Government is not matter of Revelation',[4] Johnson attempted to provoke 'Protestant' officers and soldiers in the Army 'not to serve as Instruments to enslave their Country, and to ruin the Religion they profess'd' by the distribution of a paper, 'An Humble and Hearty Address to all the English Protestants in the present Army'.[5] For such incitement Johnson was again brought before the King's Bench in June 1686. He was found guilty of high misdemeanour.

The Judge, Sir Francis Withens, imposed a severe sentence upon Johnson: he was to pay 'Five hundred Marks to the King, and to lie in prison till 'twas paid; to stand thrice in the Pillory, in the Pallace-Yard, at Charingcross, and at the Old Exchange; and to be whipt by the Common Hangman from Newgate to Tyburn'.[6] Apprehending that such punishment would bring 'scandal to the Clergy', the judges insisted that Johnson should be 'degraded from his Ministerial Function and Preferment'.[7] Johnson had become, in the words of the circular letter sent out by the commissioners for the suspended Bishop of London, 'infamous to the whole Order of the Clergy'. Summoned to the Convocation House at St Pauls on 20 November, to appear before the Bishops of Durham, Rochester and Peterborough 'with some Clergymen, and many spectators', Johnson was charged with 'great misbehaviours'. Allowed neither a copy of the libel against him nor an advocate, the sentence was pronounced against him 'that he should be declar'd an Infamous person; that he should be depriv'd of his Rectory; that he should be a mere Layman, and no clerk; and be depriv'd of all Right and Privilege of Priesthood'. Although Johnson appealed against the legality of the proceedings, his protestations were refused and the ritual of degradation was performed: 'by putting a square Cap on his Head, and then taking it off; by pulling off his gown and girdle . . . Then they put a Bible into his hands, which he not parting with readily, they took it from him by force.'[8] With the removal of his '*vestes sacerdotales*', he was reduced to the status of '*merus laicus*' (a mere layman).[9] On 22 November the sentence against Johnson was executed: he was put in the pillory, his clerical cassock having first been torn off. On 1 December, with forbearance and piety, he suffered 317 lashes 'with a whip of nine cords knotted'. Johnson's living was taken away and Thomas Berrow was granted it in his stead.[10]

After the Glorious Revolution Johnson was released from prison, and the House of Commons undertook an investigation into his treatment. His conviction and punishment were declared 'cruel and illegal', a bill was introduced to reverse the judgment and an address was 'made to His Majesty to recommend Mr Johnson to some ecclesiastical preferment, suitable to his Services and Sufferings'. Unfortunately, although Johnson regained his living at Corringham, he did not achieve further preferment: according to his friend John Hampden, this was because his continued opposition to divine right principles of passive obedience and non-resistance (especially in his account of James II's deposition) generated hostility among 'Divines of Note' who upheld such doctrine. William III did, however, settle a pension and compensation upon Johnson and his son.[11] The treatment and actions of Samuel Johnson allow some consideration of commonplace attitudes towards the status and public function of the priesthood. The evidence of his degradation indicates not only the seriousness of his 'misdemeanours', but also (ironically) the value placed upon the sacredness of the 'ministerial function'. Johnson's crime was to have meddled with the shibboleths of political ideology: in denying the injunctions of *de jure divino* obligation, he had compromised his sacred duty. 'Republican' accounts of political authority were deemed incompatible with the authority of the priesthood. In convicting Johnson of such deviance, neither the King's Bench nor the Ecclesiastical Commissioners wanted to impugn the public authority of the priesthood, and thus he was degraded to the status of a mere layman. The corporal punishment of Johnson (prompted by his excursions into political theory) at the same time as it indicated the deviance of such political ideologies, reinforced and restated the sanctity of the priesthood. Johnson the Republican was punished to preserve the authority of the 'Holy Function' of his priesthood. To those magistrates and bishops who judged him in 1686, republican political language was incompatible with the sacerdotal office. Johnson's parishioners in Corringham, Essex, saw the matter in a different light when they refused to allow the induction of his successor, 'even at a time when the Court carry'd all by violence'. Thomas Berrow, who had been nominated to the parish in 1686, had difficulty in gaining acknowledgement of the legality of Johnson's deprivation from reputable common and civil lawyers. Indeed, the three bishops who had degraded Johnson only allowed Berrow's 'institution' to the parish upon the receipt of a bond of indemnity for £500.[12] Notwithstanding these legal procedures, Berrow 'could never get entrance, but was oblig'd to return *re infecta*'. Although, technically, Johnson held no legal right to the living, the 'great respect' and 'good will' of his parishioners meant that he was restored 'both to his Orders and this Living' until his death in 1703.[13] Clearly those men and women in his cure regarded his religious conduct and performance as a priest as both acceptable and worthy. Johnson's career as a political polemicist in the 1690s, when he became the most militant of propagandists for the commonwealth cause in defence of 'revolution principles', was not perceived to compromise his status as a cleric.[14] Johnson's distinction as the pre-eminent Whig cleric was reinforced by the posthumous publication of his collected works in 1710 in a political context where the relationship between clerical status and ideological correctness had been contested during the trial of another clerical martyr, the high Tory Henry Sacheverell.

If Johnson was meticulous about keeping 'politics' out of his sermons, Benjamin Hoadly (1676–1761), Rector of St Peter Le Poor and later Bishop of Bangor, used his position in the pulpit to declaim against the false politics of contemporary churchmen. Johnson, in indicting false political dogma, such as passive obedience and hereditary succession, had cause to describe some clergy as 'pimps to divinity' for their political use of the sermon to reinforce *jure divino* conceptions of authority. Hoadly, between 1709 and 1717, contrived a series of arguments in defence of the same 'revolution principles' advanced by Johnson which ultimately undercut the sacerdotal nature of the Christian Church. As a churchman, Hoadly inspired the 'most bitter ideological conflict of the century'.[15] As another contemporary wrote, Hoadly 'had, by his writings, done more harm to the Church of Christ and the Protestant cause than any man living'.[16] Between 1705 and 1708, in a series of sermons and pamphlets, Hoadly had undertaken a defence of Bucerian readings of the key biblical injunction of Romans 13 ('Obey the Powers that be') to justify the deposition of unjust Jacobean regal power in 1689. Political obligation was due only to rulers who pursued the good of the commonwealth: popular resistance to tyranny was just. A key part of Hoadly's polemic concentrated upon the destructive nature of divine right accounts of political and religious authority. In his sermon of 1717, 'The Nature of the Kingdom or Church of Christ', Hoadly, by now a royal chaplain, articulated a fundamental critique of sacerdotalist claims. His sermon, prompted by the posthumous publication of the non-juror George Hickes's *Constitution of the Catholic Church* (1716), which defended a *jure divino* conception of Church and State, rebutted the clericalist claim that they 'stood in God's stead'.[17] The key to Hoadly's argument was the rejection of supernaturalist claims by the established Church. The Church of Christ should not be confused with the Church of England; there was no 'visible' succession from Christ, through the Apostles to the contemporary Church establishment. Contrary to assertions in favour of the sacredness of the clerical order, Hoadly insisted that 'He hath . . . left behind Him no visible, human authority; no vicegerents who can be said properly to supply His place; no interpreters upon whom His subjects are absolutely to depend; no judges over the consciences or religion of His people'.[18] The High Church-dominated Lower House of Convocation in committee was swift to contest Hoadly's arguments, characterising them as a subversion of 'all government and discipline in the Church of Christ' which would 'reduce His kingdom to a state of anarchy and confusion'.[19] Before such condemnation could be formally acknowledged and supported by Convocation, Hoadly's ministerial supporters contrived to have the institution prorogued. The suspension of Convocational discussions did not stop controversial engagement. It has been estimated that some fifty authors contributed around two hundred tracts. Most contemporary historians have been content to dismiss the intellectual content of the controversy and merely to note the formal termination of meetings of Convocation. The marginalisation of the significance of this contestation over the relationship between clerical power and political authority needs profound reconsideration. As William Law pointed out, the conceptual logic of Hoadly's arguments led to the dissolution of 'the Church as a society'.[20] The practical consequence of the controversy was the silencing of the Church as a constitutional institution.

According to the commonplace accounts of the Bangorian controversy, Hoadly is treated as a rather eccentric and perhaps treacherous cleric: a man over-enthused by Lockean, and possibly Hobbesian, understandings of the relationship between belief and authority, who reduced the Church to a voluntary society unhindered either by civil tests or sacerdotal direction. Hoadly's status as a clergyman has usually been dismissed with a few comments about his non-residence and pluralism. Such a limited appreciation of his churchmanship has licensed secularist understandings of his ecclesiology; since (it is argued) Hoadly cared little for the pastoral or spiritual duties of the cure, it seems sensible to regard his description of the Church as an essentially desacralised and anticlerical institution. Such a historiographical position makes an island of Hoadly's contribution and marginalises the importance of debates about the nature of the Church and the concomitant status of the clergy. Just as Samuel Johnson behaved like a bad priest because he denied divine right theories of government, so Benjamin Hoadly was an even worse churchman because he repudiated the sacerdotal status of the Church. Between Johnson writing in the early 1680s and Hoadly in the 1710s, there appears to have been a continuity of Whig clergymen attacking the status and authority of the Church of England. Both Johnson and Hoadly were men of 'revolution principles': many contemporaries saw this political heritage as the font of their anticlericalism. Johnson's 'republican' credentials are unimpeachable. That Hoadly drew inspiration from the same sources can be seen in the hostile prints of 1709 which represent him at his desk composing his sermon prompted by the ghost of Cromwell, and by the Devil. In the background a bookshelf complete with volumes of Hobbes, Harrington, Sidney, Toland, Locke, Baxter, Tindal and Bacon illustrates the irreligious prints Hoadly had consumed.[21] 'Republican' accounts of political government bred an anticlericalism even among Whig clergymen. Men like Johnson and Hoadly objected not just to the status of the clergy as 'men of God', but also to their perceived social and political authority.

In order to explore the meaning and significance of the anticlericalism articulated by men like Johnson and Hoadly (among many others), it is clearly necessary to understand what representations or constructions of clericalism they contested. What was it to be a priest? What functions, rights, duties, gifts, offices were associated with the cure? Were the origins of such faculties divine or conventional, apostolic or prophetic, indelible or institutional? While there have been studies of the clergy as a profession, of the economic problems of the Church and of the complex ecclesiological models adopted by different theological movements in the administration of the Church in England, there has been little historical examination of the changing construction of 'priesthood' in the early modern period. Inscribing descriptions of the rights, powers and privileges of the Church was clearly not simply a religious or spiritual matter, as thinkers like Thomas Hobbes were very well aware: priests, clergymen, rectors, lecturers, curates, deans, bishops, preachers, chaplains, all attracted, wielded and performed different types of religious and social power. Defining priesthood was one of the key moments in the politics of subordination that structured early modern society. What Johnson and Hoadly attempted was to challenge one of the dominant and commonplace understandings of what priesthood and clerical authority were. In disputing the authenticity of such status, a threat was posed to the hierarchical structure of social and political power.

Given that the nature of the priesthood was not a fixed concept but one that was continually defined, refined and contested, the intention here is to examine the most dominant concept of clerical authority.[22] One way of exploring the hinterland of belief about the nature of the clergy is to examine the various handbooks for religious practice that structured the passage of the year. Here, conceptual understandings intertwined with devotional ritual and prayer. One of the persistently popular works of this genre was Robert Nelson's *A Companion for the Festivals and Fasts of the Church of England*, first published in 1704; described by one historian as 'a complete popular manual of Anglican theology', it had achieved some twenty-eight editions by 1800.[23] Nelson, a non-juring layman, but with intimate links to the established Church, was prompted to publish his work to defend the Church from the threat of impiety and atheism. As he commented: 'Among those crying Abominations, which like a torrent, have overspread the Nation, this Age seems to distinguish itself by a great contempt of the Clergy.' In describing the 'Ember Fasts' and associated instructions, Nelson intended to refurbish clerical authority: 'If these subjects make any impression upon men's minds, as they will most certainly, if calmly and seriously considered, it will startle the boldest sinner, to find that in contemning this Order of Men, he affronts his Maker; and in despising the Minister of the Gospel, he despiseth Him that sent him.' If veneration for the Clergy could be 'early instilled into tender minds', it might be possible that the next generation could 'retrieve that respect to the sacred Order which we so scandalously want in this'.[24] In the work, Nelson, in catechetical form, detailed the dignity and power of the 'Holy Orders'. Priesthood was an honourable employment with 'the same work in kind . . . [as] that of the Blessed Angels'. Clergymen were 'ministering spirits' bringing to mankind the benefits of baptism, the sacraments and absolution. As the primitive Christians had acknowledged, 'there could be no Church without Priests', for it was 'by their means that God conveyed to men all those mighty blessings which were purchased by Christ's Death'. The clergyman was commissioned by Christ to act for God in the 'administration of Holy things'. The very titles of dignity indicated their *sacerdos*: they were 'ministers of Christ, stewards of the Mysteries of God . . . Ambassadors for Christ in Christ's stead, Co-workers with him, Angels of the Churches'. Each priest was 'empowered and authorised to negotiate and transact for God'. Priesthood was not a trade: the divine and legal rights accruing to their dignity (such as tithes) were necessary to preserve the sanctity of their status and the respect for religion. Indeed, preserving the reputation, piety and integrity of churchmen was essential to promoting the 'interests of religion, whose fate very much depends upon the reputation of those who feed and govern the Flock of Christ'. Those who opposed revelation took every opportunity to 'represent their sacred function only as a trade'.[25] The priesthood, then, was a divine and powerful order: co-workers, administrators, stewards, ambassadors of Christ and God. Such men were 'empowered and authorised to negotiate and transact for God'.[26]

Such a sacerdotal conception of the priesthood was clearly contentious even within the parameters of orthodoxy. While Article XIX (of the 39) had established the 'visible' Church of Christ, the ecclesiological dimensions and nature of such 'visibility' had varied greatly within Trinitarian Protestant discourses. In one form or another, the Church was a mechanism for the 'incarnation' of divine justice: whether placing soteriological emphasis upon pulpit or sacrament, on baptism or absolution, the 'Church' entertained an *ordo* (that is, it had a spiritual quality and function) if not a *jurisdictio* (an authority to exercise that *ordo*) made by God. The High Church ecclesiology embodied in Nelson's *Collection* was cognate with that established by the Book of Common Prayer, and stressed order, obedience and subordination. The divine apostolicity of the institution enabled the soteriologically correct administration of the sacraments: *salus extra ecclesia non est* [no salvation outside the Church]. The clergy were mediators of Christ: the spiritual succession of bishops, priests and deacons guaranteed the holiness of the two key sacraments of baptism and the eucharist.[27] As J.C.D. Clark, and more recently A.M.C. Waterman, indicated, this hierarchical and divine model of the Christian community also implied a politics of subordination in a civil context. Nelson put it succinctly: 'that the good of the state is hereby more secured, in those instructions men receive from the Ministers of God, in the necessary Duties of Obedience, Justice and Fidelity'.[28] Or, as the Book of Common Prayer enjoined, every child must learn 'to honour and obey the King, and all that are put in authority under him'. The good Christian must submit to all 'governors, teachers, spiritual pastors and masters'.[29] Just as the ecclesiastical polity was the product of Christ's incarnation, so was the civil polity: the significance of the dictum 'no bishop, no king' cannot be too heavily underscored. Priests, then, not only sanctified religion, but politics too.

Attacks upon the priesthood thus implied an assault upon the institution that 'made' political authority. The 'principle of subordination' (whether religious or political) was not just articulated as a conceptual discourse, but was a 'truth' or 'knowledge' made into belief by a complex interaction of print, practice and performance. As de Certeau has indicated, 'belief' is as much a matter of social relationship as propositional content. For example, the status of priest as 'co-worker' with God enabled a community to achieve a set of beliefs about the divinity of a structure of social relationships, not because of the 'correctness' of those 'beliefs', but because of the 'sacredness' of the cultural relationship between priest and laity. As Hobbes understood acutely, it was precisely because most people 'believed' in the divine authority of the Church that it was such a powerful political institution. Unpicking the 'authority' of the institution was a more radical and more incisive strategy than merely targeting the (corrupt) 'beliefs' that the Church instilled in the laity: thus in Chapter 42 of *Leviathan*, Hobbes deconstructed the authenticity of any claim to an apostolic, visible Church of Christ. The person of the priest, rather than just the idea of 'priesthood', was a powerful, and therefore contested, institution. To advance anticlerical suggestions within this context was a matter of dangerous import.

Treating 'anticlericalism' as the manifestation of a crisis of clerical authority, and consequently a transgression of customary structures of subordination and hierarchy, may enable a continuity of political contestation to be suggested from the 1640s to the 1720s which integrates discourses of religion into the mainstream of political debate. Surprisingly, there has been little historiographical labour devoted to the analysis of anticlericalism as a conceptual, theological or heterodox discourse in the early modern period. Admittedly there has been some entrenched engagement between Reformation scholars over the influence and meaning of 'anticlericalism'. As Dickens has pointed out: 'Anti-clericalism has become an unduly capacious word' encompassing descriptions of the systematic Erastianism of theorists like Marsiglio of Padua, to petty squabbles between parish vicars and their parishioners.[30] Arguing against Haigh, who had suggested that anticlericalism was a consequence rather than a cause of the Reformation in England, Dickens, weaving together an eclectic combination of literary, legal, economic and theological positions, insisted that anticlericalism exercised a profound and determining influence on the shape of the English Reformation. Although this is clearly not the place to attempt any arbitration of the historiographical dispute, the contours of the debate indicate both the difficulty and (consequent) importance of coming to some agreement about what anticlericalism was.

   A superficial survey of accounts of seventeenth- and eighteenth-century anticlericalism given in the current historiography would indicate a number of key concerns. One of the most obvious, and indeed most persistent, prompts to the manifestation of anticlerical activities was the particular economic grievance of tithes. Whether prompted by price inflation, dearth, the introduction of new crops, the renegotiation of rents, individual initiative or theological principle, the imposition of tithe payments was a source for the generation of hostility towards the Church and churchmen.[31] Disagreements about such a clearly material matter as tithes, when combined with the commonplace disputes focused upon the personal characteristics, corruptions or moral failings of individual clerics, might legitimately be termed 'popular' anticlericalism.[32] A second powerful moment of hostility towards the Church can be identified in the explosion of Erastian legislation against the Laudian ecclesiastical establishment in the 1640s. As Morrill has indicated, the parliamentary disestablishment of the legal, moral and theological authority of the Church of England between 1640 and 1645 was both radical and prompted by popular petitioning from the localities. The civil

legislation attacked not only the ecclesiological jurisdiction of the established
Church, but also the religious and moral failings of the 'scandalous' clergy in
each parish.[33] Such state-sanctioned anticlericalism provided the context for a
much more diffuse and virulent public assault upon 'clergy power' manifest in
the sectarian discourses examined by Hill in *The World Turned Upside Down*.
Whether articulating critiques of clerical corruption, or more fundamental
indictments of clerical vocation, Quakers, Levellers, Baptists, Diggers, Ranters et
al. implicated 'the wicked prelates' in the polemic against tyranny. Drawing from
a radical Protestant tradition that opposed conformity to episcopal authority, and
combining it with a stress on the tenderness and liberty of Christian conscience,
the connection was made between civil and priestly oppression. Public
pamphleteers like Lilburne, Walwyn, Overton and Winstanley (among many
others) inveighed against the 'blackcoats' who 'bewitched' and beguiled the
people with 'flattering, seducing words'. As William Hartley succinctly indicated
in his title to a 1649 tract, the priest's patent [was] cancelled.[34] Although the
critique of the clergy was fundamental, in many cases undercutting any notion of
apostolic *sacerdos*, it is important to note that the premise of much of this
anticlericalism (whether articulated in the Long Parliament or in the pamphlet
literature of Winstanley) was eschatological or apocalyptic.[35] In other words, such
critiques of priesthood were articulated from within a theological idiom, rather
than against a religious principle. Such a tradition of reforming polemic became
a commonplace of dissident Protestant communities after 1660, in particular in
the challenge to the apostolicity of the established Church.

   The 1640s and 1650s also saw the origins of a form of radical Erastian
anticlericalism that extended theological criticism into an attack upon the
'priestcraft' of all clerical institutions. Contrived in a historical and conceptual
form, the writings of Thomas Hobbes and James Harrington laid the foundations
for a later polemic against any notion of a 'visible and apostolic' Church.
Undercutting clerical authority in terms of hermeneutics and epistemology, later
writers like Charles Blount, John Toland, Matthew Tindal and John Trenchard
built on Hobbes's and Harrington's arguments to deny the existence of divine
sacerdos in any religious institutions. In doing so, they constructed deistical and
freethinking platforms that would influence eighteenth-century Enlightenment
anticlericalism.

   Although there is increasing historical interest in the anticlericalism of this
deistical tradition, the premise of much of the historiography is forward-looking
rather than contextual, in the sense that the significance of such writers is said to
be found in the act of transmitting a commonwealth ideology to the intellectual
culture of the eighteenth century, rather than an assessment of the place of such
anticlericalism within the debates and disputes of their own time. One of the
consequences of the current approach to anticlericalism is that it has been
identified as a marginal, radical, unstable and intellectually heterodox quantity:

'anticlericalism' is something that radical sectarians, Dissenters and perhaps 'atheists' did against the grain of traditional religious culture. Thus, the sectarian dissidence of the 1640s and 1650s has little to do with the culture of radicalism after the Restoration, and the English deists are regarded as peripheral to the political history of the period after the 1690s.[36] This marginalisation of the significance of anticlericalism is all the more extraordinary given that the most recent development in the historiography of the Restoration and after places emphasis upon the importance of religion to political conflicts.

It was commonly argued that the Restoration saw the waning of the importance and influence of religious culture and a shift towards a modern secular structure of politics. This was traditionally thought to be manifest most obviously in the increasing significance of Parliament, and in particular in the growth of party politics in both Commons and constituency. A number of recent works have suggested that religion persisted as a determining influence in national and local life. Such research substitutes a language of the politics of religious or ecclesiological crisis for that of the politics of party. The politics of religious confessionalism revolved around defences of toleration or insistence upon conformity, or of the necessity of order as against the essentially adiaphoristic nature of ceremony and forms of worship. Whether in terms of national politics or the study of local communities, 'religion' remained a powerful domain of contested authority.[37] The emphasis upon ecclesiology, and the consequent interest in Dissenting or Nonconformist cleavages, has led perhaps to an over-defined appreciation of the nature of the range of contested 'religious' positions. A characterisation of the politics of religion that represents it as a battle between Anglicans and Presbyterians, or conformists and dissenters, has tended to obscure the relevance of anticlericalism in favour of studying the implications (for example) of competing theologies of grace, or the debate over the efficacy of persecution. The conflicts that punctuated the Restoration and after were driven by a fierce competition for the appropriation of the communal language of 'true religion' to one particular platform. Although historians have designed the labels 'established' and 'dissenting', it is important not to conceive of these descriptions as fully programmatic identities: the battle for capturing the high ground of 'true religion' (especially given the powerful authority of print culture) was fought out between a mêlée of shifting, discursive allegiances. One of the central, and most contentious, definitional struggles was over the nature of the Church: anticlericalism was intimately related to these disputes. Arguments about the standing of the 'priest' were ultimately part of the mainstream of political debate about the location and distribution of authority within the communal hierarchy.

One of the achievements of the current historiography of late seventeenth- and early eighteenth-century religious culture is the underscoring of the strength of clerical involvement in both national and local society. Whether drawing from the research of John Spurr or the collection of important essays edited by Walsh,

Haydon and Taylor, it is possible to argue that from the 1660s the Church in England experienced a process of material, theological, pastoral, intellectual and cultural refurbishment. The study of the institutional performance and practice of religion in the period has indicated the importance of a range of relationships between and among (for example) clerical discourse, parochial traditions, ceremony and the material form of church buildings, individual belief and communal convictions.[38] The powers of the 'clerical' world were not simply theological or spiritual but, importantly, also practical. Churchmen exercised authority in the world of belief. Clergymen were not limited to articulation and cultivation of doctrinal or ritual positions as codified in the Thirty Nine Articles, the Act of Uniformity or the Book of Common Prayer: as Sir Keith Thomas has shown, churchmen offered counsel in a far wider range of social, moral and political concerns.[39]

One of the increasingly visible activities that clergymen undertook was periodic commentary and advice upon the principles of political subordination. Reinforcing the language of social stability and political order became a staple 'political' element in the sermonising of Restoration divines. The purpose was to inculcate the habit of obedience; consequently, one of the persistent linguistic themes of 'Anglican' sermons after the 1670s was a hostility towards theories of social contract, equality, natural rights and resistance.[40] By the 1690s and 1700s such 'political' sermons had become especially identified with the critical dates of the execution of Charles I (dismissed as 'general madding day' by John Toland), the restoration of his son, and the anniversary of 5 November (either the Gunpowder Plot, or the Glorious Revolution); again, studies of such sermons witness the increasing stridence and confidence of Anglican clergymen in reinforcing the language of divine right hierarchy in Church and State.[41] The clergymen of the established Church were more than simple voice-pieces for subordinationist ideology: Gary Bennet, writing of the early eighteenth century, described the High Churchmen as 'theorists, writers and election agents' for the Tory party.[42] The relationship between Churchmanship and politics had been forged in electoral activity during the contests for the three Exclusion Parliaments between 1679 and 1681. Although the research of Goldie and, more recently, Miller suggests that the prompt to the resurgence of clerical influence in both national and local politics was the relationship Danby forged with the bishops in the House of Lords from the mid-1670s, by the late 1670s such 'politicking' was not confined to episcopal figures.[43]

The clergy exercised for the first time the right to vote in parliamentary elections in the election of 1679. Many did so *en masse* for Court and King: two hundred 'black-coats' turned out at the poll against the Whig candidate in Essex.[44] Whether circulating letters against specific figures, haranguing the electorate at the poll or collaborating in the production of addresses and instructions, the clergy were certainly regarded by Whig parliamentarians as corrupters of political liberties. Effective authors of Whig propaganda like Henry Care launched a virulent polemic against 'the designs of some idle covetous sycophant Clergymen, who . . . do in private parlours over the Glass, whilst healths go round, as well as in their pulpits over their cushions, set up Absolute monarchy to be de jure Divino'.[45] Country priests, it was alleged, spent more time reading the absolutist writings of Roger L'Estrange than the Bible.[46] One of the pejorative neologisms coined to describe the Tory bias of clerical behaviour was that of 'Tantivy', based upon a hunting cry. The political print *The Time Servers: or a Touch of the Times* (BMC 1112) of March 1681 indicates the thrust of such language in portraying a black-coated clergyman riding alongside a Tory gentleman whipping his steed on towards Rome and the Pope. That the Whig interest perceived a profound threat from the 'Tantivee Crew' is perhaps best illustrated from the various ballads and poems of the early 1680s. As one text of 1680 made clear: 'Priests were the first deluders of mankind, who with vain faith made all their reason blind; not Lucifer himself more proud than they, and yet persuade the world they must obey.'[47] Other works denounced 'Baal's wretched curates', 'the prelate's false divinity', the 'debauched surcingled clergy', 'the tribe of Levi' and 'the proud usurping priest'; the main charge was the encouragement of 'blind obedience' to theories of divine right monarchy and hereditary succession.[48]

Such themes can be revisited with even more emphasis in the early eighteenth century. The work of Speck on voting patterns has suggested that one of the only predictable blocs of voters was the Anglican clergy. Referring to the evidence of poll books from the elections of 1705 and 1710, he argues that there was 'little doubt about the Toryism of the Clergy'.[49] Again, clergymen were involved in the preparation and distribution of election material such as addresses, letters of loyalty and newsletters like Dyer's. The clergy were, as one Whig put it in 1710, 'a standing and powerful interest' in the country. When such men heard the doctrines of passive obedience and non-resistance 'cry'd down, they think religion is at stake'.[50] The clergy again wielded influence by sermonising and by direct polling. Haranguing from the pulpit and preparation of addresses were continually noted in contemporary sources. One parson in Brentford in 1710 had 'no topics but resistance and schism, as if he was not so much afraid that his flock should be damned as that they should be Presbyterians and Whigs'.[51] Moments of religious crisis, like the 'Church in Danger' controversy of 1705 and the consequences of the 1710 Sacheverell Trial, saw churchmen swift to exploit the different forms of authority they could exercise. For example, in 1710, to rousing slogans like 'The Church, The Church', many clerics in Northampton occupied the poll booth '(though several of them had no votes), browbeating and discouraging the electors'.[52] In the Shropshire county election in the same year, the clergy 'came to poll in a body, with two Archdeacons at their head'. Defoe (in *The Review*, 1705) lamented that 'the parish vote with the parson, the people

ignorantly concluding that he who is, or ought to be, fit to guide them to heaven,
may be supposed the best judge who is fittest to direct them in choosing
members'.[53]

The clergy, then, were a powerful, if informal, political instrument on behalf of
the Tory interest. The insurgency of the High Church clericalist challenge into
national politics was also evident, from the mid-1690s, in a much more concrete
institutional form. The history of Convocation, in particular the Lower House (or
Doctors' Commons), is closely associated with the reputation of Francis
Atterbury, who was almost single-handedly responsible for bringing it political
authority with the publication of his *Letter to a Convocation Man* (1696). Brought
back to life as the political trade-off for the Earl of Rochester's support for
William III, Convocation became the forum for the advance of clericalist
programmes for reforming the nation. Although there has been much work on
the ideological intentions of the 'new High Church party', there has been little
attention paid to the institutional history of Convocation. Without exaggeration,
it could be argued that Convocation (especially the lower house) was the most
effective alternative forum for political opposition to the successive Whig
ministries of the 1700s. However, little research has been undertaken to explore
the mechanics of clerical politics, either within the Doctors' Commons or in the
spiritual constituencies. Elections to the Lower House were concomitant
procedurally with parliamentary elections. Of the 146 members, some 50 per
cent were elected *ex officio*, 27 were elected by cathedral chapters or collegiate
bodies, and the remaining 44 by the clergy.[54] Just as there was a contested politics
in the civil sphere, so too there were electoral battles in each diocese, college and
chapter. Little of this has been studied. The one thing that is certain is that the
lower house was dominated in the 1700s and 1710s by the Atterburian interest.
Although one recent commentator has dismissed the matter of Convocation as a
'dreary wasteland of strained arguments over legal precedents', it is difficult to
underestimate the significance of the institution as an indication of the strength
of the clerical world.[55] The claims of Atterbury, and associated ideologists in the
Lower House, were that the clergy were a fourth estate, a central and powerful
part of the constitution in Church and State. At the heart of Atterbury's
arguments was the assertion of the 'holy function' of the clergy as the 'ministers
of Christ'. After the 1710 electoral triumph (in both Convocation and
Parliament), the strongest platform for clericalist reform was advanced on the
constitutionalist premise of Atterbury's theory of Convocation. Establishing a link
between the lower houses in both civil and spiritual institutions, the objective was
to invoke a programme for the radical refurbishment of ecclesiastical and clerical
authority: the reinvigoration of the disciplinary and judicial power of Church
Courts, the improvement of clerical revenues and a schedule for the building of
new churches, and the strengthening of anti-heretical powers.[56] The hierocratic
ambitions of the Lower House of Convocation after 1710 were obvious. 'Clergy

power', as Winstanley might have put it, was very far from redundant. Given that the clericalist position was a powerful and effective one, entrenched both in local communities and in central offices and institutions, it is hardly surprising that those who opposed convocational models of reform articulated their views in the form of a profound anticlericalism.

It was the premise of one of the most radical post-1689 commonwealth pamphlets that false principles of divinity and government had been foisted upon the people 'from the pulpit'.[57] At the end of the first decade of the eighteenth century this radical Whig critique met head-on with the cynosure of *de jure divino* clericalists in the form of Henry Sacheverell DD of Magdalen College, Oxford. Sacheverell had established a reputation as a high-flyer in the early 1700s, when his sermons had advanced the conjoined standards of divine right in Church and State. His arguments were notorious, not only for the extremity of their conceptual content, but also for the violence and vindictive hostility towards Low Churchmen, Dissenters and Whigs. In his two most infamous sermons of August and November 1709, Sacheverell advanced the principles of non-resistance against the 'revolution principles' of 1689, at the same time as condemning 'false brethren' in Church and State. Toleration, occasional conformity, the Nonconformists, the Low Church bishops, even Whig ministers of state were lashed as corroders of true religion who should suffer punishment and reformation at the hands of the Godly priest. Prompted by the Whig John Dolben, the House of Commons indicted both sermons as 'malicious, scandalous, and seditious libels, highly reflecting upon Her Majesty and her government, the late happy revolution, and the protestant succession'. Swift considered the consequent impeachment and trial of the churchman as an attempted martyrdom.[58] Although there was some hesitation about proceeding to such a public trial of clericalist principles, for many Whig politicians it was a perfect opportunity to discipline a recalcitrant Church perhaps once and for all. Indeed, the historiographical understanding of the trial has tended to see it as a confrontation between the competing Whig and Tory ideologies: in essence, a continuity of the fundamental debate about the meaning and significance of the Revolution settlement of 1689.[59] Sacheverell had insisted upon the principle of 'the subject's obligation to an absolute and unconditional obedience to the supream power, in all things lawful, and the utter illegality of resistance upon any pretence whatsover'.[60] The threat of a Jacobite restoration made the public condemnation of *jure divino* hereditary succession an urgent necessity to the Whig ministry, and the security of a large parliamentary majority made the prosecution of Sacheverell look like a secure move. There is little doubt that the process of the trial was an opportunity to reinforce the legitimacy of moderate 'revolution principles' in a form to benefit the party advantage of the Whigs. The popular reaction to the trial, the reception (both in London and the provinces)

Sacheverell inspired after his release, and the impact the ideological
consequences of the trial had upon the general election of 1710 indicate the
critical significance of the moment.

   Although the intention here is not to downplay the importance of the political
theory under discussion during the trial, the crisis was not simply concerned with
ideological concepts, but also involved a public review of the status of priesthood.
That is: Sacheverell was placed on trial not simply for the content of his ideas, but
for actually voicing such views: in doing so, he had 'abused his Holy function'. His
crime was not just to have advanced false political ideas, but as a churchman, to
have offered a political commentary in the first place. The trial was an attempt to
rebut the clericalist idea of the 'independency' of the Church and to reassert the
principle 'by which all ecclesiastical jurisdiction . . . is made subject to the civil
power'.[61] Indeed, the opening premise of Sacheverell's *Perils* sermon had been that
his role was 'to open the eyes of the deluded people' against the view that 'the
pulpit is not a place for politics'.[62] Since doctrines of Church and State were 'so
nicely correspondent and so happily intermixt', it was incumbent upon true
churchmen to challenge all deviancy: 'heterodoxy in the doctrines of the one,
naturally producing, and almost necessarily infering, Rebellion and high Treason
in the other'.[63] Performing 'Political divinity' was Sacheverell's crime. As Robert
Walpole emphasised, the problem was amplified 'when the Pulpit takes up the
Cudgels, when the cause of the enemies of our government is call'd the cause of
God, and of the Church . . . and the people are taught for their souls and
conscience sake to swallow these pernicious doctrines'. The pulpit had been
'prostituted and polluted': the credit of the Church had been abused.[64] Sacheverell
had been insolent to suggest that civil authority could not reverse ecclesiastical
censure. Pulpits had become the 'mints of faction and sedition': Sacheverell had
compounded his pride by insisting that 'the business of a Clergyman [is] to sound
a trumpet in Sion'. Proper clerical language was 'prayers and tears', rather than
'arms and violence': Sacheverell had intended to 'raise the passions' of the public
by the 'passion, heat and violence' of his sermon. He had manipulated Scripture,
knowing the veneration and influence it held 'upon the minds of the people'. His
objective was to make the people 'fancy they hear the voice of God, when they
hear his words repeated'.[65] Sacheverell had insisted in his defence that he had
merely done his 'duty as a clergyman'. On the contrary, his prosecuters accused
him of instilling 'groundless jealousies in the minds of the people': such pulpit-
pronounced doctrines struck 'at the root of the present Government . . . [and]
disquiet the minds, and tend to pervert the obedience of the subjects'.[66]

   Sacheverell's general defence was to argue that his position was no different
from that held by the Church of England as established doctrine. Extracts from
homilies, statutes and the Fathers of the Church all confirmed the duties of
political obedience, and the idea that 'the spiritual power of Church pastors is not
derived from the Civil magistrate but from God'. This *sacerdos* enfranchised the

clergy to censure offenders against orthodoxy.[67] Given that, in Sacheverell's view, the state was inundated with blasphemy, irreligion and heresy, there were plenty of grounds 'for a preacher in the pulpit to take notice of these matters'. Citing a 'black catalogue of prophaness and blasphemy',[68] he insisted that his 'holy function' was 'to exhort and rebuke with all Authority, and without distinction'. The dignity of his function, and the seriousness of heterodoxy, excused Sacheverell's 'zeal'.[69] Indeed, in condemning impiety, Sacheverell had the cheek to suggest he was simply encouraging the enforcement of moral reformation as promoted by Royal Proclamation.[70] Sacheverell was stalwart in his self-defence: he was simply a clergyman fulfilling the 'duty of his function'. His 'sacred profession' made him God's instrument, enjoined to 'putting a stop to that overflowing of Ungodliness, and Blasphemy, which as yet no Laws, no proclamations, how well so ever design'd, and how often soever repeated, have been able to restrain'. As an 'ambassador of Christ', he was commanded 'in his name, to exhort and rebuke with all Authority'.[71] For the Whig prosecution, Sacheverell was an 'impostor and false prophet' who had betrayed the proper office of the priesthood.

Much of the exchange in the trial focused upon Sacheverell's claim that his position as a clergyman allowed and encouraged him to 'sound a trumpet'. He had used the biblical language of Kings and Lamentations both to condemn the iniquities of Whig society and to empower his critique. He had been accused by his prosecutors of deliberately mis-citing and misapplying scriptural language to denigrate 'our present circumstances'.[72] There was indeed no greater perversion of Scripture 'than to make use of the language of the Holy Ghost, to revile our *Neighbours*, to scandalize the *Government*, and to raise *Wrath, Sedition*, and *Rebellion* in the *People*'.[73] Sacheverell was also challenged over his insistence that it was a clerical duty to 'sound a trumpet in Sion'. Trumpet-blowing was a military matter, an instrument of war, a call to arms, not of the pulpit: the only priests who had blown trumpets in the Old Testament had 'literally' sounded them 'in the Army, in the field'.[74] If Scripture had been mis-cited by Sacheverell, it was the result of faulty printing rather than hermeneutical error. As a priest, Sacheverell had honestly and sincerely interpreted the meaning of Scripture. Any mistakes were genuine, not contrived to assail the Government. To control what clergymen issued from their pulpits was a devious and ungodly ambition: it was, as Sacheverell insisted, 'the avow'd design of my impeachment . . . to have the clergy directed what Doctrines they are to preach and what not'.[75]

These anticlerical themes were underscored in many of the contemporary reactions to the trial. The incident spawned a massive, controversial literature which assumed a variety of forms – ballads, pamphlets, books, broadsheets, prints.[76] The response was not merely ideological, but direct: the crowds and mobs of London were active and violent in their defence of 'The Church'. Such scenes of popular turbulence and violence directed against the Low Church, the Whigs and Dissenter communities were repeated in the provinces, often prompted by Sacheverell's visit to local churchmen and their Tory patrons. Newspapers like Swift's *Examiner* made it clear that the intentions of the Whig prosecution had been to attack the status of the clergy: 'what a violent humour hath run ever since against the Clergy, and from what corner spread and fomented, is, I believe, manifest to all men. It lookt like a set quarrel against Christianity'.[77] Antagonists like Arthur Mainwaring responded by emphasising the history of High Church misdemeanour in his paper *The Medley*. In particular, he berated the 'behaviour of the violent clergy before the Revolution' and 'all the fine sermons that they preach'd for Absolute Monarchy, the surrenders of Charters, which they influenc'd, the Abhorrences which they signed, and the Gineas which the two famous universities of our land, Oxford and Cambridge, contributed to Sir Roger L'Estrange, for writing on the side of Arbitrary Power'.[78] One of the persistent accusations made by Tories like Swift was that the contempt for the order of priesthood was sponsored by the 'public encouragement and patronage' the Whigs gave to men like 'Tindall, Toland and other Atheisticall writers'. As Wotton had commented with some concern to Wake, every 'well meaning Parson . . . thinks that every Whig is of course a disciple of Toland and Tindal'.[79] Unsurprisingly, writers like Toland and Tindal did indeed take every opportunity to lambast Sacheverell and present to the public an understanding of the trial as a necessary attempt to neutralise the authority of the pulpit and clergy. Matthew Tindal had already provoked clerical ire in the immediate aftermath of the crisis of 1705 by the publication of his *Rights of the Christian Church* (1706). Indeed, this was one of the works cited by Sacheverell as indicating the incipient blasphemy of his persecuters.[80] Tindal, among other works, was responsible for publishing a historical account of High Church atrocities against such figures as Leighton, Burton and Prynne: Sacheverell was another Sibthorpe or Mainwaring.[81] John Toland also contributed a number of commentaries upon the significance of the trial.

Those writings of Toland, directly prompted by the trial, have received little historiographical attention. He composed at least four works: three shorter pamphlets and one lengthy history of the trial itself. The latter is perhaps the most explicit condemnation of Sacheverell and clerics of his ilk. First published in 1711 and reprinted in 1713, *High Church Display'd: Being a complete history of the affair of Dr Sachaverel, in its origins, progress and consequences*, was composed as a series of seven letters to an 'English Gentleman at the Court of Hanover' written between 16 June and 27 September 1710. The didactic purpose of the volume was indicated by the title page, which noted: 'Fit to be kept in all Families as a storehouse of arguments in defence of the Constitution'. To ease such edification, the volume was completed by an alphabetical index.[82] One of its obvious intentions was to prime the Hanoverian interest against the deceit and danger of the High Church. The second edition also pointed out that it was 'abridg'd, in an easy Method, for the benefit of Common readers'.[83] In effect, Toland's book was a very close reworking of the 'official' account of the trial published by Jacob Tonson in 1710. Toland added commentary and ancillary contemporary documents to Tonson's transcription of the trial. Toland edited the material to accent the extremism of Sacheverell's hostility towards 'revolution principles', and to point to the dangerous social consequences of his inflammation of opinion in the City of London and the provinces.[84] Toland pruned much of Sacheverell's defence, and indeed censored some of the defence material which cast aspersions on the religious integrity of his own work.[85] The message was clear, if embedded in a very long-winded account: the High Church was dangerous to the political, religious and social constitution of Britain. Since history was philosophy taught by examples, so the historical account of the trial indicted the corruption of the priesthood.

If Toland's interpretation of the meaning of the trial was anticlerical but restrained by the rhetorical form of it being a piece of historical writing, his other pamphlets were shrill and unbridled in their critique of the Church. In *Lettre d'un Anglois à un Hollandais. Or Mr Toland's Reflections on Dr Sacheverell's Sermon* (1710), Toland made it apparent that the main business of the trial had been the impeachment of 'busie and seditious clergymen'. He condemned the 'pulpit orator' and the 'great company of black-gowns' who by 'cabal' promoted the deviant beliefs of 'PASSIVE, or unlimited OBEDIENCE, to all the commands of a Prince, tho' never so strange, illegal, unjust or prejudicial . . . or pretends to believe, that disobedience to that slavish maxim, is like the sin against the Holy Ghost, which will not be forgiven, either in this world or the next'.[86] In *The Jacobitism, Perjury and Popery of High Church Priests* (1710), Toland riveted the connection between the 'High Church drummers' who used their pulpits as the trumpets of sedition and the incipient threat of Jacobite restoration. Pulpits were 'wooden Engines' for the advance of passive obedience and other 'slavish notions'. Pulpits had been the 'armed instruments of Tyranny . . . in most countries'. To allow oneself to be 'prated out' of liberty and property was foolish: 'Will not the world think that we do not value as we ought our happy constitution if they see its greatest enemies permitted twice a week to banter, ridicule, libel and insult it?'[87]

Toland's anticlericalism was refined against the specific butt of High Churchmen like Sacheverell: in condemning the example of the latter, he took the opportunity to commend the good model of clerics like Hoadly. For Toland, the clergy had a clear choice between the two men.[88] In his last work related to the theme of Sacheverell's trial, *An Appeal to Honest People against Wicked Priests* (1713), Toland drew a careful distinction between good priests, who were an 'order of men not only useful and necessary, but likewise reputable and venerable', and the corrupt priesthood, who brought 'an unworthy reflection, a lasting disgrace, nay an inveterate Odium on the honest priests, and consequently on the whole order'. Just like the pre-Constantinian Church, which had been fed by ambition and party contestation, the modern Church had for its own advantage set up an *imperium in imperio*. One benefit born of the Sacheverell trial was, as Toland pointed out, 'that Clergymen shou'd not (under penalty of incapacity during life) meddle with the civil government in their pulpits, nor pretend to decide questions in Politicks'. The High Churchmen, following the examples of the early Church, had established a 'protestant popery' concerned only with 'advancing the pride and power of priests'. Sacheverell, like 'the Dunstans, the Anselms, the Becketts, the Huberts, or the Langtons', was in a long line of wicked priests who had challenged the authority of the civil state. Not only were the clergy immoral and drunk, haunting taverns and coffee-houses, but becoming riotous and seditious, they unhinged 'wholesome order and Government'.[89]

This theme of priests exploiting their social power and status, in particular the 'divine' authority of the pulpit, which had become a commonplace complaint in the early 1680s, was an especially acute problem in the 1700s and 1710s, when the politics of religion had prompted party interests to embrace sophisticated communication methods.[90] One of the legacies of the 1710 trial was the powerful mobilisation of the clergy against the Whig interest in the constituencies, which resulted in electoral victory for the Tories in the General Election of that year. Newsletters, prints, ballads, pamphlets, addresses and sermons all indicate the central role of contestation over the status of the clergy and the Church. As Arthur Mainwaring complained, once again the 'pulpit heralds' took up 'their old Topicks of Non-resistance, Hereditary Right, and the Church's danger'. Powerful use, in particular, was made of the language and meaning of Sacheverell's trial. The objective was 'possessing the minds of ignorant people', the means was the orchestration of a national campaign. Lists, addresses, printed *pro formas* were composed and distributed: 'instructions were given to their Clergy, what doctrines they were to preach'. Loyal addresses were drawn up, printed headings of subject matter for sermons were disseminated. As Mainwaring commented: 'to this end the whole power of the Party was set at work'.[91] The collections of addresses to Anne made in 1710 support this claim: indeed, they were more than likely collected and published to reinforce the theme that 'the sense of the Kingdom, whether Nobility, Clergy, Gentry or Communalty, is express for the Doctrine of Passive-Obedience and Non-Resistance, and for her Majesty's Hereditary Title to the Throne of her Ancestors'.[92] Oldmixon's *History of Addresses* for 1710 illustrates time and time again both clerical involvement in the production of loyal addresses and the penetration of the language of Sacheverell's defence into these texts.[93] The episode of Sacheverell's trial and its electoral consequences is a very powerful illustration of the centrality and importance of anticlericalism at the heart of the politics of party and religion in the period. It is evidence that the contestation for control over the definition and authority of an important symbolic institution was not simply a discursive engagement. The trial of Sacheverell was an important ritual moment that involved the disputation of different textual and conceptual accounts of the constitution, religion and society, but it did not remain confined to a purely ideological sphere. In the streets of London, mobs attacked Whig figures and Low Church chapels; in the provincial towns and rural parishes riotous behaviour was manifest, as it was in the more formal spaces of poll booths, constituency meetings and other electoral venues. The response to the trial also indicates both the polarity of conceptions about the nature of priesthood, and ultimately the abiding strength of beliefs in the 'holy function' of the clerical order. Such contestations about the status and authority of churchmen were intimately related to the perceived stability of the civil constitution.

Debates about the role of the Church and the power and authority of churchmen were not marginal to the political discourses and practices of the late Stuart period. One of the early acts of the Hanoverian George I was to issue a Royal Proclamation directing the 'clergy to refrain from preaching politics'.[94] As the examples of Johnson, Sacheverell and Hoadly illustrate, the contestation about the correct ideological behaviour of the priesthood was furious and consistently at the epicentre of national and local politics. It is possible to suggest an incremental heightening of the stand-off between clericalist and anticlerical polemics from the 1680s to the 1710s. The power of the clergy and the prevailing ecclesiological relationship between religious conformity and political orthodoxy was manifest in the enactment and enforcement of confessional statutes such as the Test and Corporation Acts and the Act of Uniformity after 1660. This power of clergymen to impose upon individual conscience was repeatedly challenged between 1660 and 1689 and after; these debates about the authority of the Church were not merely theological, but by default also about the nature of the limits and legality of state power: clericalism and anticlericalism were not simply 'religious' matters, but a key theme in the broad discourse about power and authority. Redefining the nature of priesthood held implications not only for the nature of the Church, but ultimately for the distribution of social power. In one sense anticlericalism can be thought of as part of the ideological battle defining the 'idea' of the state: in this way, it was part of the political discourse about sovereignty that originated in the Henrician delineations of an 'imperial' monarchy.[95] Deployment of arguments against the *imperium in imperio* of the Church by Whiggish commonwealthsmen (such as, for example, Trenchard and Gordon in popular works like *Cato's Letters*) in the early decades of the eighteenth century is evidence of the continuity of this theme. Importantly, as the reactions to the trial of Sacheverell and the treatment of Hoadly indicate, such critiques were not only conceptual, but directed against the practical activities and actions of the established priesthood in national and local society.

The trial of Sacheverell was contrived by the Whig prosecution to be an opportunity for resolving the political problem of the High Church clergy: this crescendo was muted by the significant and tumultuous popular reaction in defence of the 'Church'. If the trial was the high water mark of Whiggish political anticlericalism, does the reaction to it denote the essential failure of attacks upon the Church? Any answer to this question must be cautious: careful consideration must be given to the location and reception of attacks upon the Church. It is quite clear from the collective works of historians like Clark, Jacob, Taylor, Walsh and many others that a broad cultural attachment to a clericalist model of Anglican religion persisted into the nineteenth century, certainly in the local communities. Such persistence did not indicate that these communities clung to an unchanging and essentially conservative pattern of worship. The work of Langford in particular indicates the changing social status and roles adopted by the parish clergy: much of this innovation was masked by the continuity of practice, ritual and doctrinal belief in the Church of England. The efflorescence of religiosity outside the establishment of Anglicanism is similarly testimony both to the unflagging importance of religion and to the diversity of forms it assumed after 1689.

Turning from the practice of religion to assessing the institutional status of cleric or Church might prompt a different answer to the question of the significance of anticlericalism. Although sacerdotalist conceptions of the Church and churchmen were robust and extensive after 1717, the same cannot be said for the constitutional articulacy of the Church. The 'Convocation crisis' was a major and historically understated moment in the history of political anticlericalism: after 1717 the possibilities of an Atterburian-style collaboration of Church and State to reinvigorate clerical authority were limited. Between the late 1690s and 1717 the Lower House of Convocation had been a powerful forum from which clerical militants could inspire the concomitant campaigns in the pulpit and in the printed media. Compromised by the spectre of Jacobitism, political clericalism after 1717 did not have the advantage of a national platform for the declaration of its ambitions. Such silence should not be interpreted as non-existence, but what it did mean was that, in one very profound and important sense, a return to the confessional ambitions of a pre-1689 model were perhaps politically unlikely, if not ideologically unthinkable. As the anticlerical parliamentary campaigns of the 1720s and 1730s indicate, the war against priests was far from over, but the ecclesiological combination of Walpole and Gibson, for the most part, dampened down controversy about the status and authority of the Church on the national stage. The crises provoked by the Jew Bill in the 1750s and the Gordon Riots in the 1780s suggest the latent volatility of challenges to the 'Church'. Direct confrontation with clericalism (in its widest possible sense), as the trial of Sacheverell indicated, resulted in defeat; reform from within, as the example of Hoadly shows, was perhaps more successful. English anticlericalism had by 1717 won some important victories against the Church (as an ecclesiological institution), while perhaps losing the bigger war against the priests.

Notes

1   See M. de Certeau 'The Formality of Practices', in *The Writing of History* (New York, 1988), p. 155. For their thoughts and reactions to this piece, I would like to thank Margaret Jacob and Nicholas Tyacke.

2   See 'Some Memorials of the Reverend Mr Samuel Johnson; communicated in a Letter to a Friend, by one of his Intimate Acquaintance', in *The Works of the Late Reverend Mr Samuel Johnson* (2nd edn, London, 1713), pp. iii–iv. For a more recent account, see M. Zook, 'Early Whig Ideology, Ancient Constitutionalism, and the Reverend Samuel Johnson', *Journal of British Studies* 32 (1993), pp. 139–65.

3   See M. Goldie, 'The Roots of True Whiggism 1688–94', *History of Political Thought* 1 (1980), pp. 195–236, esp. 199.

4   *The Works of the Late Reverend Mr Samuel Johnson*, 151.

5   Ibid., p. viii.

6   Ibid., p. xi.

7   See J. Wickham Legg, 'The Degradation in 1686 of the Revd Samuel Johnson', *English Historical Review* (hereafter *EHR*) 29 (1914), pp. 723–42, at 726.

8   'Some Memorials', p. xi.

9   See Wickham Legg, 'The Degradation', for a transcription of the process of degradation, esp. pp. 739–40.

10   'Some Memorials', pp. ix and xi; Wickham Legg, 'The Degradation', pp. 741–2.

11   'Some Memorials', pp. xii–xiii.

12   Ibid., pp. ix–x.

13   Wickham Legg, 'The Degradation', p. 742, citing the opinion of the Proctor-General of the Arches, Richard Newcourt.

14   On Johnson's contributions, see M. Goldie, 'The Revolution of 1689 and the structure of Political Argument: An essay and an annotated Bibliography of pamphlets on the Allegiance controversy', *Bulletin of Research in the Humanities* 83 (1980), pp. 473–564.

15   J.C.D. Clark, *English Society 1688–1832* (Cambridge, 1985), p. 302.

16   See N. Sykes, 'Benjamin Hoadly, Bishop of Bangor', in F.J.C. Hearnshaw (ed.), *The Social and Political Ideas of Some English Thinkers of the Augustan Age* (1928), pp. 112–56, citing (at p. 120) Royal Historical Manuscripts Commission, Egmont Mss, I 444.

17   The best account is P.B. Hessert, 'The Bangorian Controversy' (Edinburgh University, PhD, 1951). See also H.D. Rack '"Christ's Kingdom not of this World": The case of Benjamin Hoadly versus William Law reconsidered'; Studies in Church History 12 (1975), pp. 275–91.

18   Cited in Hessert, 'Bangorian Controversy', p. 68 (Works II 404).

19   *Synodolia* II, 'A Representation of the Lower House of Convocation about the Bishop of Bangor's sermon of the Kingdom of Christ', p. 829.

20   Sykes, 'Benjamin Hoadly', p. 143.

21   See 'The Church in Danger', 1709 (reproduced in Holmes, *Sacheverell*, from Magdalen College, Oxford); 'Guess att my Meaning', 1709 (BMC 1503); M.D. George, *English Political Caricature to 1792* (Oxford, 1959), points out (at p. 68) that a later print, 'The Apparition' (BMC 1569), also represents a Low Church library with many of the same volumes.

22   For an understanding of how even 'orthodoxy' was not a fixed point, see J.G.A. Pocock, 'Within the Margins: Definitions of Orthodoxy', in R. Lund (ed.), *The Margins of Orthodoxy* (Cambridge, 1995).

23   Cited in Clark, *English Society*, p. 147, footnote 129.

24   R. Nelson, *A Companion for the Festivals and Fasts of the Church of England* (1798), Preface, p. x.

25   Ibid., pp. 481, 482–3, 487–90 and 520–30.

26   Nelson, cited by R. Cornwall (p. 78) in *Visible and Apostolic: The Constitution of the Church in High Church Anglican and Non-juror Thought* (Delaware, 1993).

27   Cornwall, *passim.*

28   Nelson, *Visible and Apostolic*, p. 483.

29   See A.M.C. Waterman, 'The nexus between theology and political doctrine', in K. Haakonssen (ed.), *Enlightenment and Religion: Rational Dissent in Eighteenth-Century Britain* (Cambridge, 1996), pp. 193–218, at p. 205.

30   A.G. Dickens, 'The Shape of Anti-clericalism and the English Reformation', p. 379.

31   See C. Hill, *The Economic Problems of the Church* (Oxford, 1956).

32   See E.J. Evans, 'Some reasons for the growth of English Rural Anti-clericalism *c.*1750–*c.*1830', *Past & Present* 66 (1975), pp. 84–109.

33   See J. Morrill, 'The Attack on the Church of England in the Long Parliament, 1640–1642', pp. 105–24.

34   See J. Maclear, 'Popular Anticlericalism in the Puritan Revolution', *Journal of the History of Ideas* 17 (1956), pp. 443–70.

35   See Morrill, 'The Attack', pp. 117–19; Maclear, 'Popular anticlericalism', p. 460.

36   For a corrective, see M.A. Goldie, 'Priestcraft and the birth of Whiggism', in N. Phillison and Q. Skinner (eds), *Political Discourse in Early Modern Britain* (Cambridge, 1993), pp. 209–31; and J.A.I. Champion, *The Pillars of Priestcraft Shaken: the Church of England and its enemies, 1660–1730* (Cambridge, 1992).

37   See D. Beaver, 'Religion, politics and society in Early Modern England: A problem of classification', *Journal of British Studies* 32 (1993), pp. 314–22.

38   See, in particular, Walsh, Haydon and Taylor (eds), *The Church of England, c.1689–c.1833. From Toleration to Tractarianism* (Cambridge, 1993), pp. 8–10.

39   See K.V. Thomas, 'Cases of Conscience in Seventeenth Century England', in J. Morrill, P. Slack and D. Woolf (eds), *Public Duty and Private Conscience in Seventeenth Century England* (Oxford, 1993), pp. 29–56.

40   See P. Harvey, 'The problem of social-political obligation for the Church of England in the seventeenth century', *Church History* 40 (1971), pp. 156–69.

41   See B.S. Stewart, 'The Cult of the Royal Martyr', *Church History* 38 (1969), pp. 175–87, and H.W. Randell, 'The Rise and Fall of a Martyrology: Sermons on Charles I', *Huntington Library Quarterly* 10 (1947), pp. 135–67.

42   G.V. Bennett, *Tory Crisis in Church and State, 1688–1730. The career of Francis Atterbury, Bishop of Rochester* (Oxford, 1975), p. 140.

43   M.A. Goldie, 'Danby, the Bishops and the Whigs', in T. Harris et al. (eds), *The Politics of Religion in Restoration England* (Oxford, 1990); Professor Miller suggested this in a seminar

communication of his research on Norfolk in the 1670s in the Institute of Historical Research.

44 Goldie, 'Danby, the Bishops and the Whigs', p. 98.

45 H. Care, *English Liberties*, p. 93.

46 H. Care, *Weekly Pacquet of Advice from Rome*, III, no. 46, 22 April (1681), p. 368.

47 *Poems on Affairs of State* (hereafter POAS) 2, *An Historical Poem* (1680), p. 157.

48 POAS II, pp. 11, 347, 353 and 370; POAS III, pp. 11, 19, 72 and 95.

49 See W. Speck, *Tory and Whig* (1970), pp. 24–9; W. Speck and W.A. Grey, 'Computer analysis of Poll Books: an initial report', *BIHR* 43 (1970), pp. 105–12, and W. Speck, W.A. Grey and R. Hopkinson, 'Computer Analysis of Poll Books: a further report', *BIHR* 48 (1975), pp. 68–79.

50 M. Ransome, 'Church and Dissent in the Election of 1710', *EHR* 56 (1941), pp. 76–89, at p. 80.

51 J. Oldmixon, *The History of Addresses*, vol. II (1711) (HOP transcripts), p. 143.

52 Cited in G.A. Holmes, *Transcripts* 396 (now in the possession of the History of Parliament), *The Flying Post*, 2–4 November (1710). Many thanks and acknowledgements to Dr Stuart Handley for allowing me access to this material.

53 Holmes, *Transcripts*, p. 417 (HOP).

54 See P. Langford, 'Convocation and the Tory Clergy, 1717–61', in E. Cruikshanks and J. Black (eds), *The Jacobite Challenge* (Edinburgh, 1988), pp. 107–22.

55 See J.A.W. Gunn, *Beyond Liberty and Property: The Process of Self Recognition in Eighteenth Century Political Thought* (McGill, 1983), p. 140.

56 See Bennett, *Tory Crisis*, pp. 125–40.

57 See R. Ashcraft and M.M. Goldsmith, 'Locke, Revolution Principles, and the formation of Whig Ideology', *HJ* 26 (1983), pp. 773–800, at pp. 776–7.

58 Ellis, *The Medley*, p. 151.

59 See H. Dickinson, 'The eighteenth century debate on the "Glorious Revolution"', *History* 61 (1976), pp. 28–45, esp. pp. 33–5.

60 *The Perils of False Brethren, both in Church and State* (1709), pp. 19–21.

61 *The Tryal of Dr Henry Sacheverell before the House of Peers, for high crimes and misdemeanours* (London, 1710), pp. 4, 24.

62 Ibid., p. 32.

63 Ibid., pp. 37–8.

64 Ibid., pp. 61 and 75.

65 Ibid., pp. 99–100, 106, 110 and 114.

66 Ibid., pp. 119, 121 and 125.

67 Ibid., pp. 156, 161–73, 185–94 and 206.

68 Sacheverell, cited from a series of heretical works (pp. 217–30). These were later published separately, to the disgust of Whig MPs, who ordered the volume burnt.

69 Ibid., pp. 215 and 223.

70 Ibid., pp. 243–6.

71 Ibid., pp. 251 and 257.

72 Ibid., pp. 114–15.

73 Ibid., p. 115.

74   Ibid., p. 116.

75   Ibid., p. 246.

76   See W. Speck's edition of F.F. Madan, *Bibliography of Sacheverell* (1977).

77   Ellis, *Examiner-Medley*, 28 December 1710, *The Examiner*, no. 22, p. 128.

78   Ibid., p. 156.

79   Ellis, *Examiner-Medley*, p. 400; Ransome, *EHR* 56 (1941), p. 80.

80   On Sacheverell's bibliographical collection, its publication and burning, see Speck, *Bibliography of Sacheverell*, p. 237; 'Collection of Passages referred to by Dr Henry Sacheverell' (1710); reprinted in A. Boyer, *The History of the Reign of Queen Anne* (1710), Appendix, pp. 137–70.

81   See POAS VII, p. 440, *The Merciful Judgements of High Church Triumphant on Offending Clergymen and Others, in the Reign of Charles I* (1710). The writings of these High Church precursors of Sacheverell were also republished with commentaries, see Speck, *Bibliography of Sacheverell*.

82   For a full bibliographical description, see G. Carabelli, *Tolandiana* (Florence, 1977), pp. 151–2.

83   Interestingly, the title page of the second edition also included a scriptural citation from James 3.5–6, 'Behold, how great a matter a little fire kindleth! The Tongue is a fire, a world of iniquity, which setteth on fire the Course of Nature, and is set on fire of Hell.'

84   So, for example, he inserted material about the mob attack on Burges' Chapel, and similar riotous behaviour in Wolverhampton and Barnstaple, pp. 95–6 and 104–6.

85   See p. 305 on 'blasphemous books'.

86   *Mr Toland's Reflections*, pp. 9, 11 and 12.

87   *Jacobitism, Perjury and Popery*, pp. 3, 4–6, 8–10, 11, 13, 14 and 15.

88   *Mr Toland's Reflections*, p. 13.

89   *An Appeal to Honest People*, pp. 2, 4–5, 11, 14, 36–7, 38, 42–7, 56 and 57.

90   For an early essay exploring the diversity and sophistication of party propaganda, see W. Speck, 'Political propaganda in Augustan England', *TRHS* (1972), pp. 17–32.

91   A. Mainwaring, *Four Letters to a Friend in North Britain Upon the Publishing the Tryal of Dr Sacheverell* (1710), pp. 6–8, 9–10, 11 and 18.

92   See *Collection of Addresses* (1710), Preface.

93   See HOP transcript, noting that the Northants, Exeter, and Abingdon addresses used Sacheverell-style arguments.

94   Speck, *Bibliography of Sacheverell*, pp. 111–12.

95   See J.A. Guy, 'The Henrician Age', in J.A.G. Pocock (ed.), *The Varieties of British Political Thought, 1500–1800* (Cambridge, 1993), pp. 13–46.

4

ANTI-CATHOLICISM AS ANGLICAN ANTICLERICALISM: NONCONFORMITY AND THE IDEOLOGICAL ORIGINS OF RADICAL DISAFFECTION

James E. Bradley

Recent research on late Stuart and early Hanoverian religion has provided us with new insights into the importance of English anti-Catholicism and various expressions of anticlericalism. We now have detailed studies, for example, of eighteenth-century anti-Catholicism and what might be called 'the anticlericalism of unbelief', and several recent monographs have touched on the anticlericalism of Dissent and Low Church Anglicans – what might be called 'believing', or Christian anticlericalism.[1] The English Nonconformists, however, who represented far greater numbers than the Deists, freethinkers or heterodox commonwealthsmen, have not received the attention they deserve, and yet their anticlericalism was arguably more influential in the long term than that of any other group. In the wake of a century of religious upheaval, the Presbyterians, Congregationalists and Baptists espoused an alternative religious culture, replete with an unsavoury history, a separate educational system, corporate meeting places and an articulate intelligentsia, and these bodies still appeared highly menacing to many Anglicans well into the early decades of the eighteenth century. Conversely, from the vantage point of the Dissenters, the Anglican Church appeared to be equally threatening, especially in the reign of Queen Anne (1701–14), and since the Anglican hierarchy seemed to behave exactly like its hated Catholic counterpart, the hostility of several High Church divines provoked a vigorous body of Dissenting anticlerical literature. Much remains to be learned about how, during the course of the century, the traditional anti-Catholic attitude of the Nonconformists veered over into a more generalised anti-Anglican or anti-Establishment attitude.[2] We can presently show, however, that much eighteenth-century anti-Catholic rhetoric was in fact directed against the Anglican Establishment, thus signalling an important shift from the old, intra-confessional warfare to a new inter-confessional debate and the early break-up of the *ancien régime*. But the connections between anti-Catholicism, anticlericalism and political disaffection in the civil realm, while often assumed to exist by the defenders of the established Church, remain to this date little studied and poorly understood.

A number of recent works have attempted to locate the ideological sources of the Dissenters' political disaffection under George III in their heterodoxy, but just as the common associations between anticlericalism and unbelief need to be challenged, the affinities often assumed to exist between heresy and civil disaffection require further investigation.[3] Recent treatments of England and the North American colonies that emphasise the heterodoxy of Dissent depend unduly on the influence of ideas and individual thinkers, and they have tended to neglect the social dislocation and minority status of the Dissenters. These efforts have also failed to plumb the long memories of the Dissenters, and the hatreds they nurtured in their embattled stance as religious outcasts. The Dissenters' dominant mentality of opposition can be traced to several defining episodes of persecution and social ostracism they experienced at the hands of High Anglicans in the first two decades of the eighteenth century. This chapter seeks to establish the importance of anti-Catholicism and anticlericalism for understanding the origins of Dissenting political disaffection, and argues that anticlericalism, not heterodoxy, was a leading ideological source of radical opposition to the government of George III. A major line of political argument is thus located in the adaptation of anti-papal rhetoric, freshly applied by Dissenters against Anglican forms of religious imposition. This study therefore attempts to adumbrate the affinity between anti-Catholic, anticlerical and anti-government thought, and to show various ways in which anticlericalism was periodically revived and sustained by anti-Catholicism, and ultimately transformed into civil Dissent during the conflict with the American colonies. Religious or 'ebelieving' anticlericalism appears to have been the most politically viable form of anticlericalism, in that it was highly malleable and readily exportable; when once transferred to the colonies and there put to radical use, it was arguably more protean than Deist and other, more secular forms of anticlericalism in England.

I

The leading political reality that united Presbyterians, Congregationalists and Baptists in their shared and profound anticlerical convictions was the common experience of political oppression in late Stuart England. From the ejection of some 2,000 Nonconforming ministers and schoolmasters in 1662, through the penal period of Dissent before 1689, and on into the early years of Queen Anne's reign, the Dissenters, heterodox and orthodox alike, were constantly under the threat of repression, and frequently experienced social and political ostracism. The Act of Toleration itself was but a small step toward liberty, in that it merely suspended the legal penalties against orthodox Dissent. Moreover, while the revolution of 1688–9 was a new beginning in some senses, for Dissenters it continued what was begun in 1662 by forcing them into a separate and politically inferior status.[4] Statements of anticlericalism among Dissenters were unavoidably tied to politics because the established Church simply represented the civil government in its religious expression. In this context, it should come as no surprise that for Dissenters, 'popery' embraced all forms of ecclesiastical imposition, including Anglican forms, because for them, impositions in religion at the hands of a clerical magistrate unavoidably entailed impositions in the civil realm as well, and thereby always invited comparisons with a Catholic past.

To support these claims, we will look briefly at three episodes of Dissenting anticlerical agitation that reveal the connections between anti-Catholic and anti-Anglican sentiment: first, the period following the Sacheverell riots up to the Bangorian controversy in 1717; secondly, the agitation in the 1730s over renewed fears of a revival of Catholicism; and lastly, the mid-1760s debate over the Stamp Act and the attempt to introduce bishops into the American colonies. The immediate occasion of the Dissenters' anticlericalism can be located in the rancorous history of party in the first decade of the century, and by examining the Anglican response to the Dissenters, we will discover how anti-Catholicism was often a thinly veiled form of anti-Anglicanism that was readily transformed from thence into political disaffection.

Having experienced some freedom after the Act of Toleration and the largely benign conditions under William and Mary, the Dissenters in the early years of Anne's reign found the attempts by Jacobites and Tories to curtail their freedom particularly galling and intimidating. We know, for example, that the debate beginning in 1702 over occasional conformity was unusually rancorous, and in its initial phase, it extended, almost without intermission, for over two years. The Tories understood the Dissenters' practice of occasionally receiving the Anglican sacrament of the Lord's Supper in order to qualify for political office as a wicked attempt of the 'sectaries' to subvert the law and undermine the proper electoral and civil influence of the Church. Conversely, for the Dissenter, the threat of closing the legal loophole to office-holding was but further evidence of tyranny supported by priestcraft. Their point seemed to be proven when, in 1703, for his clever response to Charles Leslie's attack on the Nonconformists, Daniel Defoe was fined, imprisoned and pilloried. Henry Sacheverell, High Church advocate of ecclesiastical authority and opponent of toleration, had already by this date drawn the attention of the Dissenters because of his Assize Sermons at Oxford.

A second issue centred around the Dissenters' education and the question of the legitimacy of their ministry. Since the first years of the century, there had been considerable debate over the Dissenting academies; just after the accession of Anne, the Lower House of Canterbury Convocation complained that the Dissenting academies prejudiced people against the two universities. The subject came up again in a vigorous debate in Parliament three years later, in 1704.[5] Throughout the period, in pamphlets, sermons and newspapers, High Church publicists intimidated Nonconformists with the charge of schism, and threatened them with the loss of their academies. The move to wrest the Dissenters' academies from them cut to the heart of their legitimacy, for the 'Schism Bill' – as it came to be called – would effectively destroy an educated ministry.

In 1709 Henry Sacheverell rose to national prominence through his notorious sermon at St Paul's Cathedral on 5 November on the theme 'in peril among false brethren'. The sermon blasted the Dissenters as a 'A brood of vipers' with their 'Hellish principles of fanaticism, regicide and anarchy'. The Whig prosecution of Sacheverell for sedition seemed to confirm to the majority of Anglican clergy, and many laymen as well, that the Church was indeed in danger from traitorous Low Church divines and Dissenters. The Sacheverell affair thereby marked a significant resurgence of Tory influence in the last years of Anne's reign that culminated in the abortive rebellion of 1715. In December 1711 the Occasional Conformity Bill, though liberally modified, passed into law, and in June 1714 the Schism Act finally passed both houses of Parliament, though the Queen's death subsequently prevented its implementation, and both laws were eventually repealed in 1719 under an administration that was far more friendly to Dissent.

One of the few Dissenting ministers who challenged Sacheverell's sermon in print was Daniel Burgess, a prominent Presbyterian minister whose new, enlarged meeting house in Lincoln's Inn Fields had opened in 1705. Following Sacheverell's trial for sedition in 1710, the verdict against him provoked High Church riots in London that Geoffrey Holmes ranked second in destructive power only to the Gordon riots of 1780.[6] On the night of 1 March 1710 a well-orchestrated mob involving many thousands of Londoners systematically dismantled six Dissenting chapels (two of which were large structures with three galleries each), collected the debris in the centre of the streets to avoid setting fire to adjacent houses, and burned it all in huge bonfires. The rioters began with Daniel Burgess's chapel. The emotional intimidation of the proposed Occasional Conformity Bill and the closing of the academies was here powerfully reinforced by the physical threat to life and limb. These six chapels provided seating for thousands of Dissenters, and the impact of the riots on the mentality of the victims was undoubtedly profound. If, as Holmes says, the flames and destruction of March 1710 left an indelible impression on the mind of Robert Walpole for three decades and more, what must have been the effect on the average Dissenter? If the Whigs were 'shaken', as one contemporary put it, at the terror of Sacheverell's 'inveterate expressions',[7] how must those Dissenting ministers have felt when they actually experienced the violence of Sacheverell's devoted followers? If it is true, as Holmes urges, that at least four-fifths of the parish clergy in England and Wales were sympathetic to the cause of Sacheverell, the fears and the hatreds of the Dissenters were not without foundation.[8]

We have some indication of how significantly the Sacheverell riots influenced the development of anticlericalism, and specifically the Dissenters' contribution to the growth of anticlericalism. Of the six Dissenting ministers who suffered the destruction of their meeting houses in the riots, five (Burgess, Jabez Earle, Samuel

Wright, Christopher Taylor and Thomas Bradbury) were outspoken in their zeal for religious liberty and in their criticism of the Establishment.[9] Three of them (Earle, Wright and Bradbury) later contributed to the Salter's Hall anti-Catholic lectureship in the mid-1730s, a lectureship that was construed by Anglicans to be broadly anti-Anglican. Amazingly, Samuel Wright's meeting house at Blackfriars was systematically gutted a second time in 1715 by High Anglican opponents of the Hanoverian succession.[10] It will come as no surprise that in defence of Dissent, writing as late as 1733, Wright entitled a pamphlet 'The Church in Perils Among False Brethren', mocking Sacheverell's more famous sermon of twenty-odd years past.[11] There is, in addition, a tantalising connection between the Dissenters and the more famous anticlerical writers, John Trenchard and Thomas Gordon. When Trenchard and Gordon published their *Independent Whig* in 1719, it was immediately attacked by some High Anglican clergy. In response, Trenchard wrote *The Craftsman*, with the subtitle, 'A Sermon or Paraphrase upon Several Verses of the 19th chapter of the Acts of the Apostles. Composed by the late Daniel Burgess.'[12] The 'sermon', with Burgess's name attached, went through seven editions by 1732; it was republished in Philadelphia, and only modern scholarship has revealed that Trenchard was the author, not Burgess.[13] Some indication of the salience of this publication and the abiding impact of Sacheverell and the Dissenting response is found in the fact that *The Craftsman* was republished in Birmingham in 1791 and again in 1792 in an eighth edition in the wake of the Church and King riots.

In all of the polemical literature of Anglicans and Dissenters written in the first two decades of the eighteenth century, the anticlericalism of Dissent transcended personal attacks on the evil lives of particular priests and extended to the institution, and in each case it was theologically grounded in christology and ecclesiology. When deployed for political purposes, the Dissenters' christology was orthodox, and it functioned identically in the writings of all Dissenters, whether or not the author personally espoused an Arian or Trinitarian point of view. Embracing a common theory, both the Trinitarian and heterodox Dissenters' understanding of Christ as 'sole legislator in his Church' was juxtaposed to the twentieth of the Thirty Nine Articles that declared the Church's power to decree rites and ceremonies, and its authority in controversies of faith. In all of the pamphlet wars – including those between Edmund Calamy and Benjamin Hoadly in his early career; Samuel Palmer and Samuel Wesley; Peter Dowley and Edward Wells; James Owen, George Hicks and Charles Leslie; Daniel Neal and Francis Hare; and Thomas Bradbury and Luke Milbourne – the principled basis of the Dissenters' identity and their opposition to the establishment remained the same. All the controversialist Dissenters listed here were orthodox Trinitarians; conversely, the defenders of the Church – ranging from Low Churchmen, in the case of Hoadly, to High, in the case of Leslie – were, at the time of writing, equally orthodox. There were, to be sure, differences in emphasis and tone between these authors, but in the case of Dissent, the moderation of their more enthusiastic tone can be attributed to strategic considerations. In their disadvantaged and threatened situation, most Dissenters were bound to be discreet, and from sociological studies we now know how minorities in distressed circumstances are prone to use indirect speech and *double entendre* to criticise their perceived oppressors.

II

Two extended examples, one from the controversy over education and the Schism Bill, and the other from the Occasional Conformity Bill and the debate over office-holding, will illustrate these matters. At the opening of the eighteenth century Presbyterian minister Samuel Palmer became embroiled with Samuel Wesley, the father of John and Charles Wesley, in a debate over the legitimacy of the Dissenting academies. Palmer wanted the restrictions against Dissenters removed from the universities, and he also defended full freedom for private academies. These changes should not, he argued, be seen as a threat to Anglicans, for the most learned among the Dissenters, Palmer averred, had the most generous opinion of the Church of England. So, in attempting to vindicate the legitimacy of Dissent, it was strategically crucial for the Dissenters to stress that they possessed the same essential religion as the Anglicans. Still, a vigorous anticlericalism, in most of its radical force, can be found in Palmer's pamphlets. Referring to Sacheverell's Assize sermons, Palmer observed that the Dissenters' adversaries sought to provoke the government against them by arguing that their academies taught vice and irreligion. In response to the Royal Grant to the two universities, Palmer asked: 'Does the grant force me to attend Oxford or Cambridge, or has it fixt the abode of the *science* there? No such matter, the arts and sciences we pursue in *Academies* are liberal, and will not be chain'd to a post, nor are they pleas'd their *votaries* should address 'em in fetters, or with a rope about their necks; for tho' a *university* may teach men to be slaves, yet the *sciences* always cherish and support the liberty of mankind.'[14]

   The resistance to the establishment through the language of ropes around necks and denigrating the servility of Anglicanism is here powerfully connected to a high regard for reason, science and the liberty of private judgement. In later parts of his *Vindication*, Palmer excoriated the ecclesiastical control of the press and the '*hierarchical* pomp' of the Church.[15] When his opponent, Wesley, charged the Dissenters with 'unbecoming deportment' to the Church of England, Palmer insisted that 'with very few exceptions' there was a constant decorum among the Dissenters when speaking of the Church. And when Wesley charged the Dissenters with a lack of thankfulness for the liberty they already enjoyed, Palmer reminded him that the Dissenters did address the Church 'the very instant that we receiv'd the favour, to the *King*, who was *Head of the Church*; and the *Tail* of the

Church in this very book I'm answering, has most unreasonably banter'd and buffoon'd us for it'.[16] Here, an implicit criticism of Anglican theology with respect to the temporal head of the Church was combined with an explicit denigration of Wesley himself. Palmer, like all Nonconformist authors, grounded his Dissent in theology, and he concluded his vindication with a line of raillery from the *Life of Christ* (Lib. III, ver. 215), evidently Wesley's own translation:

> Prest with your Crimes, *the Church, the Church*, you Cry
> Your meaning, *Grandure, Wealth and Policy*.[17]

The anticlericalism that arose from the issues surrounding occasional conformity is illustrated by the writings of Thomas Bradbury, by far the most outspoken of all of the victims of the Sacheverell riots. Bradbury was the Congregationalist pastor of the prominent Shoe Lane Chapel, New Street, and he had early earned the resentment of High Church Anglicans and Jacobites. He was the most inflammatory Dissenting preacher of the early eighteenth century, rivalling Daniel Defoe in his rhetorical power, yet Bradbury – like Burgess, Earle, Wright, Taylor and Palmer – was an orthodox Trinitarian. At the opening of the eighteenth century Bradbury began preaching an annual political sermon on 5 November in defence of 1689, and he published his first five sermons in 1705. In 1707 the title of his annual diatribe was *The Divine Right of the Revolution*, evidently designed to provoke a response, and in the next year he blasted the Jacobites in a highly publicised sermon called *The Son of Tabeal* that rapidly went to four editions. When the Occasional Conformity Bill was finally passed in December 1711 Bradbury preached on the Old Testament hero Daniel, and his steadfastness under the unjust decrees of the tyrant Darius. But the most offensive sermon of his career appeared on 5 November 1712, called *The Ass: or, The Serpent. A Comparison between the Tribes of Issachar and Dan, in their Regard for Civil Liberty*. This work provoked a vigorous response in the Tory press, with anonymous attacks in *The Post Boy* and *The Examiner*. There was a further furious pamphlet by another anonymous author, and in addition Luke Milbourne, the well-known High Church pamphleteer, wrote several vigorous replies, including *A Guilty Conscience Makes a Rebel* (1713) and *The Traytors Reward* (1714).[18]

A study of five of Bradbury's pamphlets between 1712 and 1717 will illustrate something of the nature, extent and motivation of Dissenting anticlericalism. Bradbury's anticlericalism is directed against Roman Catholics, High Anglicans and Anglicans broadly; indeed, his thought is anti-establishment and anti-coercion, and one can detect a fanatical element in his writing that is profoundly threatening and violent. For him, the 'popish religion' is clearly a generic term that takes in Anglican as well as Catholic.[19] To be sure, he refers to Rome by his criticism of the doctrines of merit, purgatory, absolution, intercession to departed

saints and the use of images, and he promises to testify against these false
doctrines and practices, he says, if necessary with his blood.[20] But he moves freely
from Catholic to Anglican with the circumlocution that 'We know who it is that
gives laws about religion, that have no foundation in Scripture; and 'tis in
maintenance of these impositions, that nations are involv'd in wars. The doctrine
of Christ Jesus is the doctrine of peace . . . but ceremonies have always swum in
blood, and must be driven in with force and violence.'[21] Bradbury catches both
Catholic and Anglican in his broad net, since all coercion is forbidden to
Christians: when people lay nations waste, they cannot rightly claim to derive
their authority from Christ. Writing in 1716, the year before Benjamin Hoadly's
famous sermon on Christ's spiritual kingdom, Bradbury exclaimed: 'What place
can inquisitions, massacres, and penal laws have in promoting *a kingdom that is not
of this world?* . . . Must *Zion*, the *City of our Solemnities*, be a desert? Shall the noble
frame of salvation, that he laid in the Gospel, be all brought to rubbish?'[22]

Bradbury indicts Anglican clergy directly. Quoting Isaiah 9:16 ('For the leaders
of this people cause them to err; and they that are led of them are destroyed'), he
argues that Anglican preaching is often 'mere morality'; their praying is false,
since they have to rely on 'the Book' in order to learn what to pray for, and those
are excluded from the Lord's Table who would view it as a feast of love, 'but it is
left open for those, who mean no more by it than a qualification for an office'.[23]
But Bradbury's critique, while it included the clergy, went beyond them and
embraced the established institution of the Church. The matters of the spirit and
salvation are to be kept separate from the matters of this world and its
government.[24] 'Men should not take Sacraments because they are *Officers*, but
because they are *Christians*: or *think that eating the Body and Blood of the Lord* is any
preparation for eating the Bread of the Government. This [i.e. taking the
sacrament because they are Christians] had been a fairer inference, but that was a
doctrine they were not paid for.'[25] So people who impose penal laws, and here he
indicts the Anglican alliance of Church and State, have gone the way of Cain,
'first entertaining fancies of their own, and then imposing them on others'.[26]

What makes the current alliance of Church and State so hideous to Bradbury
is that it is coercive and ends in persecution. The alliance breeds oppression. He
thinks he discerns something in the persons of Anglican rulers that hates simple
devotion to Christ: they resent 'the carriage of those that are more religious' than
they.[27] And this leads eventually to murder. Cain murders his brother Abel, who
is represented explicitly as the Dissenter, and thus human blood is shed in the
honour of superstition – 'Oh miserable effect of human inventions in the worship
of God!'[28] More importantly, Bradbury's anticlericalism led him to a broader
anti-authoritarianism that bordered on republicanism. In *The Ass: or, The Serpent*,
Bradbury likens all those who teach passive obedience and submission to
arbitrary government to the Jewish tribe of Issachar: such people are as stupid as
asses. What is said of Issachar, according to Bradbury, 'is as full of contempt as a

metaphor can be. We are to know him by his likeness to the most heavy and stupid animal in creation.'[29] Bradbury proceeded to show how vile a creature the ass is, unfit for both this world and the next. Since, according to divine law, asses cannot even be sacrificed, 'they seem to be the outcasts of both worlds'.[30] But there is a further foundation to tyranny, and it is laid in religion: 'You may always observe it, that an indifference to civil liberties goes along with a neglect of that which is [genuinely] religious. A man that throws away the blessings of providence, cannot have a due relish to those of grace.'[31] In the application, Bradbury exhorted his hearers to resent those doctrines that would argue away their liberties, and he clearly located the cause of priestcraft in tyranny. In short, Issachar is a strong ass, bowing down between two burdens: the burdens of slavery in his person, and poverty in his concerns, for he has become a servant to tribute (i.e. excessive taxes).[32]

The Jewish tribe of Dan, on the other hand, is taken to represent the wisdom of a serpent, and by extension all those who espouse true religion and let the magistrates know that they will not forfeit their civil liberties. Dan will 'undermine the foundations of tyranny'; his people are characterised by courage and resolution, rather than laziness and cowardice.[33] The 'spirit of our religion', namely Dissenting religion, is characterised by the apostles who used their privileges against the unjust encroachments of authority.[34] Bradbury seemed to relish the Old Testament event of Abraham destroying five kings,[35] and he urged his hearers that 'There's nothing in any one doctrine of Christianity that will tye up the hands of an injur'd people.'[36] Wise and well instructed, Dan is determined to have the blessing of liberty at any expense, for when the tyrant 'decides to ride over liberty and religion, if they cannot stop his career, they'll break his neck'.[37] There can be little wonder that such bold, intemperate language provoked a vigorous response.

Both the anonymous writers who responded to Bradbury understood him to be attacking monarchy and the Anglican Church, as did Luke Milbourne. *Some Short Reflections upon Mr Bradbury's Late Libel* urged that the Dissenters had used their freedom as 'a trumpet of rebellion', and the author suggested that their superiors should 'disable' them from doing any mischief.[38] Bradbury's essay excites subjects 'to rise against their princes upon every provocation'.[39] Luke Milbourne agreed with the anonymous authors. The work of Bradbury was a 'scandalous libel' against 'good Christians of all ages', and against 'all governments and governours, spiritual and temporal'.[40] As with the anonymous authors, Milbourne viewed the anticlericalism and the anti-authoritarian sentiment of a piece: our young Hugh (referring to Hugh Peters, executed as a regicide), Milbourne says, urges 'down with spiritual and temporal government', and we find in him the same spirit as 'the rebellious saints of old'. Evidently 'the devil of sedition, is not yet cast entirely out of the party'.[41] Clearly, from a High Church perspective, the anticlericalism of believing Dissent could not be distinguished from that of atheism and republicanism, for Bradbury was here likened to Hobbes, Spinosa, Collins, Tyndale and Toland for abusing and ridiculing the sacred Word, and in another place Milbourne compared Bradbury's ideas to the Sydneys, Lockes, Hoadlys and Burnets of this world.[42]

Predictably, Bradbury replied in kind. His sermon of 1714 on *The Lawfulness of Resisting Tyrants* was highly inflammatory.[43] Bradbury heartily thanked Milbourne for putting him in the company of the Sydneys, Lockes, Hoadlys and Burnets, and 'if he likes to herd with the Sibthorps, Mainwarings, Hicks, Sach—lls, Wel—ns, Lesleys, and Ropers, both sides are pleas'd'.[44] His main contention was the duty and glory of a people 'to break any yoke that is hung upon their liberty', and next to tyrants themselves, the leading opponents of this political position are 'those high-flying preachers' whose only religion 'lies in their great places', supposing godliness is gain.[45] True religion, on the other hand, is on the side of liberty and 'political equity'.

The provocative, bellicose rhetoric of Bradbury prompted Daniel Defoe's entry into the fray in 1715 under the pseudonym of a Quaker. *A Friendly Epistle by Way of Reproof From one of the People Called Quakers, To Thomas Bradbury, A Dealer in Many Words* is the first of nine pamphlets in which Defoe adopted the conciliatory persona of a Friend.[46] Defoe was not only interested in defending his moderate, though now fallen, comrades of a previous ministry, particularly Robert Harley; evidently he also hoped to mollify a fellow Dissenter and avoid further conflict, though it must be recalled that Defoe had by this time entered a period in which his political views were unclear and almost certainly duplicitous. It may indicate something of Bradbury's eminence at the time that Defoe associated him with the more famous Bishop of Salisbury in a second pamphlet: *Burnet and Bradbury, or the Confederacy of the Press and the Pulpit for the Blood of the Last Ministry*.[47] Defoe kept Bradbury's name in print for the entire period 1715–17, and gave him an eminence he might not otherwise have enjoyed. Defoe rebuked Bradbury for giving people just cause to say 'that thou wast a preacher of sedition',[48] and trampling the ministers of the Church of England under his feet, calling the people together 'to cry for Blood, Blood, under the old cant of (41) [i.e. 1641] Justice, Justice'. Defoe appealed to all sober and moderate Dissenters to 'abhor this man and his preaching'.[49]

Such admonitions, even from a Presbyterian brother, seemed to excite rather than calm the spirit of Bradbury. Beginning with his *EIKON BASILIKE*, or 'the Image of a King' – in the tradition of Milton's anti-royalist polemic of the civil war – Bradbury's works of the years 1715–17 were even more anticlerical and anti-authoritarian.[50] The anti-monarchical theme was outspoken and radical: 'Oh what are kings, when the voice of death bids them disrobe! There are but a few moments between the dazzle of a court and the horror of darkness; the softest notes of flattery, and the howlings that are supply'd from guilt and vengeance.'[51] What is of special interest to us is the way that Bradbury connected these themes: priestcraft and superstition supported wicked monarchs. The kings did not call unto God, though they were very active in superstition. Kings had temples and they had priests, but they laughed at prayer, and the comparison with Restoration England was readily made: 'they contrive all the ways they can to drive it [prayer] out of their kingdoms, either cramping it with clumsy forms, or condemning it with wicked laws'.[52] As ever in Bradbury's thought, superstition in religion and wickedness in government led to persecution.

What were the principles behind Bradbury's anticlericalism, and how did his principles cohere with his experience? His principles were grounded in his reading of the Bible, and they are, like the early Anabaptists', primitivist. His primitivism construed the faith of Christ and the apostles as simple and undeveloped; the absence of a hierarchy and a creed is not, in this view, a liability, but an indication of simplicity and purity.[53] In his sermon of 1717 called *The Primitive Tories: or, Three Precedents, of Persecution, Rebellion, and Priestcraft, consider'd*, he typified the Church party as imposing new terms of communion, while for Bradbury Scripture alone was 'a perfect rule of faith and manners'.[54] Such, however, is not enough for Anglicans: it is as if the decency and order of our worship must be derived from rules 'taken from the conceits of a whimsical priest . . . so that by Church-Authority we are to understand a sort of Supplement to the Divine Legislature'.[55]

Bradbury especially emphasised a high christology as the foundation for a true ecclesiology in his sermon *Hardness of Heart*. The devotees of Rome and High Anglicanism 'have inverted the great design of Christianity, which was to establish Christ Jesus as the *Head over all things to the Church*'.[56] Now 'The authority of Christ over his Church lies in giving them laws, and being the only Sovereign of the conscience.'[57] 'All intrusion of human authority here, is treason against his throne; and to this the martyrs in several ages have *witness'd a good confession*, that which they suffer'd for was refusing to bear the *mark of the beast*.'[58] Bradbury's traditional christology was emphatic: 'To talk of mitres, and priests, and sacrifices, and altars, and holydays, and new moons, was right enough in the Jewish dispensation, because these were a *shadow of the good things to come*: but to continue the language now, is a practical suspicion that this is not the Christ. We have no *Priest* but himself, no *Atonement* but his merit, no *Sacrifice* but his body.'[59] All of this can be proven, Bradbury contends, on the basis of the Bible alone, and his primitivism was thus complemented by a thoroughgoing biblicism.

At points Bradbury indulged in apocalyptic imagery that evoked images of holy war. When once the kingdom of the messiah extends itself, 'it will *proclaim Liberty to the Captives*', and there will be no hurting or destroying in his holy mountain. 'Again, waiting for this salvation, prepares a man for battle. A Christian does not fight upon those hazards that others do, who lose two lives at once, that which drops in the field, and that which is eternal.'[60] The recurring themes of apocalyptic christology and holy war seem to be reinforced by the opposition that Bradbury encountered. He sought to show that it is not only a people's duty to resist oppressive power; it is a glorious work.[61] 'There's no person so equal to the hazards of battle, as one that has *good hope through grace* that all is secure for his soul on the other side; that to fall is to die but once, and then to live forever.'[62] Here, indeed, are the strains of 1641; here, indeed, the reason that Anglicans justly took offence.

Beyond the collective Puritan memory of the revolution, Bradbury's preaching was also grounded in his own experience of oppression by the Anglican Church. In his sermon of 1716 called *Hardness of Heart, the Certain Mark of a Ruin'd Party*, he recollected the former harsh treatment of Dissent: priests bear rule by superstition, but this entails a sacrifice of reason, and this is what the Jacobites ask for. A nation is found in a most wretched way when people are willing to 'give up the Empire and use of their own reason' and hire it out to others.[63] The Romish religion will stop at no barrier, not 'mobs and riots', no, not even 'burning the Houses of Worship that belong'd to those who were never up in arms against them, and had given them no particular affront'.[64] Here Bradbury is remembering either 1710 or 1715, or both. 'This fury against ministers, this indignation at the places of worship, the pleasure that's taken in abusing the one, and destroying the other; are sins of that nature, that they cut deep into the conscience.'[65] These are crimes committed against the people of God, and they provoke God's judgment: God 'will argue with judgment and fury against those who thought they had a licence from him to use in the worst manner the best inhabitants of the earth'.[66] All of this is done in profession of zeal for the Church, when in fact, according to Bradbury, all of this makes the name of God contemptible.[67]

III

Perhaps one test of the importance of authors like Palmer and Bradbury and the early eighteenth-century tradition of Dissenting anticlericalism is the degree to which such ideas persisted in the remainder of the century. In the main apologetic works of the Dissenters that appeared later and went through many editions, we find numerous points of comparison with the early century. Charles Owen's *Plain Reasons for Dissenting from the Communion of the Church of England* first appeared in 1715 and went to twenty-four editions by 1736.[68] This standard, well-used text was republished as late as 1771. In Owen, we find a conception of the Church as the people of God met together with Jesus Christ as the head and only lawgiver – a view that is indistinguishable from that of Palmer and Bradbury, and accordingly, we find the same anti-Catholicism that readily shaded over into Anglican anticlericalism.[69]

Similarly, the Dissenting Arian Samuel Bourn, whose *A Vindication of the Principles and Practice of the Protestant Dissenters* provided a widely used catechism for parents, argued that the principles of Dissent inevitably entail a rejection of all ecclesiastical impositions and 'obtruded forms of worship'.[70] In a later tract published in answer to an attack on his *Vindication*, Bourn opposed human traditions that are not found in Scripture, and seemed to adopt the language of Bradbury with the imagery of slavery: 'In which case, it is acting a worthy part for Christians to assert their liberty, and to oppose impositions, made by men, without the shadow of authority from Jesus Christ. But we leave men inured to slavery, to crouch, like an ass, under their burden.'[71]

While anticlerical attitudes can thus be readily documented in Dissenting *apologias*, perhaps the viability of the Dissenting anticlerical tradition is best illustrated through an examination of two other episodes of political agitation. In the 1730s both Anglicans and Dissenters thought they perceived growth in the numbers and influence of Roman Catholics. English Protestants thought that Catholic conversions were increasing, and Anglicans as well as Dissenters worried about the threat and wrote vigorously against it. Early in 1735 the London Dissenting ministers organised a weekly sermon against 'popery' at Salter's Hall, and for four months without a break, week in and week out, they inveighed against all the wicked doctrines and practices of the Catholic Church.[72] In this lectureship, as with earlier collaborative efforts among the London Dissenting ministers, the orthodox, like Daniel Neal, laboured side by side with the heterodox, like Moses Lowman. Fifteen of the seventeen anti-Catholic sermons were published separately, and subsequently they were collected and published together in two volumes that went to several editions. Colin Haydon has investigated the social implications of the cyclical resurgence and abating of anti-Catholic sentiment, and Jeremy Black has explored the 'Catholic threat' in the British press of these years.[73] But the anti-Anglicanism of the Dissenters has not been explored. For example, Samuel Chandler's purpose in preaching was, as he put it, to expose the absurdity and 'antichristian nature of the corruptions and errors of the apostate church of *Rome*'.[74] His article displayed, however, a persistent criticism of the 'prelates of the establishment', and he clearly implied, with more than a little force, that the principles of 'popery' were resident in the established Church, since it 'oppresses' men in their religion and in their consciences. We thus, as Dissenters, he observed, have 'so long had reason to complain' of injustices from our national Church.[75]

Naturally, Catholic apologists like Richard Challoner responded to the sustained polemic of the Dissenters, though the pamphlets by Catholics that did appear were not published until the following year.[76] What has not been appreciated up to this point is that while there were only two known Catholic pamphlets written in reaction to the Salter's Hall lectureship, there were four Anglican rebuttals to the anti-Anglican sentiment of these lectures, and they appeared in print immediately, even before the lectureship concluded. In other words the anti-Catholic rhetoric of the Dissenters was understood to be Anglican anticlericalism directed against the established Church. The four anonymous pamphlets recognised that the rhetoric against popery extended to criticism of any use of secular power for the purpose of religious or spiritual ends, and this, of course, included the established church. For example, *A Scourge for the Dissenters: or, the Fanatick Vipers* was subtitled *Wherein Some of the Dissenting Teachers, who Preach'd Against Popery at Salter's-Hall, are Charged with the Blackest Ingratitude, Falsities . . . &c. Occasion'd by Their Intemperate Zeal and Invectives Against the Tenets of the Church of England. . . .*[77] Writing under the pseudonym 'Scourge', the author addressed the writings specifically of Chandler, Daniel Neal, Benjamin Grosvenor and Samuel Wright, and his response to their sermons was far more reasonable and convincing than the invective of the title might imply. 'Scourge' made several crucial observations that applied broadly to the Dissenters' anticlericalism. First, the author agreed in large measure with the opposition to Roman Catholic doctrine, and he distanced himself from a High Anglican position.[78] 'But the *Church of England* seems to be the peculiar mark of these gentlemen's spleen, and in all their exclamations against *popery* there is such a *mixture* of invective against the establishment, that it is no easy matter to say which of them, in their opinion, they take to be the greater tyranny of the two, or which is more remote from the purity and simplicity of the Gospel.'[79] 'Scourge' observed that these Dissenters accomplish this evil as much by 'intimation' as by direct statement, and the use of such a tactic, he laments, is to break the harmony of Protestants and prepare the way for sedition. Three additional Anglican pamphlets on the lectureship appeared, written by the anonymous 'Countryman', who adopted, as had Daniel Defoe, the persona of a Friend, and from the pacificist, Quaker perspective charged all the Dissenters with insinuating the wickedness of Anglican clergy generally through the circumlocution of anti-papal rhetoric.[80] In truth, argued 'Countryman', the Dissenters intend all their 'rail and rage' against the Catholic Church to be applied to the Anglican Church.[81] Further study of this lectureship will likely support the thesis that Dissenting anti-Catholic rhetoric in this period is in fact thinly veiled anti-Anglican polemic.

IV

In the study of English anticlericalism it would seem desirable not only to determine what forms of anticlericalism were persistent, but which were exportable and under what conditions. It appears, at least initially, that the more religious, 'believing' variety of anticlericalism examined here was not only, at times, more violent, but more malleable in application and more portable than the unbelieving variety. We will find that in the period of the American Revolution, in Boston, New York and Philadelphia, it was not primarily the anticlerical works of the Deists and republicans, like Anthony Collins and

Richard Baron, that were republished, but the works of Dissenting pastors. Their vigorous and bellicose brand of anticlericalism was evidently more useful to the colonists, and the reasons may be found in the common theological foundations of English Dissenters and North American colonists, especially those in the northern colonies. To be sure, in the 1720s and 1730s we do find several more or less secular English anticlerical tracts published in the colonies. For example, Thomas Woolston's *A Free Gift to the Clergy* appeared in Philadelphia in 1724. Moreover, thanks to research on the Commonwealthsmen tradition, we have full accounts of the republication of Trenchard's and Gordon's *Independent Whig* and *Cato's Letters* in North America. Editions of *Independent Whig* were published in Philadelphia in 1724 and 1740, and selections were often reprinted in the Boston newspapers throughout the 1770s. Francis Blackburne's work against bishops in America was published in Philadelphia in 1771, and John Milton's anticlerical *An Old Looking Glass* was republished there in 1770 and in New Haven in 1772.[82] But when the colonists sought out ammunition against English bishops in the colonies, they turned pre-eminently to the English Dissenters.

We thus find a final episode of English Dissenting anticlericalism in the North American colonial agitation against taxation and the introduction of bishops. The Stamp Act crisis and the excitement over an American episcopate were intimately connected, and it was the convergence of these issues that fed the heightened panic concerning bishops in 1768; in *Mitre and Sceptre*, Carl Bridenbaugh called the period 1766–70 'The Great Fear'.[83] Micaiah Towgood wrote to his colonial correspondent, Jonathan Mayhew, on the conflation of these two issues: 'Perhaps the reluctance you have shown to have episcopal bits put in your mouth, may have hastened your being saddled with that disagreeable tax. If that order of men had been established, you would probably have found not only the saddle fixed, but riders also mounted on you.'[84] I have been able to isolate four English Dissenters whose pamphlets were republished in the colonies in the 1760s to help combat the introduction of bishops in America: Thomas Bradbury, James Murray, John Macgowan and Micaiah Towgood (representing, respectively, Congregational, Presbyterian, Baptist and Arian groups).[85] Three of the four were orthodox Trinitarians, and the anticlerical language of all of them was suffused with religion and passion. With the onset of the conflict with the American colonies, there appears to be a noticeable return of a bellicose tone in the Dissenters' writings; by this date they had returned to the theme of the close association of clerical and civil tyranny.

Thomas Bradbury's earlier remarks against the Anglican establishment – or ecclesiastical tyranny – and his resistance to paying undue taxes – civil tyranny – seemed to fit the situation in the colonies perfectly, and hence his sermon *The Ass: or, The Serpent* was republished in 1768 in Boston, and again in 1774 in Newbury Port, Massachusetts. The preface by 'Concionator' stated the purpose for republication: 'It is with a design to excite in this people a just sense of the misery and guilt of slavery, and to animate them to a proper discharge of their duty, in making use of such instruments as providence has put in their hands, for the preservation of their liberties, that the following sermon makes its appearance at this time.'[86] In this sermon a virtuous, wise and free people is contrasted with a vicious, stupid and servile people; the contrast 'is so justly displayed' that it is hoped it will make an impression, excepting, of course, those 'remorseless wretches' who are hardened beyond recovery. Bradbury was selected as well for his known zeal for the truth, and his contending for 'the liberty wherewith Christ has made us free' – a qualification that could not be found among Deist writers. His sermon was republished to raise among the Americans 'Just apprehensions of their obligations to themselves, to their country, and to their offspring, and above all to that God, who has committed to them that inestimable pearl, liberty'.[87]

To Bradbury's contention that we should never fix our faith on what our 'superiors' pretend to believe, 'Concionator' made the application that American ministers had not been sufficiently attentive to their rights and liberties as Americans. On the basis of Bradbury's admonition, they were to offer their objections to the introduction of bishops and to an establishment that caused their fathers to flee.[88] The editor believed that bishops would eventually be destructive of the religious liberty of Dissenters. But religious and civil liberties were connected, and inspired by Bradbury's words 'Concionator' argued that the colonists were under no necessity to give their necks to the yoke. The only cord by which the colonies were bowed down was cowardice and a 'capricious fondness' for British goods; we can, if we wish, admonishes 'Concionator', be 'free, rich and happy'.[89] 'Concionator', drawing upon the inspiration of Bradbury, concluded that it is the duty of a good magistrate to preserve the liberties of the people. If magistrates try to persuade people to submit to the 'arbitrary infringement' of their rights, they forfeit their title to respect and 'deserve to be treated with the severity due to a traitor'.[90]

Along with *The Ass: or, The Serpent*, one of the other most outspoken anticlerical and anti-authoritarian pieces that Bradbury published was *EIKON BASILIKE*, and it is striking that James Murray (1732–82), the radical Presbyterian of Newcastle upon Tyne, published two titles in the 1760s and 1770s that closely resemble the works of Bradbury.[91] The precise lines of influence between Murray's *Sermons to Asses* and his version of *EIKON BASILIKE* and the earlier works of Bradbury are presently unknown, but there are strong parallel lines of thought. Murray's rabid anticlericalism enjoyed tremendous popularity in the colonies; in fact, far more than in England. First published in Newcastle and London in 1768, *Sermons to Asses*, a book that ran to 200 pages, was republished in Boston in 1768, and a third and fourth edition appeared in Philadelphia the next year, with a fifth Philadelphia edition in 1770. Another work, *Sermons to Doctors in Divinity; Being the Second Volume of Sermons to Asses*, appeared in Philadelphia in 1773, and it was dedicated to the great defender of the Anglican

establishment, Dr William Warburton, Bishop of Gloucester. And in 1774 his
New Sermons to Asses appeared in Philadelphia, dedicated to the petitioners against
the Dissenters' bill – 'I know,' said Murray, 'no persons to whom Sermons to
asses can, with more propriety, be dedicated than to you.' In his hatred of
ecclesiastical tyranny Murray outdid even Bradbury, and in general terms the
themes of anticlericalism may never have been expressed with greater violence or
a higher degree of rhetorical flourish than in the writings of James Murray.

Murray, like Bradbury, drew his main text from the Book of Genesis, with
Issachar, like England, bowing down between two burdens. He began his *Sermon*
with the phrase, 'A nation of slaves, is a kingdom of Asses,' and he refined
Bradbury's image of Issachar: 'All Europe – yea the greatest part of the world
have couched down between these two burdens of civil and religious
oppression.'[92] At every conceivable opportunity Murray attacked, as he put it,
the 'Dignitaries of the Church of England': he attacked them on tithes, on their
wealth, on oppression in spiritual courts and on corruption in high places.[93]

As with Bradbury, Murray connected antipathy for wicked priests to the
institution of the establishment, damning both. And like Bradbury, his
anticlericalism was constitutive of an anti-monarchical sentiment that verged on
republicanism, and it was thus, in my judgement, his anticlericalism that
provided a main source of his radicalism. Again, like Bradbury, he located the
principle of a separation of spiritual and temporal power in christology – Christ
is the sole head and supreme legislator in his Church. The North American
colonists evidently found Murray extremely useful in their struggle against the
introduction of bishops, and of course, in their struggle against Parliament. One
of Murray's last productions was his *Sermons to Ministers of State. By the Author of,
Sermons to Asses*, and it was 'Dedicated to Lord North, Prime Minister of England'
(1783).

John Macgowan (1726–80) was a relatively unknown London Baptist minister
at Devonshire Square (1766–80) who wrote under the pseudonym 'the Shaver'
and later 'Pasquin Shaveblock'.[94] Macgowan was the author of *Priestcraft Defended*,
a pamphlet that satirised the expelling of six young men, Calvinistic Methodists,
from St Edmund Hall, Oxford, in 1768 because of their praying, reading and
expounding the Scriptures.[95] Like the works of Murray, those of Macgowan
appear to have been more popular in North America than in England, and the
timing of the unfortunate episode at Oxford with the heightening of the debate
over bishops in the colonies seemed, to the colonists, providential. In England
Macgowan rapidly followed his hugely successful *Priestcraft Defended* (it went to
nine editions in the first year in London) with *A Further Defense of Priestcraft*.[96] In
the colonies *Priestcraft Defended* was reprinted three times in Boston, beginning
in 1769, and in Philadelphia the same year.[97] It appeared in a corrected edition
in Newport, Rhode Island, in 1770 with an additional 'Hymn in praise of the
University. To the tune of Down, down with hypocrisy', and 'An epitaph for the

grave of the Slain Goliath'. The book was printed in New London, Connecticut, in 1773, and as late as 1792 in Baltimore and 1794 in New York. All the purported vagaries of Anglican priestcraft seemed to come to a head in the expulsion of youthful piety from Oxford. Yet whereas Murray used biting, sometimes vicious, satire, Macgowan plied his opposition with humour, banter and mild ridicule.

In the second half of the sermon, having explained his text, Macgowan purports to defend the conduct of the Heads of Houses on the basis of 'the conduct of the clergy of all ages and countries, whatsoever snarling persons may say'.[98] Believe me, 'the Shaver' advised, the zealous Dr Sacheverell 'was not the first, nor the last, who was grieved for fear of the church'.[99] Here, he clearly generalised beyond the case to critique the principles of established religion, instancing four illustrations out of that 'old antiquated book called the Scripture', and beginning with the story of Daniel and 'the established church at Babylon'.[100] New Testament times afforded 'the Shaver' the opportunity of comparing false, State religion to the primitive Church, supported by revealed religion. Christ and the apostles were noted for their simplicity. The 'doctrine of Christ' preached in its simplicity lays 'the axe at the root of the tree of priestcraft, and throws down the importance of the parson into the dirt. If the clergy were all to observe the rules given by Christ to his disciples in his sermon on the mount, where would be all their titles, their riches and grandeur, their coaches, their liverymen, and their plate?'[101] Macgowan was also a Trinitarian, and wrote vigorously against the Unitarianism of Joseph Priestley in his *Familiar Epistles to the Rev Dr Priestley* (1771).[102]

The apologetic works of the Arian Micaiah Towgood (1700–92), Dissenting minister successively at Moretonhampstead, Crediton and Exeter, were perhaps the best known of all in the second half of the century, and in part the reputation he acquired is based on his anticlericalism. Towgood's apologetic works first appeared in the late 1730s, but his real notoriety began in 1746, when he engaged in an extensive debate with the Anglican rector John White (*c.* 1685–1755). In 1743 White had published an open letter to Towgood under the title *A Letter to a Gentleman Dissenting from the Church of England*, and a second and third letter appeared in 1745; the three were republished in 1748, and together this attack on Dissenting principles ran to almost 300 pages. Towgood's response appeared as *The Dissenting Gentleman's Answer to the Reverend Mr White's Three Letters; in which a Separation from the Establishment is Fully Justified; the Charge of Schism is Refuted and Retorted* (London, 1746). This work, 'The Dissenting Gentleman's Letters' with additions, appeared under various titles[103] and went to numerous editions in both England and the colonies.

It is hard to overstate the importance of Towgood's work.[104] For our purposes what is important here is that by mid-century the theological base of Dissenting separatism had begun to be worked into the title of apologetic works, even the apologetic works of Arians. The editions of Towgood's work in the 1750s began to appear with the title *A Dissent from the Church of England, Fully Justified: and Proved the Genuine and Just Consequence of the Allegiance Due to Christ, the Only Lawgiver in the Church.* The book went to eight editions in the eighteenth century in London and Cambridge but, like the other works studied here, it also enjoyed considerable popularity in the colonies, with editions printed in Boston and New York in 1748, and again in Boston in 1768, the pivotal year for the bishop's controversy, and in 1773.[105]

There are at least two reasons why Dissenting anticlericalism may have been more viable in the colonies than republican or Deist anticlericalism. First, believing anticlericalism was grounded in religious conviction stemming from primitivism and biblicism; moreover, the religion in which it was grounded was the common religion of the two countries, though with important differences. A vital transatlantic intellectual culture of Dissent has been amply documented by Colin Bonwick and Bartholomew Schiavo.[106] Secondly, Dissenting anticlericalism allowed, at least in theory, an Establishment. Presbyterians in Scotland depended on an Establishment, as did Congregationalists in New England, whereas unbelieving anticlericalism necessitated a thoroughgoing secularisation and allowed no softening of the blow to ministerial claims. Dissenting anticlericalism, on the contrary, was directed primarily at the hierarchy, the clerical use of secular power, and the threat of coercion for cause of conscience. To be sure, some English Dissenters did veer off into a thoroughgoing critique of the establishment, but because they wished to attain repeal of the Test and Corporation Acts, many authors felt it incumbent upon themselves to adopt a friendly appearance and thereby avoid direct attacks on the establishment. Deists were probably less inclined to adopt such rhetorical postures of reticence, though to be sure, as Justin Champion has shown, they insisted on the value of some form of civil religion for the sake of social order.

V

In conclusion, it might be useful to attempt some general remarks concerning the predictable, stable aspects of Dissenting anticlericalism, as well as those aspects that changed over time. Generally speaking, the Dissenting tradition in the period following 1720 was less anti-monarchical than the views espoused by Bradbury.[107] This fact can almost certainly be attributed to the widespread favour the Dissenters enjoyed under the early Hanoverians; in time, their experience of protection under George I and George II undoubtedly softened their attitude toward monarchy. On the other hand, in broad terms I believe that the loyalty of eighteenth-century Dissenters has been overstated, and this is because the evidence for their purported unfailing devotion to successive Whig governments has been drawn largely from sermons and voting records. The rhetoric of loyalty found in Dissenting sermons has misled us concerning the anti-Establishment sentiment of the Dissenters, and their patterns of consistent voting for government candidates betrays only the absence of any viable alternative in the local setting. A thorough study of the literature of Dissenting apologetics will, I believe, reveal a different, more disaffected, possibly even radical side to Dissenting politics, even at mid-century.

The other element that drops away by the 1730s is apocalypticism. It seems likely that the loss of the experiential base of persecution meant a general softening of the critique of the Anglican clergy. Their rhetoric becomes noticeably less rabid and bloodthirsty. On the other hand, violent rhetoric does reappear in the period of Wilkes and the American Revolution, and the bloodthirsty tone comes audibly to the surface in the period of the Gordon riots. The general theme of anti-Catholicism as anti-Anglicanism needs to be seriously examined in this later period. When we move into the 1790s, with the French Revolution and emergence of Church and King riots, the reintroduction of the experience of persecution and the growing threat of repression, the apocalyptic element becomes prominent once again. The extent of these recurring themes and their larger meaning are areas that need much further research.

Three characteristics of Dissenting anticlericalism appear to have remained largely constant throughout the eighteenth century, regardless of circumstance. First, the anticlericalism of Dissent extends consistently to anti-Establishment thought, and the rhetorical use of anti-Catholicism broadens to anti-Anglicanism. The critique of Dissent is thus not mere moralism or Puritan reformism directed against the vices of individual clergy. This means, secondly, that Dissenting anticlericalism was grounded in a separation of temporal and spiritual power that had radical political overtones; these overtones were readily grasped by Anglican antagonists, with the result, among other things, that the repeal of the Test and Corporation Acts was delayed until well into the nineteenth century. Anglican anticlericalism as espoused by the Dissenters was unavoidably political. Finally, Dissenting anticlericalism arose from a high christology that contributed to a highly spiritualised ecclesiology. Biblicism and primitivism were themes that were shared by both Arian and Trinitarian Dissenters, in the same way they shared a high, public christology that was deployed for political purposes and was clearly separable from private conviction. A public, widely agreed upon christological foundation stood behind the Dissenters' ecclesiology, and hence their anticlericalism was a direct extension of their theology. From at least the time of Richard Baxter onward, the Dissenters insisted that Jesus Christ was the sole head and supreme legislator in his Church. The phrase, 'sole head and supreme legislator' rings like a refrain in all the Dissenters' controversial works; it was a christology clearly adopted for its political salience, and it functioned identically in the mouths of both Trinitarian and Arian Dissenters. On theoretical grounds orthodox and heterodox Dissenters were equally strong in their anticlericalism; if anything, the orthodox were even more outspoken.

So, is the displacement of 'the priestly cast from the temple', as Champion puts it, a central achievement of Republican thought, or does it have something to do with Trinitarian Christians?[108] It might be argued that Dissenting polemic was more persistent and, because of its persistence, in the long term more destructive, than the anticlericalism of the Deists and unbelievers. Having stood, and sometimes fallen, by his principles, it is not surprising that many a Dissenting minister was more than a little sensitive to issues of ecclesiastical and political influence. The intractableness of this ecclesiological position led inevitably to a proclivity to Dissent in politics. For the early eighteenth-century Dissenter, religious self-determination was thus invariably linked to civil self-determination and his anticlericalism was very much at the heart of his own self-understanding. Since Dissent involved seeing the religious and political world with a fundamentally different vision from the reigning one, we find the anticlericalism of English Dissent representing a genuine counter-culture and pointing to the ultimate demise of the old regime. The Dissenters' alternate ideology, their separate meetings and rituals, their experience of alienation and exclusion from approved institutions, both educational and political, all contributed to an alien folk mentality of a dissident culture that was finally exported to the American colonies and helped to produce a rebellion there.

The Dissenters' opposition was embodied, ultimately, not in the minds of individual thinkers, as in the case of the Deists and Commonwealthsmen, but in thousands of local congregations, and in the last analysis it was the actual practice of religious pluralism that defeated the Test and Corporation Acts and produced the revolution in outlook that has come to characterise the modern world. In the end this is why the heresy–radicalism thesis fails, for in the reconstruction outlined in this chapter, the sources of the Dissenters' proclivity for radical political disaffection is located in what heterodox and orthodox ministers held in common: anticlericalism, a backward-looking prejudice common to all Dissenters and grounded in an age-old anti-Catholicism, was combined with a public, high christology, and together these elements go much further in explaining the Dissenters' civil disaffection in the reign of George III than does heterodoxy, a modern, forward-looking ideology that possesses only tenuous connections with the past.

Notes

1   J.A.I. Champion, *The Pillars of Priestcraft Shaken: The Church of England and its Enemies, 1660–1730* (Cambridge, 1992), pp. 233–6; Colin Haydon, *Anti-Catholicism in Eighteenth-century England: a Political and Social Study* (Manchester, 1993); and John Gascoigne, *Cambridge in the Age of the Enlightenment: Science, Religion and Politics from the Restoration to the French Revolution* (Cambridge, 1988), p. 18.

2   Haydon, *Anti-Catholicism in Eighteenth-century England*, p. 263.

3   The theory is an old one, and can be traced in the seminal essay by Anthony Lincoln, *Some Political & Social Ideas of English Dissent, 1763–1800* (Cambridge, 1938). J.C.D. Clark, *English Society 1688–1832* (Cambridge, 1985), pp. 252, 293, note 63, and p. 423; *idem, The Language of Liberty, 1660–1832: Political Discourse and Social Dynamics in the Anglo-American World* (Cambridge, 1994), pp. 100–1 and 111; J.G.A. Pocock, 'The Definitions of Orthodoxy', pp. 36–7, in Roger D. Lund (ed.), *The Margins of Orthodoxy: Heterodox Writing and Cultural Response, 1660–1750* (Cambridge, 1995); A.M.C. Waterman, 'The Nexus between Theology and Political Doctrine', p. 194, in Knud Haakonssen (ed.), *Enlightenment and Religion: Rational Dissent in Eighteenth-Century Britain* (Cambridge, 1996); John Gascoigne, 'Anglican Latitudinarianism, Rational Dissent and Political Radicalism in the Late Eighteenth Century', pp. 219–40, in Haakonssen, op. cit.

4   Gordon Schochet, 'The Act of Toleration and the Failure of Comprehension: Persecution, Nonconformity, and Religious Indifference', in Dale Hoak and Mordechai Feingold (eds), *The World of William and Mary: Anglo-Dutch Perspectives on the Revolution of 1688–89* (Stanford, 1996).

5   Richard Barlow, *Citizenship and Conscience* (Philadelphia, 1962), p. 60.

6   Geoffrey Holmes, 'The Sacheverell Riots: The Crowd and the Church in Early Eighteenth-century London', *Past & Present* 72 (1976), p. 56.

7   Ibid., pp. 58 and 61.

8   Ibid., p. 69.

9   David Bogue and James Bennett, *History of Dissenters, From the Revolution in 1688, to the year 1808* (London, 1810), IV, p. 395. On Burgess, Earle, Bradbury and Wright, see below, pp. 73, 80.

10   Nicholas Rogers, 'Popular Protest in Early Hanoverian London', *Past & Present* 79 (1978), p. 73. Bogue and Bennett, *History of Dissenters*, III, pp. 120–2.

11   *The Church in Perils Among False Brethren; or, the Danger of the Church from her Pretended Friends but Secret Enemies, Review'd* (London, 1733).

12   2nd edn (London, 1720).

13   First attributed to Gordon by *DNB*.

14   Samuel Palmer, *A Vindication of the Learning, Loyalty, Morals . . . of the Dissenters* (London, 1705), p. 15.

15   Ibid., pp. 28–9.

16   Ibid., p. 73; 'Thus I know of no *Dissenter* that does not think it a *sin to conform*, and I know no *church-man*, who does not think it a *sin to dissent and separate*', p. 74.

17   Ibid., p. 115.

18   *A Guilty Conscience Makes a Rebel: or Rulers no Terrour to the Good Prov'd in a Sermon Preached on the Thirtieth of January, 1712/13 being the Solemn day . . . with a Preface, reflecting on a late Pamphlet, call'd The Ass and the Serpent* (London, 1712/13); *The Traytor's Reward: or a King's Death Revenged* (London, 1714).

19   *The Primitive Tories: or, Three Precedents, of Persecution, Rebellion, and Priestcraft, consider'd. In a Sermon Preach'd November 5, 1717* (2nd edn, London, 1717), p. 14.

20   *Hardness of Heart, the Certain Mark of a Ruin'd Party: Open'd on Two Sermons, Preach'd on June the 7th and 10th, 1716* (London, 1716), p. 30.

21   Ibid., p. 29.

22   Ibid., p. 34.

23   Ibid., p. 36. And again on the Test Act: 'as if it was not enough to profane the name of God before the magistrate [swear an oath], unless he did it at his very table', p. 39. See also Bradbury, *EIKON BASILIKE, A Sermon Preach'd the 29th of May, 1715* (4th edn, London, 1715), p. 18.

24   *Primitive Tories*, pp. 15–17.

25   Ibid., p. 17.

26   Ibid., pp. 12–13.

27   Ibid., p. 19.

28   Ibid., p. 20.

29   *The Ass: or, The Serpent. A Comparison between the Tribes of Issachar and Dan, in their Regard for Civil Liberty. Nov. 5, 1712* (London, 1712), pp. 2–3.

30   Ibid., p. 4.

31   Ibid., p.4; see also p. 5.

32   Ibid., pp. 8–9, 12 and 5. The use of religion by Anglicans for social control is condemned by Bradbury.

33   Ibid., p. 14.

34   Citing Paul arguing with the centurion, and refusing to answer the summons of Festus (Acts 16:36–7, 23:3), *The Ass*, p. 6.

35   Ibid., p. 15, citing Genesis 14, the story of '*the first rebels* we read of'.

36   Ibid., p. 20.

37   Ibid., p. 18.

38   *Some Short Reflections upon Mr Bradbury's Late Libel Intitled 'The Ass and the Serpent', Wherein is shewn the Great Weakness of his Shuffling Plea, for the Resistance of the Higher Powers. Published for the better Instruction of his Dissenting Congregation* (London, 1713), pp. 3–4 and 14.

39   Ibid., p. 20.

40   *A Guilty Conscience Maketh a Rebel*, pp. i–ii.

41   Ibid., p. ii. Bradbury would have us believe 'that none can have pure hearts but rebels; and that none can have patience under a tyrannical government, but fools. This was the cant of 41', p. iii.

42   Ibid., pp. iv, vi.

43   *The Lawfulness of Resisting Tyrants, Argued from the History of David, and in Defense of the Revolution. Nov. 5, 1713. With Some Remarks on Mr Luke Milbourn's Preface and Sermon* (London, 1714), pp. ii–iii. This response to Milbourne and other critics went to four editions.

44   Ibid., p. vi. Here as well, there is a downplaying of the importance of monarchy. Bradbury's main point in this sermon is to argue on the basis of Old Testament precedent that 'the people have a right in themselves to dethrone a tyrant', p. 3.

45   Ibid., pp. viii, 1.

46   4th edn (London, 1715). See Laura Ann Curtis, *The Versatile Defoe: An Anthology of Uncollected Writings of Daniel Defoe* (Totowa, NJ, 1979), p. 57.

47   2nd edn (London, 1715).

48   *A Friendly Epistle*, pp. 7–8.

49   *Burnet and Bradbury*, pp. 9 and 11.

50   *EIKON BASILIKE*, p. 3.

51   Ibid., p. 11.This railing against wicked kings knows few bounds: see pp. 5 and 14–15.

52   Ibid., p. 13.

53   *Lawfulness*, p. 23.

54   *Primitive Tories*, p. 13.

55   Ibid.

56   *Hardness of Heart*, p. 25.

57   Ibid., p. 28.

58   Ibid.

59   *Primitive Tories*, p. 14.

60   *The Ass*, p. 21.

61   *Lawfulness*, p. 20.

62   Ibid., p. 22.

63   *Hardness of Heart*, p. 15.

64   Ibid., p. 20.

65   Ibid., p. 38.

66   Ibid., p. 39.

67   Ibid., p. 40.

68   *Plain Reasons: I. For Dissenting from the Communion of the Church of England. . . .* (London, 1736).

69   Ibid., pp. 5, 7, 8, 9, 20, 22 and 24.

70   *A Vindication of the Principles and Practice of Protestant Dissenters: . . . Designed and Fitted . . . for the Use of Dissenting Parents, . . .* (London, 1748), pp. ii and iii.

71   Bourn, *An Answer to the Remarks of an Unknown Clergyman* (London, 1750), pp. 7 and 11. Too often the clergy of the Church of England are 'so many thieves and robbers, permitted to fleece and slay a stupid priest-ridden people', p. 14. Again, churchmen unjustly 'ingross all power and preferment in State and Church, upon no better a title, than a preposterous zeal for church tyranny and foppery', *An Answer*, pp. 17–18.

72   For the plan of the lectures that ran from 9 January to 17 April and the division of labour, see the comments in Samuel Chandler's sermon *The Notes of the Church Considered: In a Sermon . . . Preached at Salters-Hall, January 30, 1734–35* (London, 1735), p. 3.

73   Haydon, *Anti-Catholicism*, pp. 128–9; Jeremy Black, 'The Catholic Threat and the British Press in the 1720s and 1730s', *Journal of Religious History* 12 (1983), pp. 364–81.

74   Chandler, *The Notes of the Church*, p. 1.

75   Ibid., p. 55. The great issue with all establishments is christology: it is Christ's authority that is usurped by the Roman Church and the Pope (p. 12). Christ is sole head of the church and legislator. We acknowledge only 'one Lord, one Lawgiver in the Christian Church' (p. 21).

76   Richard Challoner, *A Specimen of the Spirit of the Dissenting Teachers in their Sermons lately preach'd at Salters-Hall; or some remarks upon Mr John Barker's sermon against Popery, . . . and Mr S. Chandler's sermon upon the Notes of the Church* (London, 1736). John Chrysostom Gregory Sharp, *The Catholic Church Cleared from the Charge of Corruption and Novelty. A Sermon Occasioned by the Late Lecture against Popery at Salters-Hall* (London, 1736).

77   London, 1735.

78   He compares Chandler's writings *mutatis mutandis* to those of Sacheverell, and thinks they deserve as severe a reproach as his received, not, he adds, by any means implying that he recommends the views of Sacheverell. *Scourge*, p. 20.

79   Ibid., pp. 17–18. He concedes that not all the writers in the entire lectureship were equally outspoken against the Anglican Church.

80   *A Letter from a Friend to Samuel Chandler, Occasion'd by his Sermon Against Popery* . . . . (London, 1735), pp. 7–8; *Observations on the Four Last Sermons against Popery, preach'd at Salters-Hall by Mr Smith, Dr Wright, Dr Harris and Dr Hughes* (London, 1735); *Farther Observations on Several Sermons Lately preach'd against Popery, at Salters-Hall* . . . . (London, 1735).

81   *Observations on the Last Four Sermons*, pp. 7, 10 and 18.

82   Milton's work was originally 'Considerations touching the likeliest means to remove hirelings out of the Church' (1659). There was also a satirical piece attributed to Thomas Ward (1652–1708), published in Philadelphia in 1766.

83   *Mitre and Sceptre: Transatlantic Faiths, Ideas, Personalities, and Politics 1689–1776* (Oxford, 1962), pp. 260–87.

84   Cited in ibid., p. 243.

85   Bridenbaugh overlooks the contribution of Bradbury, Murray and Macgowan in the 1760s.

86   Bradbury, *The Ass: or, The Serpent* (London and Boston, 1768), preface.

87   Ibid.

88   Ibid., pp. 5–6.

89   Ibid., p. 9.

90   Ibid., p. 16.

91   For a general treatment, see James E. Bradley, *Religion, Revolution, and English Radicalism: Non-conformity in Eighteenth-Century Politics and Society* (Cambridge, 1990), pp. 128–30 and 170–2.

92   *Sermons to Asses* (London, 1768), pp. 4–5.

93   On tithes, see ibid., pp. 53, 55 and 207; on wealth, see pp. 58–9, 114, 166, 172 and 196–7; on courts, see pp. 198–9, and *passim* on corruption.

94   See his *The Shaver's New Sermon for the Fast Day. Respectfully inscribed to the Revd and Laborious Clergy of the Church of England* (New York, 1796).

95   *Priestcraft Defended. A Sermon Occasioned by the Expulsion of six Young Gentlemen from the University of Oxford. For Praying, Reading, and Expounding the Scriptures* . . . *By their humble servant, the shaver* (9th edn, London, 1768).

96   *A Further Defense of Priestcraft: Being a Practical Improvement of the Shaver's Sermon on the Expulsion of Six young Gentlemen from the University of Oxford* (London 1768).

97   7th edn. In Boston, 1769, 10th edn in 1771, and 7th edn again in 1793. The 1769 Philadelphia edition was the 6th edn. The New London edition of 1773 was the 12th edn.

98   *Priestcraft Defended*, p. 19.

99   Ibid., p. 27.

100   Ibid., p. 19.

101   Ibid., p. 28.

102   See also his *Socinianism brought to the Test* (London, 1773), and his *The Arians and Socinians Moniter* published in Boston (1774) and again in Norwich, Connecticut, in 1787.

103   *A Calm and Plain Answer to the Enquiry, why are you a Dissenter from the Church of England?* appears to be a summary of the arguments in Towgood's letters to White, and *A Dissent from the Church of England,*

Fully Justified also seems to reproduce the substance of the three letters (see the 1766 Dublin edition, which says: 'being the Dissenting Gentleman's three letters and Postscript . . .').

104 See the 1787 London edition of *A Dissent from the Church of England Fully Justified*.

105 The earlier Boston editions are under the title *A Dissent from the Church of England*, and the 1773 Boston edition is *A Calm and Plain Answer* with the subtitle, 'Dedicated to Sacred Truth; to Liberty; to the Interest and Cause of Jesus Christ, the Only King, in his Kingdom the Church'.

106 Bartholomew Schiavo, 'The Dissenter Connection: English Dissenters and Massachusetts Political Culture: 1730–1774' (Brandeis University, PhD dissertation, 1976); Colin Bonwick, *English Radicals and the American Revolution* (Chapel Hill, NC, 1977).

107 Although Samuel Bourne, while he allowed oaths to Kings, adds: 'Oaths to a king and his successors bind, I suppose, only so long and so far as they act as kings, govern according to law, and keep the coronation oath'; *An Answer*, pp. 29–30.

108 Champion, *The Pillars of Priestcraft*, p. 222. S.J. Barnett's *Idol Temples and Crafty Priests: the Origins of Enlightenment Anticlericalism* (New York, 1999) develops similar themes to those found here, but the book came to my attention too late to be engaged in this essay.

FURTHER READING

Barnett, S.J., *Idol Temples and Crafty Priests, the Origins of Enlightenment Anticlericalism* (Basingstoke/New York, 1999).

Champion, J.A.I., *The Pillars of Priestcraft Shaken: the Church of England and its enemies, 1660–1730* (Cambridge, 1992).

Haakonssen, Knud (ed.), *Enlightenment and Religion: Rational Dissent in Eighteenth-Century Britain* (Cambridge, 1996).

Haydon, Colin, *Anti-Catholicism in Eighteenth-century England: a Political and Social Study* (Manchester, 1993).

5

THE CHANGING NATURE OF ENGLISH ANTICLERICALISM, *c.* 1750–*c.* 1800[1]

G.M. Ditchfield

I

The term 'anticlericalism', in its Anglicised form, was not current in eighteenth-century England. Its first use, recorded by the *Oxford English Dictionary*, may be found in a *Times* newspaper report of the French Assembly in 1886; on the passage of bills disqualifying monks and nuns from teaching in municipal schools and enabling citizens to obtain civil funerals, the comment was: 'both these measures may be regarded as the swing of the pendulum from clericalism to anticlericalism'.[2] Some twenty years later the *Encyclopaedia of Religion and Ethics* believed that anticlericalism 'often includes a reference not so much to the clergy as to that for which they stand, viz. the profession, defence and propagation of the Orthodox Faith'.[3] In 1997 the third edition of the *Oxford Dictionary of the Christian Church* defined anticlericalism as 'a liberal movement in politics and religion which affected many parts of Europe and Latin America in the 19th and 20th centuries'. It saw anticlericalism exclusively in post-1793 terms, exclusively in anti-Catholic terms, and almost exclusively in French terms. Although conceding that 'to be anticlerical and a Catholic believer was not as a rule a contradiction', it portrays anticlericalism as fundamentally irreligious, beginning with the French Revolution's 'dechristianising movement' in 1793–4.[4]

The limitations of the definitions quoted above emphasise the need for new studies of anticlericalism – theoretically, as well as in terms of nation, state and period. Clearly anticlericalism is not a phenomenon which exists in some kind of supra-historical void. It acquires specific and varying definitions according to the particular circumstances of space and time. For the phenomenon which we recognise as anticlericalism was, of course, much older than the French Revolution. Moreover, it still seems necessary to emphasise that in the eighteenth century, and earlier, anticlericalism for the most part attacked not religious belief itself, but what it perceived as the distortion and exploitation of it by a self-serving priestly elite: the term 'priestcraft' is much older than 'anticlericalism'. The distinction between disbelief in religion itself on the one hand and opposition to the power of the Church and its clergy on the other still needs to be made.[5]

It was, admittedly, a distinction that was not always apparent to the clergy. The response, for instance, of James Ibbetson, Archdeacon of St Albans, to Francis Blackburne's *Confessional* in 1768 might be taken as a representative summary of the meaning of the term from the point of view of contemporaries who regarded it as a threat:

> It [*The Confessional*] falls in, very luckily for the bookseller, with the fashionable humour, which almost universally prevails, of finding fault with every part of the establishment, in direct opposition to truth and experience, and the most approved principles of Protestant liberty; it is manifestly the result of a wild and mistaken zeal for what is called, with little meaning and much affectation, an absolute, uncontrolled, equal and impartial Liberty; whereby infidelity and religion are placed upon the same footing, and the defence of Christianity against heathens and idolaters must be totally abandoned.[6]

Those so characterised by Ibbetson would have chosen very different terminology, and it is one purpose of this chapter to investigate the ways in which writers who may be regarded as anticlerical perceived themselves. Justin Champion demonstrated that in the Restoration and Augustan periods English anticlericalism could not be equated with secularisation or modernisation, and that the debates he examined were conducted within a framework which was fundamentally religious, if not always Christian in the orthodox sense.[7] Dr Champion's warning should be applied even more firmly to the later eighteenth century. As is well known, many of the sharpest critics of religious establishments were themselves clergy of the established Church or shared a cultural background with the clerical elite; Francis Blackburne, for instance, whose *Confessional* (1766) was widely interpreted as an attack on the Church's doctrines, was Archdeacon of Cleveland. Some critics, such as Thomas Hollis and Theophilus Lindsey, exercised ecclesiastical patronage through their rights of presentation. Anticlerical writers tended to accept many of the basic assumptions of Protestant Christianity; their objective was not to subvert or destroy Christianity, but to promote a different version of it, which they regarded as more biblically specific. An obsession of critics of the Church of England in the second half of the eighteenth century was a search for authentic Christian belief and practice in scripture and in the primitive Church; this was the theme of the Unitarian Joseph Priestley's *An History of the Corruptions of Christianity* (1782).[8] Moreover, one regularly encounters in the writing of that generation a greater stress than that laid by many of their predecessors upon revelation, with an unmistakable elevation of scriptural authority over the 'natural religion' which had been so intellectually fashionable in the early and mid-century. Revelation was presented as confirmed by reason, not vice versa. As Gilbert Wakefield, an Anglican clergyman who seceded from the Church to Unitarianism, put it in 1793:

No candid mind can desire, and no ingenuity could devise, a more convincing *internal evidence* of the validity of the *Gospel* narratives, than the SUPERLATIVE PRE-EMINENCE of their MORALITY, in competition with the doctrines of *Gentile* Philosophy, and the deductions of what is usually called *natural Religion.*[9]

Appropriately, John Gascoigne entitled one of his chapters on late eighteenth-century Cambridge 'The revival of revealed theology'. The description could be applied equally to Cambridge dissidents such as George Dyer and William Frend: 'The Bible is the rock, on which I stand,' declared the latter.[10] It could be applied more widely. On the publication in 1768 of the second edition of Richard Baron's *Pillars of Priestcraft and Orthodoxy Shaken*, the advertisement insisted that Baron, that most vehement of anticlerics, who is designated, as if by profession, in the *Dictionary of National Biography* as 'republican', was one who 'firmly believed in Revelation'.[11] Baron himself, in the Dedication, made clear that his principal weapon against priestcraft was to be scriptural authority:

Whoever compares the scriptures with the articles and canons of our national church, will see how little we have of christian truth and liberty, and what remains there still are of *popish* corruption and tyranny. Can any man reconcile the right of private judgment, and the apostolic injunction to *prove all things*, with the twentieth article of the church; by which the Priests claim a power over all human understanding, and by denying us a right to think for ourselves, treat us as brute beasts?[12]

Hence, in the controversies between anticlerical writers and their opponents during this period, the highest priority was accorded to the search for scriptural justification. The authority of the Bible was not the central point of disputation; at issue was the most accurate and plausible exposition of the received biblical text. This becomes evident in the two most important and wide-ranging of those debates: that over the question of oaths and subscriptions to creeds and articles of religion, and that over the doctrine of the Trinity. George Dyer argued at length that there was no scriptural justification for oaths or subscription. The same opinions may be found in the works of continental writers translated into English under the aegis of sponsors such as Thomas Hollis. The Bernese pastor Brian Herport, for example, denied that Christ prescribed any system of subscription in the gospels, and claimed that religious tests denied access 'to those glorious truths promised us in the last times'; even the Helvetic Confession 'was originally meant by our forefathers only as a *testimonial* and not as a *rule*'.[13] Such a dismissal of oaths was, of course, entirely consistent with Benjamin Hoadly's perception of the Church as an earthly institution, unable either to boast of apostolic legitimacy or to invoke divine sanction for its articles and creeds, and hence amenable to reform in the interests of human expediency and utility. But as Martin Fitzpatrick has shown, for many later eighteenth-century critics, such as Francis Blackburne, the ultimate criterion was not the utilitarian one, but that measured by proximity to biblical truth.[14] The aim of the vast majority of anticlerical writers was to promote a more fully Christian society, purged of what they saw as the accretions of priestcraft. This was the spirit, for example, of Caleb Fleming's *Civil Establishments in Religion a Ground of Infidelity: or, the Two Extremes shewn to be united* (1767). It was for this reason that many of those stigmatised by James Ibbetson gave so high a priority to textual accuracy and even to new biblical translations, such as that sponsored by the Unitarian Society in London in 1807–8.

This objective, of purifying the Christianity of their day, took priority even over the further defence of at least some form of organised religion advanced by most anticlerical authors, namely the argument that it tended to promote order and social harmony. To Frend, 'Social worship is a very desirable thing', while the flood of replies in 1792 from Dissenters and their sympathisers to Gilbert Wakefield's attack on public worship as inconsistent with Christian duty reiterated the same point: religious services communicated biblical knowledge to those to whom it might otherwise have been unavailable, and such knowledge could be expected to instil higher standards of morality. The Dissenting minister John Simpson replied to Wakefield by quoting Mark 11:17.[15] Sylas Neville reflected on the point in an unpublished section of his diary; after discussing it with an (unnamed) admirer of Algernon Sidney, he noted:

> This Gent. thinks that, if civil establishments in religion were abolished, as they ought, there wd. be no occasion for preaching, as the teachers, if permitted to explain scripture, might raise martyrs &c. But tho' I agree that reading the word, praying & singing praise are the only essential parts of true Xstn worship, I am apt to think that preaching wd. be productive of no bad consequence, but wd. rather be useful for the instruction of the ignorant, if the teachers were made dependent on their respective flocks only, & deprived of all power of meeting in Ecclesiastical Courts or enacting regulations of any kind.[16]

Behind this predictable antipathy to a state religion and any claim to temporal power on the part of the established clergy or their defenders lay a virulent aversion to Catholicism. The Catholic Church was the ultimate source and sanctum of 'clericism' at its worst, and every effort was to be made to eradicate its last vestiges in England and to forestall their reappearance. Hence Richard Baron's prime targets were '*Popery*, the *Inquisition*, the *Bastile*',[17] and any hints of 'popish' practices in England. There was an equally strong suspicion of the English Catholic minority and – from the 1760s – paranoia about its supposedly increasing numbers. Above all, however, mid-century anticlericalism was both politically and socially respectable; its doyen, Samuel Clarke, had been patronised by royalty, while the prospect of a Jacobite restoration supported by Catholic powers had conferred an aura of approval even upon unorthodox writers who were pro-Hanoverian. It had successes to its credit: the repeal of the Schism and Occasional Conformity Acts, the suspension of Convocation, the political defeat of the High Church Anglicanism of the Atterbury type, and an acceptance, and indeed extension, of the legal toleration of Dissent which had certainly not been present in the reign of Queen Anne.

II

It is necessary to ask at this stage what had made such a state of affairs possible? What had made mid-century anticlericalism, despite its lack of a popular base, relatively assured and effective – and how was this to change after 1750? This chapter seeks to answer both questions.

To this purpose it is possible to identify three leading components of English anticlericalism in mid-century.[18] The first is the effective presence of a group of anticlerical Whigs in Parliament. Their influence reached its height in the Parliaments of 1727–34 and 1734–41, and to a lesser extent in that of 1741–7, when anticlerical legislation of a fundamental kind was either passed (such as the Mortmain Act of 1736) or threatened (such as the bills attacking Church Courts, Church rates and tithes). Some of the anticlerical 'Old Whigs' achieved high office: Charles Talbot became Lord Chancellor, Sir Joseph Jekyll Master of the Rolls, and even lesser lights such as William Glanville and John Hampden secured minor office.[19] It was partly due to their influence that Convocation remained suspended for all but formal purposes (despite efforts in 1741 to revive it) and that suspicious eyes were cast upon the clerical privileges of the English universities, with Tory Oxford in particular danger from the possibility of a hostile parliamentary inquiry. A series of Whig ministries enjoyed harmonious relations with mainstream Protestant Dissent; Newcastle urged his successors in 1765 to make plain that they would ensure that 'it is His Majesty's Intention to give his Royal Protection to the Protestant Dissenters'.[20] Newcastle himself, as a devout member of the Church of England, was able to offer at least some reassurance, especially after 1740, to the Anglican clergy while containing parliamentary anticlericalism within the network of patronage. This was a period in which the values of those who admired the anti-Church policies of the Stanhope administration did not predominate, but those who adhered to such values were close to the centre of power and could not be ignored by the ministry.

The second component is to be found in the Anglican latitudinarian tradition, which, though hardly an organised 'party', remained powerful in mid-century. While commanding the allegiance of only a minority among the clergy as a whole, latitudinarianism was still well represented in higher circles, was intellectually dominant in Cambridge and had constructed a weighty body of political argument: Hoadly was alive until 1761. While recent scholarship has insisted upon the fundamental orthodoxy of most latitudinarians in matters of doctrine, at least in their earlier years they were generally characterised by a leniency and sympathetic understanding towards the heterodox.[21] Martin Fitzpatrick has drawn particular attention to the latitudinarian quest for simplicity, its insistence that the Bible alone was the repository of vital Christian truths, and that differences of opinion in lesser matters were of secondary importance.[22] The articles of religion were best seen as 'articles of peace', designed to secure a measure of consensus in the face of internal and external enemies. Only a very few latitudinarian clergy refused subscription to the articles; even Francis Blackburne subscribed on becoming Archdeacon of Cleveland in 1750. Indeed, personal assent was widely seen as unobjectionable and not necessarily conducive to a disingenuous approach to the articles.[23] Such clergy and their lay friends were hardly likely to make subscription a cause of division or to confront those who subscribed according to their own – very limited – interpretative terms. The latitudinarian mentality, in its rejection of notions of a Church as independent of the State, could lead to the Erastianism often attributed to Warburton; spiritual matters should not be the concern of the civil magistrate, and social utility was the prime justification for the alliance between Church and State. As Stephen Taylor has observed, the argument that the Church in fact gained relatively little from the alliance apart from material perquisites for its well-connected clergy had been exploited by such radical anticlerical organs as *The Old Whig*,[24] an allegation given some credence by the career of the likes of Edmund Pyle, chaplain-in-ordinary to George II and a noted pluralist. It followed that mid-century latitudinarians were hostile to any proposals to augment clerical powers, and would resist attempts to present the Church in a sacerdotal rather than a socially useful light. As long as the latitudinarian tradition remained intact and reasonably united, anticlerical opinion was assured of a measure of acceptance and, within the Church at least, of protection. The very orthodoxy of that tradition in theology conferred a vital element of respectability upon anticlericalism.

The third element is best described as the Commonwealth tradition, or the ideology of those whom Caroline Robbins memorably portrayed as 'Old Whigs' or the 'Club of Honest Whigs'. Combining the values of classical republicanism with those of the champions of the seventeenth-century English republic, the commonwealthmen, for all their diversity and lack of coherent organisation, contributed powerfully to a climate of opinion among the political elite which favoured a libertarian approach to matters of conscience; Professor Robbins went so far as to claim that they 'rescued England from uniformity and intolerance even in a period of conservatism and indifference'.[25] It is true that one might suggest that religious belief, often of a heterodox kind, was more central to the Commonwealth ethos than Professor Robbins allowed, and that many eyebrows would rise at the suggestion that mid- or late eighteenth-century public opinion was apathetic. However, it would be difficult to deny the conclusion that, through the diffusion of the printed word, the 'Honest Whigs' reached a considerable readership; over sixty separate works, for instance, are credited to Caleb Fleming, one of its relatively minor figures. By the mid-eighteenth century a guiding influence was Thomas Hollis, whose ability to widen the circulation of favoured texts and obtain access to the newspaper press was second to none, and has been very well documented.[26] The Hollis connection spread both its influence and its interests beyond England; it followed events in Scotland and North America – territories without an Anglican establishment – closely. Possessing some affinity with the civic humanism propagated at the Scottish universities, and sharing with the Anglican latitudinarians a suspicion of creeds and religious texts, the Hollis connection kept a kind of watching brief against what it regarded as a revival of clerical power. This, too, extended beyond England, and Fleming's sympathy with those in the Church of Scotland who sought to abolish compulsory subscription to the Confession of Faith was matched twenty years later by the concern in English Dissenting circles over the prosecution of the heterodox William M'Gill, minister at Ayr.[27] Many of the associates of Hollis were, of course, Dissenters: Hollis himself sprang from a prominent Baptist family in Yorkshire. For all their disapproval of religious establishments, however, a factor central to an understanding of their role in mid-century is that they were very close to the political establishment; they identified their interests with those of the state, especially during the Seven Years War, and were strongly pro-Hanoverian. Hollis, in particular, was on terms of close personal friendship with Pitt the Elder.

Each of these three components of English anticlericalism underwent fundamental changes in the second half of the eighteenth century, and with those changes the whole character of anticlericalism itself was forced into new and less comfortable patterns. These changes require a brief analysis.

The first of them was the marginalisation of parliamentary anticlericalism. As mid-eighteenth-century Whiggism gradually shed its court element, moves against the clergy in both houses of Parliament fell far short of those in the 1730s and 1740s. Even in the Parliament of 1768–74, the most explicitly anticlerical of those elected between the 1740s and the 1830s, the proposal to abolish the observance of 30 January failed, the Feathers Tavern petition was twice rejected and bills to reform the subscription laws for Dissenters miscarried in the House of Lords. The North ministry, for all its emollience, was more than willing to defend the Church. There was no more talk, as in 1719 and 1749, of inflicting hostile visitations upon the clerical strongholds in the universities or of placing restrictions upon lay gifts to the Church. Later examples of successful measures in Parliament which threatened the authority of the Church, however marginally, were rare; in 1786–7, for instance, when J.P. Bastard introduced a bill to reform the ecclesiastical courts, he encountered several strong defences of the clergy, and his bill, passed only after its references to tithes were removed, merely limited the period of time in which relatively minor suits could be brought in the Church Courts.[28] Thereafter, for all their radical implications, motions which threatened the privileges of the Church had to be clothed in the language of moderation. Their proponents were forced on to the defensive. Beaufoy, in 1789, when moving for the repeal of the Test and Corporation Acts, went to considerable lengths to try to reassure the House that his motion would not place Anglican endowments in any danger. A year later, when moving a similar motion, Fox, too, for all his strictures upon what he called the 'High Church Party', adopted a defensive tone: 'he trusted that no observation whatsoever had fallen from him, since the first moment of having risen, which did not discover that he was a decided friend to an Established Religion'.[29] It was the duty of Parliament 'to extend their protection to that which, more than any of the others, approached to *Universality*, and to secure for it some of the chief emoluments of the state'.[30]

Just as the Old Corps Whigs were separated from their virtual monopoly of office and moved into opposition, their successors, at least in their Rockinghamite and Foxite manifestations, rediscovered their 'country' or libertarian past via attacks on the Crown and on the influence of the Anglican clergy. Despite the interruption of 1783–4, they reaffirmed and made more explicit their alliance with Dissent, at the very time when Dissenting numbers were increasing, when the Dissenting leadership with the highest public profile was acquiring a reputation for heterodoxy, and when Dissenting voters were becoming increasingly radicalised.[31] Fox, for all his public professions in 1790, was in fact highly critical of the Church hierarchy, and in the early 1790s took up other issues contrary to its interests. But by then the Foxites were a small and dwindling rump in both Houses, and with the Church of England at the forefront of the defence of order in the American War, and even more so during the revolutionary years after 1789, anticlericalism in Parliament was a minority affair, far further removed from the levers of power than had been the case in 1750.

The second change concerns the deteriorating fortunes of latitudinarianism in the reign of George III. The publication of Blackburne's *Confessional* forced many latitudinarian clergy to face the awkward question as to the course of action to be followed by those who rejected the Thirty Nine Articles test in principle. Blackburne strongly implied that private doubts were insufficient; it was necessary for convictions to be acted upon.[32] Very few followed that implication to its logical conclusion of resignation, and it is testimony to the width of eighteenth-century Anglicanism that latitudinarianism was still contained and comprehended within it – but at a price. The impact of *The Confessional* was a divisive one for latitudinarian opinion. If resignation were rejected, the alternatives were to campaign for a reform of the Articles, or to remain silent and avoid controversy. The limited support for the Feathers Tavern petition in 1771–2 reveals the extent to which the latter alternative was adopted by the majority. Theophilus Lindsey, its chief promoter, admitted a lack of support from the clergy: 'I find every where the Laity as we call them more ready to promote this deliverance from impositions upon conscience than those whose grievance it is immediately and directly.'[33] After 1772 some of his radical associates among the clergy angrily repudiated the latitudinarian compromise and moved from the Warburtonian camp to a complete rejection of state support for any religious denomination. William Frend put it succinctly:

> The Alliance between church and state is a fiction, which could not be realised in this country, without subjecting the abbettours of it to the penalties of high treason.[34]

However, by the time Frend wrote these words in 1793 more conservative latitudinarians were moving in the opposite direction and rallying to the establishment. William Paley, for instance, while advocating 'a comprehensive national religion, guarded by a few articles of peace and conformity', accepted also 'the right of the magistrate to establish a particular religion' not only in the national interest, but in order to balance what he termed 'the progress of truth with the peace of society'.[35] With the French Revolution, as Dr N.U. Murray convincingly demonstrated, most latitudinarians retreated from their former – now exposed – 'liberal' positions and 'edged closer to the orthodox mainstream'. Threatened on the one hand by the evangelical revival and on the other by association with allegedly subversive Dissent, old-style latitudinarianism disintegrated.[36] By the end of the century it could count on the support in elite politics only of such as Shelburne, the most unpopular politician of his generation, and the Duke of Grafton, who left the Church to become an avowed Unitarian. On the bench of bishops its only open sympathisers were Graftonian survivals such as Edmund Law (d. 1787), Jonathan Shipley (d. 1788) and John Hinchliffe (d. 1794), while Richard Watson was preoccupied with warding off the threat from Paine. This was no longer a safe haven, or source of strength, for anticlerical opinion.

Thirdly, the Commonwealth tradition faded away or was transmogrified into 'Rational Dissent'. To Caroline Robbins, one of its key features was its eclecticism: 'In a study of the Commonwealthmen', she wrote, 'sect is unimportant.'[37] The later eighteenth century, however, was a period of more rigid sectarian definition, with the emergence of Unitarianism as a distinctive denomination, and the transformation of much of the Old Dissent as a result of evangelicalism. For the commonwealthmen, the transition from a generalised heterodoxy to a more focused and dogmatic Socinianism was bound to have a narrowing effect upon their influence and appeal.[38] It is apparent, both from his diary and from his will, that Thomas Hollis in his later years took up a number of avowed Socinians as his true spiritual heirs.[39] The Hollis connection itself decayed; the heir to his estates, Thomas Brand Hollis, identified himself completely with Rational Dissent and was a trustee of Lindsey's Essex Street Unitarian Chapel. Hollis's nephew John Hollis, who felt himself cheated of his due legacy by Brand Hollis, complained bitterly: 'If the property of the Family had come into my hands I will not pretend to say what I should have done. Thomas Hollis however thought proper to alienate it in favour of a very unworthy person.'[40] John Hollis withdrew even from Unitarianism, and horrified Lindsey in the later 1790s by publishing deist pamphlets.[41] Caleb Fleming's congregation at Pinners Hall disappeared after his death in 1779, while Sylas Neville became a sycophantic would-be client of Windham, Lord Liverpool, and even Sir Robert Peel, whom he inundated with begging letters before rounding off a picaresque existence with burial in Norwich Cathedral.[42] The Hollis connection, so central in mid-century to the perpetuation of the Commonwealth ideal, had depended heavily upon personal relationships and access to men in high office. But its heirs and successors in Rational Dissent increasingly acquired the appearance and mentality of outsiders. They were well connected only with the Whig opposition in Parliament and maverick peers, such as the 3rd Earl Stanhope, the 8th Lord Lauderdale and the lapsed Catholic 11th Duke of Norfolk. Their connections with the political establishment became almost completely attenuated. Thomas Hollis had enjoyed a close personal friendship both with the Archbishop of Canterbury, Thomas Secker, and with the Speaker of the House of Commons, Arthur Onslow, encapsulated in his diary entry for 4 April 1760: 'Received a very fine pina apple as a present from the Speaker. Dined at a tavern with Mr Brand[?]. Sent the pine apple to the A.[rch]bishop.'[43] It is difficult to imagine Joseph Priestley, for instance, on such terms with Archbishop John Moore and Speaker Henry Addington. When Brand Hollis formed a friendship with Thomas Hardy of the London Corresponding Society in 1792, it was very far from the patron–client relationship of Thomas Hollis and the authors whose works he sponsored; Hardy addressed Brand Hollis as an equal.[44] These tentative approaches towards popular radicalism showed how far the old, elite, Commonwealth tradition had withered, and how far this branch of anticlerical opinion had removed itself from the political mainstream.

III

How are these changes to be explained? For the purposes of this chapter, two explanations seem to stand out.

First, it is well known that a familiar motivation behind anticlericalism is the aggressive assertion of its antithesis. In the later eighteenth century there was, in some quarters, an understandable, if misplaced, perception of clerical aggrandisement in terms both of ideology and of practical politics. When Lindsey deplored what he called the 'obstinate churchism' of Edmund Burke,[45] he had in mind a growing disposition to conceive the basis of society in sacerdotal terms and the invocation of *iuro divino* as sanction for the existing order, together with the failure to secure either reform within the Church of England or reform of the Test Laws. I have tried to show elsewhere that the extent of this clerical reassertion was much exaggerated.[46] In responding to the Evans judgment of 1767, in which the House of Lords ruled that Protestant Dissent was no longer to be regarded as a crime at law, Blackstone in his *Commentaries* was trying to salvage something of the previous position, not to thrust Dissent back into an age of intolerance, when he wrote that 'the crime of nonconformity is by no means universally abrogated'.[47] His Dissenting critics, on the other hand, regarded the Evans judgment as a famous victory which – if pushed further – promised a considerable advancement of their interests. George Dyer's interpretation of the Evans judgment was a truly radical one: 'Dissenters are very numerous: and, as they now have a title in law, it would not be accurate to say, the church of England and the people of England are the same people.'[48] Of course, to Dyer and those of his ilk, an increase in Dissenting numbers weakened the case for an Anglican Establishment; but he and others also believed that the Church's reaction to the unwelcome evidence of growing religious pluralism was a clerical rallying. Such an alleged rallying was detected in incidents great and small, from the fundraising for the American episcopalian clergy in 1776 to the withdrawal of the invitation to Priestley to serve as scientist on the second voyage of Captain Cook. With the Hutchinsonian George Horne's elevation to the Deanery of Canterbury in 1781 and Samuel Hallifax's bishopric in the same year, it appeared – mistakenly, in the author's view – that 'High Churchmen' in substantial numbers were receiving the preferment hitherto withheld from them. 'Generous liberal sentiments are not now the passport to the mitre,' lamented the Dissenter Samuel Kenrick in 1792.[49] Even the Scottish Episcopalians, with their Jacobite past, secured a Relief Act in that year. In reality, there was no flood of old-style High Churchmen to positions of seniority; the careers of William Jones of Nayland and many of his High Church contemporaries show plainly how little preferment they were accorded. However, the perception of an assertion of clerical authority was of much historical importance. It is typified by the Unitarian lawyer and Foxite Whig Samuel Heywood in his *High Church Politics* (1792), and by allegations in some Dissenting circles that there had not been so great a danger of persecution since the time of Henry Sacheverell. This perception – and genuine fear – induced many anticlerical writers to suppose that they no longer commanded the ear of the Establishment, and a heightened sense of exclusion drove them into positions which were more radical and at the same time less representative and less politically influential.

The second explanation concerns the declining force of traditional anti-Catholicism among the elite, so ably depicted by Colin Haydon.[50] Although some Rational Dissenters of the later eighteenth century acquiesced in the relaxation of the penal laws against Catholics in the British Isles, the older generation of Commonwealth anticlerics did not. This was a serious development in a period when anti-Catholicism had exerted a unifying effect and when attacks on popish survivals and on alleged revivals of Catholic influence had been central to the anticlerical case. By the later eighteenth century, and especially after the Gordon riots, virulent anti-Catholicism was something of an embarrassment, and caused a gap to develop between some elements of anticlericalism and the Establishment. William Cole, for instance, pounced on the opportunity to denounce Thomas Hollis, an advocate of toleration, as a hypocrite for his belief that the state had a right to curb Catholicism.[51] The same stricture was levelled against the opponents of the Quebec Act. In the 1790s there was a temporary easing of official anti-Catholicism, to such an extent that the elderly Horace Walpole, no friend to monarchs and bishops, told Hannah More that he had 'been persuaded, much against my will and practice, to let my name be put to the second subscription for the poor French clergy'.[52] But this was of no benefit whatever to anticlericalism as far as public opinion was concerned; so clearly identified with support for the French Revolution were many leading anticlerical writers that they suffered a 'transference of hatred' from Catholicism to themselves. It is true that at the popular level, anti-Catholicism retained much of its force in the early nineteenth century, and perhaps even gained in strength. But the result was that when Rational Dissent and the successors to the old-style latitudinarians shed most of their anti-Catholicism, they remained out of touch with public opinion. Nevertheless, a vital change had taken place. The author hopes to examine in a separate paper the campaigns of Christopher Wyvill for 'universal toleration' in 1806–13. It becomes plain immediately that the anticlericalism was of a quite different order from that of Blackburne, despite their geographical proximity in Richmond, Yorkshire, and the involvement of members of Blackburne's own family in Wyvill's subsequent moves for religious reform. Not only did Wyvill resign his benefice (though not his Anglican orders), but he included Catholics in his campaigns for 'universal toleration', and worked closely with representatives of the Catholic elite.

IV

Finally, what conclusions might one draw about the character of English anticlericalism at the end of the century? One of its characteristics, undoubtedly, was a guarded and coded republicanism. Of course, the connection between anticlericalism and republicanism was not a necessary an ineluctable one. Many of the best-known anticlerical initiatives in later eighteenth-century Europe emanated from monarchies: one thinks of Joseph II's dissolution of the religious orders, the imposition of 'royalism' in Spain, and the expulsion of the Jesuits from major Catholic monarchies. In England, by contrast, there was an increasing identification of Crown and Church. No one could doubt the genuine nature of George III's personal Anglican convictions, and there was no stronger defender of the Test and Corporation Acts. By 1800 the Hanoverian monarchy was far more closely associated with clerical privilege than in mid-century. Hence anticlerical opinion turned, at least implicitly, in a more anti-monarchical direction. The clergy themselves were usually the first nervously to detect republicanism among their critics. In Kent the Revd Joseph Price noted: 'Mrs Macaulay much followed and admired by Lord Nuneham and all the republican party.'[53] By the 1790s, if not earlier, 'republicanism' had become almost exclusively a term of abuse. Hence its expression was often cautious and veiled. Private contempt for the royal family could co-exist with public statements to the effect that the values of republicanism could be achieved within a limited monarchy.[54]

Moreover, there were, at least before the 1790s, republican examples to admire. In addition to the Protestant cantons of Switzerland (Thomas Hollis bequeathed financial legacies to the public library of Berne and to the University of Geneva[55]), there was the much-admired Corsican struggle for independence, and most of all there was the fledgling republic in North America, with the Virginia Statute of 1786 as exemplar. As George Dyer put it:

> There is a modern government where the office of supreme magistrate is so frugally supported, so wisely directed, and where the electing powers arise from so prudent an arrangement, that I venture to affirm, the evils charged on elective governments are never likely to happen.[56]

Frend was more explicit and strident in condoning the execution of Louis XVI: 'if all the crowned heads on the continent are taken off, it is no business of ours'.[57] The immediacy of these examples reduced the dependency of republican sympathisers upon the seventeenth-century intellectual legacy lovingly preserved by Hollis. However, with republicanism no longer a remote and theoretical possibility, and with the spoliation of the Gallican Church, anticlericalism in England experienced an outburst of hostility which sought to defend Crown as well as Church. The public identification of critics of the Church with republicanism reached its height at the very time when the popularity of George III – not merely the creation of elite propaganda – also reached a climax.[58] To quote Dyer again, this time in a mildly satirical verse about London landladies:

> For Gaia loves King and her Church
> And thinks it a maxim most true,
> Who leaves a poor priest in the lurch
> Would soon rob the King of his due.[59]

However, this was a republicanism which embodied an idealised version of a Christian society, not a secularised state. As Sylas Neville reflected: 'Rational religion is one of the best foundations of liberty.'[60] In her entry for Catherine Macaulay in her volumes of *Female Biography* in 1803, Mary Hays took care to point out that in middle age, her subject had found solace in 'rational religion', with a 'prepossession in favour of the christian revelation', at the very time of her laudatory visit to America. A study of the unpublished diary of Sylas Neville suggests that she had always had such a prepossession.[61] An 'aristocratic' form of republicanism which possessed its own branch of theological conviction and embraced the ethical values of Christianity naturally appreciated a need to inculcate public morality as well as to encourage the individual search for biblical truth. The essentially religious dimensions of later eighteenth-century English republicanism deserve recognition.

This point leads on to a second important characteristic of anticlericalism in this period. For most anticlerical writers succeeded in keeping the debate within a religious – indeed, Christian – context, despite the efforts of their opponents to exclude them from it. Hence Lindsey warmly accepted the suggestion of Robert Tyrwhitt that the title of the Unitarian Society founded in 1791 be amended in its aim from 'promoting religious knowledge' to 'promoting christian knowledge'; he was relieved, for 'we are already called a Society of Deists'.[62] John Disney complained that 'to impute to rational notions of the christian religion any tendency, either directly or remotely, to promote infidelity is greatly to wrong our faith'.[63] A noteworthy feature of such writers is their avoidance of the relativism beloved of early eighteenth-century Deists. Christianity was the only road to truth. Replying to Paine's allegation that 'every national church has established itself by pretending some special mission from God communicated to certain individuals. The Jews have their Moses; the Christians their Jesus Christ . . . the Turks their Mahomet', Gilbert Wakefield commented:

> We affirm of the *Jewish* and *Christian* dispensations, that *they* only were *the way* to any man desirous of entertaining rational notions of God and human duty . . . [T]he natural inference from these indubitable positions is clearly, *some* degree of supernatural communication, which we stile *Revelation*, to the founders of *Judaism* and *Christianity*, *Moses* and *Jesus*; and the denial of such communication leaves a problem, I apprehend, of much more arduous solution.[64]

Samuel Kenrick dismissed *The Age of Reason* more summarily: 'As to Pain's notions abt. revelation & the real christian doctrine, nothing can be more groundless. It is not christianity – but its abuses wch he attacks.'[65] There was a touch of bewilderment and injured innocence in Lindsey's complaint about Burke's *Reflections*:

It is a curious accusation which Mr Burke brings formally and with all seriousness against the projectors of the French revolution, of a design to overthrow the christian religion. His grand proof of it is, their curtailing of the hierarchy and appropriation of the vast surplus of the revenue of the church to civil purposes . . . His assertions from his own imaginations of a similar design in our revolution society and its abetters at home . . . will tend to inflame and excite the zeal of churchmen and set us at a greater distance from Reformation.[66]

It was indeed 'reformation' of the Church which Lindsey and his fellow (former) latitudinarians such as Wyvill sought, and in that aim they received the implicit support of most Rational Dissenters, who came to regret Priestley's talk of gunpowder. The atheist politician, even in Whig circles – such as Lord Holland – was a rarity; far more characteristic was Lord Althorp, later the 3rd Earl Spencer, whose Anglican paternalism is well illustrated in E.A. Wasson's biography.[67] Indeed, it was precisely for this reason that the types of anticlerical writers who had been most prominent in the second half of the eighteenth century diverged from Painite radicalism, and from the world of freethinking, deism and 'infidelity' described by Iain McCalman which characterised the semi-plebeian radicalism of the early nineteenth century.[68] They were much more at ease in the socially exclusive world of Foxite Whiggery. Indeed, they bitterly resented imputations of 'guilt by association' with the latter phenomena, especially after the legal toleration afforded to Unitarians by the Trinity Act of 1813 was also exploited by plebeian freethinkers. The dilemma of English anticlericalism by 1800 was that it had lost much of its previous intellectual and political respectability – a process under way *before* the French Revolution – without achieving any compensating gain. In this chapter the same names have tended to recur. Anticlerical writers frequently belonged to small coteries of the educated. They could not move easily into a world of mass political activity.

   How, then, was the primarily intellectual anticlericalism of the later eighteenth century transformed into the type of plebeian, material and socially aggressive anticlericalism of the 1830s vividly depicted by Eric Evans?[69] As the material perquisites of the clergy re-emerged as political targets, with renewed attacks on tithes, clerical magistracy and the Game Laws, and as the Act of Union brought the endowments of the Church of Ireland closer to the centre of politics, the nature of the argument shifted dramatically. Admittedly these issues are not completely absent from the works of the writers examined here, but they were far from leading priorities. Material questions had not been a vital feature of eighteenth-century anticlericalism. The tithe grievance should not be exaggerated: there was much local accommodation in practice, and the specifically Quaker objection to tithes was confined to a small number of high-profile cases.[70] There was little about tithes in Dissenting polemic over the Test and Corporation Acts in 1787–90, or even in 1828. Many subsequent attacks upon tithe as a clerical perquisite uttered by radical Whigs such as Francis Horner, while adopting a sharp anticlerical tone, were based more upon the need for agricultural improvement, a *laissez-faire* concern for unhampered efficiency, than upon social grievances.[71]

Much of this is evident in the degree of emphasis placed by the opponents of anticlericalism upon the standard arguments against it. The sense of priority with which those arguments are deployed provides some indication as to which aspects of anticlericalism its potential targets find most threatening. In the later eighteenth century the argument most frequently used was the complaint that anticlericalism led to heresy and infidelity, with a consequent breakdown of ethical values; only the clerical elite could be trusted to preserve the integrity of soul-saving doctrine. Next in order of priority was the charge that anticlericalism was politically subversive, a threat to the rule of law and to property: this is the familiar 'no bishop, no King' argument, lampooned by George Dyer in the doggerel quoted above. Third, there was the 'charity' argument, that attacks on clerical privilege and property would cause immense harm to the poor, robbing them of philanthropic relief and basic religious education, and would threaten social stability. Fourth in order of priority was the assertion of a need for authority on matters of doctrine and discipline, a final court of appeal.

One is accustomed to read both of contempt for clerical poverty on the one hand[72] and resentment at clerical wealth on the other[73] as reasons for anticlericalism. The common factor, of course, was clerical distinctiveness. Perhaps the later eighteenth century was a period of balance between these two extremes, a period of slow transition from one to the other. In this process one can point to the consolidation of the clerical profession,[74] growing clerical wealth, or much more important, a hostile depiction of growing clerical wealth, unequally distributed, spatial separation from parishioners, and the increasing number of clerical magistrates, not to mention the scandals caused by such splendid mavericks as Edward Drax Free.[75] But this was a very lengthy process, it belongs much more to the early nineteenth than to the later eighteenth century, and it was subject – in common with enclosures and the incidence of clerical magistracy – to very wide regional variations. If clergymen received threatening anonymous letters during the food crises of 1795, 1800–1 and 1816,[76] they also received favourable publicity as leading contributors to funds for the relief of the attendant hardship.[77] Similarly, it is difficult to regard as nationally representative the five clerical diaries upon which John Phillips drew in his critique of notions of deference in late Georgian England.[78] That critique raises the further methodological issue: what critical problems are raised by the use of clerical sources, and especially clerical pessimism, as evidence of a widespread anticlericalism?

In the later eighteenth century denominationalism and theology remained vital features of English anticlericalism. For anticlericalism took the form of conflict not only between denominations, but also *within* denominations. Four main examples may be cited. First, the extent of mild heterodoxy and opposition to priestcraft within the Church of England has been demonstrated recently by Brian Young, and serves to emphasise the Anglican achievement in comprehending so wide a diversity of opinion.[79] Secondly, the anticlerical agenda of some of the Cisalpine writers of the English Catholic community has been well documented.[80] The hostility towards papal authority and to the role of the Vicars Apostolic expressed by Joseph Berington and others at the time of the Relief Act of 1791 is unmistakable. The Catholic lawyer John Joseph Dillon complained in 1810 of the way in which the Catholic petition of that year had called for an amendment to Lord Hardwicke's Marriage Act: 'Proceeding upon the supposition that it is unlawful for Catholics to apply to the Protestant clergyman for marriage, we can be in future married only by a licensed minister of our persuasion.' When he demanded, rhetorically, 'Are any of us prepared to concede such an authority to our Clergy?', he was not referring to the Anglican clergy.[81] Thirdly, the growth of more popular, plebeian types of Methodism led to opposition to ministerial control, and there was a clear anticlerical motive behind the Kilhamite and Primitive secessions from the main Wesleyan body. Fourthly, James Bradley's essay cites the vehemence of Dissenting anticlericalism, which took the form less of a material grievance than of a theologically driven opposition to the concept of a State Church, a wish to free religious observation, especially the communion service, from use as a test of citizenship, and the ideological assertion of the voluntary principle. But in the later eighteenth century one also detects hints of a Dissenting anticlericalism which took the form of lay distrust of heterodox ministers, fresh from the academies with allegedly heretical ideas, which caused divisions within and secessions from Dissenting congregations.[82]

Hence, although English anticlericalism had a primary target in the late eighteenth and very early nineteenth centuries, it did not have a single target. Similarly there was no united anticlerical programme, rather a series of aspirations. Just as the *Oxford Dictionary of the Christian Church* was rather misleading in depicting anticlericalism only in anti-Catholic terms, so there was more to English anticlericalism at this time than an attack on Anglican perquisites. This, perhaps, is one reason why the transition to the world depicted by Eric Evans took so long, and did not become fully apparent until the 1830s, and perhaps also why anticlericalism of the more material sort fell into decline after the 1830s.[83] In the early nineteenth century English anticlericalism entered the world of genuine religious pluralism, as well as that of the Industrial Revolution. The more one studies anticlericalism, the more impressed one is by the ability of the clergy to survive it.

Notes

1   I am grateful to the Houghton Library, Harvard University, for permission to quote from the diary of Thomas Hollis; and to His Grace the Archbishop of Birmingham, the John Rylands University Library of Manchester, Cambridge University Library and the Trustees of Dr Williams's Library, London, to quote from manuscripts in their possession. I have benefited greatly from discussions of this subject with Nigel Aston, James E. Bradley, Matthew Cragoe and Stephen Taylor.

2   *The Times*, 31 March 1886.

3   J. Hastings, J.A. Selbie and L.H. Gray (eds), *Encyclopaedia of Religion and Ethics* (12 vols, Edinburgh, 1908–21), vol. III, p. 689.

4   E.A. Livingstone (ed.), *Oxford Dictionary of the Christian Church* (3rd edn, Oxford, 1997), pp. 76–7.

5   For a recent lucid statement of the distinction, see *The Spectator*, 6 April 1996 (editorial by Frank Johnson, 'Keeping Faith').

6   James Ibbetson, *A Plea for the Subscription of the Clergy to the Thirty-nine Articles of Religion* (3rd edn, 1768), preface to the 3rd edn, p. v.

7   J.A.I. Champion, *The Pillars of Priestcraft Shaken: The Church of England and its Enemies, 1660–1730* (Cambridge, 1992), esp. pp. 22–4, 228ff.

8   Joseph Priestley, *An History of the Corruptions of Christianity* (2 vols, 1782): 'What I object to is really a corruption of genuine christianity, and no part of the original scheme' (vol. I, preface, p. xiv).

9   Gilbert Wakefield, *Evidences of Christianity: or a Collection of remarks intended to display the excellence, recommend the purity, illustrate the character, and evince the authenticity . . .* (1793), p. 24.

10   William Frend, *A Second Address to the Inhabitants of Cambridge and its Neighbourhood, exhorting them to turn from the false worship of Three Persons, to the worship of The One True God* (St Ives, 1788), p. 12.

11   Richard Baron, *The Pillars of Priestcraft and Orthodoxy Shaken* (2nd edn, 4 vols, 1768), Advertisement to vol. I.

12   Ibid., p. viii.

13   George Dyer, *Inquiry into the Nature of subscription to the thirty-nine Articles* (references are to the 2nd edn of 1792); Brian Herport, *An Essay on Truths of Importance to the Happiness of Mankind. Wherein the Doctrine of Oaths, as relative to Religious and Civil Government, is impartially considered* (1768), pp. 192 and 189. The bindings of the latter work in Dr Williams's Library reveal its provenance under the patronage of Thomas Hollis.

14   Martin Fitzpatrick, 'Latitudinarianism at the Parting of the Ways: a Suggestion', in John Walsh, Colin Haydon and Stephen Taylor (eds), *The Church of England c.1689–c.1833: From Toleration to Tractarianism* (Cambridge, 1993), pp. 209–27.

15   William Frend, *An Address to the Inhabitants of Cambridge and its Neighbourhood* (St Ives, 1788), p. 10; John Simpson, *Christian Arguments for Social and Public Worship* (Bath, 1792), p. 1.

16   Norfolk Record Office, MC7/349 (Neville MSS); diary of Sylas Neville, 2 November 1767.

17   Baron, *Pillars of Priestcraft*, vol. I, p. ix.

18   Stephen Taylor adds a fourth, and much smaller, element: the Erastian legal anticlericals, represented by politicians such as Sir Michael Foster. Dr Taylor also finds a rather surprising Tory initiative in the presentation of the Ecclesiastical Courts Bill of 1733, no doubt indicative of Tory hostility to a Whig-dominated episcopal bench. See Stephen Taylor, 'Whigs, Tories and

Anticlericalism: Ecclesiastical Courts Legislation in 1733', *Parliamentary History* 19 (2000, forthcoming). I am most grateful to Dr Taylor for allowing me to consult this article before publication.

19   See T.F.J. Kenrick, 'Sir Robert Walpole, the Old Whigs and the Bishops, 1733–1736: a study in eighteenth-century party management', *Historical Journal* XI (1968), pp. 421–45.

20   BL Add. MS 32967, ff. 177–80, partly quoted in F. O'Gorman, *The Rise of Party in England: The Rockingham Whigs 1760–82* (1975), p. 588, note 88.

21   R. Emerson, 'Latitudinarianism and the English Deists', in J.A. Leo Lemay (ed.), *Deism, Masonry and the Enlightenment* (Delaware, 1987); W.M. Spellman, *The Latitudinarians and the Church of England, 1660–1700* (Athens, GA, 1993).

22   Fitzpatrick, 'Latitudinarianism at the Parting of the Ways', pp. 212–14.

23   I am grateful to Dr Nigel Aston for his comments on this point.

24   Stephen Taylor, 'William Warburton and the Alliance of Church and State', *Journal of Ecclesiastical History* 43 (1992), p. 275.

25   Caroline Robbins, *The Eighteenth-century Commonwealthman: Studies in the Transmission, Development and Circumstance of English Liberal Thought from the Restoration of Charles II Until the War with the Thirteen Colonies* (New York, 1968), p. 386.

26   For Thomas Hollis, see particularly Caroline Robbins, 'The Strenuous Whig, Thomas Hollis of Lincoln's Inn', *William and Mary Quarterly*, 3rd series, 7 (1950), pp. 406–53; and W.H. Bond, *Thomas Hollis of Lincoln's Inn: A Whig and His Books* (Cambridge, 1990).

27   Norfolk Record Office, MC 7/349, Neville MSS., Fleming to Neville, 3 January 1771; Dr Williams's Library, MS 24.157, Kenrick Papers, Samuel Kenrick to James Wodrow, 1–2 March 1791.

28   Cobbett, *Parliamentary History of England*, vol. XXV, pp. 1,053–4; vol. XXVI, pp. 623–6. The measure was passed in 1787 as 27 George III, c. xliv.

29   *Two Speeches, delivered in the House of Commons, on Tuesday the 2nd of March, 1790, by the Right Honourable Charles James Fox, in support of his Motion for a repeal of the Corporation and Test Acts* (London, 1789), pp. 37 and 46.

30   Cobbett, *Two Speeches*, p. 47.

31   See especially James E. Bradley, *Religion, Revolution and English Radicalism: Non-conformity in Eighteenth-century Politics and Society* (Cambridge, 1990), Part Three.

32   This subject is very well covered in Fitzpatrick, 'Latitudinarianism at the Parting of the Ways', pp. 216ff.

33   Literary and Philosophical Society of Newcastle upon Tyne: Lindsey to the Revd William Turner, 19 November 1771.

34   William Frend, *Peace and Union recommended to the Associated Bodies of Republicans and Anti-Republicans* (St Ives, 1793), p. 25.

35   William Paley, *Principles of Moral and Political Philosophy*, in *The Works of William Paley, with a Life by Alexander Chalmers* (5 vols, 1819), vol. II, pp. 51 and 58; and see Taylor, 'William Warburton', p. 280.

36   N.U. Murray, 'The Influence of the French Revolution on the Church of England and its Rivals, 1789–1802' (Oxford, DPhil, 1975), pp. 95–6 and 124.

37   Robbins, *Eighteenth-century Commonwealthman*, p. 231.

38   For these developments, see G.M. Ditchfield, 'Anti-Trinitarianism and Toleration in late eighteenth-century British politics: the Unitarian Petition of 1792', *Journal of Ecclesiastical History* 42 (1991), pp. 39–67.

39   Diary of Thomas Hollis, Houghton Library, Harvard (microfilm copy consulted at the Seeley Library, Faculty of History, Cambridge); PRO PROB 11/994, ff. 123–4 (Will of Thomas Hollis).

40   BL Add. MS 24869, f. 146: John Hollis to Revd J. Hunter.

41   John Hollis, *Sober and Serious Reasons for Scepticism, as it concerns Revealed Religion. In a Letter to a Friend* (1796); *An Apology for the disbelief in Revealed Religion: being a Sequel to Sober and Serious Reasons for Scepticism* (1799); John Rylands University Library of Manchester (JRULM), Lindsey Correspondence, Lindsey to John Rowe, 2 May 1786.

42   BL Add. MSS 38264, ff. 266–7 and 268; 38265, f. 173; 38266, f. 3; 38267, f. 153; 38269, ff. 36 and 273; 38270, f. 260; 38425, f. 45 (Neville to Lord Liverpool); Add. MSS 40356, ff. 343–4, etc. (Neville to Peel); B. Cozens-Hardy (ed.), *The Diary of Sylas Neville 1767–1788* (Oxford, 1950), p. 332.

43   Thomas Hollis diary, 4 April 1760.

44   BL Add. MS 27811 (Letter Book of the London Corresponding Society); Hardy to Brand Hollis (copy), 10 April 1792.

45   Cambridge University Library, Frend Papers, Lindsey to Frend, 23 April 1791.

46   G.M. Ditchfield, 'Ecclesiastical Policy under Lord North', in *The Church of England, c.1689–c.1833*, pp. 228–46.

47   William Blackstone, *Commentaries of the Laws of England* (10th edn, 4 vols, 1787), vol. IV, p. 54.

48   Dyer, *Inquiry into the Nature of Subscription*, p. 239.

49   Dr Williams's Library, Kenrick Papers, Samuel Kenrick to James Wodrow, 2 July 1792.

50   Colin Haydon, *Anti-Catholicism in Eighteenth-century England: A Political and Social Study* (Manchester, 1993).

51   BL Add. MS 5852, f. 469.

52   W.S. Lewis et al. (eds), *Horace Walpole's Correspondence*, vol. 51, p. 383. Walpole contributed £50 to the fund for the relief of the emigré French clergy.

53   G.M. Ditchfield and B. Keith-Lucas (eds), *A Kentish Parson: Selections from the Private Papers of the Revd Joseph Price, Vicar of Brabourne, 1767–1786* (Stroud, 1991), p. 142.

54   On Catherine Macaulay's contempt for royalty, see the diary of Sylas Neville, 21 November 1767 (unpublished), Norfolk Record Office MC7/349. On her moderate republicanism and acceptance of limited monarchy, see B. Hill, *The Republican Virago: The Life and Times of Catherine Macaulay, Historian* (Oxford, 1992), Chapter 8.

55   PRO PROB 11/994, f. 123 (Will of Thomas Hollis).

56   Dyer, *Inquiry into the Nature of Subscription*, p. 265.

57   Frend, *Peace and Union*, p. 46.

58   Linda Colley, 'The Apotheosis of George III: Loyalty, Royalty and the British Nation, 1760–1820', *Past & Present* 102 (February 1984), pp. 94–129.

59   Dyer, 'Gaia, or Willy Rhymer's Address to his London Landladies', *Poems* (1801), p. 29.

60   Norfolk Record Office, Neville MSS: unpublished diary, 21 November 1767.

61   Quoted in Hill, *Republican Virago*, pp. 149–50; unpublished diary of Sylas Neville, e.g. entry for 30 April 1768.

62   Frend Papers, Lindsey to Frend, 14 February 1791.

63   John Disney, *A Caution to Young Persons against Infidelity. A Sermon preached in the Unitarian Chapel, in Essex Street, London; Sunday, April III, MDCCXCVI* (1797), p. 10.

64   Gilbert Wakefield, *An Examination of the Age of Reason, or an Investigation of true and fabulous theology, by Thomas Paine* (1794), p. 12.

65   Kenrick Papers, Kenrick to Wodrow, 21 December 1795.

66   Frend Papers, Lindsey to Frend, 2 November 1790.

67   E.A. Wasson, *Whig Renaissance: Lord Althorp and the Whig Party, 1782–1845* (New York and London, 1987), pp. 50 and 97–8.

68   Iain McCalman, *Radical Underworld: Prophets, Revolutionaries and Pornographers in London, 1795–1840* (paperback edn, Oxford University Press, 1993), esp. pp. 87ff.

69   Eric J. Evans, 'The Church in Danger? Anticlericalism in Nineteenth-century England', *European Studies Review* 13 (1983), pp. 201–22; 'Some Reasons for the Growth of English Rural Anticlericalism, *c.*1750–*c.*1830', *Past & Present* 66 (February 1975), pp. 84–109.

70   Eric J. Evans, *The Contentious Tithe: The Tithe Problem and English Agriculture 1750–1850* (London, 1976); G.M. Ditchfield, 'Parliament, the Quakers and the Tithe Question, 1750–1835', *Parliamentary History* 4 (1985), pp. 87–114.

71   *The Horner Papers: Selections from the Letters and Miscellaneous Writings of Francis Horner, M.P., 1795–1817*, eds Kenneth Bourne and William Banks Taylor (Edinburgh, 1994), pp. 177–80.

72   W.M. Jacob, *Lay People and Religion in the Early Eighteenth Century* (Cambridge, 1996), p. 48.

73   Evans, 'English Rural Anticlericalism', pp. 94–100.

74   Penelope Corfield, *Power and the Professions in Britain 1700–1850* (London and New York, 1995), Chapter 5.

75   R.B. Outhwaite, *Scandal in the Church: Dr Edward Drax Free 1764–1843* (London and Rio Grande, 1997).

76   Evans, 'The Church in Danger?', p. 213.

77   For some examples, see Frank Panton, 'Finances and Government of Canterbury: Eighteenth to Mid-nineteenth Century' (University of Kent, unpublished PhD dissertation, 1999), pp. 141–3.

78   John A. Phillips, 'The Social Calculus: Deference and Defiance in Later Georgian England', *Albion* 31, 2 (Fall, 1989), pp. 426–49. The diaries are those of William Cole of Bletchley, James Woodforde of Norfolk, William Jones of Broxbourne, and John Skinner and William Holland, both of Somerset.

79   Brian Young, 'A History of Variations: the Identity of the Eighteenth-century Church of England', in *Protestantism and National Identity: Britain and Ireland c.1650–c.1850* (Cambridge, 1998), pp. 105–28.

80   Eamon Duffy, 'Ecclesiastical Democracy Detected: I (1779–87)', *Recusant History* 10, 4 (January 1970), pp. 193–209; J.C.H. Aveling, *The Handle and the Axe: The Catholic Recusants in England from Reformation to Emancipation* (London and Tiptree, 1976), chapter 15.

81   John Joseph Dillon, *A Letter to Edward Jerningham, Esq., respecting the Inexpediency of a Petition in the present Moment on the Part of the English Catholics to Parliament* (Bath, 1810), p. 10. Although this is a printed document, it is marked 'not published'; Birmingham Archdiocesan Archives, R195.

82   Twenty-eight examples of Congregational secessions from what had been Presbyterian meetings are conveniently listed in Michael Watts, *The Dissenters: From the Reformation to the French Revolution* (Oxford, 1978), p. 468, note 3.

83   Evans, 'The Church in Danger?', p. 208.

FURTHER READING

Bradley, James E., *Religion, Revolution and English Radicalism: Non-conformity in Eighteenth-century Politics and Society* (Cambridge, 1990).

Clark, J.C.D., *English Society 1688–1832: Ideology, Social Structure and Political Practice During the Ancien Regime* (Cambridge, 1985).

Corfield, Penelope, *Power and the Professions in Britain 1700–1850* (London and New York, 1995).

Cozens-Hardy, B. (ed.), *The Diary of Sylas Neville 1767–1788* (Oxford, 1950).

Evans, Eric J., 'Some Reasons for the Growth of English Rural Anti-Clericalism, c.1750–c.1830', *Past & Present* 66 (February 1975).

——, 'The Church in Danger? Anticlericalism in Nineteenth-century England', *European Studies Review* 13 (1983).

Haydon, Colin, *Anti-Catholicism in Eighteenth-century England: A Political and Social Study* (Manchester, 1993).

Robbins, Caroline, *The Eighteenth-century Commonwealthman: Studies in the Transmission, Development and Circumstance of English Liberal Thought from the Restoration of Charles II Until the War with the Thirteen Colonies* (New York, 1968).

Taylor, Stephen, 'William Warburton and the Alliance of Church and State', *Journal of Ecclesiastical History* 43 (1992).

Walsh, John, Haydon, Colin, and Taylor, Stephen (eds), *The Church of England c.1689–c.1833: From Toleration to Tractarianism* (Cambridge, 1993).

Young, Brian, 'A History of Variations: the Identity of the Eighteenth-century Church of England', in Tony Claydon and Ian McBride (eds), *Protestantism and National Identity: Britain and Ireland c.1650–c.1850* (Cambridge, 1998).

6

ANGLICAN RESPONSES TO ANTICLERICALISM IN THE 'LONG' EIGHTEENTH CENTURY, *c.* 1689–1830

Nigel Aston

Responses by members of the Anglican clergy to anticlericalism in the 'long' eighteenth century is a topic yet to be systematically assessed by historians. It may be that this relative neglect owes much to the enduring perception – despite the wealth of recent scholarship – of Anglicanism's institutional torpor in this period. Precisely who or what did the Anglican Churches threaten sufficiently to make attacks on the clergy a priority for its foes? In Scotland episcopalians were outside the pale altogether as the revolutionary regime aligned itself, for exclusively political reasons, with presbyterians;[1] in Ireland, despite the sometimes desperate attachment of Anglicans to the sacramental test marking them out from other denominations,[2] the clergy were, in the last resort, part of a common Protestant front, and even in England the Church was a legal corporation steadily being divested of exclusive privileges unacceptable to the lay political elite. A vast proportion of its landed estates had passed into their ownership at the Reformation; it had abandoned its right of independent taxation in 1660; in 1689 it gave up denying the rights of Protestant dissenters to licensed worship, then it had seen its representative assemblies, the Convocations of Canterbury and York, silenced in 1717 in the wake of the Bangorian controversy. As one Dissenter writing later in the century saw it: 'It is well known how great a clamour that memorable controversy excited. The Church did not want for able and valiant defenders of the faith; but alas! the fatal blow was given, and CHURCH AUTHORITY, that mighty DAGON, was at Length thrown prostrate on the ground.'[3] In these circumstances, what need was there for Anglican apologists to blow the trumpet in Zion?

By comparison the Gallican Church across the Channel gave up none of these entitlements until after 1787,[4] yet in France anticlericalism – or the attack on 'priestcraft' as contemporaries would have recognised it – was a fundamental part of Enlightenment culture. The leading *philosophes* deprecated its every manifestation as mere intellectual obscurantism designed to shore up the Gallican Church's institutional status by playing upon the susceptibilities of the credulous. The charge was exaggerated and unfair, but it was a brilliant tactic intended to caricature religion and help reduce the Church's influence to a strictly pastoral role predicated on 'usefulness'. The ploy was inimitably articulated by Voltaire, whose best-selling play *La Pucelle*, telling the story of Joan of Arc, deplored the extent to which 'before civilisation and enlightenment, manners were dissolute, religion was fanatical, and superstition massive'.[5] As Justin Champion has shown, Voltaire and other French protagonists of the Church were heavily indebted to English seventeenth-century precedents for their war on priestcraft.[6] They polished and refined its jibes and barbs to deploy against the power and pretensions of their own First Estate, but they were unable to return their matured, modernised antagonism to its country of origin.

The intensification of anticlericalism in France and some other parts of continental Europe after about 1770 had only a muted counterpart in the British Isles. The Church of England and its sisters in Scotland and Ireland were less threatening targets; for a start monks and nuns were non-existent. Yet there assuredly were challenges to Anglican clerical status in the eighteenth century, often as one front in a general assault on the Christian faith by Deists or sceptics. For although the Church of England had resigned much of its institutional independence by about 1720, enough remained for the Hanoverian polity throughout its existence to be classifiable as something resembling a confessional state, where rivals to the established Church had only limited rights (as Scottish Anglicans knew to their cost). Its landed wealth, the bedrock of clerical power, remained impressively intact; all the King's subjects, irrespective of denomination, were required to pay tithes, and the influence of the clergy over the majority of them from cradle to grave in England and Wales was reinforced by the Sunday School movement and the Evangelical revival.[7] The Anglican Church was neither strong enough to ignore anticlerical tirades, nor weak enough not to attract them in the first place. Indeed, the willingness of the clergy to make do with a semi-Erastian establishment (the norm in eighteenth-century Europe) in itself made disaffected Dissenters and 'freethinkers' alert to any tokens of excessive priestly influence. Defenders of the clergy could easily be uncomfortable and angry in response. As one West Country controversialist, himself lashing out wildly, noted in 1750:

> There is scarce a Libel upon Christianity, which has lately been published by Infidels, Jesuits, or Heretics of any Denomination, but what has been stuff'd with Invectives against the established Church . . .[8]

There could be no room for complacency in the face of this multiform challenge and its ill-assorted perpetrators, men who drew on old tropes and invented new ones. And murmurings about minor aspects of Anglican practice could be symptomatic of deeper discontents. As Anthony Ellys, a prebendary of Gloucester, wrote in 1736:

She [the Church of England] cannot but fear what might be, at proper conjunctures, the workings of such Spirits, as *can* take offence at the colour and shape of a decent vestment, or at a posture of the Body expressive of fitting Humility and Reverence in the Worship of God. She has found by experience, that they who have *strained* at things of this sort, have made no scruple to *swallow* her Revenues, and lay waste her sanctuaries.[9]

If anticlericalist strategies and targets alike had a greater intensity in England compared to the other component states of the kingdom, the phenomenon was none the less present in them all, and prone to surface at times of stress in British public life. The Revd George Henry Glasse sounded a recurrent warning for churchmen in the first months of the French Revolution:

That there are, even in this country, busy, restless, malicious adversaries – that they have long been secretly meditating our destruction, and that, of late years, they have attempted it in a more open and decisive manner, is a truth, which we must be blind indeed not to acknowledge.[10]

This intimation was hardly fresh news to the majority of clergy, alert to challenges that had come and gone since the seventeenth-century sectarians had overthrown the Church in the 1640s. They had introduced a spectre of an anarchy which could never be finally excised and thereafter afforded a lingering inspiration to malcontents.[11] Contestation which reawakened uncomfortable memories of the Interregnum recurred at intervals throughout the 'long' eighteenth century: the 'Church in Danger' scares of Queen Anne's reign; the threat to the privileges of the Anglican establishment apparently posed by Walpole's government in the 1730s; the cry for reform of the Thirty Nine Articles and the liturgy inaugurated by Archdeacon Blackburne's *The Confessional* in 1766; and the associated Feathers Tavern petitions to Parliament of 1772–4. Watchfulness was historically ingrained, and we should not underestimate the institutional power of Anglicanism to absorb anticlerical criticism, and to reply in kind. Clergy insisted on the right to speak out, their entitlement, in the words of Cambridge professor John Mainwaring in 1776, with 'great propriety [to] both exercise and declare their judgment on any question of public concern'.[12] And, in defence of their own order, they showed a continuing inventiveness. This chapter will look briefly at that defence in three key areas where it was challenged: their relationship, as ministers of the established Church, with government; the linked issues of Christian doctrine, academic culture and the character of their holy orders; and finally their material standing. The chapter will end with an assessment of their success – or otherwise.

Of course, it took time for the majority of the clergy to adjust to the implications of 1688, and there were those – the Nonjurors – who could not do so. For everyone the confessionalism of the 1680s became a fond memory of what might have been. For the English majority who took the oaths, there was some continuity with the pre-revolutionary situation, in that the new Supreme Governor continued to be a non-Anglican, albeit this time a Calvinist rather than a Catholic, but otherwise they had to come to terms with a polity that was the particular patrimony of the Whigs who, by definition, were on guard against priestly intrusions into public life, the exponents of a political creed which, as Mark Goldie has lately reminded us, 'was born as much in anticlericalism as in constitutionalism'.[13] If half a century after the Revolution, the legal privileges of the English clergy remained broadly in place, their precarious existence could hardly be doubted. They had exchanged a state in which crypto-Catholic politicians were less the problem than overt anticlericalist ones.

What forms did Anglican responses take to the anticlericalist colouring of most administrations down to about 1740? First, it confirmed an overwhelming sense that the Church was 'in Danger' from the refashioned monarchical state itself, with anticlericalism only one of the symptoms for the expression of that antipathy. With the brief exception of Queen Anne's reign, the alliance with the state was anything but a source of strength and comfort. Indeed, Norman Sykes famously referred to the spirit of anticlericalism in the Parliaments of the 1730s as on a scale unparalleled since the Reformation Parliament of exactly two centuries earlier.[14] Swift put the matter well in *The sentiments of a Church of England man*, finding himself unable to see 'how that mighty passion for the church, which some men pretend, can well consist with those indignities, and that contempt they bestow on the persons of the clergy . . .'.[15]

Secondly, it induced a tendency among many priests to overlook the unshakeable attachment of the Stuarts to Roman Catholicism and think the best of Jacobite alternatives to Williamite and early Hanoverian governments which, at intervals, wanted to diminish and confine the role of the Anglican clergy, dilute the Church's confessional purity by such strategies as Occasional Conformity, and police the universities, especially Oxford. For most clergy, such an outlook seldom led to openly treasonable acts or the heroic example of Bishop Francis Atterbury during the Layer Plot of the early 1720s,[16] but it at least bestirred them to defend more vigorously what remained of the Church's statutory privileges against the Whigs and their Nonconformist allies. In such unpropitious circumstances as the period *c.* 1714–40, as Ian Higgins has said, 'defence of the Test [Act of 1673] was almost an act of faith' for High Churchmen and Tories.[17]

Thirdly, it confirmed the willingness of the lower clergy to act in their own defence rather than expect the bishops to defend the spiritual and material privileges of the Church, for the moderate Whig character of the episcopate of the 1690s swiftly became clear (as Gary Bennett pointed out back in the 1960s[18]) to all, and was not much modified or tempered by the long archiepiscopate of John Sharp at York or the limited Tory appointments of Queen Anne's reign.[19]

Anticlericalism as part of party warfare was classically embodied in the Sacheverell affair – this was clerical martyrdom handled with a public relations panache never afterwards equalled by the Tories.[20]

Lastly, and the concomitant of the first three points, was the association of clericalist defences with High Churchmen and the willingness of their Low Church brethren to connive in the anti-sacerdotalist tendencies of 'revolutionary' government. The latter was that crucial – and under-researched – section of the clergy which, as James Bradley has shown, fostered working alliances at local level with Dissenting ministers, never wavered in their support for the Protestant Succession, and accordingly derived the benefits from it in terms of patronage throughout the period.[21] In defending the Church, 'high flyers' were, often explicitly, combatting the enemy within, the 'false brethren' who were the beneficiaries of Whig patronage, but whose concern to protect the Church from further violation appeared minimal.

Relations between State and Church thawed only gradually. Whig politicians had no desire to throw up another Henry Sacheverell, though their insensitive reform plans of the 1710s and 1730s nearly succeeded in doing so. Thereafter the instinctive anticlericalism of some government supporters was contained. *Per contra*, a degree of clericalism in the maintenance of lawful authority in the state became politically acceptable at mid-century, even if the revolutionary partnership between Church and State remained inherently unequal. Cabinet moderates among them – and here, of course, the Duke of Newcastle is the vital architect in *rapprochement*[22] – saw the sense in not offending churchmen if it could safely be avoided (and it usually could), and they were ready to extend the hand of friendship to the majority of disaffected parsons, especially after the fiasco of ministerial support in 1736 for the Mortmain and Quakers Tithe Bills. In the words of Horace Walpole, writing in 1751, ministers believed that the 'High Church party' was:

> so numerous, & warm and ready . . . to lay hold of any occasion to [weaken the] Church of England, would be . . . a dangerous attempt, as productive of greater troubles, than ye good expected from it could compensate.[23]

His elder brother Sir Robert early appreciated the sense of this strategy, and had found first Archbishop Wake and then Bishop Gibson willing partners, until he in time marginalised both by policy choices that showed the enduring vulnerability of the Church to the kind of diminished importance favoured by the 'Old Whigs'. But the last five years of his ministry restored the policy of *quiete non movere* towards the established Church, and anticlericalism became much less programmatic.

The extent to which the recast Church–State alliance sustained by Newcastle and Hardwicke won the blessing of the thousands of disillusioned High

Churchmen the length and breadth of England remains unclear. It may well be the case, as Richard Sharp has contended, that their principles 'were more widely diffused than is often supposed'.[24] Certainly, it is no oxymoron to talk of Whig High Churchmen in George II's reign, such as Bishop Richard Smalbroke of Lichfield, a defender of the spiritual and material privileges of the Church against the claims of Hoadly and the Dissenting Deputies. But we should be careful about overestimating either their numbers or their influence. Only a minority of High Churchmen followed the lead of respected figures like Bishop Thomas Sherlock and gained preferment. But even a man of Sherlock's prominence (he turned down the offer of Canterbury) could do little to protect the Scottish Episcopalians from the state repression initiated in the wake of the '45. The majority of 'high flyers' north of the border were not appeased, and stayed true to their Tory politics – and often their Jacobitism[25] – but at least they could conduct their pastoral ministry in the 1740s and 1750s in the knowledge that the Church of England was more secure than at any point since Queen Anne's death.

Only after George III's accession in 1760 did the Church as a whole cease to fret that the King's government might be the primary source of anticlericalism. The new monarch was, throughout his reign, a devout son of the Church, who never doubted the moral influence for good which the established Church should wield over the vast majority of his subjects in England, Wales and Ireland, and he took his coronation vows of protecting the same with unmitigated seriousness. Clergymen, in their turn, for the most part delighted in their protector, and for the first time in half a century preached obedience to the King *and meant it*, frequently resorting to the polarised imagery and declamations of the Civil Wars, as in the Fast Day Sermons of the 1770s.[26] These usually drew the fire of critics away from the government on to itself, as the ferocious attack on Archbishop Markham of York in 1777 suggests. With the clergy, to quote Professor Bradley, 'clearly the most consistently pro-government body in the nation',[27] to what extent did their conspicuous enjoyment of political power lead critics of Lord North's administration to draw afresh on anticlericalist commonplaces? Quite considerably, I would contend. If clergy were returning to a militant vocabulary in the interests of conformity and obedience, then Dissenters supportive of the American rebels were ready to return the compliment and reawaken the confrontational echoes of the 1640s. The resurgence of English clericalism in the 1770s with High Churchmen in the vanguard stimulated its opposite: taken together, the trend exacerbated confessional distinctions and played a neglected part in causing the deterioration in goodwill between Anglicans and Dissenters to a degree unparalleled since the Sacheverell affair, and one that was perhaps never thereafter healed.[28]

Its traces can be found in a new sense of aggression among Rational Dissenters that would find its classic embodiment in the Unitarian Joseph Priestley's writings in the 1780s, but also in the preaching of other ministers like James Murray and Caleb Evans. By 1780 warnings about High Church, even popish revivals were not uncommon in these quarters.[29] The clergy interpreted attacks on lawfully constituted authority – which, by definition, included their own order – as symptomatic of a world in which moral decline and infidelity were making irreversible progress. For Priestley himself, they had nothing but contempt. George Horne, the leading High Churchman, Oxford don and Dean of Canterbury, commented tersely on learning of Priestley's preference for putting a powder keg to the Church of England: 'the person . . . should be considered (if a gentleman) as a person of unsound mind; if not a gentleman, then as an object of the penal laws of his country . . .'. Horne ably seconded Samuel Horsley's pamphlet campaign of the 1780s against Priestley, but considered it in a sense superfluous, for 'one, who is so wild and dangerous in his politics, must be a counterfeit in his Christianity; who being detected, is thereby sufficiently answered'.[30] Horne was one of the most famous preachers of his age, and seldom failed to remind his congregations in Oxford, Canterbury and elsewhere of the duties of obedience.

The usefulness of the established clergy in the defence of the realm during the long struggle against France which began in 1793 gave them another generation of security; they could preach national loyalty and the moral and religious qualities associated with it, confident of their safety through ministerial protection.[31] Churchmen came to rely on the good offices of politicians who looked to the pulpit for encouragement to Britons not to abandon the struggle against the French Revolutionaries and then Napoleon; to remind their people through the example of France of what they risked losing in terms of social cohesion if an institution like the established Church was overthrown. The sister Churches also appeared in no imminent danger. In Scotland episcopalians had never wavered in their defence of the justice of the Revolutionary War, and had attracted minimal unfavourable notice for it from Kirkmen.[32] In Ireland the Act of Union had confirmed the privileges of the established Church, and thus to some extent offset uncertainties over the Catholic Question; moreover, there was some interest in government circles for the new missionary endeavours among the Papists.[33] The end of the Napoleonic wars, the final breakdown of Pittite politics in the 1820s and the formidable Catholic Association of Daniel O'Connell in Ireland overthrew this Anglican expectation of effective clerical purchase on government. In England and Ireland alike it was a withdrawal of the protection they had come all too easily to rely on from the state, a rude discovery of the priorities within Whig political culture, that lent such shrillness to the complaints of the first Oxford apostles as they faced up to the consequences for the establishment of the dismantling of the Revolution settlement.[34] It was too easy to forget that the comfortably protective pall of the state had only been in place during the second half of the century onwards, and the loss of Anglican privileges in the 1830s signalled a return by the state to the policies of a century earlier.

To an appreciable extent eighteenth-century anticlericalism was the corollary of the intellectual assault on those Christian doctrines which the Church was commissioned to teach, an intrinsic by-product of a desacralising culture of derision,[35] and as such an inseparable dimension of the Enlightenment experience in much of Europe and, arguably, of the accelerating process of secularisation from the mid-century. With these came the forces of social displacement, as the new polite, lay elites of the drawing room and the study discretely denied the established clergy an automatic right to intellectual pre-eminence. These trends were associated with a doctrinal challenge, one that if successful would necessarily reduce the academic credibility of the clergy and break their institutional dominance in contemporary intellectual life – to declericalise it in fact. It may be the case that Anglican clergy were here better placed to defend themselves than their Gallican counterparts, or that the main challenge came earlier (in the first four decades of the century) and was better withstood. Even if that point is conceded, success in saving their places in the academy was due less to the superior talents of its protagonists than to the inherently moderate character of the Church order they defended. For this was a Church that was widely held up to be, as William Frampton proclaimed it in Oxford in 1769, 'in doctrine truly catholic, in government truly apostolical, in worship truly rational, in temper truly moderate'.[36] But putting all one's glory in moderation was not how it struck the predominantly lay critics of clerical ascendancy in academy and parish alike, by no means die-hard Deists. Take, for instance, the figure of Sir Joseph Banks, whom John Gascoigne has urged us to regard as a representative voice of the 'English' establishment, unable to see the Church as having a constructive role in intellectual life and wishing to marginalise it.[37]

Banks encountered the stout opposition of Bishop Samuel Horsley, that great champion of late eighteenth-century Anglicanism from a stable of talent nurtured by Archbishop Thomas Secker. His primacy of 1758–68 was crucial in setting the tone for English Anglicanism for the rest of the century, and in securing its defences. Gone was the good-humoured, intelligent inactivity of Herring and Hutton, in favour of what the new primate's opponents took to be a prickly conservatism, all the more conspicuous in an ex-Dissenter. Secker's discreet but determined pressure on ministers to defend the interests of the established Church at home and in the colonies was seconded by talented younger protégés and often attracted favourable notice from the new King. And he was always careful not to provoke anti-Anglican sentiment by inappropriate policy choices. Thus the Archbishop in the last resort set his face against reviving Convocation as a vehicle for reforming Church discipline, for fear of reviving the party strife of Anne's reign.[38] This did not stop regular and extravagant comparisons with Laud, but Secker's episcopal charges, both at Canterbury and earlier at Oxford, classics of their kind, showed his watchfulness about the issues at stake, and the vindictiveness of the Church's enemies:

The rule which most of our adversaries seem to have set themselves is, to be at all adventures as bitter as they can, and they follow it not only beyond truth, but beyond probability; asserting the very worst things without mercy; imputing the faults, and sometimes imagining faults of all particular persons, to the whole order; and then declaiming against us all promiscuously with such wild vehemence, as, in any case, but ours, they themselves would think in the highest degree cruel and unjust.[39]

Secker's counter-offensive was intended to flush out the enemy, and it did so with a vengeance in Richard Baron's *The Pillars of Priestcraft and Orthodoxy Shaken* (1768), a book which featured in four volumes his representative selections of priestly power over the ages, and in so doing echoed the vituperative anticlericalism of the *philosophes*.[40] Had Secker lived, there might have been a direct riposte. Instead, this vulgarised tract met with a contemptuous silence: the conservative polemicists of the mid-century declined to imitate the Nonjuror Charles Leslie, in his monumental collection of High Church journalism, the *Rehearsal* (published 1700–8), and engage in debate with Grub Street anticlericalists like Baron. Such practice obviously offended the conventions of polite if acerbic learned exchanges between social equals, and instead Secker's protégés made a reply to Blackburne's *Confessional* their priority.

Ecclesiology was at the centre of the eighteenth-century debate about the power of the clergy, part of a wider discourse about authority and the Anglican understanding of the historic ministry based on bishop, priest and deacon was always a point of vulnerability to critics like Baron. This tripartite distinction invited attack as a popish survival, an authoritarian and unscriptural aberration unjustly and unjustifiably accorded legal supremacy everywhere in the British Isles but Scotland. The powers claimed for the priestly office were always the subject of attack, not just by Deists, but by Protestant critics of the Anglican establishment, men eager for further reformation, who tried – in vain – to persuade clergy to reform their office as the best way of disarming critics:

Is it strange, if sagacious Deists ridicule the Christian Priesthood; insult a character and an office so surreptitiously obtained; and treat all their pretended zeal about doctrines and truth as mere form and grimace![41]

At no point, however, were the majority of clergy inclined to agree with this critic and give up 'the out works [of religion] which we know to be untenable'.[42]

What might be called the sacerdotal residue of the Restoration tradition persisted in vigorous life well into the next century, reaching a climax in Queen Anne's reign with a restless Convocation and the whole Sacheverell business, with works like Leslie's *The Case of the Regale and of the Pontificat* (1700) and George Hicks's (another Nonjuror) *Treatise on Christian Priesthood* (1719), marking perhaps the pre-Tractarian high watermark of English sacerdotalism. But this militant clericalism was itself in many ways a defensive reaction. Those who propped up the ramparts of the Church of England, confronted by continuing assault from the likes of Tindal and Collins, were stung to fury by what they saw as the insidious, disingenuous efforts of their adversaries to lambast their Church as a bastion of 'priestcraft' where the clergy, according to Tindal, employed a 'thousand sophistical and knavish methods of defending their opinions',[43] instead of having the honesty to name it as a communion unique in its kind for purity, at once catholic and reformed. Collins's reference in *Priestcraft in Perfection* (1710) to a 'most excellent and pure Church' was deemed nothing but humbug by clergy who read on to find him holding up the twentieth of the Thirty Nine Articles (the power of the Church to decree rites and ceremonies, and acknowledging its authority in matters of controversy) as a forgery, a popish survival, all part of a plan whereby divines too readily promoted the 'Interest of the clergy' disguised as the 'Good of the Church'.[44]

The Anglican defence to such slurs commonly rested on an exhaustive resumé of the Elizabethan historical background to the Articles, and took in previous disputes on the same issue. There was a keen awareness of precedent, and if it was potentially embarrassing to cite William Laud in their cause, clergy were unhesitating in deploying the Archbishop's defence of the self-same Twentieth Article and claiming his disputed authorship as genuine. Defence also took the form of denying the enemy had anything much to say. An unpublished reply of 1707 by Swift to Tindal's *Rights of the Christian Church* (1706) asserted its absence of merits. In addition to 'the most impudent Sophistry and false Logick', Tindal 'hath added a paltry, traditional Cant of Priest-rid and Priest-craft, without Reason or Pretext as he applieth it'.[45] These tactics could be supplemented by arraigning the motives and good faith of the critics. Could anyone seriously believe they had the Church's best interests at heart? 'To imagine that these Pretenders to Reformation are in good earnest, is to expect to gather Grapes of Thorns, or Figs of Thistles,' declaimed one clerical vindicator. If anyone was misguided enough to mistake Collins as a defender of true religion, he went on, let the public be in no doubt about what Collins's wish list would lead to:

a Church much better establish'd upon the Chymerical notions of a few enthusiasts, whose Rights are to be found in the incomparable Works of Dr Tindal, Mr Whiston, Mr Lock, Mr Le Clerc, Mr Bayle, and to name no more, in his own . . .[46]

The clergy made the most of their case, and the further decline of the Church's institutional power in George I's reign seemed to confirm their view of things: what survived for the most part was a muted rather than a triumphalistic sacerdotalism, enough in itself to disarm most potential critics but also an incentive for country Whig extremists like John Trenchard and Thomas Gordon to drive home the attack in publications like *Cato's Letters* and *The Independent Whig*.[47] Most would-be allies were not drawn in to any appreciable extent. They had a sense of how much the institutional power of religion had been confined since the Revolution. Even Collins had, by the early 1720s, toned down his hostility – more, I would argue, for this reason than Robert E. Sullivan's unconvincing suggestion in his book on Toland that Anglicans were cultivating the amity of their putative foes.[48] By the death of George I in 1727, the Whigs had infiltrated the highest offices of the Church of England in such numbers that the process drew the teeth of the attacks on the establishment. Furthermore, the habitual refrain of churchmen, that Deists were blatantly and unfairly exaggerating the true nature of the case, also made a forceful public impact on most shades of Protestant opinion. Clerical insistence that the Church of England was not a powerful, independent agency in the state, nor its priests oppressors, was accepted. As Berkeley noted *à propos* of Collins, wittily turning against him the proto-Gothick terrors he had claimed to find in the Church of England and its servants:

> But, as I drew near, the terror of the appearance vanished; once the castle I found to be only a church, whose steeple with its clock and bell-ropes was mistaken for a tower filled with racks and halters. The terrible giants in black shrunk into a few innocent clergymen.[49]

For all his humorous disclaimers, Berkeley was no more prepared than other clergymen in early eighteenth-century England to relinquish such priestly powers as could be found in the Articles and liturgy, or to abandon the Anglican tradition of restraining every man from interpreting religion solely according to his own lights. Thomas Bray, chief founder of the SPCK, had emphasised the importance of priestly leadership and direction, especially for young people:

> You shall seek the law at his Mouth, that is, you must apply your selves duely to those whom God has Ordained to open and Interpret the Scriptures, for the discovery of his Will, and of what he has Prescribed, as necessary to Salvation.[50]

The SPCK itself was a practical response to perceptions of declining respect for the clergy; Bray hoped that esteem would be increased by other no less practical measures, such as the funding of parochial libraries to ensure churchmen in the remotest parts had access to books that could deepen their learning and intensify their piety.

By contrast, Anglican attempts to suggest that critics of the role and powers of the ordained ministry might have a case received short shrift. Peter Maurice, fellow of Jesus College, Oxford, tried this approach in a sermon of 1718 before the University. He pleaded for changes, especially abolition of the pretended right to priestly absolution, as a means of lifting from 'men's shoulders those heavy Burdens which our Fathers were not able to bear; and which the great Author of Christianity never design'd they should . . .'.[51] The sermon gave such offence that the vice-chancellor instigated judicial proceedings against Maurice for breach of Article Twenty Six (refuting the belief that the validity of the Sacraments depends on the worthiness of those who minister them). He refused to recant, but it was hardly an encouragement for others to return to the theme. As far as most Oxford clerics were concerned, Maurice's High Church contemporary Charles Wheatly had the matter right: ecclesiastical authority was inviolable – even an Act of Parliament could not reach it.[52] That authority was, by definition, bound up with the commissioning of the clergy, the powers they were thereby deemed to have received from the Holy Spirit, and the priestly gift of absolution that was associated with it.

Of course it was left to individual clergy to decide how much emphasis to give their sacerdotal status, with Low Churchmen keen on continuing Reformation uneasy about any suggestion of 'priesthood' within a visible Church. Their unwillingness to entertain a fundamentally different doctrine of ministry from Protestant Dissenters made them suspicious of any claims to special powers of absolution and excommunication.[53] High Church colleagues felt exactly the opposite. It was not a matter that appears to have concerned the majority. Clerical stress on their 'priestly' status was rare, and had little to do with that growth of professionalism which Geoffrey Holmes and Penelope Corfield have noted.[54] For the most part the clergy discountenanced attempts by those outside the establishment to portray their *esprit de corps* as in any way redolent of a powerful, priestly caste. As one recent scholar has emphasised, it was a splendid antidote to the asperities of the Stuart age: 'This is what soothed away anticlericalism and healed the bitter memories of the seventeenth century, torn with religious dissension.'[55] Did these tactics always work? Perhaps we should not rely too much on Horace Walpole, but his suggestion that this approach could be counter-productive may be worth following up:

> I remember some years ago Dr Kaye preached a sermon in York Minster in which he praised the excellence of our ecclesiastical constitution, its purity simplicity etc. so highly that I whispered [to] the Residentiary that sat next to me 'Almost thou persuadest me to be a Presbyterian.'[56]

Even a High Church prelate like Thomas Sherlock was ready to admit the limitations to the clergy's mediatory role in the Christian life. In a sermon preached at the Temple Church, he conceded that even if the various charges levelled against the clergy by the proponents of natural religion were admitted, this would not in itself absolve Christians from acknowledging the tenets of their faith:

> Suppose the People deceived, and the Priests either ignorant or superstitious; what then? Does the Error of one, or the Ignorance of the other destroy the Relation between you and God, and make it reasonable for you to throw off all obedience? The Fear of God will teach you another sort of wisdom.[57]

But if parsons troubled themselves little after ordination with their 'priesthood', they were not disposed to minimise the essential episcopal character of Anglicanism, one that distinguished it from the majority of Protestant Churches, that had been its glory throughout the seventeenth century and that continued to act as a focus of unity for all shades of opinion within its branches. The inherently hierarchical nature of Anglicanism meant there was no getting away completely from sacerdotalism, if only because of the Church's unswerving commitment to episcopacy and the hierarchical underpinnings on which it rested. Churchmen were perhaps fortunate that in England few anticlericalists attacked the Church for retaining bishops; the debate had moved on. Not so in Scotland, where episcopacy was at the heart of a distinctive Anglican identity, or in Ireland, with a confident Presbyterian presence that worked against complacency on the part of the established Church. What does all this say for the sense of the Apostolic Succession within Anglicanism, as stressed by recent historians? Simply, one might argue, that it was just another useful weapon in defence of the Church's constitution, one that usefully – if very generally – acted as a legitimising token in any war of words, but which was not defined in the strictest historical terms by more than a minority of High Churchmen.

Rising clerical numbers on the English magistrates' bench from the 1760s onwards was in one sense a visible denial of sacerdotal distinctiveness, in another an affirmation of the principles of the confessional state. However interpreted, it generated its own forms of tension in clergy–laity relations, and heightened the perception of clerical aggrandisement in the later eighteenth century. Priests in most counties were quick to fill other local government offices, including surveyors of highways, enclosure commissioners and turnpike trustees, and protests were provoked.[58] As other contributors to this volume emphasise, the scale and incidence of these outbursts between about 1760 and 1830 should not be exaggerated. In this context, charges of 'priestcraft' were scarcely relevant and criticism tended to be more loosely focused on clerical magistrates as exacting, and often unfair agents of propertied authority in the countryside at times (as during the French wars) when the majority of the population was suffering sometimes acute material hardships. The clergy scarcely bothered to notice such complaints. A tinge of complacency there might be in this omission, but it also points up the difficulty complainants had in mounting a sustained attack on parson JPs, both in terms of maintaining community interest or deciding the most effective line of invective. And there is evidence to suggest that many parson JPs saw their role on the bench as complementing their pastoral labours. James Ibbetson, for instance, Archdeacon of St Albans and prebendary of Lincoln, preaching in 1778, was also convinced that clerical justices were as well placed as anybody to stand up for the interests of the rural poor, especially necessary with enclosure.[59]

A related flank was of more immediate concern to most clergy: the defence of the Church's material power in the localities – its tithe, in particular – against lay encroachment, especially after about 1750, when new enclosure and tithe commutation turned many parsons into substantial farmers as glebe holdings benefited.[60] It remains important to guard against seeing tithe (certainly in an English context) as necessarily the occasion for the most vituperative manifestations of anticlericalism in the 'long' eighteenth century, and not to overestimate the extent of conflict it generated. Thus, in the Canterbury diocese, tithe disputes decreased over the course of the century.[61] Tithe conflicts were as old as the parochial system, and there were at least two distinct strands to them. The first created tensions within the elite, to the great benefit of the lawyers, as the numerous disputes coming before the courts testify; secondly, and perhaps more significant over the medium term, was the irritation and sometimes anger of the tithe-payers, especially if they were non-Anglicans. Admittedly popular religion had always had a sediment of resentment at the assured if variable income of the beneficed clergy, but it was reaching new levels of intensity for the Church of England by the turn of the nineteenth century, and tithe was often a contributory factor.[62]

Of course, looked at from the parochial level, the privileges of the clergy seemed impressive enough to critics at any point in this period. They resented the opportunities for social control these offered (one habitually utilised by preachers in the 1790s), and sought, concurrently, to reduce the sources of material well-being which, as was claimed, militated against effective pastoral ministry. The legal requirement for folk of every religious persuasion to contribute to the clergy's growing prosperity was much resented. Here is the radical Dissenting minister James Murray:

> Ah ye *priests!* Ye make us pay for all things; ye catch us as soon as we come into the world, and ye never lose sight of us until we return to dust. Our mothers must pay for bearing us, our fathers for having us baptized. When we are married, and when we are buried, ye must be paid.[63]

To spokesmen for the clergy, these payments were merely their legal dues. Who benefited within their order from the enhanced value of tithe was a secondary consideration: what *really* mattered was their symbolic significance in confirming the Church's place in the polity by reminding those outside it of the definite limitations to toleration. Beneficed clerics were uncompromising in their assertion of entitlement throughout the 'long' eighteenth century, and as rising incomes after *c.* 1780 excited fresh clamour, the clergy resorted to conjuring up ferocious images of Jacobin-inspired complaints against them. Such exaggerations did not signally impress fellow members of the propertied public, and the pressure on the clerical order endured. Radical propagandists drew constant attention to financial inequalities within the Church of England, and its clergy found themselves tainted with membership of 'Old Corruption' by the 1820s. If the politicians could gradually curtail the abuses of the patronage state, the pressures on the Church to do likewise were increasingly hard to evade.

The clergy were thus not disposed to sacrifice any shred of their increased income in the face of criticism, but their stubbornness should not be explained on the grounds of self-interest. Until well into the eighteenth century it was the sense of undeserved poverty that aroused clerical apologists to call on an ungrateful nation, for the first time since the Reformation, to pay its clergy what they deserved. William Wake, for instance, while Bishop of Lincoln, had no doubt that disrespect for the priesthood and clerical poverty went together, noting in his Visitation Charge of 1709:

> The debasing of the Clergy, having not only lestened their Authority, but sunk their esteem too, and made their Very Doctrine like the Poor Man's Wisdom, despised, and their Instructions not heard.[64]

His episcopal plea called forth many an echo in parsonages across England whose incumbents faced an agonising choice between fostering good relations with their parishioners by not insisting on every last small tithe legally due, or financially damaging the value of the living for their successors. The Revd John Clendon, Rector of Harlestone in Northamptonshire (1710–39), reluctantly decided to avoid acrimony:

> And severall concessions of this nature I have (I confess) made for the sake of peace; which if I have when I first came, broke, it would have been better by some pounds to me & not made me less uneasy than I am now after such concessions.[65]

The reluctance of the average parishioner to pay up, men like Clendon feared, was fostered by too many members of the elite. In sermons, tracts and doubtless day-to-day pastoral work, clergy probed the guilty consciences of the wealthy laity and the attitudes which were, as it seemed, condemning so many of their brethren to poverty. Some laymen spoke out with them. 'If there is a national sin,' opined one anonymous pamphleteer of 1711, catching the heady mood of

Tory revival during the Harley ministry (1710–14), 'it is that of Sacrilige in the dispossession,' and he went on to recommend the abolition of firstfruits and tenths, and the legal obligation for impropriators to make provision for the clergy from their great tithes.[66] That was never a realistic possibility for Anglicans anywhere. One only has to think of Irish landlord jealousy of clergy entitlements, as when in 1736 the levying of tithe on cattle caused Archbishop Boulter to complain of 'a rage stirred up against the clergy that they thought equalled anything they had seen against the popish priests, in the most dangerous times they remembered'.[67] In England the litigious wrangling between parsons and squires over tithing endured throughout the century, until the French Revolution fortuitously came to the clergy's rescue (here as in other respects) and enabled them to make a convincing case for a tithe truce in the interests of social solidarity. With the fate of the Gallican Church to act as an awful warning, parsons played unashamedly on the fear of levelling principles:

> Once take away the rewards which are due, and have been cheerfully given to the advancement of learning and the cultivation of the minds and manners of men; once deprive them of those advantages which are fairly expected from all laudable exertions; and you will soon see the Church fall into decay: you will hear the services of it literally read in the vulgar tongues of men of the lowest orders of the people, and perhaps your places of worship may be seen appropriated to work-shops, for six days out of the seven! A fine triumph this to the enemies of our Church, who see its prosperity with a jealous eye, and would rejoice in the impending ruin from the removal of its corner stone.[68]

But the enemies of the Church were not to interfere with clerical enjoyment of prosperity for another two generations. Here, as on other vulnerable fronts, the Anglican establishment of the early nineteenth century was bloody but unbowed, by no means having defused resentment at clericalist hegemony in the civil, religious and educational spheres, but at least having justified its persistence so long as alien forces (whether internal or external) troubled the kingdom's stability, especially those blown in by the storms raging on the other side of the Channel. It showed itself sufficiently self-confident not to buckle under assault, with the English and Irish Churches tied closer together than ever by the Act of Union, and the Scottish Episcopalians enjoying greater privileges by the early nineteenth century than they had known for the best part of a century.[69]

By that date the pastoral effectiveness of the Church of England was more evident than it had been for a generation, encouraged both by legislation and by a bench of bishops keen to tighten up the mechanisms of diocesan government and not to relax their pastoral oversight. The Church had always been acutely vulnerable on this ground. One Oxford don had attempted to turn the attack around by arguing that critics of the clergy's pastoral labours had, 'by ill-grounded Invectives against the Constitutions of our Church, and unmerited Slanders of the Body of Her Ministers', been most to blame for lessening their influence,[70] but his efforts were probably unpersuasive to any but his congregation. That was in 1758; fifty years later it was hard to argue with the proposition that perhaps the most effective antidote of all to anticlericalism at parish level was a resident clergyman putting the pastoral needs of his people first; the ideal of John Keble was actually being adumbrated by bishops like Fisher of Salisbury over a decade before the Tractarian movement started. The process also involved a reduction of the burden on curates, those packhorses of the Georgian Church, essential to its functioning and frequently the sole visible representative of the Church on the ground, yet often given little thanks, either by the incumbent or by his parishioners.[71] They might have been expected to act as a source of anticlericalism *within* the established Church, but, as far as the present state of research suggests, their loyalty to the Church held, perhaps in the hope that one day, against the odds, a benefice would be theirs to enjoy.

The Jeremiahs within Anglicanism had never been far away, the cry of '*ubi sunt*'? always sounding somewhere in the eighteenth century. Here was one priestly warning to the Bishop of Chester in 1782:

> The ministerial order sinks daily into deeper contempt. Even the episcopal authority and character have lost much of that esteem and popularity in which they were formerly held.[72]

Yet the Church had defied them and given less ground to its anticlerical critics than its gloomier prognosticators were foretelling in the quarter-century after 1688. The same Bishop of Chester, one of the most talented Anglicans of his generation, Beilby Porteus, used the set-piece occasion of the annual meeting of the Sons of the Clergy in St Paul's Cathedral in 1776 to review favourably the progress of the clergy since the Revolution of 1688. He insisted that they were still 'in general, faithful, diligent, and regular in the discharge of their sacred functions'. While not denying that their profession, like any other, held its unworthy members, for the most part their moral life had withstood the general contagion of the times. They were:

> Contented, humble, modest, patient and laborious, their lives are divided between fulfilling the duties of their profession and struggling with the difficulties of their situation.[73]

Yet the impression persisted that the Church establishment might be riding its luck, a sense that wider social trends were moving against it, not least the soaring numbers attracted to Dissent from the 1780s onwards.[74] But these folk were drawn not because of anticlerical polemic – or despite clerical responses to the same – but because of the vibrant Gospel preaching of the new but orthodox denominations. Although they might have quarrelled with the pulpit commonplaces uttered throughout the Hanoverian period affirming the excellences and moderate character of the Church, it was that very moderation which was allowing them to go elsewhere to worship.

The appeal to moderation was a card the clergy played well against their detractors, and it had a credibility that was difficult to deny, albeit one that was insufficient in the face of the Evangelical revival. One should not forget, however, that for many observers of the ongoing debate, anticlericalist manifestations were reassuringly ritualised, no less so the ripostes to them. As suggested above, there could be an element of shadow-boxing in the debate, where the images of a threatening *sacerdotium* mattered more than the reality to combatants on both sides. The tenacity of the clergy in defending new-found wealth delighted the caricaturists with the image of the fat-bellied 'master-parson' contrasted with the worthy but scraggy curate that one finds, for instance, in the drawings of Robert Dighton (1752–1814). And one should perhaps be wary about seeing good humour and the age-old urge to detect clerical lives at odds with their profession as concealing a more serious if gradual disaffection from the established Churches. In the end other issues in the life of the Anglican Churches counted for more than the status and role of their priests. Anti-Christian tendencies were felt to be widely diffused, but anticlerical ones rather less so. And if religion was under attack, then the clergy might expect to be, and vice versa. 'For,' as one Suffolk parson noted, 'in our spiritual warfare, men judge of the goodness of our cause by the abilities of the defenders of it.'[75]

That could require pastoral persistence despite personal intimidation of the kind experienced by the Vicar of Epworth, Samuel Wesley, father of John and Charles, who was 'ran-tanned' by his parishioners for voting Tory in 1705, and after being briefly imprisoned for debt in Lincoln prison, came home to find three of his cows had been stabbed.[76] Such experiences were, of course, commonplace on a much bigger scale for Church of Ireland clerics. In combat against the detractors of the cloth, they had shown both a truculence that cannot be accounted for exclusively in terms of self-interest and the survival instinct, and abilities which were invariably the equal of their numerous adversaries. So, even if considered as an exercise in stifling the opposition, or as a delaying action, the clerical response to anticlerical manifestations proved surprisingly effective. Only when British governments found internal political pressures for action against the Church irresistible (as they were from the mid-1820s onwards) did the clergy find their defence of the sacerdotal *status quo* of little use. It showed how, in the last analysis, the success of clericalist defences depended on the identity of the enemy: the Church might be capable of withstanding plebeian threats of dispossession but was less successful if the challenges originated from the state itself.

Notes

I am grateful to Grayson Ditchfield, Peter Nockles, Richard Sharp, John Walsh and W.R. Ward for their comments on an earlier version of this essay.

1   For Tory efforts to remedy the Scottish episcopalians, see D. Szechi, 'The Politics of "Persecution": Scots Episcopalian Toleration and the Harley Ministry, 1710–12', in W.J. Sheils (ed.), *Persecution and Toleration*; Studies in Church History xxi, (Oxford, 1984), pp. 275–87.

2   For Swift's view of the issue, see J.C. Beckett, 'Swift as an Ecclesiastical Statesman', in H.A. Cronne, T.W. Moody and D.B. Quinn (eds), *Essays in British and Irish History in Honour of James Edie Todd* (London, 1949), pp. 134–51, at 142–4; Louis A. Landa, *Swift and the Church of Ireland* (Oxford, 1954), p. 51.

3   W. Belsham, *Essays Philosophical and Moral, Historical and Literary* (2 vols, 1799), vol. II, p. 225.

4   Norman Ravitch, *Sword and Mitre: Government and Episcopate in France and England in the Age of Aristocracy* (The Hague/Paris, 1966); Michel Péronnet, *Les Evêques de l'ancienne France, 1515–1790* (2 vols, Paris, 1977); Nigel Aston, *The End of an Elite. The French Bishops and the Coming of the Revolution 1786–1790* (Oxford, 1992).

5   There were as many as sixty editions between 1762 and 1790. Gérard Cholvy, *La religion en France de la fin du xviii siècle à nos jours* (Paris, 1991), p. 6.

6   J. Champion, *The Pillars of Priestcraft Shaken: the Church of England and its Enemies 1660–1730* (Cambridge, 1992).

7   Jonathan Clark, *English Society 1688–1832: Ideology, Social Structure and Political Practice During the Ancien Regime* (Cambridge, 1985); A.D. Gilbert, *Religion and Society in Industrial England: Church, Chapel and Social Change 1740–1914* (London, 1976), p. 133.

8   A Presbyter of the Church of England (Mr Bosswell of Taunton), *Remarks upon a Treatise, intituled Free and Candid Disquisitions Relating to the Church of England, etc. in some Letters to a Worthy Dignitary of the Church of England* (London, 1750), p. 7.

9   Anthony Ellys, *A Plea for the Sacramental Test as best Security for the Church established, and very conductive to the Welfare of the State* (London, 1736), p. 132.

10   George Henry Glasse, *Sermons on Various Subjects* (London, 1798), p. 13, 'The Clerical Character': Titus 2:7 and 2:8.

11   Christopher Hill, 'Freethinking and Libertinism: the legacy of the English Revolution', in Roger D. Lund (ed.), *The Margins of Orthodoxy: Heterodox Writing and Cultural Response 1660–1750* (Cambridge, 1995), pp. 54–70.

12   John Mainwaring, *A Sermon preached before the University of Cambridge . . .* (Cambridge, 1776), p. 1.

13   Mark Goldie, 'Priestcraft and the Birth of Whiggism', in Nicholas Phillipson and Quentin Skinner (eds), *Political Discourse in Early Modern Britain* (Cambridge, 1993), p. 214. See also his 'John Locke and Anglican Royalism', *Political Studies* 31 (1983), pp. 61–85; 'The Roots of True Whiggism 1688–94', *History of Political Thought* I (1980), pp. 195–236.

14   N. Sykes, *Edmund Gibson, Bishop of London, 1669–1748* (Oxford, 1926), p. 149.

15   H. Davies et al. (eds), *The Prose Works of Jonathan Swift* (Oxford, 1939–68), vol. II, p. 8.

16   G.V. Bennett, *The Tory Crisis in Church and State 1688–1730: The Career of Francis Atterbury, Bishop of Rochester* (Oxford, 1975).

17   Ian Higgins, *Swift's Politics: A Study in Disaffection* (Cambridge, 1994), p. 36.

18   G.V. Bennett, 'King William and the Episcopate', in G.V. Bennett and J.D. Walsh (eds), *Essays in Modern English Church History, in memory of Norman Sykes* (1966).

19   A. Tindal Hart, *The Life and Times of John Sharp, Archbishop of York* (London, 1949); G.V. Bennett, 'Robert Harley, the Godolphin Ministry and the bishoprics crisis of 1707', *English Historical Review* 82 (1967), p. 726.

20   Geoffrey Holmes, *The Trial of Doctor Sacheverell* (London, 1973).

21   James E. Bradley, *Religion, Revolution and English Radicalism. Non-conformity in Eighteenth-century Politics and Society* (Cambridge, 1990).

22   Stephen Taylor, 'Church and State in England in the mid-Eighteenth Century: the Newcastle Years 1742–62' (Cambridge, PhD, 1987).

23   Horatio, Lord Walpole, *A letter on a proposed alteration of the 39 Articles* (London, 1863).

24   Richard Sharp, 'New Perspectives on the High Church Tradition: Historical background 1730–1780', in G. Rowell (ed.), *Tradition Renewed: The Oxford Movement Conference Papers* (London, 1986), p. 5.

25   Linda Colley, *In Defiance of Oligarchy. The Tory Party 1715–1760* (Cambridge, 1982), p. 107.

26   Henry P. Ippel, 'British Sermons and the American Revolution', *Journal of Religious History* 12 (1982–3), pp. 191–205, at 197; Paul Langford, 'The English Clergy and the American Revolution', in E. Hellmuth (ed.), *The Transformation of Political Culture* (Oxford, 1990), pp. 275–307; James E. Bradley, 'The Anglican Pulpit, the Social Order, and the Resurgence of Toryism during the American Revolution', *Albion* 21 (1989), pp. 361–88.

27   Ibid., p. 363.

28   J.E. Bradley, *Religion, Revolution and English Radicalism. Non-conformity in Eighteenth-century Politics and Society* (Cambridge, 1990).

29   The subject is well discussed in ibid., 169–72. Professor Bradley notes: 'The local Anglican priest was a symbol of authority and an ever-present reminder of the oppressive national Church and its restrictive laws,' p. 170.

30   William Jones, *Memoirs of the Life, Studies, and Writings of the Rt. Rev. George Horne, D.D., late Lord Bishop of Norwich* (London, 1795), pp. 144–5.

31   Robert Hole, *Pulpits, Politics and Public Order in England 1760–1832* (Cambridge, 1989).

32   Colin Kidd, 'The Kirk, the French Revolution, and the Burden of Scottish Whiggery', in Nigel Aston (ed.), *Religious Change in Europe 1650–1914: Essays for John McManners* (Oxford, 1997), pp. 213–34.

33   David Hempton, *Religion and Political Culture in Britain and Ireland: From the Glorious Revolution to the Decline of Empire* (Cambridge, 1996), pp. 79–83.

34   Owen Chadwick, *The Spirit of the Oxford Movement: Tractarian Essays* (Cambridge, 1990).

35   Most recently, James Byrne, *Glory, Jest and Riddle: Religious Thought in the Enlightenment* (London, 1996).

36   William Frampton LLD, *A Sermon preached before the University of Oxford at St Mary's, on Act Sunday, July 9th 1769* (Oxford, 1769), p. 17.

37   John Gascoigne, *Sir Joseph Banks and the English Enlightenment: Useful Knowledge and Polite Culture* (Cambridge, 1994).

38   Stephen Taylor, 'Whigs, Bishops and America: the politics of Church reform in mid-eighteenth-century England', *Historical Journal* 36 (1993), pp. 331–56.

39   Secker, in B. Porteus and G. Stinton (eds), *Eight Charges, delivered to the Clergy of the Dioceses of Oxford and Canterbury* (London, 1769), p. 5.

40   They were based on the collection made – and in part written – by Thomas Gordon, formerly secretary to Trenchard, and first published in 1752. J.M. Robertson, *History of Freethought* (2 vols, London, 1915), vol. II, note 320.

41   A Christian (Micaiah Towgood), *Serious and Free Thoughts on the Present State of the Church, and of Religion* (4th edn, London, 1774), p. 19.

42   Ibid., p. 44.

43   Matthew Tindal, *Rights of the Church Vindicated against Romish and all other Priests*, quoted in Charles J. Abbey, *The English Church and its Bishops 1700–1800* (2 vols, London, 1887), vol. I, p. 33.

44   Anthony Collins, *Priestcraft in Perfection* (3rd edn, London, 1710), pp. 9, 45 and 46.

45   Herbert Davies et al. (eds), *The Prose Works of Jonathan Swift* (Oxford, 1939–68), ii, p. 72.

46   A Priest of the Church of England, *A Vindication of the Church of England from the Aspersions of a late Libel Intituled, Priestcraft in Perfection* (London, 1710), pp. ii, 1–2, 210–11 and 215.

47   David L. Jacobson (ed.), *The English Libertarian Tradition* (Indianapolis, IN, 1965); Marie P. McMahon, *The Radical Whigs, John Trenchard and Thomas Gordon: Libertarian Loyalists to the New House of Hanover* (Lanham, New York and London, 1990).

48   Robert E. Sullivan, *John Toland and the Deist Controversy. A Study in Adaptations* (Cambridge, MA, 1982), p. 266.

49   Sir Richard Steele, Joseph Addison, et al., *Guardian*, no. 39 (7th edn, London, 1740).

50   Thomas Bray, *A Pastoral Discourse to Young Persons* (1704), unpaginated.

51   Peter Maurice, *The True Causes of the Contempt of Christian Ministers. A Sermon preach'd before the University of Oxford at St Mary's Church, on November 30, 1718*, citing Titus, 2:15, 'Let no man despise thee' (Oxford, 1718), p. 9.

52   Charles Wheatley, *A rational illustration of the Book of Common Prayer* (1880 edn), p. 33.

53   See the rather Hoadlyan offering by William Bowman, Vicar of Dewsbury, *A sermon preach'd at the Visitation held at Wakefield in Yorkshire June 25th 1731* (5th edn, London, 1731), 'The Traditions of the Clergy destructive of Religion. With an Enquiry into the Grounds and Reasons of such Traditions'.

54   Geoffrey Holmes, *Augustan England, Professions, State and Society, 1680–1730* (London, 1982); Penelope Corfield, *Power and the Professions in Britain, 1700–1850* (London, 1995).

55   Peter W. Whitfield, 'Change and Continuity in the Rural Church: Norfolk 1760–1840', (St Andrews, PhD, 1977), p. 103.

56   Walpole to Mason, 1780, *The correspondence of Horace Walpole [. . .] and [. . .] the Rev. W. William Mason*, ed. J. Mitford (London, 1851, 2 vols), vol II, pp. 153–4.

57   Thomas Sherlock, *Discourses preached at the Temple Church* (4 vols, London, 1764), vol. IV, p. 147 (Proverbs 9:10).

58   Paul Langford, *Public Life and the Propertied Englishman 1689–1798* (Oxford, 1991), pp. 411–20 and 30–6.

59   James Ibbetson DD, *A Sermon Preached within the Peculiar of Nassington* (London, 1778), pp. 11, 12, 14, 19 and 20. He also saw hopes from clerical prosperity for a return of 'the ancient hospitality'.

60   E. Evans, *The Contentious Tithe: The Tithe Problem and English Agriculture, 1750–1850* (London, 1976); 'Some Reasons for the Growth of English Rural Anti-Clericalism *c.*1750–*c.*1830', *Past and Present* 66 (1975), pp. 84–109; W.R. Ward, 'The Tithe Question in England in the Early Nineteenth Century', *Journal of Ecclesiastical History* 16 (1965), pp. 67–81; Peter Virgin, *The Church in an Age of Negligence: Ecclesiastical Structures and Problems of Church Reform 1700–1840* (Cambridge, 1989). See generally E. Le Roy Ladurie, *Tithe and Agrarian History* (London, 1982).

61   Jeremy Gregory, 'Archbishop Secker's Speculum for Canterbury, 1758', unpublished paper. Evans himself showed that the Quaker tithe grievance was much exaggerated.

62   For the nasty encounters tithe disputes gave Parsons Cole, Woodforde, Jones of Broxbourne and Skinner, see John A. Phillips, 'The Social Calculus: Deference and Defiance in Later Georgian England', *Albion* 21 (1981), pp. 426–49, at 440–3.

63   James Murray, quoted in Bradley, *Religion, Revolution and English Radicalism*, p. 171.

64   *The Bishop of Lincoln's charge to the clergy of his diocese in his triennial visitation, June the 1st, 1709,* citing Ecclesiastes 9:16 (London, 1710).

65   Quoted in Margaret Forrest, 'John Clendon's Tithe Book', *Northamptonshire Past & Present* 52 (1999), pp. 32–40, at 38.

66   A Lay-Hand, *The Clergyman's Advocate: or an Historical Account of the Ill Treatment of the Church and Clergy, from the Beginning of the Reformation to this Time* (London, 1711), pp. 59, 62 and 65.

67   Boulter to the Earl of Anglesey, 8 June 1736, *Letters*, ii, p. 92, quoted in S.J. Connolly, *Religion, Law and Power. The Making of Protestant Ireland* (Oxford, 1992), p. 191. Swift noted ruefully in 1736, soon after the Irish Commons had passed a resolution against the collection of agistment (tithe due from grazing land): 'As to the church, it is equally the aversion of both kingdoms: you for the quakers' tithes, we for grass, or agistment as the term of art is,' Swift to Ford, 22 June 1736 (*Swift corr.*, V, 351). And see his brilliant satire against principal members of the Irish Commons leading the attack on the Church in 'A Character, Panegyric, and Description of the LEGION CLUB. Written in the Year 1736'.

68   A clergyman of Suffolk, *Remarks on the Temper of the Present Times. Addressed to the Gentlemen, Yeomanry and Common People* (Ipswich, 1792), p. 14.

69   F.C. Mather, 'Church, Parliament and Penal Laws: Some Anglo-Scottish Interactions in the Eighteenth Century', *EHR* 92 (1977), pp. 540–72.

70   George Fothergill DD, *A Sermon preached before the University of Oxford at St Mary's Church, on Friday, February 17, 1758* ('The Violence of Man subservient to the Government of God: Isaiah 62:24) (London, 1758), p. 29.

71   Politeness to the clerical proletariat of Georgian England – the curate – was often denied by tradesmen enjoying their office as churchwarden on a Sunday. One poet noted:

> Will treat all curates with contemptuous air,
> Although the livery of Christ they wear;
> 'Servant to Christ! and what is that to me?
> I keep a servant too, as well as He:'
> Step to the Vestry – view the offic'd Fool,
> You'd swear that there the beast was hard at stool,
> So close he keeps his seat, nor deign to stir,
> When curate comes, nor scarce 'your Servant, Sir' –

> And tho' they are but sweepers of the pews,
>
> The Scullions of the Church, they dare abuse,
>
> And rudely treat their betters, urg'd by pride
>
> As Grooms, tho' Horses' Servants, mount and ride.

E. Lloyd, *The Curate: A Poem* (London, 1766), pp. 16–17.

72   *Free and Apposite Observations on one very evident and indecent cause of the Present Rapid Decline of the Clerical Credit and Character; in a letter addressed to the Right Reverend the Lord Bishop of Chester* (2nd edn, London, 1782), p. 65.

73   Beilby Porteus, *A Sermon preached at the Anniversary Meeting of the Sons of the Clergy, in the Cathedral Church of St Paul on Thursday, May 9, 1776* (2 Kings 4:1) (London, 1776), pp. 13, 15 and 16.

74   W.R. Ward, *Religion and Society in England, 1790–1850* (London, 1972).

75   John Clubb, *Miscellaneous Tracts* (2 vols, Ipswich, 1770), vol. II, p. 15.

76   Charles Brears, *Lincolnshire in the 17th and 18th Centuries* (London, 1940), p. 113.

FURTHER READING

Champion, J., *The Pillars of Priestcraft Shaken: The Church of England and its Enemies, 1660–1730* (Cambridge, 1992).

Clark, J.C.D., *English Society 1660–1832: Ideology, Social Structure and Political Practice during the Ancien Regime* (2nd edn, Cambridge, 2000).

Evans, E., *The Contentious Tithe: The Tithe Problem and English Agriculture, 1750–1850* (London, 1976).

——, 'Some Reasons for the Growth of English Rural Anticlericalism *c*.1750–*c*.1830', *Past & Present* 66 (1975), pp. 84–109.

Goldie, Mark, 'Priestcraft and the Birth of Whiggism' in Nicholas Phillipson and Quentin Skinner (eds), *Political Discourse in Early Modern Britain* (Cambridge, 1993).

7

ROTAVATING THE KAILYARD: RE-IMAGINING THE SCOTTISH 'MEENISTER' IN DISCOURSE AND THE PARISH STATE SINCE 1707

Callum G. Brown

The Sassenach can have an uncomfortable time in the Scottish Highlands in late summer. Non-Highlanders are often beset by the midge – a tiny biting insect that swarms in thousands beside water and under trees, being particularly ravenous for exposed human skin on slightly damp, windless days. Consider the plight of the Revd John Morrison. On 1 March 1711 he was appointed as the first Presbyterian minister to the parish of Gairloch in Wester Ross, where the people of all social ranks at that time, as in much of the Highlands, were strongly episcopalian and resented Lowland Presbyterians 'without the Gaelic'. He reported to his supervising presbytery that within two days of starting to tour the massive parish, he had been assaulted by local men, held prisoner for three days in a cottage full of cattle and dung, and only released by the episcopalian landowner after being told that 'no Presbyterian should be settled in any place where his [the landowner's] influence extended'. Six months later, in September, according to local tradition, matters got much worse. While travelling on the east side of Loch Maree, he was attacked by the inhabitants, who stripped him naked and bound him to a tree by the lochside. There his body suffered the midges until evening, when a woman took pity and released him. The midges accomplished what three days in a cowshed could not: he abandoned his parish, local tradition has it, for several years.[1]

Anticlericalism has been an alien concept in late modern Scotland. As a term, it is entirely absent from Scottish historiography of the eighteenth, nineteenth and twentieth centuries. None of the standard ecclesiastical histories of Scotland contains index entries for anticlericalism, and the theme of popular or civil hostility to clergy *per se* seems entirely unknown.[2] In this context, the tale of the minister and the midge has significance on two counts. First, it was symbolic of early modern Scotland, when episcopalians and Presbyterians were struggling for control of the Scottish Church; the latter had won in the 1690 settlement, but with the Highlands only being fully presbyterianised during the course of the eighteenth century, the midge story is emblematic of a disappearing period in

Scottish history. Secondly, it was significant because it was told in an 1885 tourist guide to the Highlands, when such stories were not only historical curios, but when the Presbyterian minister was being widely depicted as a hapless victim. The vision of the minister as victim had become a very important ingredient in Scottish popular culture in the nineteenth century, especially in the unjustifiably maligned 'Kailyard' novels of the 1880s and 1890s. This chapter explores the reasons why Presbyterian Scotland, unlike England, France or indeed most of Europe, failed to develop or sustain any significant notion of anticlericalism after 1700. It is divided into two parts. In the first, the structural framework of the life of the Presbyterian minister is examined to show how he was a vulnerable figure in the constitution of Scottish civil life. In the second part, discourses on the minister will be examined to show how the clergyman was depicted in sympathetic terms in Scottish culture.

THE MINISTER AND THE PARISH STATE

The parish was critical to civil order and identity in Scotland between the Reformation and the late eighteenth century. The country was predominantly rural, relatively economically backward in West European terms, lacking a powerful central state, and with mountain, moor and over seven hundred islands, it was bedevilled by poor communications and intense localism. In such circumstances there was a reliance placed on the established Church of Scotland to provide stability and uniformity, and this it did by being powerful locally, not centrally. With rapid agricultural improvement setting in from the early eighteenth century, and industrialisation and urbanisation befalling its central zone with even greater rapidity after 1770, the parish state retained significance as the backbone of the nation, with the minister as its key civil figure.

The parish state was constituted in civil and ecclesiastical law. The governing institution in each parish was the board of heritors, composed of the landowners; as a statutory body supervised by the Court of Session in Edinburgh, the board was required to provide a church of set proportions, a manse, parish school and glebe, and was required to ensure arrangements for the payment of the minister, schoolmaster and beadle. A second body was the kirk session, composed of the minister as chair (or moderator) and lay elders (usually farmers and larger tradesmen), which held responsibility for imposing Church discipline on the people and dealt with offences that were considered both religious and civil (ranging from fornication, adultery and witchcraft to assault, infanticide and even, on occasion, murder).[3] By involving the local elites in all levels of civil governance of the Church, the distinction between the religious and the secular was blurred to an extraordinary extent.

The position of the minister in this system was both central and vulnerable. He was a critical figure in that he was responsible for delivering a religious service, which was fairly rigorously interpreted as being 'sermon and superintendence': a Sabbath sermon, and teaching and testing of parishioners' knowledge of the catechism. The sermon was and remains the acid test of the Presbyterian minister; to fill a pulpit vacancy, it is still the custom today to invite applicants to preach on separate Sundays to the congregation, in order that he (and, since the late 1960s, also she) may be judged by the worshippers and appointment board.[4] Failure to provide a sermon – most often by being absent, though occasionally for want of speaking in the congregation's language – was ground for legal action to discipline or remove a minister.[5] As catechising declined in the late eighteenth and early nineteenth centuries, it was the sermon as a performance by which the minister was being increasingly judged. There was a sense of common ownership of the kirk, and this meant that the minister was vulnerable because he was viewed in popular culture as a figure subject to constant performance indicators assessed by the parishioners.

The minister's relationship to his parishioners was not, however, confined to religious provisioning. For his livelihood he depended on his relationship to the board of heritors. Church taxes were the main source of income, of which the principal one was the teinds. These were heritable property, granting the right to collect a tax on the rateable value of productive land and fisheries – including sea catches landed. The teind-holder had the right to collect the tax in cash or kind – usually kind, mostly barley, oats or fish, but also butter, wool and other commodities. The bulk was collectable at harvest time. The teind-holder was obliged to pass a proportion of the teinds to the board of heritors, to be paid to the minister. In practice, the minister tended to go straight to the fields and agree with the farmers what proportion of the harvest was to be his. As heritable property, the teinds could be bought, sold and bequeathed, and were generally held by large landowners – often with no property actually in the parish. This meant that the Church was dependent on a privately owned tax.

This made the minister potentially very vulnerable. He was vulnerable over the size of the teinds, over the complex way they were calculated and 'augmented' (that is, increased), and over the state of the relationship between himself and the board of heritors and between the board of heritors and the teind-holder. While tithes in England were calculated as a proportion of produce, teinds were calculated as a proportion of the rateable value of agricultural land set against current prices of the produce. This also made ministers vulnerable; after the poor harvests of 1799–1800, clergy and their families were, according to Alexander Carlyle, faced with ruin, and only a change in the method of calculation saved them.[6] From the eighteenth to the mid-twentieth century, parish ministers all over Scotland were involved in often very lengthy negotiations with these parties for increases in teinds and improvements to manse, church and glebe.[7] Ministers were constantly in correspondence with solicitors and clerks to heritors' boards, and the church pulpit was the medium for broadcasting official notices regarding board meetings, legal arrangements and formal notification of negotiations over such things as the state of the manse toilet.[8] The system also had the potential to create conflict with ordinary parishioners. At harvest time ministers met tenant farmers in their fields to negotiate which stooks of corn were bound for the manse; expansion of the glebe could cause consternation, and service dues in the form of collecting the minister's own harvest from the glebe or thatching the manse could be causes of friction. With further taxes payable to minister, kirk session and church beadle in the form of dues for pew renting, baptisms, marriage and funerals (notably the renting of mortcloths), the parish state was a complex financial institution in which civil and ecclesiastical law were indistinguishable.

This system seemed, on the face of it, capable of arousing considerable antipathy towards the minister of a parish church. Church taxes did cause protest. The major object of protest was the system of pew rents which spread from urban churches after 1720 to virtually all parish churches – as well as to most Dissenting churches. The system caused protest at its initiation when traditional rights to 'sit under a minister' on a stool or chair were withdrawn as heritors obtained permission from civil courts for the churches to be divided up among them in proportion to their landholdings in the parish, and for fixed pews to be installed and annual rents exacted for parishioners to sit in them. This led to much protest, leading in some extreme cases to years or even decades of conflict in the parish kirk. Parishioners objected by squatting in churches, instituting pew rent strikes, and eventually deserting to Dissent; heritors retaliated by drafting in their land stewards and ground officers as 'bouncers' at Sunday worship, and on occasion by even closing the church off.[9] By contrast, protest about teinds – surprisingly – was almost negligible. While there were national campaigns against pew rents,[10] there were no organised campaigns at regional or national level against teinds. The only well-documented case we have is from Eyemouth in the south-east of Scotland, where the fish-teind of one-tenth of catches was never fully exacted by the minister in the 1820s and 1830s because of the hatred of the tax, the difficulty in collecting it, and its baneful impact on churchgoing. In the 1850s this led on to major local controversy with rioting by fishermen, culminating in all twenty-eight Eyemouth skippers being summoned to court for non-payment. A boycott of Eyemouth port by fishing boats ensued, ending only in 1863 with the fish-teind being redeemed by a capital payment to the Church (and the fishermen themselves taking over operation of the teind to pay off the costs).[11] This case certainly showed how the minister could become alienated from his flock and the object of very intense anticlerical feeling. Unfortunately, this is the only case that has been discovered and researched. Others may exist, but even so it is quite clear that there was no general, organised hostility to clergy because of the teind system.[12]

The conundrum, given the obvious potential for hostility to this system of
Church taxation, is how the Scottish minister avoided becoming the object of
widespread anticlericalism. The key is how the minister came to be seen not as
the *culprit* of the system, but as the primary *victim*. And the cause of this was yet
another part of the ecclesiastical system – patronage, the issue which dominated
ecclesiastical politics and much of Scottish popular culture between the late
seventeenth and late nineteenth centuries.

The patronage system in the Church of Scotland was the most contentious
issue of Scottish government and religion between 1690 and 1874. The right to
select the minister of a parish church in Scotland was governed by the system of
patronage, which – like teind-holding – was a piece of heritable property that
could be bought, sold or bequeathed. The patron was a layperson; in around
one-fifth of Scottish parishes it was the Crown, but in the others it was a variety
of individuals (usually landowners or wealthy merchants) or institutions (like town
councils or universities). Patronage was associated with episcopacy, and those
who regarded themselves as 'true Presbyterians' believed in popular election,
where ministers were selected by the congregation (or male members of it); they
adhered to the injunction in the First Book of Discipline of 1560: 'It appertaineth
to the people and to every several congregation to elect their minister.' At the
1690 Presbyterian settlement, the system adopted was a compromise – ministers
were selected by elders and landowners. But in 1712 the Westminster Parliament
restored the right of patronage, and from then until 1874, when it was repealed,
clergy could be selected by patrons.

From the 1720s the types of minister selected by patrons started to differ
significantly from that which congregations wished to have. The ministers
favoured by patrons tended to be less harsh in their Calvinist beliefs, less
puritanical and didactic in their preaching, and more urbane and comfortable in
the new social setting the large landowners created. They became known for
drinking, gaming, dancing and indulging in sport. The speaking of Scots was
disfavoured by them as with their patrons, and a more Anglicised approach in
language and social pretension was in vogue. From the 1750s such ministers
were classified as members of the Moderate Party, while the others were
classified as the Evangelical or Popular Party. Evangelical clergy opposed
patronage on theological grounds because 'it restricted the likelihood of faithful
ministers of the gospel being appointed who would preach for the salvation of
their parishioners' souls'.[13] By the 1740s congregations were also opposing
patrons' choice of ministers, protesting both against the man chosen and against
the system which denied them choice. Legal methods would be pursued in both
Church and civil courts to oppose the selection, and the upshot was invariably
that the actual presentation of the minister was opposed by parishioners barring
entry to the kirk on the induction day. Occasionally troops were called, and there
were minor skirmishes and court cases for mobbing and rioting.[14] By the third

quarter of the eighteenth century such disputed patronage cases were very common – perhaps ten per year. By the 1790s there was probably no parish in the whole of Scotland (excluding the Highlands) where there had not been a disputed presentation – and sometimes there had been two or three in a single parish. In those decades parish disputes over the choice of clergy were ingrained in Scottish popular culture as a major feature of the life of nearly all the 984 parishes of Scotland. When they failed to stop a presentation taking place, opponents seceded to form a Dissenting Church – usually the Secession Church or the Relief Church.

Such disputes erupted with renewed vigour between 1833 and 1843, when the Evangelical Party controlled the General Assembly of the Church for the first time. With the government refusing to overturn the patronage system, and with the civil courts backing the rights of patrons, in May 1843 most Evangelicals were driven to secede from the Church of Scotland to form the Free Church. Thus by 1850 the Church of Scotland had lost at least 60 per cent of the Presbyterian clergy and more than three-quarters of the people of Scotland, almost entirely due to the patronage system.

Presbyterian ministers were hero-victims in Scotland. Very large numbers had given up secure stipends in the Church of Scotland for the unknown liberality of Dissenting congregations. When clergy left, they took many if not most of their people with them. Scottish ecclesiastical life became in the eighteenth and nineteenth centuries a politics of the popular. Essentially the Scottish minister had to make a choice at some point in his career between being with the congregation or with the patron, and by 1850 the majority of clergy had sided with the forces of congregational democracy. And they had done so overwhelmingly on the basis of a decision against the patronage system. As a result the very structure of the Scottish ecclesiastical system after 1712 obviated the development of anticlericalism in Scotland.

THE MINISTER IN SCOTTISH MYTHOLOGY

To avoid anticlericalism, the Presbyterian minister needed a benign image in popular culture. While he himself could have an influential role in his own social construction, discourses on the minister in modern Scotland should not be regarded as manufactured from the pulpit. As Foucault observed, the authorship of discourses is less the critical issue than the manner of their existence, circulation and appropriation.[15] In this respect the treatises of the clergy reflected, rather than invented, the discourse on the Scottish minister. And the primary medium for disseminating the discourse was the narrative of the minister's life – the biography, autobiography, published diary and fictional novel.

The study of narrative structures is a growing and productive area of historical research. It reveals how societies imagine their own configurations, how they typecast and stereotype the individuals in social dramas. Two historians of narrative have written that scholars of narrative are showing that 'stories guide action; that people construct identities (however multiple and changing) by locating themselves or being located within a repertoire of emplotted stories; that "experience" is constituted through narratives . . . and that people are guided to act in certain ways, and not others, on the basis of the projections, expectations, and memories derived from a multiple but ultimately limited repertoire of available social, public and cultural narratives'.[16] As Patrick Joyce has persuasively argued, the melodrama was a narrative form which began as 'populist' in the early decades of the nineteenth century, but which was adopted for the mass-circulation 'improving' magazines of the 1840s, 1850s and 1860s. In these, an audience already accustomed to the melodramatic form were invited to identify with the virtues of social improvement – teetotalism, churchianity, hard work, thrift, rational recreation, imperial patriotism, and so on – through the narrative tales of individual lives and social commentaries. Stories of heroes and heroines overcoming insuperable odds – poverty, crime, drunken husbands – were allegories of social redistribution and social reconciliation, a 'probing of the moral drama of an unequal society'.[17] This melodramatic literature of 'improvement' laid out the burning questions of moral relations in a society of manifest inequalities of income, wealth, opportunity and gender. It turned over these questions, investigated them, and postulated through narrative example (supported by straight exhortation) the triumph of morality over inequality. Judith Walkowitz has shown the centrality of the melodrama for sexual narratives in late Victorian London, narratives which in newspapers, court cases, learned journals and elsewhere imagined women almost exclusively as victims.[18]

The structure of this melodramatic form was widely adaptable, and was well known in religious improving literature in the nineteenth and twentieth centuries. Indeed much of the material in the stories of the popular as well as religious magazines of the Victorian period was founded on implicit Christian interpretations of 'improvement' and of life 'dramas' as obstacles to that improvement. In essence, moral 'improvement' became synonymous with Christian 'salvation', and the journey – often melodramatic – to that state of grace acquired exemplars. These exemplars were used to express the nature of male and female irreligion and religiosity, and the means of progress from the first condition to the second. Female religiosity acquired diverse types of exemplar – women from many backgrounds, historical and contemporary, fictional and real. Male religiosity, on the other hand, acquired the minister as the key paradigm in Scotland. It was the minister's tale that told how men should behave.

The process started in the eighteenth century with the establishment of the narrative of the clerical hero-victim of Presbyterian Dissent. The clergy of the Secession and Relief Churches, formed in 1733 and 1756 respectively, became mythologically established as the successors to the Covenanters of the seventeenth century who had resisted the Catholic and episcopal intrusions of Charles II and James VII.[19] The Seceders established a very thorough 'victim culture' from the 1730s onwards. Their puritan millenarianism was especially evident in the culture of the fast days – the day of 'fast and humiliation' which preceded the day of communion, in which manifestos were issued decrying their own 'conformity to the world in sinful customs, particularly in promiscuous dancings; levity of spirit, and uncleanness of various kinds; injustices in matters of trade; lying, backbiting, and covetousness . . . and the late unfavourable harvest . . . with the many other spiritual strokes we are lying under – while there is no suitable viewing of the Lord's hand in these strokes'.[20] With many suffering the ravages of agricultural improvement, the Seceders felt themselves estranged from the elite positions of the Church of Scotland's leadership in the eighteenth century. They were the object of much criticism from the Church of Scotland, their ministers charged with being ill-educated rustics who had no right to preach the Gospel, and – as one critic pointed out in evidence – having no doctors of divinity among their number; in response, one Secession minister openly acknowledged: 'their ministers have been too poor to purchase the title and too illiterate to deserve it'.[21] In such circumstances ecclesiastical histories of the Dissenting Churches well into the nineteenth century portrayed the clergy as upholders of principle, but victims of the system.[22]

Ministers and congregations were leaving the Church of Scotland with sustained regularity by the last quarter of the eighteenth century. Patronage was usually the trigger, but by then parish ministers had a whole catalogue of complaints with patrons and heritors. This was nowhere more apparent than in the unique document of late eighteenth-century Scottish life, *The Statistical Account*, published in over twenty volumes between 1790 and 1798. The minister of each of Scotland's more than nine hundred parishes gave accounts of the economic, social, religious and climatic life of their parish, and many took the opportunity to describe their own position as luckless clerics. They complained of parsimonious heritors leaving their manses and churches in dilapidated condition; as one minister from Argyllshire wrote: 'with us of the church of Scotland, many of our country kirks are such dark, damp and dirty hovels, as chill and repress every sentiment of devotion'.[23] The civil support system for the state Church was evidently failing, and parish ministers were increasingly siding – and being perceived as siding – with congregations in fights with heritors for church improvements, extensions and reduced pew rent charges.[24] The effect of this was to extend the perception of the clerical 'victim' from Dissenters to all Presbyterian ministers.

As a result the minister became one of the first 'hero-victims' of the Scottish novel. This was perceptible with the rise of the popular novel in Scotland from the 1810s, and from the 1840s of the popular magazine. The Scottish minister became a major focus of fictional narratives in which he started to emerge as an endearing figure of Scottish history and culture. Extremely influential in this was John Galt's novel *Annals of the Parish*, published in 1821, which takes the form of the diary of a minister of an Ayrshire parish between 1760 and 1810. In the very first chapter the minister, the Revd Micah Balwhidder, recounts how he was a selection of the patron, and 'intruded' into the pulpit against the wishes of the congregation. From the very outset, then, the reader is invited to sympathise with the minister's plight:

> It was a great affair; for I was put in by the patron, and the people knew nothing whatsoever of me, and their hearts were stirred into strife on the occasion, and they did all that lay within the compass of their power to keep me out, insomuch, that there was obliged to be a guard of soldiers to protect the presbytery; and it was a thing that made my heart grieve when I heard the drum beating and the fife playing as we were going to the kirk. The people were really mad and vicious, and flung dirt upon us as we passed, and reviled us all, and held out the finger of scorn at me; but I endured it with a resigned spirit, compassionating their wilfulness and blindness.[25]

By describing this violent induction, Galt draws on the well-known history of patronage presentations over the preceding hundred years – violent occasions familiar in nearly every parish of the country. With this resonance to Scotland's common cultural heritage, Galt cultivates through his first-person narrative a sympathy for not just a minister who sided with the congregation, but one who was intruded against its wishes. Galt was not shifting public sympathy here: he was reflecting it. Whether a clergyman of popular choice or not, the Scottish Presbyterian minister by the early nineteenth century was being perceived as a victim of the ecclesiastical system.

In the 1830s and 1840s the place of the minister in the imagining of religion rose to a new prominence. In those decades new forms of literature appeared in which the lives of 'model ministers' became widely disseminated in Scottish society. There were three main forms of new literature: the cheap, popular 'improving' magazine, the religious tract and tract-magazine, and the book-length biography (which included the formats of autobiography and memoir). What shaped the incorporation of the clergyman's life within each of these was the evangelical narrative. This was a formulaic structure within which the narrative of a person's life was located.

Hundreds if not thousands of ministerial biographies appeared in Scotland in the nineteenth and early twentieth centuries, mostly between the 1840s and the 1920s.[26] The subjects almost always began their lives in godly and dignified poverty, invariably in rural or Highland cottages. One biographer said of his subject:

It was no slight advantage to the future minister that his education was thus begun at a common school and in the companionship of the children of the poor. Indeed it is one of the secrets of the power which the Scottish clergy exercise among their flocks that the great majority of them have enjoyed a like advantage. No subsequent part of their training, at grammar school, college or [divinity] hall, is more valuable than that which makes them feel their oneness with the class that generally forms the major portion of Scottish congregations. They can preach the gospel to the poor all the better that they know them as only schoolboys learn to know each other.[27]

They were invariably portrayed as good boys: 'While Robert Hood bore a good character outside his home, he also bore a good character inside it. It was the testimony of his mother than he never once said no.'[28] The struggle through university and divinity school, and the part-time jobs taken as home missionaries are common themes.[29] But the issues of conversion and continual rebirth are often the constant themes on which the biographies hang. They become the dramas – the personal melodramas, if you like – upon which the life-stories hinge in these volumes. For some it is a process, beginning, as with Robert Hood, after a period of Sabbath School attendance:

> The young lad began now to be seriously concerned about religious things, and especially about the salvation of his own soul. He used to tell in after days that when he was a boy he sometimes went with his father to see an old bed-ridden man in Green Street, Calton, and that this made a deep impression upon his mind. The sight of the good old man as he lay in bed, and the patience which he exhibited under suffering, had a greater influence upon his mind than all his subsequent studies. It was, however, at the age of seventeen that his conversion really took place. His conversion was not a sudden thing, but a gradual growing into the light. Some conversions come like a flash of lightning across a midnight sky, while others come like the sunrise. Robert Hood's conversion came like the sunrise. He had always been good, with his face towards the sun-rising, and at last the blessed beams of the Sun of Righteousness arose upon his soul.[30]

However, there were some ministers who resisted the excesses of evangelical conversionism. John Watson recalled that his three months as assistant minister at Barclay Free Church in Edinburgh in 1874, shortly after it had been the stage for the inaugural fame of the American revivalists Moody and Sankey, were the most miserable of his whole life:

> I was reserved for the work of visiting elderly ladies and trying to bring young men into Church who did not attend. On rare occasions I was allowed to

enter the pulpit. The crisis in my life came on a Friday. I was told my chief was suffering from a sore throat, and that I should have to prepare to preach the following Sunday. What should I do? I had usually consumed two weeks in preparing a sermon from Hodge. As I had recently lost my mother the miracle of Nain appealed to me, and I preached about a man's relation to his mother. I know it was real, for I felt what I said. But my chief told me he had had a bad report of me – I did not preach conversion.[31]

This was unusually candid. The evangelical themes of temptation, resistance and sustaining the state of grace invariably dominated. Of Robert Hood, a minister of the Evangelical Union, his biographer wrote: 'When he would be on his way to visit among the closes and alleys on a fine summer evening, he would see hundreds of young people like himself betaking themselves for a walk in the outskirts of the city. On such occasions the devil would say to him, "Why can't you go and have a walk too?" But he always told the devil to get behind him, saying, "No; Christ's work is first."'[32] The biographer of a leading minister in the Free Presbyterian Church, Donald Macfarlane, wrote of him that: 'He was not ignorant of Satan's devices, and by being sifted as wheat he became a succourer of many who passed through fiery temptations.'[33] Macfarlane's diary dwells on three years of temptation from atheism after he left divinity college, 'a temptation from the evil one. It left me as weak as a feather before the tempest. It was only gradually I got rid of it.'[34] These biographies tend to give full exposure to weakness and – in diary form – to the self-remonstrance of the minister. Norman Macleod of the Church of Scotland wrote in his journal in 1837: 'I have got a most irritable temper. I have got a loose way of talking and of using slang words, most unbecoming my profession.'[35]

The grievances of ministers with their paymasters feature a lot. At Paisley High Kirk one minister left very embittered at not being paid £80 he was due in 'hard cash'. His published letters state in 1861: 'The loss of it won't ruin me, but it will embitter me. I have no hesitation in saying to you that I have done far more for the High Kirk than it has done for me.'[36] Struggles with heritors over parsimony feature strongly in these biographies. The demands of the office – especially in towns – could be onerous for what was perceived to be little pay. Thomas Chalmers wrote on coming to Glasgow in the 1810s:

The peculiarity which bears hardest upon me is the incessant demand they have upon all occasions for the personal attendance of the ministers. They must have four to every funeral, or they do not think it has been genteelly gone through. They must have one or more to all the committees of all the societies. They must fall in at every procession. They must attend examinations innumerable, and eat of the dinners consequent upon these examinations. They have a niche assigned them in almost every public doing, and that niche must be filled up by them . . . I long to establish it as a doctrine that the life of a town minister should be what the life of a country minister might be, that is, a life of intellectual leisure . . .[37]

The conditions of service in town pulpits were often criticised by ministers. Norman Macleod turned down the opportunity of a Glasgow pulpit because 'the system of competition in Scotland, both for pulpits and for churches, and against the dissenters' led to a chasing after popularity not just to fill the pews but to fill them with high-paying pew-renters, resulting in 'effort, and froth, and turgidity, and an attempt after grand generalisations are required to gain popularity'.[38] The loss of Church members through schism is tackled in most biographies very diplomatically; the Revd Fergus Ferguson of the Evangelical Union lost large sections of his congregation twice in two years, and his biographer notes that 'the pastor acted in the kindest way, as they left and implored the divine blessing on their enterprise'.[39] One remarkable and popular biography of 1877, *The Life of a Scottish Probationer*, was actually about a man who failed, a 'stickit minister' who never received 'a call' to a congregation, but instead wrote poems and ended his life as an invalid. 'It would be unjust to [Thomas] Davidson,' wrote his biographer, 'to represent him as having been a professional failure. The fact that he did not receive a call is neither to be attributed to his lack of power as a preacher, nor altogether to lack of ability, on the part of the congregations to which he preached, to discover and appreciate his gifts.'[40] The Presbyterian system of congregational democracy created noble victims.

The Scottish clergyman's vulnerability was perceived as increasing after the 1860s, when a surfeit of clergy emerged from the Evangelical revivals of the period. Congregations were willing to stand up to their ministers and elders if need arose, but equally were sensible of the loyalty due to those who were now so dependent on congregational acceptance and liberality. Equally, greater educational opportunity extended doctrinal and theological knowledge deep into the laity, and clergy no longer had a monopoly over ecclesiastical wisdom. In the absence of apostolic succession, the ministers of both Establishment and Dissent in Scotland shared many of the job insecurities of their congregations during the rise of capitalist individualism. The lives of the ministers mirrored the destiny of the country's people. Father-and-son ministers became famous for the sense of continuity in a country so ravaged by clearance, industrialisation and urban slums. The great dynasty of the Macleods, stretching through at least five ministers over four generations as they shifted from eighteenth-century Highland manses to urban Glasgow congregations of the nineteenth and twentieth centuries, symbolised the same great migrations and social changes of their hearers, making their chain of biographies – the one about the other – immensely popular.[41] Theirs was a moral tale of how ultimate worth was established in the manner of the attempt, not in the fact of achievement. Each biography becomes a personal melodrama against temptation and congregational fickleness. This made them figures for emulation, whether in success or failure – no more apparent than in the remarkable number of clergy (let alone laity) of the period 1850–1920 who were baptised with Christian names taken from the first names and surnames of famous ministers – especially with the names 'Thomas Chalmers'.

The minister rose in the later nineteenth century to be a key figure of the Scottish novel – especially of the so-called 'Kailyard' school of Scottish romantic stories of the late Victorian and Edwardian periods, notably in the novels of J.M. Barrie, S.R. Crockett and Ian Maclaren. These have been much condemned by Scottish historians and literary critics of the late twentieth century as part of the 'Brigadoon'-style romantic falsification of Scottish national heritage and culture. Gillian Shepherd is of the opinion that 'it was commercialism that perverted any sense of moral purpose that the kailyarders might have had'. She condemns them for formula-writing for English and American markets which 'increased the distance between observers and observed'. 'The result', she concludes, 'was that Barrie, Crockett, and Maclaren ceased to write as Scots within a Scottish nation,' and instead wrote 'with increasing detachment and cruelty and decreasing plausibility' in the form of 'ridicule', 'sadism' and 'downright falsity' about Scots in Scottish communities.[42]

This analysis is not merely harsh, but ill-founded. Modern Scottish critics take exception with the Kailyard writers for promoting a parochialism that mocked Scottish people and culture. But this is to completely misunderstand these novels. They were essentially about Presbyterianism in Scottish society, and their humorous tales were very well-informed and tender explorations of the rhythms of puritan culture in industrialising small towns. Such criticism fails to appreciate this, and fails to engage with the Scottish Presbyterian heritage of conflict which informs most of these novels, and specifically fails to perceive the central function of the minister in these tales. The Kailyard authors had strong links to the Churches. Maclaren (real name Revd John Watson) was actually a Presbyterian minister (latterly in Liverpool), and, like Barrie, was intensely interested in the nature of the Church in Scottish life in the early twentieth century. They were deeply concerned with issues of secularisation and ministers as victims of poverty, heritors and fickle congregations, and were far from frivolous in their view of Presbyterianism's place in Scottish culture.[43] Their novels were also, as Ian Maclaren pointed out, located in the emotional world of the minister and death-bed scenes: 'We ministers rarely see the brighter side of life. We are tolerated at weddings I admit; we are more at home at funerals. People do not ask a minister to share family festivities. He most often hears painful disclosures, and meets death from day to day.'[44] Their novels were rooted in this experience.

Indeed, many of the Kailyard novels are fictionalised versions of the ministerial biography, encompassing the same themes and dramatic structures.

Crockett's *The Stickit Minister and Some Common Men*, published in 1893, was the first to use the term 'kailyard',[45] and was made up of twenty-four short stories – almost all of them about Presbyterian ministers – set in the Galloway hills of the Scottish south-west. The title of the book is a hint to the theme: ministers are 'common men' in Scottish culture, men of humble origins, often from poor families, who have struggled to pay their son's way through parish school and university. The minister is the ultimate 'lad o' pairts', the gifted child who, in the mythology of Scottish intellectuals from the late nineteenth century, could work his way through the 'democratic' educational system of Scotland to success. Yet the stories are ones of struggle and – for some – indefinite half-success in their careers. Such was the fate of the 'stickit minister', a university graduate who had trained for the ministry, spent time as a schoolmaster or dominie, became a licentiate but was never inducted as a minister as he couldn't find a charge. The stories are constructed around the lives of student and graduate ministers: their studies, their examinations and their experience as ministers. The congregational experiences of the ministers are fraught with problems. One character, the Revd Hugh Hamilton, 'awakened memories of that young James Renwick who died in the Edinburgh Grassmarket, last of them who counted not their lives dear for the sake of the Scottish Covenant'. His life as a minister was ravaged by an evil-wishing rumour-monger:

> . . . in the secret dark of the stairs, in the whispered colloquy of the parlous, an enemy was at work; and murderous whispers, indefinite, disquieting, suggesting vague possibilities of all things evil, brought with them the foul reek of the pit where they were forged, paralysing his work and killing his usefulness. But Hugh Hamilton wotted [knew] not at all of it. What threats came to him by the penny post or were slipped into his letter-box on dark nights, were known only to himself and his maker . . . At least, he made no sound and none knew if he suffered. Elders dropped away, members lifted their lines and went to other communions. Only his Sabbath School remained unimpaired.[46]

Hamilton was prosecuted before the presbytery on a 'fama' – an accusation on the basis of gossip. Crockett's volume is devoted to such tales of the suffering minister, maligned and impugned, poverty-stricken but valiant, and persistent in faith and social purpose. It shows the minister as the often unwitting victim of circumstance and human badness. But he was also noble; one of Crockett's characters refers to the Disruption of 1843, which created the Free Church, as 'the forty-three', thus comparing it to the Jacobite Rebellion of the 'forty-five' (1745).[47] Sacrifice to seemingly lost causes is the Presbyterian minister's lot.

The term 'lad o' pairts' originated in a novel by another Kailyard writer, Ian Maclaren.[48] In *Beside the Bonnie Brier Bush*, the role of the minister and the kirk in the Scottish community is again colourfully and intimately presented – this time by an author who was himself a minister. He paints the people of his fictitious small town of Drumtochty as learned: 'Drumtochty read widely – Soutar was soaked in Carlyle, and Margret Howe knew her "In Memoriam" by heart – but our intellectual life centred on the weekly sermon.'[49] Like the other Kailyard novelists, Maclaren dwells on the rigours of the sermon by which Scottish ministers were judged: 'There was a tradition that one of the Disruption fathers had preached in the Free Kirk for one hour and fifty minutes on bulwarks of Zion, and had left the impression that he was only playing round the outskirts of his subject.'[50] Evangelical preachers described the town as 'dead', but this was a false view: 'It was as well that these good men walked in a vain show, for, as a matter of fact, their hearers were painfully alive.'[51] The novel recounts at length worshippers' couthy and incisive criticisms of ministers' sermons. Of one:

> . . . he hes mair material than he kens hoo tae handle, and naebody, hearin' him, can mak head or tail o' his sermon. Ye get a rive at the Covenants ae minute, and a mouthfu' o' justification the next. Yir nae suner wi' the Patriarchs than yir whuppit aff ate the Apostles. It's rich feedin', nae doot, but sair mixed, an' no verra tasty.[52]

But Maclaren also used his fiction to explore the emotional as well as intellectual power of the sermon. In his second Drumtochty novel, *The Days of Auld Langsyne*, he wrote of one sermon that 'the minister exalted those things that endure for ever above those that perish in the using, with such spiritual insight and wealth of illustration – there was a moral resonance in his very voice which made men's nerves tingle – that Mrs Macfadyen, for once in her life, refused to look at heads, and Donald Menzies could hardly contain himself till the last psalm'.[53]

Barrie's trilogy of Thrums novels, *Auld Licht Idylls* (1887), *A Window in Thrums* (1889) and *The Little Minister* (1891), concerns a small Dissenting congregation and its minister, the Revd Gavin Dishart. In the first of these, Barrie locates the Auld Licht Seceders in 'victim culture': 'There are few Auld Licht communities in Scotland nowadays – perhaps because people are now so well off, for the most part devout Auld Lichts were always poor, and their last years were generally a grim struggle with the workhouse.'[54] Mostly handloom weavers in the novels' 1840s' location, the Auld Lichts 'have been starving themselves of late until they have saved up enough money to get another minister'.[55] The Scottish community is described in its Presbyterian divisiveness: 'Small though Thrums used to be, it had four kirks in all before the Disruption, and then another, which split into two immediately afterwards.'[56] The story of Church-splitting is central to Barrie's novels. In *Auld Licht Idylls* he recounts how the predestinarian Auld Lichts in the congregation, outvoted by the more evangelical New Lichts, left from Sunday worship with the minister at their head: 'Follow me to the commonty [common fields], all you persons who want to hear the Word of God properly preached.'[57] As Barrie adds: 'It was the Covenanters come back to life.'[58] The construction of new churches and the hiring of new ministers were always financial struggles. 'On Saturday nights the Thrums shops are besieged for coppers by housewives of all denominations, who would as soon think of dropping a threepenny bit into the plate as of giving nothing.'[59] The clergy made a poor living and had a poor dying:

> Every few years, as one might say, the Auld Licht kirk gave way and buried its minister. The congregation turned their empty pockets inside out, and the minister departed in a farmer's cart. The scene was not an amusing one to those who looked on at it. To the Auld Lichts was then the humiliation of seeing their pulpit 'supplied' on alternate Sabbaths by itinerant probationers or stickit ministers. When they were not starving themselves to support a pastor the Auld Lichts were saving up for a stipend. They retired with compressed lips to their looms, and weaved and weaved till they weaved another minister.[60]

Barrie records the vulnerability of the clergy, especially the young and the new, to the congregation: 'For the first year or more of his ministry an Auld Licht minister was a mouse among cats. Both in the pulpit and out of it they watched for unsound doctrine, and when he strayed they took him by the neck.'[61] But the minister's greatest vulnerability was to women. In *A Window on Thrums* it was taken 'for granted that a minister's marriage was womanhood's great triumph and that the particular woman who got him must be very clever'.[62] In the last of the Thrums trilogy, *The Little Minister*, the Revd Gavin Dishart falls for the bohemian 'Egyptian woman', Babbie. The modern critic might find the tale perhaps a touch unbelievable,[63] but Babbie becomes a device for exploring the moral strains and contradictions of the clergyman of a strict Presbyterian congregation. Babbie's sexual potency bears a much stronger likeness to the 'new woman' of Barrie's time in the 1890s than to the 'tink' or gypsy-woman of the 1830s and 1840s in which the novel is set. Indeed, *The Little Minister* proved to be immensely popular, being turned into an oft-revived play in both Britain and the United States, and generating three American film versions. With a melodramatic conclusion set in a flood, the story was one with widespread resonance on both sides of the Atlantic for its exploration of the theme of personal conduct in the context of 'old-time religion', liberalising values and sexual attraction. In the end, the minister 'preached to them till they liked him again, and so they let him marry her, and they like her awful too'.[64] It was a moral narrative of its time deploying the ultimate exemplar of male religiosity, the minister of a puritan sect, as its central character.

The Kailyard novels of the 1880s and 1890s created a genre of romance for the place of Presbyterianism in Scottish society at the very time when Church affiliation was at its peak but showing signs of crisis.[65] But they were built upon a longer and vibrant discourse on the minister, drawing especially from the ministerial biography of earlier decades. There were also many cheap publications of anecdotes and light biographies on the lives of ministers, elders and church beadles in the late nineteenth century – books in which the vulnerability of the 'stickit minister' and the probationer were dwelt upon.[66] The clerical biography had also generated synoptical extracts and summaries in popular magazines and religious tracts from the 1830s – magazines such as *Chambers Edinburgh Journal* and tracts and tract-magazines like those from the massive Drummond Tract Enterprise of Stirling. The Kailyard novels topped off, but did not create, the romanticisation of the minister in his community and congregation. It was a powerful and irresistible discourse on the nature of the Scottish community, the 'douce burgh', during industrialisation. The minister became a man of the people, symbolising in his own vulnerability within the Church system the vulnerability of the country's people during immense social changes. He was the symbol of Scotland's 'victim culture'. This was nowhere more strikingly portrayed than in nineteenth-century Scottish painting, in which the minister was a common figure. Sir George Harvey produced many Disruption pictures of the minister 'with his people': Thomas Guthrie *Preaching in the Glens*, and especially his *Leaving the Manse*, which shows a minister, his mother, wife and children being watched by parishioners leaving the door of their manse in 1843; Thomas Chalmers said of the picture: 'It will do more for our cause than a hundred of our pamphlets.'[67] John Phillip's *Presbyterian Catechising* depicted the minister in the home of a peasant family, testing and teaching them on knowledge of the catechism, while John Lorimer's *The Ordination of the Elders in a Scottish Kirk* (1891) provided a brooding view of dark-suited Calvinism. There was a huge market for monochrome prints of such Scottish religious themes, some still hanging in kirk vestries in the 1990s. They represent a period when the Presbyterian minister was figured – rightly or wrongly – as the embodiment of Scottish experience.

CONCLUSION

Alexander Carlyle of Inveresk felt in the eighteenth century that the state did not reward Church of Scotland clergy as it did their Church of England brethren. Observing that 'no country has ever been more tranquil, except the trifling insurrections of 1715 and '45, than Scotland', he felt a great deal was owed to 'the unwearied diligence of the clergy in teaching a rational religion': 'surely enough appears to entitle them to the high respect of the state, and to justice from the country, in a decent support to them and their families, and, if possible, to a permanent security like that of the Church of England, by giving clergy a title to vote on their livings for the member of Parliament for the country'.[68] In theology, the civil constitution, economics and the discourses of popular culture, the Scottish minister had a significantly less privileged, less segregated and less elevated place in Scottish society than most other countries of Western Europe. With no apostolic succession, with annually changing moderators, with no head of the Church but Christ and with a hotly disputed system of ministerial appointment, Scottish Presbyterianism conferred upon all its clergy – whether of Establishment or Dissent – a vulnerability surely rarely matched in Christendom. The minister became, during the rapid economic change and social turmoil of the eighteenth and nineteenth centuries, an enduring signifier of a vulnerable people suffering the vicissitudes of industrial capitalism. Anticlericalism did not, perhaps could not, enter the country's heart. Church taxes were, for the most part, 'tholed' (put up with) in a way probably unique in Europe over the last three centuries. The minister was democratised with his people, his popularity assured. The Kailyard novels, which need to be relocated by modern critics within that religious popular culture, drew on that heritage at the point around 1900 when the religiosity of the Scottish people started, very slowly, to decline. The minister retained a lingering place as an icon of the Scottish community – notably as a councillor, provost and even MP of early twentieth-century burghs – but his status withered with the dwindling of his Sabbath congregations, to be replaced by the kilt, the football team and political nationalism.

Notes

1   J.H. Dixon, *Gairloch in North-west Ross-shire* (Edinburgh, 1886), pp. 65–6.

2   This applies equally to ecclesiastical and social history. See J.H.S. Burleigh, *A Church History of Scotland* (Oxford, 1960); A.L. Drummond, *The Scottish Church 1688–1843* (Edinburgh, 1973); *The Church in Victorian Scotland 1843–1874* (Edinburgh, 1975); *The Church in Late Victorian Scotland 1874–1900* (Edinburgh, 1978); and T.C. Smout, *A History of the Scottish People 1560–1830* (London, 1969).

3   C.G. Brown, *Religion and Society in Scotland since 1707* (Edinburgh, 1997), pp. 67–76.

4   The system is explained in detail in A. Herron, *A Guide to Congregational Affairs* (Edinburgh, 1978), pp. 105–30.

5   For a case from Lochalsh parish in the west Highlands in 1790–1808, see C.G. Brown, 'Protest in the Pews: Interpreting Presbyterianism and Society in Fracture during the Scottish Economic Revolution', in T.M. Devine (ed.), *Conflict and Stability in Scottish Society 1700–1850* (Edinburgh, 1990), pp. 94–6.

6   Revd A. Carlyle (1722–1805), *Autobiography* (Edinburgh and London, 1860), p. 502.

7   A.A. Cormack, *Teinds and Agriculture* (London, 1930).

8   H. Gilbert, *As a Tale That is Told: A Church of Scotland Parish 1913–1954* (Aberdeen, 1983), pp. 2.1–2.32.

9   Brown, 'Protest in the Pews', pp. 91–5.

10   C.G. Brown, 'The Costs of Pew-renting: Church Management, Churchgoing and Social Class in Nineteenth-century Glasgow', *Journal of Ecclesiastical History* 38 (1987).

11   This singular event is well told in P. Aitchison, 'The Eyemouth Fish Tithe Dispute: the State Church Promoting Voluntaryism', *Records of the Church History Society* 23 (1988).

12   Compare this with the role of tithes in arousing anticlericalism in England: E.J. Evans, *The Contentious Tithe: The Tithe Problem and English Agriculture, 1750–1850* (London, 1976).

13   J.R. McIntosh, *Church and Theology in Enlightenment Scotland: The Popular Party, 1740–1800* (East Linton, 1998), p. 237.

14   K.J. Logue, *Popular Disturbances in Scotland, 1780–1815* (Edinburgh, 1979), pp. 168–76 and 191–217.

15   M. Foucault, 'What is an Author?', in P. Rabinow (ed.), *The Foucault Reader* (Harmondsworth, 1984), pp. 119–20.

16   M.R. Somers and G.D. Gibson, quoted in P. Joyce, *Democratic Subjects: The Self and the Social in Nineteenth-century England* (Cambridge, 1994), p. 153.

17   Joyce, *Democratic Subjects*, p. 189.

18   J.R. Walkowitz, *City of Dreadful Delight: Narratives of Sexual Danger in Late-Victorian London* (London, 1992), esp. pp. 81–120.

19   C. Harvie, 'The Covenanting Tradition', in G. Walker and T. Gallagher (eds), *Sermons and Battle Hymns: Protestant Popular Culture in Modern Scotland* (Edinburgh, 1990); Brown, *Religion and Society*, pp. 22–5 and 78–83.

20   Stirling General Associate (Antiburgher) Presbytery minutes, 11 February 1783, Stirling Archive Services CH3/286/2.

21   J. Peddie, *A Defence of the Associate Synod against the Charge of Sedition* (Edinburgh, 1800), p. 7.

22   A good example is T. Brown, *Annals of the Disruption* (Edinburgh, 1884).

23   J. Sinclair, *The Statistical Account of Scotland*, vol. 8 (Edinburgh, 1793), p. 352.

24   Brown, 'Protest in the Pews'.

25   J. Galt, *Annals of the Parish* (orig. edn 1821, reprinted Edinburgh, 1978), p. 5.

26   The University of Glasgow Library Catalogue lists at least 206 biographies with 'Rev' in the title. Many others omitted this term.

27   J. Brown, *Life of William B. Robertson, D.D.* (Glasgow, 1889), p. 14.

28   D. Hobbs, *Robert Hood, the Bridgeton Pastor: The Story of His Bright and Useful Life* (Edinburgh, 1894), p. 31.

29   See for instance J.G. Paton, *Missionary to the Hebrides: An Autobiography* (London, 1889), p. 59 et seq.; Hobbs, *Bridgeton Pastor*, pp. 40–2; F. Balfour, *Life and Letters of the Reverend James MacGregor D.D.* (London, 1912), pp. 1–13.

30   Hobbs, *Bridgeton Pastor*, pp. 33–4.

31   W.R. Nicoll, *'Ian Maclaren': Life of the Revd John Watson D.D.* (London, 1908), pp. 67–8.

32   Hobbs, *Bridgeton Pastor*, pp. 45–6.

33   D. Beaton, *Memoir, Diary and Remains of the Rev. Donald Macfarlane, Dingwall* (Inverness, 1929), p. 64.

34   Ibid., p, 11.

35   D. Macleod, *Memoir of Norman Macleod D.D.: Volume One, by his Brother* (London, 1876), p. 103.

36   Quoted in Balfour, *Life and Letters*, p. 98.

37   Quoted in ibid., p. 147.

38   Macleod, *Memoir, Volume 1*, p. 106.

39   W. Adamson, *The Life of the Rev. Fergus Ferguson* (London, 1900), p. 76.

40   J. Brown, *The Life of a Scottish Probationer: Being a Memoir of Thomas Davidson* (1838–1870) (Glasgow, 1877), pp. 173–4.

41   N. Macleod, *Reminiscences of a Highland Parish* (London, 1867), a best-seller by one minister about his ministerial father and grandfather; D. Macleod, *Memoir of Norman Macleod D.D.*; S. Smith, *Donald Macleod of Glasgow: A Memoir and a Study* (London, 1926); R. Ferguson, *George Macleod: Founder of the Iona Community* (London, 1990), about Norman's grandson.

42   G. Shepherd, 'The Kailyard', in D. Gifford (ed.), *The History of Scottish Literature, Volume 3: Nineteenth Century* (Aberdeen, 1988), pp. 315–16. See also L. Paterson, *The Autonomy of Modern Scotland* (Edinburgh, 1994), pp. 60–1.

43   For their documentary analyses of Scottish Church life, see I. Maclaren, *Church Folks* (London, 1901), and J.M. Barrie, *The Kirk in Scotland* (reprinted Dunbar, 1985).

44   Quoted in Nicoll, *'Ian Maclaren'*.

45   Shepherd, 'The Kailyard', p. 309, cites its origin as a year later when Maclaren quoted Burns in *Beside the Bonnie Brier Bush*. In Crockett's story, a minister snubs a bailie's wife in the street, and she rages to her husband at how he 'slichtit her' (slighted her), 'a laird's dochter'. Her husband replies: 'I wadna work the auld man's kail-yard ower sair!' – meaning: 'Stop using your father's small bit of land as a source of social power.' S.R. Crockett, *The Stickit Minister and Some Common Men* (orig. edn 1893, reprinted London, 1905), p. 13.

46   Ibid., pp. 15–16.

47   Ibid., p. 103.

48   I. Maclaren, *Beside the Bonnie Brier Bush* (orig. edn 1894, reprinted London, 1895), p. 3. On the development of the mythology, see R.D. Anderson, 'In Search of the 'Lad o' Parts': the Mythical History of Scottish Education', *History Workshop* 19 (1985).

49   Maclaren, *Brier Bush*, p. 200.

50   Ibid.

51   Ibid., p. 201.

52   Ibid., p. 210.

53   I. Maclaren, *The Days of Auld Langsyne* (London, 1896), p. 48.

54   J.M. Barrie, *Auld Licht Idylls* (orig. edn 1888, reprinted London, *c.* 1910), pp. 11–12.

55   Ibid., p. 12.

56   Ibid., p. 20.

57   Ibid., p. 60.

58   Ibid., p. 75.

59   Ibid., p. 64.

60   Ibid., p. 73.

61   Ibid., p. 79.

62   J.M. Barrie, *A Window in Thrums* (orig. edn 1889, reprinted London, 1938), p. 152.

63   'This "faery woman" is almost a sexual fantasy figure and like all fantasies when exposed to the light of day, seems faintly embarrassing. Her exoticism sits rather uneasily in the Auld Licht

setting and what attracts her to the rather colourless minister is never adequately explained.' Alasdair Cameron, 'Scottish Drama in the Nineteenth Century', in Gifford (ed.), *Scottish Literature*, p. 439.

64 J.M. Barrie, *The Little Minister* (orig. edn 1891, reprinted London, 1909), p. 298.

65 Brown, *Religion and Society*, pp. 61–5.

66 See, for instance, Nicholas Dickson, *The Auld Scotch Minister* (Glasgow, 1892), and his accompanying volumes on *The Elder at the Plate* and *The Kirk Beadle*; J. Martin, *Eminent Divines in Aberdeen and the North* (Aberdeen, 1888); J. Davidson, *Old Aberdeenshire Ministers and Their People* (Aberdeen, 1895).

67 Quoted in G.N.M. Collins, *The Heritage of Our Fathers: The Free Church of Scotland: Her Origin and Testimony* (Edinburgh, 1976), p. 61.

68 Carlyle, *Autobiography*, pp. 502–3.

FURTHER READING

Brown, C.G., *Religion and Society in Scotland since 1707* (Edinburgh, 1997).

Drummond, A.L., *The Scottish Church 1688–1843* (Edinburgh, 1973).

The Church in Victorian Scotland 1843–1874 (Edinburgh, 1975).

8

DID ANTICLERICALISM EXIST IN THE ENGLISH COUNTRYSIDE IN THE EARLY NINETEENTH CENTURY?

Frances Knight

INTRODUCTION: THE PROBLEM OF DEFINING ANTICLERICALISM

During the first third of the nineteenth century – and particularly the years from 1815 to 1831 – there occurred a small number of well-documented flashpoints when certain clergy and bishops, or their property, became the objects of verbal abuse or physical attack. These incidents include the East Anglian disturbances of 1816, the Swing Riots of 1830–1 and the attack on the Bishop of Bristol's palace in October 1831. These events have usually been understood as evidence of English anticlericalism, but it will be argued here that they represent a sudden response to extreme circumstances, and were untypical of the general pattern of relations between parsons and people. Although there is little evidence of a general climate of violent hostility towards the clergy in the early nineteenth-century English countryside, there were tensions. The clergy maintained a strong presence in rural society, and this could provoke irritation, jealousy and sometimes intense animosity. The most potent tensions, unsurprisingly, concerned money, particularly in the form of tithe payments, and the involvement of clergy in what were increasingly seen as essentially civil matters, such as the magistracy and the registration of births and marriages, and burial.

The Church was the largest profession in early nineteenth-century England,[1] and its clergy were easily identifiable. It was the ambiguity in their role that was at the heart of many of their difficulties. They were set apart from other business and professional men by being publicly committed to a religious ideal, rather than simply to the making of money. In early nineteenth-century terms that religious ideal included an expectation of active involvement in local society, whether through philanthropy, the magistracy, the organisation of schools or other means. It is likely that a clerical class that had opted for withdrawal from the early nineteenth-century world would have been severely censured by people of all classes. Nevertheless land enclosure meant that many of the clergy were newly wealthy, or appeared to be so. The most obvious sign of this was the construction of new rectories and vicarages, with their elegant reception rooms, extensive servants' quarters and large gardens providing eloquent testimony to the aspirations of a rising class. The clergy were part of a society in which a gentle pattern of upward mobility was a notable trend.[2] But this was more problematic than it would have been if the clergy had been members of any other burgeoning professional group, for were not the clergy supposed to be storing up treasure in heaven, rather than in the English countryside? Active involvement in the parish was all very well, but it was impossible that they could fulfil the roles of magistrate, tithe-owner and landlord without falling foul of at least some of their parishioners. The resulting conflicts contained the seeds of most of the anticlericalism that existed in the English countryside in the years before 1835. After the mid-1830s a combination of parliamentary reform, tithe reform, a reduction in the number of clerical magistrates and an improvement in labourers' living standards caused some of the tensions to disappear.

The variety of roles that a clergyman was expected to fulfil in the early nineteenth century, and the conflicts that arose between them, make discussion of anticlericalism particularly difficult. When a clergyman was attacked, was it because he was a clergyman, or because he was a magistrate, or a tithe-owner, or an unpopular landlord? Perhaps it was because he seemed ostentatiously wealthy, living in comfort cheek by jowl with those who had never been as poor or as hungry as they were in the aftermath of the Napoleonic wars. A clergyman might also be publicly criticised because people perceived in him some weakness or shortcoming which they believed unfitting to his clerical office. This implies the expectation of a higher standard, rather than antagonism to the Church.

The clergy were sometimes keen to describe the hostility that they had encountered in their parishes, but it is hard to know how much weight to put upon the clergy's own reports of anticlericalism directed against themselves. They probably tell us more about the clergy's own anxieties than about the realities of popular attitudes. Furthermore, 'anticlericalism', a term coined in the second half of the nineteenth century, was not in their vocabulary. They tended to prefer words like 'infidelity', 'disloyalty', 'sedition', 'radicalism' – all words that convey different shades of meaning. Indeed, it is very difficult to gauge when a differing political viewpoint, or an unfriendly attitude, should be interpreted as actual 'anticlericalism'. Did there always need to be violence or the threat of violence? To require violence or threats may limit the definition of anti-clericalism too narrowly, but to give weight to every less-than-friendly encounter may make the term so broad as to be meaningless. The clergy occasionally displayed distinctly anticlerical attitudes themselves. What are we to make of these displays of unfraternal feeling, which intensified as the rise of mutually hostile Church parties caused the clergy to lose much of the common ground that they had previously shared? Indeed, if we define anticlericalism as an attack on clergy as churchmen, rather than as unpopular agents in local society, we may be hard-pressed to find a single example. Attacks on clergy as churchmen belong more to the second half of the century, exemplified by the anti-Ritualist riots of the late 1850s and 1860s.[3] Although the focus of this chapter will be on the Church of England, it should be remembered that anticlericalism was not just an Anglican problem. It was particularly in evidence in Methodist groups that split from the Wesleyan parent in order to resist what they saw as the corruption of Wesley's ideal, which they believed was inherent in Wesleyan Methodism's drift towards denominationalism.[4]

RECENT DISCUSSIONS OF THE CHURCH OF ENGLAND AND ANTICLERICALISM

In the 1990s a shift in the interpretation of the nature and function of religion in nineteenth- (and also eighteenth-) century Britain took place among historians of English and Scottish religion. Put simply, this was a shift from a so-called 'pessimistic' thesis that portrayed the Church of England as in a downward spiral of decline from the beginning of the industrial age, to a more positive evaluation that stressed the extent to which the Church retained, and in some cases increased, its support.[5] This, as we shall see, has implications for the notion of anticlericalism, and it is noticeable that anticlericalism has, until now, been very little discussed by the proponents of the 'optimistic' thesis. If an earlier generation of historians sometimes seemed to take for granted the existence of an anticlerical working-class culture, so there is a danger in the present generation assuming a rather too harmonious view of people's attitudes towards the Church. It is timely to revisit and perhaps to reassess the less positive aspects of popular attitudes to religion.

In the 1970s and 1980s the historian most responsible for advancing in detail the view that there was significant anticlericalism among the English people in the first half of the nineteenth century was Eric Evans, who argued that a number of changing circumstances – predominantly agricultural and social – caused levels of anticlericalism to increase.[6] Evans explained this in a trio of inter-related developments: tithe, enclosure and the rising number of clerical magistrates. Although, as Evans pointed out, lay impropriators were often the most assiduous collectors of tithe, 'it was the image of the bloated parson clutching his tithe pig which influenced opinion when the tithe question began to be seriously agitated'.[7] This underlines the way in which images of anticlericalism, then and later, were manufactured by means of the satirical cartoon. The cartoon in question was Cruickshank's 'Clerical Anticipation' (1797), depicting a fat parson leaning over a pigsty. To add to the friction, some tithe-owners began to demand tithes on crops that had never before attracted them, such as potatoes, which were grown by the poor. There was the potential here not just for local animosity, but for bitter and lengthy tithe disputes, and some resulted. Many clergy decided, however, for a mixture of practical and pastoral reasons, that it was not worth pressing their claims.

The second element that Evans identified as contributing to anticlericalism was the move towards land enclosure, which often took place in exchange for collecting unwieldy tithe. Enclosure was naturally unpopular because it deprived people of their common land. From the clerical point of view, one of the advantages of reaping the benefits of enclosed land was that it permitted clerics to emerge rapidly as men of property. This, combined with their literacy and perceived reliability, made them seem particularly suitable for promotion to the magistrates' bench. Evans notes that there was a doubling of the number of clerical magistrates in the period from 1761 to 1831.[8] 'In many counties, rectors had become moderately prosperous over a very short period; they were now dispensing justice in laws and codes formulated by rich men whose prime concern was the protection of property.'[9] Clerical magistrates were also a favourite subject for satire. In the radical literature and cartoons of the period, the clerical magistrate was one of the stock figures of ridicule and contempt.[10] More harsh and more zealous than his fellow justices, he was portrayed as bent on sniffing out the most trifling misdemeanours, and crushing the poor. The reality was perhaps rather different; Peter Virgin has argued that some clerical magistrates were very lenient, but to portray them otherwise clearly suited the propagandists.[11] Tithe, land enclosure and the rise of the clerical magistrate were the cocktail of circumstances which, according to Evans, produced a swelling undercurrent of anticlericalism in England. It was particularly evident during the food crises of 1795, 1800–1 and 1816, and reached a crescendo in October 1831, the moment when the second Reform Bill was lost in the Lords as a result of the block vote of the bishops. There was, Evans notes, 'a pronounced anti-clerical tone' pervading the riots which followed, and the clergy were victims during the 'Captain Swing' agricultural disturbances of 1830–1.[12]

Evans has provided the most detailed discussion so far of anticlericalism in early nineteenth-century England.[13] Although some historians would challenge the basic pessimism of his view of the Church's role in rural society,[14] most would probably endorse his point about the social tensions caused by the clergy's increasing wealth in the face of enclosure, and the ambiguities that resulted from widespread clerical involvement in the magistracy. The weakness of his argument is that he does not distinguish between when a clergyman might have been mobbed as a tithe-owner or as a magistrate rather than as a churchman. Evans tells us more about the causes and character of anticlericalism, and about the moments of maximum tension, than about the extent to which anticlericalism pervaded the thought forms of the English people, or whether it had any specific religious content at all.

When Evans began writing about anticlericalism over twenty-five years ago, he could hardly have anticipated the historiographical shifts of the 1990s. Yet the tradition that began with Horace Mann's lament on the irreligion of the working classes in his *Report* on the 1851 religious census, and which in the mid-twentieth century found expression in the work of E.R. Wickham and K.S. Inglis, has now been comprehensively challenged. Perhaps the most complete challenge so far has come from Mark Smith, so it is worth considering anticlericalism from his perspective. His study of religion in Oldham and Saddleworth over a 125-year period of rapid industrial growth effectively demolished what had already become an outdated notion of the Hanoverian Church as gripped by lethargy and spiritual torpor. Instead, Smith depicts a rapidly expanding, working-class community, where support for the Churches remained at high levels, and where the clergy, both individually and collectively, enjoyed considerable respect.[15]

Mark Smith found 'no evidence of any sustained popular anti-clericalism in Oldham and Saddleworth', although sometimes individual clergymen courted temporary unpopularity.[16] Smith's account of clerical popularity is interesting, and it is important to emphasise it because it must have contributed significantly to the absence of anticlerical feeling. In particular, there was no massive economic gap between clergy and parishioners; the clergy were mostly poorly paid by contemporary standards, 'not too far removed from the position of skilled cotton workers'.[17] Furthermore, of the thirteen benefices in the area, only one, the rectory of Middleton, was in receipt of tithe.[18] Also of interest is the fact that the local clergy were almost totally absent from the magistracy; there were never more than two of Oldham's incumbents serving on the bench after 1830, and as Smith notes, 'this certainly removed one potential source of unpopularity in a period of considerable turbulence'.[19] Although Eric Evans and Mark Smith may appear to be at opposite ends of an interpretative spectrum, they do in fact share significant common ground, Evans by emphasising the presence of certain factors, Smith by emphasising their absence.

WHEN WAS VIOLENCE ANTICLERICAL?

We have established so far that historians of differing perspectives have highlighted some of the same tensions as triggers for anticlericalism. The next task is to re-examine some of the issues surrounding allegedly 'anticlerical' flashpoints to see what they tell us about anticlericalism. First, attention will be given to the East Anglian disturbances of 1816, which appear to endorse Evans's view that tithes, enclosure and the presence of clerical magistrates did indeed play a crucial part in fomenting disturbance. It will be argued, however, that the riots were not primarily anticlerical.

On the evening of 22 May 1816, at about 11 o'clock, 'a mob' arrived at the house of the Vicar of Littleport. It was the second visit they had made to the house that evening, having called earlier to demand work and bread – 2*s* a day in wages, and flour at 2*s* 6*d* per stone. The Vicar, the Revd John Vachell, stood at the door with a pistol, threatening to shoot anyone who attempted to enter. He offered the crowd £2 and a barrel of beer to disperse, but they were unsatisfied. After being easily overpowered, he was forced to flee on foot to Ely with his wife and two daughters. The intruders then set about the house, stealing 20lb of flour, breaking windows, destroying furniture, plate and papers, ripping up feather beds, smashing a greenhouse – damage that was estimated at about £2,000. When Vachell's gardener returned to the scene two hours later, he found the contents of the house largely destroyed, and a man in the dining room helping himself to the plate chest. Within a few hours the Vachells' belongings had been dispersed around the village, silver spoons concealed in thatched roofs, Mrs Vachell's gold rings given to a rioter's mother.[20]

The disturbance that became known as the 'Littleport and Ely Riots' began with a visit to a clergyman and was ended three days later by the intervention of another, the magistrate Sir Henry Bate-Dudley, a prebend of Ely, who was sent down from London by the Home Secretary, Lord Sidmouth. The riot was the climax of disturbances that broke out across East Anglia in April and May 1816, involving incidents in Bury St Edmunds, Brandon, Norwich and Downham Market, before moving south-west to the adjacent fenland towns of Littleport and Ely. About 300 people were active in rioting in those places, and over seventy arrests were made. One rioter was shot dead in Littleport during Bate-Dudley's intervention. Five of the principal rioters were executed, and many more were imprisoned or transported.[21] The incident entered local folklore as the most significant moment in Littleport's history, and is spoken of still.[22] It is recorded in both local and national history as an occasion when a popular uprising was put down harshly by the Church through the intervention of clerical magistrates.[23]

Eric Evans claims that 'anti-clericalism was a prominent feature' of the riot;[24] this view is also shared by A.J. Peacock.[25] This claim does not, however, stand up to re-examination. Its basic character was that of a food riot, the principal demand being cheaper flour, and its perpetrators were spurred by the news that the magistrates at Downham appeared to have capitulated to the demands of rioters there. Remarkably, Vachell was the only clerical target. There were many other targets, but they were farmers, shopkeepers, millers and those with property. If the rioters' intention had been primarily anticlerical, it might have been expected that when they marched on Ely, as they did early on the morning of Thursday 23 May, they would have targeted the cathedral, the bishop's palace or the homes of the dozen clergy who resided in the city. The prebendal houses would have been easy prey from which rich pickings could have been had. Instead, the rioters headed for the market square, where a number of magistrates (all clergy) had gathered. Clearly terrified by the armed and furious body, the magistrates, led by the Dean, Peploe Ward, agreed to the rioters' demands for flour at 2s 6d a stone, an allowance of 2s per week for each family member on parish relief, and wages of 2s a day.[26] The magistrates were divided, however, on whether they could grant 'forgiveness for what had passed', a suggestion, perhaps, that the negotiators were trying to appeal to their clerical rather than to their magisterial side. Initially they promised no prosecutions if everyone went home peaceably,[27] but this, along with the rest of their offer, was later retracted, and the following evening the riot was ended by force.

Despite the absence of a general targeting of clergy at Littleport and Ely, important elements of Eric Evans's thesis hold good. The enclosure movement was spreading rapidly in East Anglia at this period,[28] and newly erected fences had been destroyed at the nearby parish of Feltwell a few weeks earlier.[29] The Revd Vachell was probably targeted because he was an over-zealous collector of tithes and other dues, and had on at least two occasions in the previous years successfully prosecuted non-payers.[30] Littleport had a history of tithe disputes involving the vicar; in 1772 the Lord Chancellor had found in favour of the Vicar of Littleport after a three-day hearing in a case that established the Vicar's right to corn tithe.[31] Vachell was not only an unpopular tithe-owner, he was also a magistrate, and a rich man living alongside the poor. This was the substance of the rioters' grievance against him; they had little interest in him as a cleric.

Another useful context in which to understand the Littleport and Ely Riots is that provided by John Bohstedt in his extensive study of six hundred riots in the period 1790–1810.[32] Rioting, he suggests, had its own protocols, and was usually conducted according to rules of engagements that were understood by all the participants, including the magistrates, who often played a conciliatory role.[33] It was part of the protocol of riot to avoid provocative excesses of violence that were likely to result in the capital punishment of offenders. It would seem that in the Fenland riot, the lack of coordinated leadership caused this protocol to be breached.[34] As a result the amount of violence unleashed meant that the riot did not develop in a way that might have led to at least some of the rioters' demands being met, although at an early stage (perhaps before the full extent of the crimes perpetrated at Littleport became known), the magistrates did make an attempt at conciliation.

Bohstedt's study is also relevant for a general investigation of anticlericalism, because it reveals that the clergy were almost never the targets of rioters during the period from 1790 to 1810. Sometimes, indeed, rioters might warn others against attacking clergymen, on the grounds that they were wasting time.[35] On another occasion noted by Bohstedt, at Barrow-on-Soar in 1795, rioters used first the churchyard and then the belfry for the storage of grain. He suggests that this might imply a desire on the part of the rioters to appropriate the moral high ground, and to 'sanctify' their actions.[36] As at Littleport, the Barrow riot was a serious disorder resulting in fatalities, and it entered local tradition as the 'Barrow butchery'. Rather than attacking a clerical magistrate, however, the Barrow crowd at an early stage contacted the nearest one, the Revd Mr Storer, in order 'to solicit [his] friendly interference'.[37] Positive intervention by clerical magistrates on behalf of rioters and protesters was evidently not unusual at this period, and is also attested by Roger Wells.[38]

Hobsbawn and Rudé, in their classic account of the agricultural disturbances of 1830–1 known as the Swing Riots, cite a number of instances where clergy came under attack.[39] In all these cases the clergy were singled out over the issue of tithe, the demand being that they should either reduce or abandon their collection of it. The experience of Mr Cobbold, Vicar of Selborne in Hampshire, seems to have been typical; he was visited by some rioters who demanded that he should reduce his tithe by a half, which he agreed to do.[40] In Horsham a church was used for a tithe-and-wage demonstration, but this revealed uncharacteristic hostility towards the building, which was described afterwards as 'much disfigured'.[41]

Hobsbawn and Rudé did not have much to say about clerical magistrates, but suggested that in certain areas, such as the Weald and along the Norfolk–Suffolk border, parsons were more often the victims of attack than any other group.[42] This implies that in the large number of other locations where Swing was active, the parsons were not the principal victims. Perhaps it was the proportion of clerical magistrates in both areas that caused them to be targeted. In 1831 one incumbent in every six was also an active magistrate.[43] This was the high point of the clerical magistracy; it was not a position that would be sustainable for much longer, as enquiries began to be commissioned by an anxious government about the names and professions of those on the bench.[44]

The function of the clergy in the Swing Riots is therefore complicated, once again, by the issues of tithe and the magistracy. In Roger Wells's more recent evaluation of the Swing disturbances in southern England, the clergy do not appear as the victims of popular anticlericalism. He suggests that when parsons and landlords were attacked, it was often farmers that were to blame, as they attempted to side-step 'their employees' anger . . . in opportunist attempts to wrench tithe and rent reductions'.[45] He argues that farmers, both overtly and secretly, gave Swing far more support than was previously supposed.

Hard on the heels of the Swing Riots came the news that on Saturday 8 October 1831 the House of Lords had rejected the Reform Bill, and that the opposition of the bishops had been decisive. Demonstrations and protests broke out in various parts of the country, many of them directed at bishops.[46] The most serious incident was in Bristol, and although this represents the expression of urban, not rural, anticlericalism, it merits brief mention here. One of the principal rioters was the articulately anticlerical Christopher Davis, known in Bristol as a champion of the poor, and a man who seldom missed the opportunity at public meetings of expressing his disapproval of bishops, anti-reformers and the Bristol Corporation. He had been seen on the afternoon that the bishop's palace was destroyed, waving his hat and a silk umbrella, shouting that 'this is the end of your damned magistrates and bishops'.[47] A few hours later, when the palace lay in smouldering ruins, the physical manifestation of early nineteenth-century English anticlericalism had reached its zenith.

Although controversies concerning Church rate continued to focus discontent for several more decades, the cocktail of anticlerical grievances identified by Eric Evans began to be resolved by the mid-1830s. Parliamentary reform was secured at the third attempt in 1832. Tithe commutation occurred in 1835. The number of clerical magistrates went into sharp decline from about the same time. The working poor experienced a modest increase in their living standards which made riot less likely. Other factors also altered the nature of rural life. Roger Wells points to the scores of agricultural societies that were created from the mid-1830s, arguing that they played a crucial role in pacifying the English countryside in the years after the passing of the much-hated 1834 Poor Law. These societies were under aristocratic or gentry patronage, were frequently managed by clergy and offered valuable prizes to those whose lifestyles extolled what would become known as Victorian values. 'Moral restraint, thrift, cleanliness, industriousness and deference . . . brought their rewards in cash, clothing, fuel, seed potatoes, suckling pigs and allotments, ceremoniously handed down at annual meetings. Many of the benefits paid as right under the old poor law were now bountifully bestowed by the affluent as rewards under the new.'[48] All these circumstances contributed to creating a changed atmosphere in which the parson ceased to be regarded with animosity.

THE INFLUENCE OF ANTICLERICAL LITERATURE

The expanding world of cheap print in the early nineteenth century provided a medium for disseminating printed attacks on the clergy, although publishers of such material risked imprisonment for seditious libel. Indeed, it can be argued that anticlericalism in its published form was rather more effective than the mobbing of the tithe-collecting parson. The production and circulation of anticlerical literature was largely an urban phenomenon; its significance in the countryside is harder to evaluate. Nevertheless brief consideration will be given here to the anticlericalism of three important and very different early nineteenth-century radicals, Richard Carlile (1790–1843), William Cobbett (1763–1835) and John Wade (1788–1875), whose writings provide an insight into a variety of different positions within the spectrum of anticlerical print.

Richard Carlile was probably the most extreme public critic of the Church at this period, and his attacks on the clergy as 'black slugs' resonate with the rhetoric of violent European anticlericalism. Reared as an Anglican, Carlile moved through deism to the espousal of atheism in 1822. Unlike Cobbett and Wade, Carlile viewed the destruction of Christianity as the prelude to all other reform, and sustained attacks on Christianity became a regular feature of his writing. He believed in nothing supernatural, and he told the readers of the *Republican* 'that every account that exists about the appearance of a God or Gods, angel or angels, spirit or spirits, to any man or men, woman or women, is a fabricated and false account, [since] no such beings did exist, nor ever will exist'.[49] 'Oh, horrible religion,' he wrote, 'what havoc hast thou made of the earth! Thou are a pestilence, more destructive of life, happiness, and peace, than all other pestilences combined.'[50] He took delight in debunking the Bible as an 'obscene, voluptuous, false, scandalous, malicious and seditious book'; its publishers and sellers, he suggested, no doubt with heavy irony, should be prosecuted.[51] Hardly surprisingly, he hated those 'enemies of mankind' the clergy, and he demanded the abolition of tithes and Church rates, and the disestablishment of the Church of England. Carlile's supporters, who numbered several thousand, were mainly urban-dwellers. They were most numerous in London, but were also to be found in Manchester, Halifax, Leeds, Bradford and Birmingham.[52] The countryside did not provide Carlile with a fertile core of support.

It was partly Carlile's anti-religious views that caused strain in his relationship with William Cobbett, although Cobbett was also appalled by Carlile's republicanism and his frank discussion of birth control.[53] Unlike Carlile, religion was not central to Cobbett's plans for reform. His own critique of the Church, powerful though it was, operated from the perspective of being a life-long member. He continued to belong because he believed in religious uniformity and because he hated Protestant Dissenters; his approach was practical and unmetaphysical. 'The Christian religion,' he wrote near the end of his life, 'is not an affair of preaching, or prating or ranting, but of taking care of the bodies as well as the souls of people . . . not an affair of fire and brimstone, but an affair of bacon and bread, beer and a bed.'[54] Cobbett's hatred of features of Church life such as tithe, non-residence and establishment intensified as he became older and more disillusioned.[55]

His anticlericalism took a number of less usual forms, which included advocating clerical celibacy; the children of clergy constituted 'an enormous national evil', as they expected to be kept like ladies and gentlemen – at great expense to the tithe payer. If the clergy had no children and fewer social pretensions, he reasoned, they would place less of a financial burden on those tithe payers who had to support them, and the money could be used to help the poor.[56] He was a stern critic of the wealth of the clergy, believing that it marred their effectiveness: 'Did [Christ] ever say or insinuate, that the success of his saving word depended on the teachers of it having palaces for their places of residence; having parks well stocked with deer; having retinues of servants . . .?'[57] Cobbett came to the conclusion that the government should take over all the property of the Church, and pay the working clergy salaries. He died in the year that the Ecclesiastical Commission came into existence, but would presumably have approved of its formation.

Cobbett attended church somewhat irregularly, believing that although attendance afforded him 'a very good opportunity of making an estimate of the condition of the people', it would be 'hypocrisy' to go if it cut into his writing time. He believed, probably with justification, that he could understand the contents of the Bible as well as any parson, and pointed out that he had written a dozen 'good thumping' sermons himself.[58] These sermons began as articles in the *Political Register*, and were later republished as a book. They had titles like 'Hypocrisy and Cruelty' and 'On the Duties of Parsons, and on the Institution and Object of Tithes'. In this context the importance of Cobbett is that he illustrated that it was possible to combine vehement anticlericalism with membership of the Church of England.

The publication of John Wade's widely circulated *Black Book* marked a significant moment in the history of anticlericalism in its printed form.[59] First published as *The Black Book, or Corruption Unmasked!* in 1820, it was reissued with revisions as *The Extraordinary Black Book* in 1831, 1832 and 1835. The Church, however, was only one of Wade's targets; he was equally concerned with unmasking corruption in Parliament, charitable foundations, the civil list, the legal profession, the Bank of England and the East India Company. As Philip Harling has put it: 'Wade's exhaustive chronicles of élite cupidity mark the climax of the post-war radical critique of Old Corruption.'[60]

Wade's position was to want to appear to defend Christianity while launching a fulsome attack on what he termed 'Church of Englandism'. Speaking up for those who were more Christian than the clergy was a common device of anticlerical rhetoric at this period,[61] and was safer than causing offence to those who wished to see reform but also had religious sensibilities. 'It is not Christ, but Anti-Christ, the Anti-Christian Church of England, that we are going to unmask,' wrote Wade. 'Tithes are not Christianity, nor bishops, nor archdeacons, nor prebendaries, nor canons, nor the catechism, nor the liturgy. These are all innovations – corruptions unknown and unordained by Christ.'[62] Wade's anti-Church rhetoric was a mixture of the outrageously exaggerated and the relatively accurate. Some exaggerations were rather bizarre, as when he declared that the revenues of the priesthood exceeded the public revenues of either Austria or Prussia, or when he asserted that the see of London was worth £100,000 a year.[63] Other observations, however, were rooted in a firmer grasp of reality. He wrote eloquently about the poverty and suffering of curates (just as Cobbett did), giving expression to views that we know from other sources were sometimes shared by the curates themselves.[64] The importance of Wade was that his encyclopaedic fulminations did sting the Church into a response. It came in the form of the recognition of the need to compile accurate statistics that would put paid to allegations about the 'fabulous wealth' of the Church. The statistics were published as the Report of the Ecclesiastical Revenues Commission of 1835, which provided an important foundation for the work of the newly formed Ecclesiastical Commissioners.

ANTICLERICALISM ARISING FROM ECONOMIC IMBALANCE: THE RESENTMENT OF RICH CLERGY

At whatever level of society anticlericalism existed, and whether it took the form of physical violence, verbal abuse or the printed squib, allegations of clerical money-grabbing were invariably present. As we have seen, the clergy were caricatured as idle and useless, growing fat on their tithes – and yet they were also expected to be lax and inefficient, and were immediately vilified as avaricious if they revealed any aptitude in financial matters.

The popular belief was that the clergy were very wealthy. The propaganda put out by Carlile, Cobbett, Wade and others, and the fact that many clergy had private means, did much to promote this misconception. Recent research has demonstrated, however, that the wealth of the clergy was often not derived from Church sources.[65] Peter Virgin's analysis of the 1835 Ecclesiastical Revenues Report revealed the median income of English incumbents was just £275 a year, or £5 10s a week.[66] Shrewd contemporary observers knew this was true; W.J. Conybeare asserted that 'the clergy, while poor as a profession, are rich as a class'.[67] For parishioners, however, it was difficult to know whether the money being spent on improving the rectory was coming from their tithe payments or from private means. It remained a strongly held article of belief that they had a just claim on a share of the money which their incumbent derived from his living, and that it was his duty to use his clerical income to relieve the poor. In 1849 the parishioners of Whaplode in Lincolnshire protested against the non-residence of their vicar on the grounds that 'their' money was being spent elsewhere. They claimed that the parish was worth £550 a year, which was clearly an exaggeration, but that the curate was receiving only £70 a year, and was therefore struggling financially; it was 'quite impossible for him to relieve the wants of the needy, or the distress of the suffered' (*sic*).[68] The accuracy of the figures is largely immaterial; what is important is the parishioners' indignation at being denied a share in the living's revenues.

For similar reasons the disclosure of debt among the clergy could provoke an outbreak of anticlerical feeling. Not only were clerical debtors seen to have squandered the money that should have been used in the parish, they had often obtained credit on the strength of their clerical status. An example from Creeton in Lincolnshire well illustrates this strain of indignant, but ultimately self-controlled, English anticlericalism. It is a letter written by a parishioner named Millington to a curate in debt in 1835:

> Revd Sir,
> Being very little in the habit of writing especially writing letters I feel a sort of reluctance but as you seem to demand an answer to yours I will try my hand, but must first promise that I am not accountable to any human Being for my conduct in matters of Religion provided I do not offend against the Law. It is

not my intention however to recede [*sic*] from the established Church. You have thought proper to give me an history of your private affairs from your setting out in life with which I have nothing to do. You have made arrangements (it appears) for the payment of your debts, which appear fair enough and which if acted upon your creditors may I hope get paid eventually – but the misfortune of it appears to have been that that (sic) while these were and are in operation to extricate you, you have contrived to get into fresh debts . . . I should rather be inclined to think the misfortune is with those industrious tradesmen and others who have been induced by your appearance to give you credit and who are thus held out of their money that the Problem is easily solved – When a man lives beyond his income it requires no Mathematical demonstration to prove the result.[69]

It was the impact of clerical debt on local businesses that was frequently the main issue in similar cases. Few traders, apparently, would refuse credit to a clergyman, and some had their fingers burned as a result.[70]

OTHER FORMS OF RESENTMENT:
CLERICAL INVOLVEMENT IN CIVIL MATTERS

Another aspect of English anticlericalism needs to be touched upon: the strong dissatisfaction at the apparent slowness of the changes in the law to give non-Anglicans equal rights. This feeling expressed itself in hostility towards the necessity for clerical performance of baptisms and marriages (before 1837), and particularly funerals.[71] Whereas civil registration was introduced for births and marriages in 1837, it was not until 1880 that the grievance was rectified concerning burials. Until that time, if there was not a Dissenters' graveyard in the parish, non-Anglicans were forced to bury their dead according to the service in the Book of Common Prayer, or in total silence.

As a result clergy sometimes became caught up in graveside skirmishes. Friendly societies could provide a platform for intervention in Anglican burial services, when the deceased member was commemorated at a special graveside oration. Rex Russell has established a link between Lincolnshire friendly societies and temperance and Methodism, suggesting that they often developed side by side.[72] At Weston in Lincolnshire a butcher read an address at the conclusion of the burial of a Wesleyan who was a member of the Foresters' Club in 1849, despite being warned by the vicar that he was committing an illegal act.[73] At Kirton-in-Lindsey a similar incident occurred when the burial took place of a member of the newly formed lodge of the Society of Ancient Foresters.[74] On this occasion the officiating curate insisted that the address be read outside the churchyard wall. No reference is made to the religious affiliation of the deceased Forester of Kirton, but it is likely that societies such as this provided an ideal opportunity for expressing dissatisfaction at the continued Anglican monopoly on burial services. A mourner at Tydd St Mary in Lincolnshire revealed much about attitudes to funerals when he complained bitterly to the Bishop of Lincoln at the lax conduct of a curate at the funeral of his friend:

> The Poor desire to have the same Service performed as the rich, for though poor in this world we shall be Rich in another, and, the friends of [the] departed person feel hurt at anything that may seem slighting to survice [*sic*] which ought to be performed at that aughfull [*sic*] moment.[75]

The outpouring of grief at a funeral may sometimes have given voice to a latent anticlericalism which would otherwise have remained unrecorded.

ANTICLERICAL FEELING AMONG THE GENTRY

Most members of the gentry probably had a clergyman somewhere in their family circle, and their view of the Church may have been partly filtered through their relative's experience, and their attitudes to him. There is plenty of evidence of antipathy towards individual clergy, or less commonly towards the clergy as a whole, but it is difficult to know how much weight to place on the former. In Buckinghamshire Lady Lovatt, widow of the baronet Sir Jonathan Lovatt, tried (unsuccessfully) to get rid of the lawful incumbent at Soulbury shortly after she became patron in 1829.[76] Presumably she disliked his preaching, or his personality, or she thought that Soulbury needed a change. A few miles away, in a case that suggests a more generalised dislike of the clergy, the 2nd Duke of Buckingham blocked the building of a parsonage at Foscott because he considered it too near to his own estate. It was also alleged that he had pulled down the parsonage at nearby Stowe without consulting the incumbent.[77] A squire resented the one man in the parish that he was powerless to remove.[78] Some squires believed that their domination of the parson was a natural expression of the established nature of the Church of England.

James Obelkevich identified a strong streak of anticlericalism running through the gentry of South Lindsey in Lincolnshire. Like the Duke of Buckingham, the 6th Baron Monson was a powerful landowner, and a prime example of the aristocratic anticlerical mentality.[79] Monson considered that the clergy were only interested in money, and this belief, as we have seen, was deeply rooted in the mentality of English anticlericalism. He complained that 'the Church at this time [1856] are more eager after money than any other profession'.[80] So it must have appeared, for it was the period when people were being asked for more and more money to fund ambitious church-building projects, as well as to prime the pumps of a large variety of Church charities. Monson declined to become a vice-president of the Church Building Society on the grounds that it was merely a clerical mode of extorting money, and he was disgusted at what he described as the shoals of impudent and extortionate begging letters which he claimed (quite plausibly) to receive from the clergy.[81] Monson's dislike of parsons was not accompanied by any favourable feelings towards Nonconformity. 'As for Dissenters,' he wrote to his son in 1850, 'I agree in the main with you. I detest them all, Catholics included.'[82]

Monson's fears about avaricious 'fellows in black coats' had clear precedents in the past,[83] and blended easily with new, distinctively nineteenth-century anxieties. The authority of the aristocratic layperson, who believed that he (or she) had absolute power in the parish, was becoming undermined by other factors, particularly the rise of Church parties, whether High Church or Evangelical, which asserted that the authority of the clergy rested on supernatural rather than social grounds. Monson disliked Evangelicals, and he blamed High Churchmen for destroying moderation:

> The fact is [he wrote in 1851] as the principle of High Church is to throw an undisputed power into the hands of the parsons and make the laity nothing, weak minds are led astray by the intoxication of power. The good old days of the moderate Country Clergyman are passing away and we shall have only fanatics of both extremes.[84]

CONCLUSION

It was hardly surprising that Lord Monson should lament the passing of the 'good old country clergyman' who was as closely implicated in the management of local society as Monson was himself. The rise of Evangelical and Tractarian self-consciousness fostered a growth in clerical independence, and a movement away from assimilation between clergy and laypeople. As such, it contained the seeds which would later germinate as anticlericalism of a different, more sectarian and more theologically focused type. In contrast, early nineteenth-century anticlericalism was, as Evans showed us, fuelled by non-theological issues. These were principally resentment of tithe and of magistrates. The fact that neither tithe-collection nor the magistracy were confined to the clergy muddies the definition of 'anticlericalism' and makes it an ambiguous concept. Historians who use the word should be ready to distinguish whether it was the clergy as clergy to whom objection was being made, or the clergy as magistrates, tithe-collectors or landlords. With the notable exception of the writings of Richard Carlile, English anticlericalism conveys little of the violence of its European counterparts.

In addition to the causes identified by Evans, dislike of the clergy might also be fuelled by other issues, particularly resentment of clerical wealth, and scandal at clerical debt. There were also other, non-financial issues at stake; some people were likely to become particularly infuriated when, unbidden, the Church became entangled in their own moments of private grief, as a result of the continuing monopoly on funerals. The most important point, perhaps, is that in early nineteenth-century rural English anticlericalism, it was the clergy who were the subject of attack and not Christianity itself. It was integral to the rhetoric of anticlericalism at this period that usually it appeared to operate within the context of Christianity.

Notes

1　Alan Haig, *The Victorian Clergy* (London, 1984), pp. 6–7. Penelope J. Corfield, in *Power and the Professions in Britain 1700–1850* (1995), p. 32, provides a table delineating the state of the professions in 1851. She notes 26,235 clergymen in England and Wales, second only to 28,304 teachers. It must be noted that a significant proportion of teachers, especially at grammar and public schools and universities, would also have been clergy at this date. It is not clear how Nonconformist ministers are represented in Corfield's table.

2　Ian R. Christie, 'Conservatism and Stability in British Society', in Mark Philp (ed.), *The French Revolution and British Popular Politics* (Oxford, 1991), pp. 171–3.

3　Owen Chadwick, *The Victorian Church: Part I* (3rd edn, London, 1971), pp. 491–501.

4　David Hempton, *Methodism and Politics in British Society 1750–1850* (London, 1984), pp. 197–202; Deborah Valenze, *Prophetic Sons and Daughter: Female Preaching and Popular Religion in Industrial England* (Princeton, 1985), pp. 134–5 and 208–10.

5　For the 'pessimistic' thesis, see E.R. Wickham, *Church and People in an Industrial City* (London, 1957); K.S. Inglis, *Churches and the Working Classes in Victorian England* (London, 1963); A.D. Gilbert, *Religion and Society in Industrial England: Church, Chapel and Social Change* (London, 1976). For more recent, 'optimistic' interpretations (listed in order of publication, and concentrating on contributions to the nineteenth, rather than the eighteenth, century) see: Callum Brown, 'Did Urbanization Secularize Britain?' *Urban History Yearbook* (1988); A.M. Urdank, *Religion and Society in a Cotswold Vale: Nailsworth, Gloucestershire, 1780–1865* (Stroud, 1990); Jeremy Morris, *Religion and Urban Change: Croydon 1840–1914* (Woodbridge, 1992); Mark Smith, *Religion in Industrial Society: Oldham and Saddleworth 1740–1865* (Oxford, 1994); Frances Knight, *The Nineteenth-century Church and English Society* (Cambridge, 1995); Callum Brown, 'The Mechanism of Religious Growth in Urban Societies', in Hugh McLeod (ed.), *European Religion in the Age of Great Cities* (London, 1995); Hugh McLeod, *Religion and Society in England 1850–1914* (Basingstoke, 1996); Arthur Burns, *The Diocesan Revival in the Church of England c. 1800–1870* (Oxford, 1999).

6　Eric J. Evans, 'Tithing Customs and Disputes: the Evidence of Glebe Terriers', *Agricultural History Review* xviii (1970), pp. 17–35; 'A Nineteenth Century Tithe Dispute and its Significance: the Case of Kendal', *Transactions of the Cumberland and Westmorland Antiquarian and Archaeological Society* lxxiv (1974), pp. 159–83; 'Some Reasons for the Growth of Anti-clericalism in England', *Past & Present* 66 (1975), pp. 84–109; *The Contentious Tithe: The Tithe Problem and English Agriculture* (London, 1976); 'The Church in Danger? Anti-clericalism in nineteenth-century England', *European Studies Review* 13, 2 (1983).

7　Evans, 'English Rural Anti-clericalism', pp. 86–7.

8   Ibid., pp. 97–109; see also Evans, 'The Church in Danger?', pp. 212–13.

9   Ibid., p. 213.

10   Examples are found in the two Cruickshank cartoons, 'The Clerical Magistrate' and 'Preachee and Flogee Too'.

11   Peter Virgin, *The Church in an Age of Negligence: Ecclesiastical Structure and Problems of Church Reform 1700–1840* (Cambridge, 1989), pp. 91–3.

12   Evans, 'The Church in Danger?', p. 207.

13   Reg Ward has provided the most detailed discussion of the tithe question, however. See W.R. Ward, 'The Tithe Question in England in the Early Nineteenth Century', *Journal of Ecclesiastical History* 16 (1965), pp. 67–81.

14   See particularly Evans, 'English Rural Anti-clericalism', pp. 108–9.

15   Smith, *Religion in Industrial Society*, pp. 56–7.

16   Ibid., p. 105.

17   Ibid., p. 48.

18   Ibid., p. 47.

19   Ibid., p. 105.

20   Account based on evidence given against the rioters by Vachell, his gardener, and others: Cambridgeshire County Record Office (CCRO), Ely and Littleport Riots, 283/L4/9, 283/L4/11, 283/L4/49, 283/L4/69, 283/L4/89 and *Cambridge Chronicle and University Journal*, 31 May 1816, p. 3.

21   The fullest account is found in A.J. Peacock, *Bread or Blood: a Study of the Agrarian Riots in East Anglia in 1816* (London, 1965). The strengths of this book are the contextualisation of events in the Fens within the broader picture of East Anglia, its useful attention to the detail of the primary sources and its appendices. The major weakness is the author's ignorance of the structures of the Church of England (he thought that a parish clerk was a clergyman, p. 59), coupled with a willingness to assume that the rioters were engaged in class struggle and were hostile to all forms of religion, without providing much concrete evidence that this was the case.

22   Today the five executed rioters are commemorated by the Littleport Society as the 'Littleport martyrs' (exhibition at Littleport Show, 24 July 1999). A plaque remembering the rioters that was originally placed in St Mary's Church, Ely (as a warning to others) now has pride of place in the newly built Littleport Community Centre.

23   C. Johnson, *An Account of the Trials and Executions of the Ely and Littleport Rioters in 1816* (Ely, 1893); Paul Muskett, *Riotous Assemblies: Popular Disturbances in East Anglia 1740–1822* (Ely, 1984), pp. 53–60; Robert Hole, *Pulpits, Politics and Public Order in England 1760–1832* (Cambridge, 1989), p. 186.

24   Evans, 'English Rural Anti-clericalism', p. 105.

25   Peacock, *Bread or Blood*, pp. 60–2.

26   Ibid., pp. 102–3.

27   CCRO 283/L49/1.

28   See Ward, 'Tithe Question in England', pp. 71–3.

29   Peacock, *Bread or Blood*, p. 20.

30   *Vachell v. Crabb*, Cambridge Chronicle, 24 July 1812, p. 3; *Vachell v. Martin*, Cambridge Chronicle, 13 August 1813, p. 3.

31   *Cambridge Chronicle*, 29 February 1772, p. 3.

32   John Bohstedt, *Riots and Community Politics in England and Wales* (Cambridge, Mass., 1983).

33   Ibid., pp. 34 and 202, *passim*.

34   Peacock, *Bread or Blood*, pp. 52 and 95–100. Peacock suggests that the rioting at Littleport remained entirely uncoordinated until John Dennis, a licensed victualler who was subsequently executed, was persuaded to join in late on the first evening. It seems that he took control of organising the march on Ely. It may be significant that the Revd Vachell was attacked at an early stage, before Dennis took over. The amount of alcohol consumed over the three days also caused some rioters to become less focused on their original aims.

35   Bohstedt, *Riots and Community*, p. 34.

36   Ibid., pp. 1–3.

37   Ibid., p. 1.

38   Roger Wells, 'English Society and Revolutionary Politics in the 1790s: the case for insurrection', in Philp, (ed.), *The French Revolution and British Popular Politics*, pp. 216 and 222.

39   E.J. Hobsbawn and George Rudé, *Captain Swing* (London, 1969), pp. 112–13, 120, 153–4 and 158.

40   Ibid., p. 120.

41   Ibid., pp. 112–13.

42   Ibid., p. 229.

43   Virgin, *Church in an Age of Negligence*, p. 8.

44   *Parliamentary Papers* 1836 (583) XLIII, 161.

45   Roger Wells, 'Rural Rebels in Southern England in the 1830s', in Clive Emsley and James Walvin (eds), *Artisans, Peasants and Proletarians, 1760–1860. Essays presented to Gwyn A. Williams* (London, 1985), pp. 131–2.

46   Throughout Hampshire on 5 November 1831 the Bishop of Winchester displaced Guy Fawkes to be burnt in effigy, but his palace in Farnham was not attacked, despite earlier fears. (Wells, 'Rural rebels', p. 139). The Bishop of Bath and Wells was treated to some 'earthy epithets' and pelted with mud by a crowd who shouted 'reform, we will have reform' when he emerged from consecrating a church in Bedminster (Geoffrey Amey, *City under Fire: The Bristol Riots and Aftermath* (Guildford, 1979), p. 31). Chadwick, *The Victorian Church: Part I*, pp. 26–9, provides further examples of post-Reform Bill attacks on bishops and clergy, and discusses the riot at Bristol.

47   Amey, *City under Fire*, pp. 125–6. Davis was a relatively wealthy man with a lucrative business as a carter.

48   Wells, 'Rural Rebels in Southern England', pp. 148–9.

49   *Republican*, 24 March and 5 May 1820. Cited in Joel H. Weiner, *Radicalism and Freethought in Nineteenth-century Britain: The Life of Richard Carlile* (Cambridge, 1983), p. 107. This discussion of Carlile is based on Weiner's work.

50   *Republican*, 16 June and 11 August 1820.

51   Weiner, *Radicalism and Freethought*, p. 108.

52   Ibid., p. 112.

53   Ibid., p. 129.

54   *Cobbett's Weekly Political Register*, 15 February 1834, col. 386.

55   John W. Osborne, *William Cobbett: His Thought and His Times* (New Brunswick, NJ, 1966), pp. 196–224. See also Ian Dyck, *William Cobbett and Rural Popular Culture* (Cambridge, 1992), pp. 96 and 128–30.

56   William Cobbett, *Two Penny Trash*, 1 January 1831, pp. 164–5; *Political Register*, 21 July 1827, cols 220–1, cited by Osborne in *Cobbett*, pp. 205–6.

57   *Political Register*, 14 July 1822, cols 653–4.

58   *Political Register*, 14 July 1832, col. 78, and 12 April 1828, col. 464, cited in Osborne, *Cobbett*, p. 206.

59   The original edition was published in several 6*d* parts, and around 10,000 copies of each part were sold. See Philip Harling, *The Waning of the 'Old Corruption': The Politics of Economical Reform in Britain, 1799–1846* (Oxford, 1996), p. 143n. According to Chadwick, *The Victorian Church: Part I*, p. 33, the total sales reached 50,000.

60   Harling, *Waning of the 'Old Corruption'*, p. 144. Harling is critical of Wade for constructing his case against sinecures from what he should have known was obsolete evidence. See pp. 143–50.

61   G.F.A. Best, *Temporal Pillars: Queen Anne's Bounty, the Ecclesiastical Commissioners, and the Church of England* (1964), p. 95.

62   John Wade, *The Black Book; or Corruption Unmasked!* (London, 1820), p. 274.

63   John Wade, *The Extraordinary Black Book: An Exposition of Abuses in Church and State, Courts of Law, Representation, Municipal and Corporate Bodies; with a precis of the House of Commons, Past, Present and to Come* (new edn, London, 1832), pp. 5 and 47.

64   Lincolnshire Archives Office (LAO) CorB5/3/26, E. Price to J. Kaye, December 1837. Edward Price, the curate of Steeple Claydon in Buckinghamshire, informed the Bishop of Lincoln that 'curates are an order of men who suffer much and say little'. For curates, see Knight, *Nineteenth-century Church*, pp. 116–30.

65   Haig, *The Victorian Clergy*, p. 307.

66   Virgin, *Age of Negligence*, p. 90. For the figures for Buckinghamshire, Cambridgeshire, Lincolnshire and Nottinghamshire, see Knight, *Nineteenth-century Church*, p. 131.

67   W.J. Conybeare, *Edinburgh Review* 99 (1853), pp. 105–6.

68   LAO CorB5/4/54/1, Whaplode parishioners' petition to Kaye, December 1849. See Knight, *Nineteenth-century Church*, pp. 132–3.

69   LAO CorB5/19/2/6, Millington to H. Daniel, n.d. (1835).

70   Knight, *Nineteenth-century Church*, pp. 134–5.

71   A fuller version of this material on funerals first appeared in Knight, *Nineteenth-century Church*, pp. 102–5.

72   Rex C. Russell, *Friendly Societies in the Caistor, Binbrook and Brigg Areas in the Nineteenth Century* (Barton-on-Humber, 1975), p. 5. See also Ambler, *Lincolnshire Returns of the Census of Religious Worship 1851* (Lincoln Records Society, 72, 1979), p. xxxii.

73   LAO CorB5/4/67/7, E. Moore to Kaye, 9 November 1849.

74   LAO CorB5/4/79/4, R. Ousby to Kaye, 25 February 1840.

75   LAO CorB5/4/68/3, Robert Burman to Kaye, 8 April 1832.

76   LAO CorB5/3/6/7, W. Wodley to John Kaye, 27 July 1829.

77   LAO CorB5/3/22/5, E.A. Uckwatt to John Kaye, 3 February 1844, and R.N. Russell to

Kaye, 2 July 1845. The Duke had fewer scruples about the presence of clergy further away from his own estate; he built a new parsonage house at Wootton Underwood. See LAO CorB5/3/24/4, Benjamin Hill to Kaye, n.d. (1838).

78   James Obelkevich, *Religion and Rural Society: South Lindsey 1825–1875* (Oxford, 1976), p. 40.

79   Ibid., p. 39.

80   Ibid., p. 40.

81   Some clergy wrote thousands of letters requesting aid for church-building projects. It was the only way many churches could be funded. See Smith, *Religion in Industrial Society*, pp. 82 and 84.

82   R.J. Olney, *Rural Society and County Government in Nineteenth-century Lincolnshire* (Oxford, 1979), pp. 38–9.

83   Best, *Temporal Pillars*, pp. 96–101.

84   Obelkevich, *Religion and Rural Society*, p. 39, citing LAO MON25/10/3/1/89, 10 June 1851.

FURTHER READING

Gilbert, A.D., *Religion and Society in Industrial England: Church, Chapel and Social Change* (London, 1976).

Knight, Frances, *The Nineteenth-century Church and English Society* (Cambridge, 1995).

McLeod, Hugh, *Religion and Society in England, 1850–1914* (Basingstoke, 1996).

Obelkevich, James, *Religion and Rural Society: South Lindsey 1825–1875* (Oxford, 1976).

9

ANTICLERICALISM AND POLITICS IN MID-VICTORIAN WALES

Matthew Cragoe

In the closing pages of his magisterial *History of Protestant Nonconformity in Wales* (1861), the Revd Thomas Rees proclaimed a truth that was a commonplace among Dissenters of his generation: Wales, he said, was 'emphatically a nation of Nonconformists'.[1] Nonconformity did indeed dominate the religious landscape of mid-Victorian Wales. At the Religious Census of 1851, ten years before Rees's book appeared, fully 80 per cent of those counted as having attended a place of worship did so under the auspices of one or other of the Nonconformist denominations. The Church of England, meanwhile, was not only the spiritual home of the minority, but of a minority that seemed to be shrinking perceptibly with each passing decade, as new chapels sprang up all over the principality.[2] Yet in Wales, as elsewhere, the Church of England retained its status as the established Church and claimed certain privileges, including the right to tax the local community for the upkeep of its buildings through a church rate, and the right to prevent Nonconformist ministers officiating at burials in Anglican churchyards.

The potential for friction to develop between clergymen and parishioners, and thus for anticlerical sentiment to flourish, is clear. In this chapter, however, it will be argued that anticlericalism in the principality was at its most prominent not in the parishes but at the level of party politics. The chapter will suggest that the period between 1832 and 1867 saw the growth of a new political discourse unique to the principality. Within this new rhetoric, anticlericalism had an important place, and although it drew heavily on ideas of anticlericalism familiar in England and Ireland it grew specifically from the tensions evident within Welsh politics. Relations between clergymen and Dissenters at the level of the parish, ironically, appear to have remained tolerably good throughout the period.

The chapter begins by exploring the antipathy towards the Anglican clergy expressed by Nonconformist and liberal politicians, and examines the extent to which their anticlericalism was affected by the growth of Welsh national identity. In the second section attention turns to the Conservative party, and offers an exploration of the ways in which it developed a recognisably anticlerical rhetoric to criticise the involvement in politics of Dissenting ministers.[3] The chapter ends by focusing on events at the parish level, and examining whether controversial political issues such as education, burials, and Church rates generated a widespread sense of anticlericalism in this period.

NONCONFORMISTS AND ANTI-ANGLICAN ANTICLERICALISM

The contours of English anticlericalism in the early nineteenth century are well known. In his seminal article on the subject, Eric Evans ascribed the unpopularity of the Anglican clergy at this period to three factors: their role as magistrates, their increased wealth from enclosure and their opposition to reform.[4] In Wales the land enclosed during the late eighteenth and early nineteenth centuries was generally poor,[5] and no large-scale enrichment of the clergy is likely to have occurred; otherwise Nonconformist hostility to the clergy doubtless had similar roots in Wales as it did elsewhere. Even in the 1850s, when the great days of the clerical magistracy had passed, approximately one-fifth of all active magistrates in Wales were Anglican clergymen. In some areas the administration of local justice lay almost entirely in clerical hands: at Bangor in Caernarfonshire, for example, five of the seven active magistrates were clergymen,[6] as were both JPs in the Uwchaled division of Denbighshire, the Revds John Jones and John Evans. In political terms, meanwhile, the Anglican clergy in Wales were overwhelmingly Conservative. Of the sixty-eight subscribers to the Anglesey Conservative Registration Club in March 1837, for example, twenty-three were Anglican clergymen.[7] The clergy in the Glamorganshire election of 1837 similarly appeared on the hustings with the Conservative candidates and played a prominent role in proceedings.[8] And in Wales, as in England, such naked involvement with politics was roundly condemned by the Nonconformist interest. The denominations which were politically active in the early 1830s, principally the Baptists and Independents, denounced the actions of the bishops in the House of Lords in opposing the Reform Bill with as much gusto as their English counterparts,[9] and agitated for the immediate disestablishment of the Church of England.[10]

It was in the 1840s, however, that the unique character of Welsh anticlericalism began to take shape. In 1847 the Royal Commission established to investigate the state of education in Wales and to comment on the morality of the people in the principality published its findings. Its report was deeply unflattering. The commissioners accused the native population of gross immorality, intemperance and dishonesty, and singled out two causes as being chiefly responsible. The first was the Welsh language: the inability of the native population to converse in anything other than their native tongue, they argued, meant that the people were cut off not only from all the philosophical advances of the age, but also from any beneficial intercourse with their social superiors. This insularity was aggravated by the prevalence of Nonconformity, the second cause identified by the commissioners. Here, their strictures were severe. Instead of inculcating sound moral principles based on religious teaching, it appeared that Nonconformity did no more than pander to the love of excessive emotionalism so prevalent among the Welsh. The hell-fire sermons aimed to excite rather than educate their audiences, argued the commissioners, and the consequences were seen in the high bastardy rates which were (allegedly) a peculiarity of the principality. Not only did Nonconformist religious teaching fail to put a brake on this sort of immorality, but the chapels' midweek prayer meetings, after which young men and women mixed freely on their way home, impassioned by what they had heard, seemed to the commissioners to be its occasion.[11]

The evidence upon which the report was based had been gathered from a wide range of witnesses across the principality, including landowners, farmers and Nonconformist ministers. It was the information provided by Anglican clergymen, however, that excited particular hostility in Wales itself. A sample of their comments on Welsh morality and irreligion provides a context for the anticlerical reaction which followed.

The Revd R. Harrison, incumbent of Builth, considered the Welsh 'very dirty' and 'more deceitful than the English', while the Revd James Denning, curate of St Mary's, Brecon, was struck by the 'very great similarity' he witnessed 'between the lower orders of Welsh and Irish': 'both,' he said, 'are dirty, indolent, bigoted, and' (one can almost sense his disapproval!) 'contented'. The Revd J. Pugh of Llandilo took the list further: 'habitual lying and low cunning,' he maintained, 'are very commonly met with, and unchastity is so prevalent that great numbers are in the family-way previous to marriage'.[12] The overall import of the evidence given by Anglican clergy to the 1847 Commission can be encapsulated in that presented by Revd John Griffiths, Vicar of Aberdare. He denounced the insobriety of the Welsh miners, the lax morals of their womenfolk, drew attention to their love of religious excitement and lack of mental discipline, and concluded with the observation that although there were sixteen chapels in the town, 'properly speaking, there is no religion whatever in my parish'.[13]

The report was greeted with a furious outcry in Wales when it appeared in a popular one-volume abridgement in 1848, and a large number of books and pamphlets appeared in subsequent years denying the charges made against the Welsh people.[14] Considerable hostility was naturally directed at the commissioners themselves, but an equal measure was reserved for their informants, the Anglican clergy. The depth of popular animosity can be gauged from a famous collection of ten prints by Hugh Hughes, a North Wales artist and journalist.[15] Entitled 'Pictures for the Million of Wales', the prints were commissioned in 1848 by the arch anti-Blue Books newspaper *The Principality*, edited by the radical journalist Ieuan Gwynedd, and to each was attached a sizeable paragraph of commentary intended to drive home the picture's satirical import.

The pictures in the set covered a variety of topics relating to the Commission, its foundation, its methods of gaining evidence and the hypocrisy of its representatives. For the study of anticlericalism, however, two of the set are particularly relevant. One depicts a commissioner enjoying a cosy *tête-à-tête* with a parson, and savouring a 'tolerable' glass of wine, paid for out of the Church rate. The cartoon is entitled 'Evidence Given', and the parson's views mirror closely those of the Revd John Griffiths of Aberdare and the Revd J. Pugh of Llandilo noted above. He reports that there exists no religion in the parish, that all Welsh women are prostitutes, and the men drunken, cheating, thieving liars. These sentiments are music to the commissioner's ears (which are those of an ass): 'I thank you Rev. Sir,' he replies, 'that is exactly what I want,' explaining that he could not return to London without evidence proving that all Dissenters were immoral and their meetings nurseries of crime.

The other cartoon, entitled 'Jones Tredegar exhibiting one of the black clouded wolves, lately stripped of their sheep's clothing by the commissioners', shows a gigantic black wolf imprisoned in a cage. The text explains that the wolf is of the 'genus Sacerdotus' and was captured in Aberdare, although it was originally from 'Ordovici'. 'Ordovicis' was the *nom de plume* of the Revd John Griffiths of Aberdare, and the point of the cartoon is his derogatory comments about Welsh women. The text goes on to say that the 'Ordovici' was nastier even than the specimens from Nefyn and Troedyraur: readers would have known at once that the vicars of these two parishes had also impugned the morality of Welsh women. The central thrust of the cartoon is driven home by the crowd arrayed in front of the cage consisting entirely of women.

The 'Pictures for the Million of Wales' provide good evidence for the depth of hostility aroused by the evidence given by some Anglican clergymen to the Royal Commission. The commissioners' report, however, had a more far-reaching effect than simply the demonisation of the clergy. One consequence of the welter of refutations that followed its appearance was, arguably, the development of a new Welsh national identity. For the first time people began to think about what it meant to be 'Welsh', and what the nation of Wales might legitimately demand from Parliament. While the commissioners would doubtless have denied the existence of any meaningful Welsh 'nation', and associated Welshness with immorality and religious deviancy, those who sought to defend their countrymen offered a more positive vision of what being Welsh involved. The extent to which their more positive view of Wales internalised the notions of anticlericalism generated by the controversy of the 1847 report can be gained by examining the work of two mid-century writers, Thomas Rees and Henry Richard.

Both Rees and Richard were themselves ordained Nonconformist ministers. Rees spent his life ministering to a congregation in Swansea, while Richard was pastor at a chapel on the Old Kent Road in London until 1847, when he became Secretary of the Peace Society. As a consequence they were among that group most pilloried by the commissioners in 1847, and this clearly had its influence in their writings. In the works of both men, the impact of Nonconformity in the principality was represented as being precisely the opposite of what the commissioners had suggested. The Welsh that emerged in their pages were more, not less, religious and moral than the peoples of any other part of Britain, and possibly of Europe.

Rees's defence of the Welsh took the form of a major statistical rebuttal of the commissioners' claims.[16] The legacy of anticlericalism with which the controversy left him, however, is more clearly visible in his magnum opus *A History of Protestant Nonconformity in Wales*, published in 1861. The book, the first properly historical account of Dissent to appear in Wales, had great appeal and quickly sold its first run of 2,000 copies.[17] It offered a highly coloured account of the rocky path travelled by Dissenters in the principality from the seventeenth century onwards, and was at pains to emphasise the hostility shown to their case by the Church of England and her clergymen. Indeed, the Anglican clergy were repeatedly singled out for vituperative comment: Rees spoke of the 'hosts of clergymen . . . preaching persecution and heading violent mobs' against the Dissenters in the seventeenth and eighteenth centuries, and of the extent to which such men still regarded Nonconformity as 'a great evil'.[18] Despite the fact that the Welsh had become 'emphatically a nation of Nonconformists', Rees's readers were left in no doubt as to who the chief enemies of the nation had been and remained.

Important though Rees's work was in shaping Welsh views of their past, the work that crystallised the identity of the emergent Welsh nation was Henry Richard's *Letters on the Social and Political Condition of Wales*. These letters were received with considerable acclaim when they appeared as a series of articles for the Cobdenite *Morning Star* in 1866 and were republished in a collected edition the following year. The scope of Richard's argument was broad.[19] He defended the Welsh against the strictures of the commissioners' report and developed a sophisticated model of an almost 'ideal' Welshman to refute their claims. A mirror image of the degraded caricature presented by the commissioners, the ideal Welshman was law-abiding, highly moral, culturally sensitive and, above all, deeply religious. He was not, however, without his enemies: on the one hand he was constantly oppressed and abused by the tyrannical, Anglicised class of landlords who owned the soil of Wales; on the other, he was spied upon, defamed and antagonised by the landlords' creatures, the Anglican clergy.

Richard's hostility to the clergymen of the Anglican Church pervades every page of his *Letters*. He dwelt at length on the iniquitous role played by the Anglican clergy in Wales. Ever since the Reformation, he argued, the Church had neglected its duty in the principality: the clergy of the eighteenth century were 'ignorant, irreligious, immoral and in every way utterly incompetent to fulfil the duties of their office', he wrote.[20] Small wonder that the people had embraced Nonconformity so wholeheartedly. Yet the Anglican Church remained, and the present generation of clergymen were, if anything, worse than their predecessors. They were, complained Richard, 'the ministers of a Church imposed by the State, but repudiated by the people', a 'hostile garrison from which the population receives only provocation and annoyance, instead of protection and succour'.[21] He especially condemned them for having 'hoodwinked and misled' the 1847 commissioners as to the true character of the Welsh people, and laid the blame for the 'gross and hideous caricature' contained in the report firmly on their shoulders.[22] And if this latest betrayal was not sufficient evidence of their cultural alienation from the hearts of the people, Richard then introduced a political note: 'with exceptions as rare as black swans,' he announced, they were 'Tories of the rankest description', who used all their influence on behalf of their landed masters.[23] Scattered across the county, continued Richard, the clergy formed a huge 'Dionysius' ear . . . to gather and convey to the landlords every whisper of disaffection against their political despotism'; after an election they were then the foremost to counsel and instigate severe measures of retribution against the recalcitrants.

Richard's *Letters* offer the most extensive political condemnation of the Anglican clergy in mid-Victorian Wales. The significance of his work, however, and of the works of the Revd Thomas Rees considered earlier, was that they all developed their sense of anticlericalism within a specifically Welsh set of reference points: the 1847 report, the rise of Dissent in the principality, the power of the Welsh landowners. As a consequence their anticlericalism took on a depth of meaning that was not, indeed could not, be present in anticlericalism over the border in England: the enemies of the Nonconformists in Wales were *ipso facto* enemies of the people of Wales; and, to the extent that Wales recognised itself by 1867 as 'emphatically, a nation of Nonconformists', they were also the enemies of the Welsh nation itself.

ANGLICANS AND ANTI-NONCONFORMIST ANTICLERICALISM

Although the hostility of Nonconformists towards the Church of England and its clergy remained a touchstone of radical politics in the principality for the rest of the century, theirs was not the only brand of anticlericalism to be found in Wales. Many Anglicans, the vast majority of whom identified their cause with that of the Conservative Party, displayed a strong dislike and distrust of the Nonconformist ministers which amounted to nothing less than another version of the same phenomenon. As with its Nonconformist counterpart, Conservative anticlericalism developed gradually over the period. It was largely a South Wales phenomenon in the 1830s, and only became an important factor in the politics of North Wales after 1852. However, by the general election of 1868 it had become a well-established part of Conservative political rhetoric in all parts of Wales, and remained so for the rest of the century.

The anticlericalism of the Conservative Party first became evident in the 1830s in response to the political activism of Dissenting clergymen in South Wales. As noted above, Baptists and Independents were politically vocal throughout the early 1830s, but it seems to have been at the general elections of 1835, and more particularly of 1837, that the ministers of these denominations became openly involved in the Liberal Party's electioneering effort. In 1837 Conservative candidates publicly criticised the ministers for their actions in both Pembrokeshire[24] and Brecon,[25] but it was in Carmarthenshire that the most dramatic events occurred. The scale of Dissenting organisation was unprecedented. A circular was apparently sent to all Nonconformist congregations in the county, inviting each to send a delegate to a meeting at Carmarthen designed to hit upon the best way of promoting the return of the Independent Whig candidate Sir James Williams.[26] As the campaign progressed, reports surfaced that the Dissenters were actively canvassing the estates even of landlords known to be hostile to Williams, and had addressed a circular to the tenantry urging them to resist landlord pressure and 'BREAK THROUGH ALL RESTRAINTS TO VOTE FOR SIR JAMES!' The circular reminded the recipients that they had prayed for a candidate like Sir James in the chapels, and that failure to support him now, when God had granted their wish, was effectively to hold up their arms against God himself.[27]

Such tactics certainly alarmed Conservatives. The encouragement given to the tenants to vote against their landlords seemed to the *Carmarthen Journal*, a newspaper with strongly Conservative sympathies, to represent 'the introduction of the thin end of the wedge into that mutual bond of sympathy and good will which ever ought to exist between landlord and tenant'.[28] More worrying, however, was the Nonconformists' intrusion of concepts of religious duty into the secular political arena, and the representation of the vote as an issue of conscience. This the *Journal* described as an 'atrocious Irish tactic', and the parallel also struck others. By the time of the election, for example, the party's chief agent in Carmarthenshire, Charles Bishop, considered the situation critical: 'Our contest,' he wrote to his Breconshire counterpart, 'is assuming a desperate character: the Dissenting Ministers emulate the Irish Priests in every particular.'

In associating the activities of the Nonconformist ministers with the actions of the Irish priesthood, Conservatives invoked a well-established set of stereotypes to explain the threat they had encountered.[29] Throughout the 1830s Conservatives all over Britain made much of priestly influence in Ireland, and linked it to the disloyalty and rebelliousness of the Irish politicians led by Daniel O'Connell. Especially controversial elections, such as that for the county of Carlow in 1837, 'where the power of the Priest is triumphant, and the legitimate influence of the landlord is completely prostrate',[30] provided them with plenty of ammunition for a representation of voters behaving as mindless automatons at the behest of their cynical and manipulative clergymen.[31] By describing the activities of the Welsh Nonconformist ministers in similar language, therefore, the Tories laid bare their fears as to the consequences the same combination of demagoguery and rebelliousness as existed in Ireland might have in Wales.

Something of the same tension can be discerned in the evidence given by Anglican clergymen to the 1847 Commission. Although their derogatory comments applied strictly to the Dissenting clergy, an unspoken parallel was drawn between the activities of the Nonconformist ministers and the priests of Ireland. Both, for example, were accused of perpetuating the superstition and ignorance of their flocks by their refusal to use the English language.[32] Furthermore, the implication in both cases was that having established a hold over their ignorant congregations, the priests manipulated them at election times and forced them to vote for opponents of the established Church on pain of everlasting damnation. Thus, although the involvement of Dissenting ministers in the Chartist movement and Anti-Corn Law League also helped fuel Conservative distrust during the 1840s,[33] the Irish parallel was perhaps the key to understanding their instinctive fear of the Welsh preachers' political activities.

Before 1852, however, Conservative anticlericalism appears to have been confined largely to the southern counties of Wales. It was only at the general election of 1852 that Dissenting clergy in North Wales came to play a prominent role in electoral politics and that Conservatives had recourse to the language of anticlericalism. In explaining this development, the 1847 report occupies a key role. Its tone of blanket hostility to Nonconformity in the principality was a crucial factor in persuading the Calvinistic Methodists, the largest denomination in the north, to throw in their lot with the Baptists and Independents on the Liberal side. Hitherto, they had tended to stand aloof from political conflict, but their entry into politics introduced a new tone to electoral warfare. The *Chester Courant*'s condemnation of the 'reckless temper of religious fanaticism' exhibited by the Liberals in 1852, and its accusation that ministers had denounced the Conservative candidates in Denbighshire and Flintshire from the pulpit were to become standard fare in Tory-inspired reports of North Wales elections, as they had long been in those of the south and, of course, Ireland.[34]

The two essential characteristics of Conservative anticlericalism in Wales were thus well developed by the mid-1850s. On the one hand they deplored what they saw as the ignorance and lack of enlightenment among the Dissenting clergy, and the blind obedience they expected from their congregations. On the other, they felt grave misgivings about the involvement of the Nonconformist ministers in politics, and the social ends towards which they might use their influence. However, the peak Conservative concern about the activities of the Nonconformist ministers came at the general election of 1868, when they claimed that Dissenting ministers had mixed their religious and civil roles in pursuit of Liberal votes as never before.[35]

The election was the first to be held under the terms of the Second Reform Act, passed in 1867, and saw both sides adopt a new approach to the business of electioneering. The increase in the number of voters meant that the old methods by which candidates had reached them, through canvassing and the exercise of influence, were less efficient than once they had been. Although such methods remained important, they were now supplemented by a far greater number of political meetings at which candidates and their supporters addressed the electorate directly. Such meetings had long been a feature of political life in urban areas, but in the remote rural regions of county constituencies, they represented a new departure.

It was in such areas that Conservative fears of the influence wielded by the Nonconformist clergy became most acute.[36] Many such meetings were held, for want of any suitable alternative, in one of the local chapels. Conservatives feared that when the minister of the chapel appeared on a political platform to speak on behalf of a candidate at election time, some among the congregation would not be able to distinguish between his opinions as a citizen and his teachings as a preacher. This was especially the case since the language used to deliver these opinions was often rich in religious allusion. If Nonconformist voters understood the preacher's opinions at a political meeting to have the same value as his teachings on moral subjects, the preacher's political influence was thereby increased dramatically.

The principal issue at the election, the disestablishment of the Irish Church, certainly lent itself to such exploitation. This question was held to enshrine a central tenet of the Nonconformists' faith – the idea that religion should not be subject to state control – and the Dissenting clergy were at great pains to educate their flocks on this point. Reports such as that depicting the minister of a Cardiganshire chapel telling two men who wished to vote for the Conservative candidate that it was a 'matter of the soul', and that 'neither of them had a chance of being saved in the day of the Lord' if they voted against the Liberal, were common.[37] Others were apparently threatened with exclusion from the chapel if they failed to vote for the Liberal candidate.[38] Conservatives claimed that tactics of this sort, in which a voter's eternal spiritual welfare was presented by the minister as riding on his vote at the election, had been a crucial factor in securing Liberal success at the polls: the election had been won and lost, in the eyes of one contemporary, by the 'unbridled play of interested bigotry and sectarian hate . . . upon the side of the Liberal candidates . . . exercised by Nonconformist Ministers throughout the country'.[39] In Caernarfonshire, meanwhile, scene of perhaps the most spectacular Conservative reverse, the defeated candidate, Colonel Pennant, spoke of the 'formidable combination' of preachers that had opposed him, and likened the current state of Wales to 'the dark days in Spain and Ireland [when] the people were held in thraldom by the priests'.[40]

However one views these allegations – and they were hotly denied – what is significant in the context of this chapter is the extent to which Conservatives had recourse to a well-established rhetoric of anticlericalism to discredit their opponents. Nor did their hostility to the Dissenting clergy die away after 1868.

Until the end of the century, defeated Conservative candidates could be found inveighing against the illegitimate influence wielded by Dissenting ministers at election time. Like the Liberals' accusations against the Anglican clergy, however, these allegations first became a central part of a distinctively Welsh politics in the mid-Victorian period.

POPULAR REACTIONS TO THE CLERGY

Although both Liberals and Conservatives made considerable use of anticlerical rhetoric in their political campaigns, it is difficult to judge the extent to which such ideas had a resonance at the grassroots level in the period between the First and Second Reform Acts. Finding reliable information on the relationship between clergymen and parishioners or ministers and congregations is very difficult. However, there appears to have been little obvious anticlerical sentiment expressed within the ranks of either the Anglicans or Dissenters concerning their own clergy. Anglicans in Wales could sometimes be found deploring the appearance of ritualism, though this was comparatively rare, or lamenting the lowly social origins of the poorer clergy, just as an older generation of Dissenters came to deplore the effects of too much college training on the preaching style of some mid-Victorian ministers.[41] But in neither case could this be said to have amounted to a criticism of the whole order of clergymen, or of the authority they wielded within their respective Churches.

Yet some indication of feelings at the grassroots can be obtained by tracing popular reactions to the Anglican Church and its privileges at parish level. A wide range of impressionistic evidence could be cited either for the argument that relations were generally good, or that they were not. Thus reports that Dissenting parishioners had been among the most anxious participants in projects to repair the local parish churches were not uncommon: many, as it was pointed out, had ancestors lying in their graveyards, and so felt a personal connection with the church.[42] In other cases a more personal bond with the officiating clergyman often developed, as in the parish of Llansantffraid, where Dissenters were among those who had subscribed to a silver vase for the curate, who was leaving to take up a living elsewhere.[43] Equally, one might cite evidence from the Rebecca Riots. The riots, ostensibly focused on opposition to the proliferation of toll gates in West Wales, provided a focus for a wider range of grievances. Interestingly, in the context of anticlericalism, although some meetings of farmers called for the disestablishment of the Church, no grievances against the clergy in particular were cited. Indeed, it is striking that no clergymen or their property were attacked in the course of the disturbances. The riots provided cover for the settling of many old scores, yet the only action taken against a clergyman was the forcible reunion of the Vicar of Bangor Teifi with Mrs Walters, his estranged wife: the rioters made them swear publicly 'to be loving and dutiful partners' thereafter.[44]

If such evidence might suggest good relations between clergymen and parishioners at parish level, many other stories can be found where a rift had clearly developed. The range of subjects over which disagreement developed at the parish level was surprisingly wide, and by no means confined to religious matters. At a time when local government was centred in the Parish Vestry, a forum in which all parishioners who paid rates had a vote, issues such as the implementation of the New Poor Law could prove divisive. At Abernant in Carmarthenshire a decision was taken in the Vestry in August 1836 not to pay the required contribution to the new Carmarthen Union of which the parish was now a part. The vestry book was signed by nine members of the parish: the only dissenter was the vicar, the Revd J.D. Lewis, who entered a protest in the vestry book 'against the above illegal combination' established to 'gratify factious feelings'.[45] What impact this disagreement had on relations between vicar and parishioners is impossible to say: the parish had begun to contribute to the Union by December 1837, and the Church rates do not seem to have been challenged in this period. That some ill-feeling had arisen, however, is plain.

Vestry books also reveal tensions on other more obviously religious issues, such as education. At Llanbadarn Trefeglwys, for example, the community was clearly split in 1847 over a plan to appoint one David Davies as the village schoolmaster, to 'bring up the Children with sound & solid knowledge in the Principles and Practices of the Church of England'.[46] Five people were recorded as being in favour of this motion, including the vicar and one of the parish's churchwardens; however, the minutes also record a list of twenty-seven dissenters, who were not happy with the new arrangement. Clearly, here was a case when the vicar and his supporters had set the Nonconformist majority of his parish at defiance. To mid-century leaders of Dissent like the Revd Thomas Rees and the Calvinistic Methodist Revd John Phillips, this would doubtless have seemed an archetypal illustration of the ill-feeling between Anglicans and Dissenters at parish level. Both men were keen to represent the proliferation of Anglican-inspired National Schools in the principality as merely the latest weapon of the clergy in their ongoing vendetta against the Nonconformist people of Wales.[47] Phillips went further, denouncing the clergy and arguing that they cared nothing about the education of the poor, establishing National Schools only to turn the minds of children against Dissent. 'The clergy,' he concluded, 'had they the power, would even now thrust us out of existence.'[48] For Phillips and Rees, the education question provided a powerful illustration of the divorce between the clergy and their Dissenting parishioners.

The question of burials was another issue on which feelings sometimes ran high, and which undoubtedly had a profound impact on relations between clergy and parishioners in some communities. The story told to the House of Commons by George Osborne Morgan, MP for Denbighshire, when introducing his Burials Bill in 1870, for example, was certainly one which roused Dissenting outrage. It involved the funeral of the Revd Henry Rees, one of the foremost Calvinistic

Methodist preachers of his generation. The burial took place in the churchyard at Llandyssilio, but, said Morgan, 'the rector of the parish – standing no doubt on his strict rights – positively refused to allow any expression of feeling on the part of the vast multitude assembled, except the singing of a hymn selected by himself, and this being declined, the body was deposited in the grave amid that enforced silence'.[49] 'It was impossible to describe the painful impression created by this incident,' Morgan went on, 'not only in the neighbourhood where it occurred, but throughout the whole of Wales – no single circumstance which had occurred within the last ninety years had done more to . . . shake the already weakened and tottering fabric of the Church in Wales.' Such an incident could hardly have failed to sour relations.[50]

However, if examples of undoubted tension at the parish level can be unearthed, it is difficult to extrapolate a more general picture of grassroots hostility from such examples. Indeed, in the cases of both education and burials, the gravity of the crises becomes less obvious if a broader approach is taken. The limited extent to which Welsh parishioners took the opportunity to rid themselves of Anglican schools after the 1870 Education Act, for example, is surely indicative of a situation which was not felt to be intolerable.[51] Similarly, although events at the funeral of the Revd Henry Rees had undoubtedly scandalised opinion throughout Wales, such situations must have been fairly isolated if the statistics relating to the implementation of the Burials Act of 1881 provide any indication. According to the Bishop of St Asaph, in the first five years after the Act's passage, only 7 per cent of interments in the principality took advantage of its provisions.[52]

A similar conclusion can be reached from a consideration of what was perhaps the most consistently divisive issue at parish level between 1832 and 1868: the church rate. The church rate was a tax that the Church of England had a right to levy on all occupiers of property in a parish for the upkeep of the church. Many Dissenters objected to the tax on the grounds that since there was no scriptural authority for an established Church, there could be none for any taxes or levies demanded for its upkeep.[53] In addition, there were complaints that the money raised in this way was misspent.[54] The controversy rumbled on throughout the period between the First and Second Reform Acts. From the 1830s a succession of remedial and repealing measures were brought before the House of Commons, supported by waves of well-signed petitions from the localities.[55] As bill after bill foundered in Parliament, however, the front line of the church rates battle moved into the parishes themselves. Here, in the vestries, Dissenters could organise opposition to the imposition of a rate, forcing a vote to be taken on whether a rate should be set or not. The atmosphere often became extremely heated during these meetings. One contemporary, speaking of Church rate disputes in his own parish of Whitechapel, recalled that when the pro-Church rate party defeated their opponents, 'they absolutely had a hurrah in the middle of the Church': 'it was', he concluded, 'a war, and a most unholy war'.[56]

To judge from newspaper accounts of battles over the church rates, vestry politics were every bit as heated in Wales as in Whitechapel. Interestingly, newspaper reporters on both sides had recourse to the familiar language of anticlericalism when describing church rates conflicts. To the *Carmarthen Journal*, for example, the significant feature of a contest over church rates in one Glamorganshire parish was the presence of three 'cowardly' Baptist preachers, who were portrayed as attempting to disrupt the harmony of the community.[57] In another report, the defeated Dissenters were depicted retiring to a local public house to drown their sorrows and 'expatiate upon the good qualities of some of their most *forcible* preachers', who, by implication, had put them up to opposing the rate in the first place.[58] An article reflecting generally on the fight against church rates in Wales, in the leading Welsh-language newspaper *Baner Ac Amserau Cymru*, however, chose a different peg on which to hang its interpretation of events: here, it was the punitive activities undertaken by the Archdeacon of Monmouth and the clergy of the county in pursuit of those who had defaulted on their church rate payments that was highlighted.[59] Elsewhere the notable features of vestry conflicts were the actions of the clergymen themselves.[60]

Yet on the relatively rare occasions when detailed reports of the proceedings were reproduced in the newspapers, a rather different picture emerges. It appears that the real lines of hostility revealed by the church rates were drawn between the Dissenters and the churchwardens charged with collecting the rates, rather than between the incumbent of the parish and his parishioners. An extremely controversial Vestry at St Peter's, Carmarthen, in 1838 provides a case in point.[61] After a long and highly charged battle which had seen both pro- and anti-rate parties doing everything they could to muster support in the weeks prior to the Vestry meeting, including fly-posting the town, the churchwarden, Mr Jeffries, proposed to make a rate of 2*d* in the pound for the forthcoming year. Out of the sum raised were to come, *inter alia*, the salaries of the organist and parish clerk. This provided a focus for the opposition of the Dissenters and provoked the following exchange between William Philipps, the ex-Mayor of the town, and Jeffries:

Mr W. Philipps:– You may depend upon it, Mr Jeffries, that, if you include those salaries in your estimate, the rate will not be legal, and can be successfully resisted.

Mr Jeffries:– Very well, Mr Philipps; if we carry the rate, I shall give you an opportunity of resisting, for I promise you I will call upon you first for the rate; and if you resist, I will take out a citation in the Bishop's Court directly. You are just the man we should like – you have plenty of money, and are a very influential man among the Dissenters; and you may depend upon it, I will give you an opportunity of resisting.

The subsequent amendment calling for consideration of the rate to be postponed by twelve months – tantamount to a refusal – was defeated in a poll. What the exchange between Jeffries and Philipps suggests, however, is the extent to which the battle over the church rates was a focal point for the wider conflict between the two religious parties in the town, rather than a simple proxy for anticlerical sentiment.

Occasionally a hint emerges in church rate cases that the cause of tension was indeed the personality of the clergyman. In the visitation return for Aberyskyr in Breconshire in 1866 for example, it was said: 'There have been no church rates for several years owing to a coolness between the late incumbent and some of the population'; it added, however, that since the arrival of a new incumbent, payment of church rates had been resumed, implying that the hostility was to the incumbent as a man, and not as a clergyman.[62] In any case the clergyman's role was usually secondary, since the setting and collection of the rate was the business of the churchwardens, not the incumbent. The anticlerical shorthand used by newspapers in describing many church rate battles presents an overly simplistic version of events.

As with the questions of burial and education noted above, the church rate question is amenable to statistical analysis. An enquiry into how well the Church rates had been paid was a standard question put to the churchwardens of every parish during the bishops' Triennial Visitations of their dioceses. The records for most of Wales are tantalisingly incomplete for the period between 1832 and 1868, but fortunately those for the diocese of St David's allow a picture of church rate payment to be constructed. In the following table, the percentage of parishes within each Archdeaconry still paying the rate at two key dates is shown. The first column refers to those parishes still paying in 1854, a year after the so-called Braintree Judgment had effectively ended the ability of the authorities to compel parishes to make a rate, having allowed a majority of ratepayers in a Vestry the right to refuse to do so.[63] The second column records parishes still paying in 1866, the last date for which we have information prior to the repeal of church rates in 1868. The number of parishes in each Archdeaconry included in the sample is indicated in parentheses.

Parishes in St David's Diocese paying church rates in 1854 and 1866 (%)		
Archdeaconry	**1854**	**1866**
Radnor & Brecon (130)	82	58
Carmarthen (74)	81	47
St David's (100)	67	45
Cardigan (82)	71	29
Source: NLW, Bishop's Visitation Returns, St David's Diocese, 1845–69		

The table shows clearly the extent to which most parishes kept paying the church rate until the Braintree Judgment removed the practical obligation to do so. Thereafter, the speed with which rates were abandoned differed markedly from region to region. In Cardiganshire, which was heavily Nonconformist and radical in its politics, rates were quickly abandoned: fewer than one-third of parishes were still paying rates by the time of their abandonment. In the more Conservative areas of Brecon, Radnor, Pembrokeshire (the area covered by the Archdeaconry of St David's) and, somewhat surprisingly, Carmarthenshire, a rather different picture emerges. In these areas, nearly half the parishes continued to pay the rate until its abolition in 1868.

Conclusion

The pattern revealed by the table provides a fitting opportunity to offer some conclusions about anticlericalism in Wales between 1832 and 1868. The table suggests strongly that grassroots levels of hostility to the established Church varied widely from region to region; it seems likely that levels of anticlerical feeling would have done so too. It may be that in areas where Dissent was strong and militant, the figure of the Anglican clergyman was naturally more hateful to parishioners. It is perhaps significant, for example, that Henry Richard, whose strictures on the Anglican clergy were noted earlier, hailed from the small town of Tregaron in Cardiganshire, a county where church rates were quickly abandoned. In other areas, however, where the church itself was a more acceptable part of the landscape and the obligation to pay rates to assist with its upkeep met with fewer objections, clergymen were not so odious to the population.

It would be mistaken to think that relations between the clergy and parishioners were everywhere amicable and conciliatory. During the late-century protest against tithes in North Wales, there was considerable evidence of antipathy having developed between parishioners and resident tithe-receiving clergymen. J.P. Dunbabin records several species of anticlerical activity, including the display of clerical effigies. A Merionethshire distraint sale, for example, was enlivened by the presence of a cart in which had been placed an effigy of a parson placarded with sentiments such as 'the parson to feed himself'. At a farm near St Asaph, meanwhile, a crowd of labourers chanting anti-tithe ballads was seen carrying about an effigy of the local vicar which they later knocked to pieces with sticks.

The ballads in which the labourers joined may well have been from the set commissioned and published by the famous newspaper editor Thomas Gee. This collection, designed to be sung to popular tunes at distraint sales, included verses offering some distinctly anticlerical sentiments. One typical example ran:

> Apostolic Priests indeed!
> Judases in heart and deed;
> Traitors steeped in fraud.

Yet what is perhaps most striking about the display of anticlerical feeling manifested during the tithe war is how unique such an exhibition was. There were no other examples during the nineteenth century of this broadly based symbolic assault on the clergy, when songs, broadsides, effigies and ritual violence all combined to demonstrate popular hostility to the tithe-taking parson. While issues such as education, burial and Church rates produced isolated incidents of great drama and controversy, they do not appear to have precipitated the concerted anticlericalism encountered during the tithe war. And during the Rebecca Riots, as noted above, little took place to encourage the view that popular anticlericalism was rife in the localities.

Instead, anticlericalism remained a largely rhetorical phenomenon in Wales, of use to politicians and the propagandists and activists who supported them. Indeed, what is striking about the nature of the anticlerical sentiments bandied to and fro by Anglicans and Nonconformists, is the extent to which they charged the clergy of the other side with the sins that both might have most readily associated with Roman Catholic priests. Dissenters accused Anglican clergy of worldliness and a love of power and riches; Anglicans responded by accusing the Dissenters of aiding and abetting the superstitious beliefs of their flocks, and of then exploiting this credulity for sinister political ends. Thus anticlerical sentiment in mid-Victorian Wales is best understood as part of that distinctively Welsh political vocabulary which developed in the mid-Victorian period. The image of the rapacious priest offered both Liberals and Conservatives a convenient shorthand for describing complex contemporary religious and political divisions. It does not, however, offer an accurate portrayal of the everyday relationship between priests and people in the principality for uncritical consumption by the historian.

Notes

1   T. Rees, *A History of Protestant Nonconformity in Wales: From its Rise to the Present Time* (London, 1861), p. 485.

2   Ibid., pp. 483–4; and see figures in 2nd edn, published 1883, pp. 454ff.

3   I have used 'Dissent' and 'Nonconformity' interchangeably throughout this article, as was customary in the Victorian period.

4   E.J. Evans, 'Some Reasons for the Growth of Anti-clericalism in England', *Past & Present* 66 (1975), pp. 84–109.

5   D.W. Howell, *Land & People in Nineteenth Century Wales* (London, 1977), pp. 37–8; M. Cragoe, 'Welsh Electioneering and the Purposes of Parliament: "From Radicalism to Nationalism" Re-considered', *Parliamentary History* 17 (1998), pp. 113–30.

6   *Parliamentary Papers* 1856, L, pp. 479ff., 'Returns relating to Justices of the Peace'.

7   University College of North Wales, Bangor, General Papers, 29534, 'Subscriptions . . . 7 March 1837'.

8   'Election for the County', *Merthyr and Cardiff Chronicle* 5 August 1837.

9   R.L. Hugh, 'The Theological Background of Nonconformist Social Influence in Wales, 1800–1850' (University of London, unpublished PhD thesis, 1951), pp. 218–19.

10   R. Tudor Jones, 'The Origins of the Nonconformist Disestablishment Campaign', *Journal of the Historical Society of the Church in Wales* xx (1970), p. 44.

11   For a fuller account of the commissioners' views, see M. Cragoe, 'A Question of Culture: The Welsh Church and the Bishopric of St Asaph', *Welsh History Review* 18 (1996), pp. 232–5.

12   *Parliamentary Papers* 1847, XXVII, *Reports of the Commissioners of Inquiry into the State of Education in Wales*, pp. 191 and 513–15.

13   I.G. Jones, '1848 and 1868: "Brad Y Llyfrau Gleision"', in *Mid-Victorian Wales: The Observers and the Observed* (Cardiff, 1992), pp. 147–8.

14   Sir Thomas Phillips, *Wales: The Language, Social Condition, Moral Character, and the Religious Opinions of the People* (London, 1849); T. Stephens, 'Sefyllfa Wareiddol y Cymry', *Traethodydd* (Merthyr, December 1857), p. 385; Revd T. Rees, 'Anniweirdeb Cymru', *Baner Ac Amserau Cymru* (3 September 1863), p. 611.

15   The paragraphs that follow are based on Prys Morgan, 'Pictures for the Million of Wales, 1848: The Political Cartoons of Hugh Hughes', *Transactions of the Honourable Society of Cymmrodorion* (1994).

16   T. Rees, 'The Alleged Unchastity of Wales', in *Miscellaneous Papers on Subjects Relating to Wales* (London, 1867), pp. 29–40.

17   A.J. Johnes, *An Essay on the Causes of Dissent in Wales* (1834), pre-dated Rees's work, but the latter was the more comprehensive account. Sales figures quoted from the preface to the 2nd edn of Rees's *History*, published in 1883.

18   Rees, *A History of Protestant Nonconformity in Wales*, p. 485.

19   H. Richard, *Letters on the Social and Political Condition of Wales*, ed. M. Cragoe (Penzance, 2000).

20   Ibid., p. 5.

21   Ibid., pp. 25 and 104.

22   Ibid., pp. 2–3.

23   Ibid., pp. 101–5.

24   'Pembroke election', *Carmarthen Journal*, 4 August 1837.

25   Powys Record Office, Wood/A/29/1/4/85, *Speech of Col Wood, MP for the County of Brecon . . . August 10 1837* (Merthyr Tydfil, 1837), pp. 5–6.

26   *Carmarthen Journal*, 21 July 1837.

27   Editorial, *Carmarthen Journal*, 4 August 1837.

28   Editorial, *Carmarthen Journal*, 28 July 1837.

29   For the origins of this, see Justin Champion, '"To govern is to make subjects believe": Anti-clericalism, Politics and Power, *c.* 1680–1717', supra, chapter 3.

30   Editorial, *Carmarthen Journal*, 4 August 1837.

31 Tory suspicion of the electoral activities of Catholic priests did not fade: 'Political Parsons', *Chester Courant*, 4 August 1852.

32 For a modern exploration of the links between Dissent and superstition, see Owen Davies, 'Methodism, the Clergy, and the Popular Belief in Witchcraft and Magic', *History* 82 (1997), pp. 252–65. Thomas Rees, never one to let Anglicans have the last say, mocked the superstition of those clergymen who believed in the Apostolic Succession: *History of Protestant Nonconformity in Wales*, p. 459.

33 R. Wallace, *Organise! Organise! Organise! A History of Reform Agitations in Wales, 1840–1886* (Cardiff, 1992), pp. 41 and 49; *Welshman*, 9 July 1841.

34 'Talk in the Rows', *Chester Courant*, 28 July 1852.

35 See M. Cragoe, 'Conscience or Coercion? Clerical Influence at the General Election of 1868 in Wales', *Past & Present* 149 (1995), pp. 151–63, for greater detail.

36 This paragraph is based on Cragoe, 'Conscience or Coercion?', pp. 151–63.

37 Letter of 'Truth and Justice', *Welshman*, 2 September 1869.

38 Cragoe, 'Conscience or Coercion?', pp. 159–60.

39 Letter of 'A Briton', *Welshman*, 27 November 1868.

40 *Carnarvon and Denbigh Herald*, 28 November and 30 December 1868.

41 Cragoe, *Anglican Aristocracy*, p. 206; W. Conybeare, 'The Church of England in the mountains', *Edinburgh Review* XCVII (April 1853), pp. 343–79; *Memoir and Sermons of the Late Rev. David Lloyd Jones*, ed. Revd R. Hughes (Wrexham, 1912), pp. 38–9.

42 Letter of 'Cambrensis', *Carmarthen Journal*, 25 February 1842.

43 *Carmarthen Journal*, 13 April 1836.

44 D.J.V. Jones, *Rebecca's Children: A Study of Rural Society, Crime, and Protest* (Oxford, 1989), p. 269.

45 Carmarthen Record Office (CRO), Abernant Vestry Book, entries for 18 August 1836, 21 May 1837 and 27 April 1838.

46 National Library of Wales (NLW), Llanbadarn Trefeglwys 1/4, ff. 349–51.

47 Rees, *History of Protestant Nonconformity in Wales*, *passim*; see 'Llangeinwen British School', *Carnarvon and Denbigh Herald*, 30 January 1847, for the sentiments of the Revd John Phillips on the same theme.

48 Phillips was the North Wales agent for the British and Foreign School society: W.J. Owen, *Cofiant y Parchedig John Phillips, Bangor* (Caernarfon, 1912), p. 21.

49 *Hansard*, 3, 23 March 1870, cols 513ff.

50 Deborah Wiggins, 'The Burial Act of 1880, the Liberation Society & George Osborne Morgan', *Parliamentary History* 15 (1996), pp. 173–89, for a modern view of Morgan's campaign.

51 Robert Smith, 'The Forster Education Act of 1870: the Experience of its Implementation in the Llanelli Area', *Carmarthenshire Antiquary* xxxv (1999), pp. 66–81; Cragoe, *Anglican Aristocracy*, pp. 200–2.

52 Bishop of St Asaph, *A Handbook of Welsh Church Defence* (London, 1895), p. 57.

53 See the *Cambrian*, 4 January 1834, for a list of Dissenters' grievances drawn up at a public meeting in Abergavenny.

54 *Parliamentary Papers* 1859 (Sess 2), V, House of Lords Select Committee on the Assessment and Levy of Church Rate, qq. 147–8, Revd J. Cale Miller; *Carmarthen Journal*, 24 November 1837,

Dissenters in Llangattock sought to disallow expenditure for killing of foxes; CRO, St Peter's, Carmarthen, Vestry Book, 17 November 1836. The fact that some of the money went on wine for communion also offended teetotal Nonconformists: 'Tregaron a'r Dreth Egwlys', *Baner Ac Amserau Cymru*, 1 August 1866, p. 13.

55   See Editorial and 'Monmouthshire', *South Wales Reporter*, 27 May 1837, p. 100, for the activities of the Pontypool Church Rate Abolition Society.

56   Lord Stanley, *The Church Rate Question Considered* (London, 1853), p. 10.

57   'The Church Triumphant', *Carmarthen Journal*, 27 May 1836.

58   'Llechryd', *Carmarthen Journal*, 1 April 1836. Nonconformist ministers were well to the fore in such meetings: *Baner Ac Amserau Cymru*, 14 June 1865, p. 377.

59   'Sir Fynwy a'r Dreth Eglwys', *Baner Ac Amserau Cymru*, 18 October 1865, p. 11; 'Bryngwyn, Bronynwy, a'r Dreth Eglwys', by 'Rhyddfrydwr', *Baner Ac Amserau Cymru*, 19 June 1867, p. 10.

60   'Llangranllo a'r Dreth Eglwys', *Baner Ac Amserau Cymru*, 20 June 1866, p. 13. Ibid., 'Llanerfyl a'r Dreth Eglwys', 13 November 1867, pp. 9–10; 'Y Treth Egwlys – Trelech', *Seren Gomer*, 1837, p. 117.

61   CRO, St Peter's, Carmarthen, Vestry Book, entries for 19 and 21 April 1838. This passage is based upon the account of the meeting in the *Carmarthen Journal*.

62   NLW, Church in Wales Mss, SD/QA/224: Brecon, Aberyskyr, p. 6, q. xii.

63   J.P. Ellens, *Religious Routes to Gladstonian Liberalism: The Church Rate Conflict in England and Wales, 1832–1868* (Pennsylvania, 1994), p. 113.

FURTHER READING

Cragoe, M., *An Anglican Aristocracy: The Moral Economy of the Landed Estate in Carmarthenshire, 1832–95* (Oxford, 1996).

Davies, E.T., *Religion and Society in the Nineteenth Century* (Llandyssul, 1981).

Harvey, J., *The Art of Piety: The Visual Culture of Welsh Nonconformity* (Cardiff, 1995).

Howell, P., 'Church and Chapel in Wales', in C. Brooks and A. Saint (eds), *The Victorian Church: Architecture and Society* (Manchester, 1995), pp. 118–32.

Jones, I.G., *Explorations and Explanations: Essays in the Social History of Victorian Wales* (Llandyssul, 1981).

——, *Communities: Essays in the Social History of Victorian Wales* (Llandyssul, 1987).

10

VARIETIES OF ANTICLERICALISM IN LATER VICTORIAN AND EDWARDIAN ENGLAND

Hugh McLeod

Wherever there is a distinction within the Church between 'clergy' and 'laity', there is likely to be at least some tension between them; and in any society where the Church is a powerful institution, exercising a degree of control over many areas of life apart from the purely 'religious', there is likely to be at least some degree of tension between the clergy and the population in general, including those who have very little involvement in the Church. The severity of these tensions will be influenced by many different factors, including most notably the extent and nature of the clergy's political activity, their individual or collective wealth, and the degree to which their separation from the laity is emphasised by such things as distinctive dress, a distinctive way of life (e.g. celibacy), exclusive access to important religious functions (e.g. preaching or administration of the sacraments), or the exercise of special controls over the laity (e.g. through the confessional). Anticlericalism played at least some part in all Christian societies in the later nineteenth century.[1] But one needs to distinguish between those like France, Spain or many Latin American countries, where it was central, and those like the United States, where it was of minor significance. England lay about midway between these extremes.

The high point of hostility to the clergy during the last two centuries is generally reckoned to be the burning down of the palace of the Bishop of Bristol in 1831, in reprisal for episcopal opposition to the Reform Bill. During the same period, rioting rural labourers threatened or attacked the homes of numerous country clergymen.[2] There is no doubt of the unpopularity which the Anglican clergy suffered during the years around 1830 because of their wealth, their identification with political conservatism and frequently their direct involvement as magistrates in the defence of the social order and the suppression of protest. However, the leading authority on the history of modern English anticlericalism, Eric Evans, argues that there was a precipitous decline in animosity towards the clergy after about 1840. He attributes this partly to the effects of the Church reforms of the 1830s and 1840s, but mainly to increasing religious apathy: it was not that the people came to love the clergy any more, but simply that what the clergy did or did not do seemed to matter less.[3]

Many historians would reject Evans's view of the later Victorian period as a time of religious apathy,[4] but most would accept his view that anticlericalism was in decline. While the literature on Victorian religion is now very extensive, and there is a growing body of work on the clergy,[5] very few historians have shown any interest in anticlericalism in the later Victorian and Edwardian periods. The major exception to this is Eugenio Biagini, whose study of popular radicalism in the age of Gladstone accords anticlericalism a centrality which no other historian has given it.[6] He notes the support given by the radicals of the 1860s and 1870s to the cause of religious freedom generally, and specifically to the disestablishment of the Anglican Church in England and Ireland, non-sectarian education and the right of the atheist Bradlaugh to sit in Parliament. He mentions their involvement in the agricultural labourers' movement of the 1870s, and their attacks on the Anglican clergy who were regarded as its chief foes. And he highlights the interest taken by British radicals in the struggles against the power of the Papacy and the Catholic Church in Italy. But it would be hard to claim any similarly central role for anticlericalism in British politics for any period after the 1880s.

However, the lack of any very powerful anticlerical *movement*, and the fact that except for a brief period in the 1870s anticlericalism was not a major political issue, should not obscure the existence of anticlerical *sentiments* of various kinds, which could have a significant influence both on the collective mentalities of certain groups and on the outlook of many individuals. Anticlerical attitudes remained significant in the private sphere, even if they tended to be pushed out of the public sphere.

Take the example of Charles Booth's monumental *Life and Labour of the People of London*, published in seventeen volumes, of which seven were devoted to 'Religious Influences'.[7] The published volumes maintained a stance towards the clergy that was generally respectful, even if quite critical in individual cases. When, however, one turns to the unpublished notebooks on which the volumes were based, one finds that some members of Booth's team of researchers held views themselves, and reported views expressed by others, that were much more frankly hostile. This was notably true of Arthur Baxter, a London barrister, who ran a boys' club in a working-class district of the city, and who was responsible for many of the interviews with clergymen on which the volumes were partly based. He concluded a report on the East End of London by writing:

The only point on which the evidence suggests any new thoughts is the often repeated remark that there is no hostility to religion: in a broad sense this is probably true, but it may be well to remember that nearly all our testimony on this point comes from ministers of religion, and the growing politeness and urbanity produced by education would make such hostility less patent to them even if it existed: but even from the clergy (e.g. Mr Dalton) one hears that the general opinion of the working man is that the clergy are either knaves or fools, while Mr Bray, a school-master of unusual culture, emphasises this point and seems rather to approve the verdict which he quotes that ministers of religion are 'rather a poor lot', worse rather than better than their fellow men. There is no doubt that this feeling is widespread, and if it does not constitute hostility to religion it does at least show a very considerable prejudice against the churches, a hostility which even men of the undeniable strength and goodness of Dalton or Howard have the greatest difficulty in breaking down. And is not this attitude to some extent justified? No doubt it is due in no small measure to the fact that the churches, with their restrictive doctrines, are bound, even when represented by saints, to be regarded with distaste by the mass of ordinary men. But is it not also largely the result of the sins of the churches? Has not the average man who stands outside the churches some reason for thinking that the intemperance, the impurity, and the gambling against which ministers of religion are always thundering are no worse than the fighting, the lying, and the uncharitableness which fill so large a place in the daily lives of so many of these good people?[8]

In a later report, Baxter went on to claim that the prejudice against the clergy was such that they would be more effective as lay social workers:

at the back of their minds they must all know that whatever the attitude of the working classes to religion in the abstract, in the concrete there is a feeling towards the minister of religion for which it is difficult to find any other word than hostility: the feeling that 'we don't want nothing to do with no bloody parsons'.[9]

Baxter's assessment of the views of London working men gains some support from the studies by Paul Thompson and Stan Shipley of metropolitan radicalism in the later Victorian period. For instance, Shipley, who has studied working men's clubs, suggests that 'a strong current of anti-clericalism ran through most of the [London radical] clubs'. He quotes the example of the Borough of Hackney Club in the 1870s, where a lecture on science took a strongly anti-religious character, with many 'sly drives at the clergy, chiefly those of the Church of England, which were highly appreciated by the audience'.[10]

This chapter will aim to present a typology of anticlericalism in later nineteenth- and early twentieth-century England, and to explore the changes over time in the relative significance of the various types. Included in this typology will be most of the forms of hostility referred to by Arthur Baxter or exemplified in his own remarks in the course of the diatribe quoted above. We shall concentrate on hostility to the clergy of the Anglican and Nonconformist Churches – those to which the great majority of the population belonged – and will leave on one side the rather different issues raised by hostility to the Roman Catholic clergy. In particular, it should be noted that much of the abuse and ridicule heaped upon Catholic priests was an aspect of anti-Catholicism.[11] Anticlericalism is interpreted as suspicion of and hostility to the clergy of *one's own church*, rather than a means of attacking *other people's churches*.

The forms of explicit or implied critique of the Anglican or Nonconformist clergy that were current in England during this time can be categorised as follows:

(1) the radical, according to which the clergy were condemned as reactionaries;
(2) the plebeian, which accused them of being snobs;
(3) the Protestant, which accused them of priestcraft;
(4) the liberal, which condemned religion, and thus most of the work of the clergy, as intrinsically opposed to science and reason;
(5) the anti-puritan, which presented the clergy as killjoys;
(6) the masculinist, according to which clergymen were not 'real men';
(7) the realist, according to which the clergy were hopelessly idealistic and did not live in 'the real world'.

The *radical* critique was directed mainly at the clergy of the Church of England, who were frequently depicted as the supreme enemies of progress, as oppressors of the poor, as preachers of submission to authority.[12] This kind of criticism was most frequently heard in rural areas, and had obvious roots in the fact that the clergy were so frequently a principal pillar of the rural power structure. In the earlier part of the century an important aspect of this was the role of clergymen as magistrates. The proportion of magistrates who were clergymen peaked at over 20 per cent of the total around 1830, rising as high as 47 per cent in the rural county of Lincolnshire.[13] Clerical magistracy subsequently declined, partly because it conflicted with the growing emphasis on the set-apartness of the clergy, and partly because of the realisation that the exercise of often highly controversial judicial functions could have an adverse effect on their relations with their poorer parishioners. But the country clergyman continued to be a figure of considerable and highly visible power, exercised through control over large numbers of village schools and charities, and through personal links with landowners, as well as through the dominant influence which the Anglican clergy still had on the religious life of many rural areas. In a rural parish it was still possible for the parson to be personally known to all of his parishioners through, for instance, visiting their homes, in a way that was seldom possible in the towns. Strong feelings, whether of admiration, respect or affection, or of resentment or even hatred, frequently resulted. For instance, interviews conducted by oral historians with people brought up in the rural working class during the later

Victorian and Edwardian years frequently elicited quite detailed memories of clergymen. A Devon farm labourer's daughter, born in 1898, remembered that: 'the Vicar was the most important one in our village. We always looked on him as being the head of the village.' He visited everybody, especially the sick: she believed that emergency treatment provided on one such sick visit had saved her father's life.[14] An Essex man, born in 1904, the son of a shepherd and a dressmaker, had less flattering, but equally detailed, memories:

> Mother and her friends would pass out of the church door, the vicar would stand near the church door, and would just nod and smile, perhaps not that, even. But when the higher class people came out he would shake hands and beam to every one of them as if they was something very superior to my mother and her friends, the poor, the very poor.

In spite of his snobbery, this man was at least 'a nice kindly old vicar', but his successor was remembered as 'a keep fit fanatic', who devoted much of his time to running round the fields, and whose apparent indifference towards his parishioners was said to have emptied the church.[15]

In the towns both the power exercised by the clergy and the intimacy of their relationships with their parishioners were considerably diluted, not only by the size of urban parishes but also by the existence of many other figures of power, including, not least, the ministers of other denominations. The religious census of 1851 showed that there already existed a high degree of religious pluralism in English towns, and in the great majority of cases, the majority of church-goers were Nonconformists. This process had gone a step further by the 1880s. The Anglican Church could still attract large congregations, and in most towns there were Anglican clergymen who were powerful and respected figures. But this respect had to be earned: it was not inherent in the clergyman's position, in the way that often happened in the village. In so far as anticlericalism was directed against the *power* of the church, it was simply less relevant in the towns.[16]

Throughout the nineteenth century criticism of the Anglican clergy had been a constant element of radical rhetoric, rising and falling in its extent and importance, but always there. After about 1890, as older forms of radicalism declined and socialism increasingly took its place, the older style of radical anticlericalism also declined. This was partly because socialists were self-consciously rejecting many of the old radical shibboleths, and concentrating their attack on capitalism, the true root of all evil. It was partly, too, because the Church of England was responding to radical criticism by becoming more politically flexible, adapting its style of ministry to the demands of different environments. In this period a new type of 'slum parson' was coming to the fore, who adapted not only his preaching and ritual, but often his politics as well, to what he identified as the needs and demands of his working-class parishioners.[17] But the same kind of logic which had driven radicals to attack the Anglican Church sometimes led socialists to attack the Nonconformist Churches. In the industrial and mining districts where socialism had its early strongholds, Nonconformity, most commonly some form of Methodism, was generally the dominant form of religion, and it was as closely identified with the Liberal Party as rural Anglicanism was with the Conservative Party. Many of the pioneers of the Independent Labour Party were themselves Nonconformists, and many of them had experienced opposition from their ministers or from the lay elite of their chapels. From the 1890s to the 1920s chapels were bitterly divided between proponents of the older liberalism and the newer socialism, and more often than not it was the liberals who came out on top, at least in the short term, as they were more likely to hold key offices, and their higher incomes also gave them leverage.[18] It is significant that Robert Tressell's famous socialist novel *The Ragged Trousered Philanthropist* (1914) directs all of its anticlerical venom at the ministers of the Shining Light Chapel: the Anglican clergy are simply ignored. Tressell's book has enjoyed lasting popularity because of the realism and humour with which he presented the everyday lives of an impoverished working class. But subtlety and nuance are conspicuous by their absence. So far as religion is concerned, Tressell's message is a simple one: working-class churchgoers are pathetic dupes, and the Nonconformist ministers whose chapels they attend are enjoying a life of comfort by exploiting the naivety of their followers. Tressell has particular fun at the expense of the enormous, balloon-like Revd John Belcher, whose health is of such concern to his congregation that they are continually paying for him to have holidays in the south of France.[19]

However, radical anticlericalism was of rapidly diminishing importance in the twentieth century. Indeed, in working-class areas, it was increasingly the case that those clergymen who intervened in politics did so from a radical or socialist standpoint.[20] One consequence of this was the emergence of a conservative anticlericalism, which lambasted the clergy for giving moral authority to the Left. This reached a high point in the 1980s, when Margaret Thatcher's government was subjected to frequent attacks by ministers of religion, and Conservative politicians periodically counter-attacked with criticism of the clergy.[21]

A more constant phenomenon has been *plebeian* anticlericalism, which also was directed primarily at Anglicans, though again Nonconformist ministers were sometimes targeted. This arose from the perception of the clergy as members of the social elite – linked most commonly with landowners in the countryside, and with businessmen or doctors in the towns. Even the best-intentioned clergyman could cause suspicion on the part of his poorer parishioners by his manner of speaking, appearance and way of life. Anglican clergymen tended to live in large houses, they went on holidays, their wives dressed as 'ladies' and their children went to fee-paying schools. They spoke an 'educated' English, often with a distinct 'upper-class' accent, and even their physique could be intimidating: Anglican clergymen were frequently tall, healthy, athletic men, towering above their half-starved parishioners.[22] All of this applied less often to Nonconformist ministers, many of whom came from working-class families, and whose income was frequently that of a skilled workman or clerk. Nevertheless there were also 'pulpit princes', commanding very large salaries and usually living in very comfortable suburban villas.[23] So there were aspects of the lifestyle of most Anglican and many Nonconformist clergymen which established a wide gulf between them and the mass of working-class people. More important than this, however, were questions of how the clergy were seen to treat the various classes of their parishioners. A clergyman who was himself a 'nob' could be acceptable if he was felt to treat everyone alike[24] and to take a personal interest even in the poorest member of his congregation: indeed, the latter might be especially appreciative of kindness shown by a clergyman who was evidently 'a real gentleman'. On the other hand any perceived slight by the clergy could leave a lasting burden of resentment. Complaints of this kind may not often be reported in published literature, but they have often been recorded by oral historians. Here, for instance, are the comments of a Tyneside coach-driver, born in 1900. He stated that the Anglican clergy:

> mixed with a certain class. They didn't do what they're supposed to do, not in my opinion. Because there's nobody loved the church more than I did. And that's one of the things that turned me against – well, I didn't turn against the church, but it certainly didn't help me with the church. In a church there was a clique, and if there was a clique, and you weren't in that clique, you was as well out . . .[25]

'They didn't do what they're supposed to do.' 'Plebeian' and 'radical' anticlericalism, unlike some other forms, were not necessarily irreligious. Indeed, they frequently stemmed from a particular conception of Christianity as democratic, egalitarian and humanitarian, and from the belief that clergymen were failing to live up to the standards of the religion they professed, and that they were therefore 'hypocritical' and indeed 'unchristian'.

Many of the same points apply to the third form of critique, which I have termed *Protestant*. This was an attack on the clergy from within Christianity, and often from within the Church. Antipathy to 'priests' and 'priestcraft' was widespread among the laity both of the Church of England and of the Nonconformist Churches in the nineteenth century. Indeed, various Nonconformist denominations, including the Quakers, the Brethren, the Churches of Christ and the Independent Methodists, had no clergy, and opened all offices in the Church at least to all male members (though some of these Churches continued to place considerable restrictions on their women members). The Salvation Army also had no clergy, though they distinguished between those who worked full-time for the Army, known as 'officers', and those who provided voluntary labour in the evenings or on Sundays, known as 'men'. The central figure in a Baptist, Congregational or Unitarian church was the minister, who was pastor and preacher, conducted services and chaired church meetings. But since he also was elected and paid by the congregation, and could be dismissed by them, clericalism and anticlericalism seldom became major issues, whatever the views on individual ministers might be. Some of the most fervent anticlericals were themselves ministers, like D.W. Dale, the famous Birmingham Congregationalist, who made a point of dressing like a lawyer or doctor, and who repudiated the title 'Reverend'. However, it was a different story in the Anglican and Methodist Churches,[26] where throughout the century discord between clergy and laity was a major source of conflict, and sometimes schism.

In the Church of England the key event was the emergence of the Oxford Movement in the 1830s and the subsequent development of 'ritualism' and 'Anglo-Catholicism'. By the later years of the century Anglo-Catholicism was the most dynamic force in the Church of England, and its influence was spreading to all areas of the Church. But when 'ritualism' was imposed in a previously 'Protestant' parish, the resistance could still be fierce.[27] Certain Anglo-Catholic practices, such as the hearing of confessions, clerical celibacy and the formation of Anglican monasteries and convents, were a cause of special suspicion. All were regarded as manifestations of 'sacerdotalism', and were thus especially suspect to those who believed in 'the priesthood of all believers'.

Clericalism was an even more explosive issue within Methodism, where the very word 'priest' was an insult. The tensions between the 'travelling preachers' (increasingly termed 'ministers') and the 'local preachers' (those who had another profession on weekdays and went out to preach on Sundays) was a central issue in the successive schisms which tore Methodism apart in the period from the 1790s to the 1850s. One of the breakaway groups in the 1820s had pointedly named themselves the *Protestant* Methodists, and the union of a number of the dissident bodies in 1857 assumed the title of United Methodist *Free* Churches. Freedom meant principally freedom from 'Conference', the governing body of the Wesleyan Methodist Connexion, and the supreme bugbear of Methodist radicals and democrats. But since (until 1878) the Wesleyan Conference was made up exclusively of ministers, opposition to its dictates can be seen as a form of anticlericalism. In this instance it was the 'tyranny' of the clergy which was the main focus of criticism, and certain aspects of the ministerial role took on special symbolic significance – for instance, the claim to monopolise the administration of the sacraments, or the question of whether travelling preachers should be separated from those who were merely 'local' by a special training.[28]

By about the 1880s, however, 'Protestant' anticlericalism was losing some of its edge.[29] Within the Church of England the militant Protestantism of such bodies as the Protestant Association and the Protestant Truth Society was coming to be regarded as 'fanatical' and 'extreme'. Anglo-Catholicism was achieving respectability, and some Anglo-Catholics were becoming bishops. Even Roman

Catholicism was winning a degree of reluctant acceptance – which would be
definitively confirmed by the First World War, when the Catholic hierarchy was
impeccably patriotic, and Catholic army chaplains won respect at the Front.
Meanwhile, the trend towards 'higher' forms of worship, which was by then long
established in the Church of England, was even influencing many
Nonconformists. It was reflected in the building of more magnificent and more
richly decorated churches, the more extensive use of music in services, more
formal liturgies and a greater emphasis on the sacraments.[30] The spirit of the age
was against Protestantism, which seemed incompatible with the new ethos of
aesthetic awareness, sensitivity to 'tradition' and nascent ecumenism.

   But if Protestant anticlericalism was beginning to seem old-fashioned, *liberal*
anticlericalism was advancing. There were, of course, many liberals who were also
Nonconformists, and whose anticlericalism was an aspect of their demand for
religious freedom and equality. In terms of the typology adopted in this chapter,
their form of anticlericalism was a mixture of the 'radical' and the 'Protestant'.
'Liberal' anticlericalism refers to the kind of liberalism which harked back to the
Enlightenment, which saw reason and science as the only basis for truth, and
presented education as the supreme panacea. In the third quarter of the
nineteenth century this form of liberalism was, of course, very widespread in
France, and it had a considerable following in many other parts of continental
Europe and Latin America. It was less popular in England, where the principal
bastions of the liberal middle class were not masonic lodges as in France, but
Nonconformist chapels. However, in England too there was a significant minority
of religious sceptics in this class, and by the 1860s and 1870s they were gaining
ground in scientific, literary and academic circles. Naturally anticlericalism was
most attractive where there was a visible and apparently dangerous clerical
presence. Probably nowhere in England was this presence so conspicuous as in the
old High Church stronghold of Oxford University, and by the 1870s it was alleged
to contain England's thickest concentration of 'argumentative agnostics'.[31]
Throughout the 1850s and 1860s High Church conservatives had been locked in
battle with university reformers, many of them liberal Anglican 'Broad
Churchmen', who wanted to open the university completely to non-Anglicans and
to broaden the range of subjects taught. Similar battles were taking place within
the scientific world, where until about 1860 Anglican clergymen had a prominent
role. In the eyes of the younger generation of professional scientists, led by the
inexhaustibly bellicose Thomas Huxley, these clergymen-scientists were doubly
objectionable, and should be cleared out. In the first place they were 'amateurs',
and their continued prominence in bodies like the British Association for the
Advancement of Science undermined the efforts of those who were trying to
establish the claims of science to be regarded as a profession on a par with, for
instance, medicine or law. And secondly, their allegiance to God potentially
diverted them from those lines of scientific enquiry that might lead to a

questioning of religious orthodoxy.[32] Of course, the Darwinian theory of evolution appeared to be a prime example of such a situation, and the theory thus became a shibboleth for Huxley and his allies. Huxley's clash with Samuel Wilberforce, the Bishop of Oxford, at the British Association in 1860 has passed into national folklore. It is still periodically cited as evidence for the proposition that clergymen are necessarily obscurantist and anti-scientific – although historical research has suggested that the public memory of this event is as inaccurate as the memory of most other legendary episodes in national history.[33]

Another leading propagandist for science, Francis Galton, wanted scientists to become 'a new priesthood'.[34] According to Frank Turner scientific anticlericalism diminished after about 1875, as scientists, who had apparently won their battle against the clergy but failed to achieve the degree of public recognition and financial support that they demanded, increasingly directed their attacks against politicians and businessmen, who were now identified as the chief 'enemies of science'.[35]

But it was not long before the clergy were under similar attack from social scientists and advocates of scientifically based schemes of social reform. A key institution during the period from its foundation in 1884 up to the First World War, and one that reflected powerful trends in contemporary social thinking, was Toynbee Hall, the settlement in the East End of London.[36] Politically, it was mainly Liberal, and religiously it tended towards agnosticism.[37] It helped to shape some of the most significant figures in twentieth-century British history, including the later Labour Prime Minister Clement Attlee, and the 'father of the Welfare State', William Beveridge. The tolerant, undogmatic Anglicanism of the founders had created a haven in which those of little religious faith could pursue what really interested them, which was the reconstruction of society on more rational and scientific lines.

While not on the whole hostile to the clergy, Toynbee men tended to regard their efforts as irrelevant. Typical here was Ernest Aves, vice-warden in the 1890s, and later an important Board of Trade official, who assisted Charles Booth in his classic study of poverty, industry and religion in London during the 1880s and 1890s. Aves wanted the Churches to concentrate on producing better citizens for a better society. He was not over-optimistic about human capacity, but neither did he believe in the need for a sense of sin or a radical change of heart. He wanted facts, social surveys, skilful social engineering. The chief instruments of social improvement were schools and an actively interventionist local government, but clergymen could help by inspiring those around them with high ideals. In most cases, he believed, they failed to do this because they were too busy either trying to save souls, or pursuing a kind of ecclesiastical imperialism, according to which a big and 'successful' Church was something good in itself.[38]

If the nineteenth century had been a great age of English puritanism,[39] by the 1890s the *anti-puritan* reaction was in full swing, and clergymen were often among its major targets. In this instance Nonconformist ministers were attacked with special frequency. Their critics could, of course, draw on a range of hostile stereotypes from literature, and especially from the novels of Charles Dickens. Since Nonconformist ministers were often the most outspoken critics of drinking and gambling and the most fervent defenders of the sabbath, they naturally came under attack from all those who saw the way forward as lying through 'emancipation', 'the divine right of self-development' or 'hedonism'.[40] One of the most popular routes to such 'emancipation' was through sport, which became a national obsession in the period from the 1870s to the First World War. There was no necessary conflict between religion and sport. Indeed, a characteristic figure of this period was the 'muscular Christian', equally at home in a prayer meeting or a boxing ring.[41] But there were those on both sides who did see a tension. While relatively few Christian preachers at the end of the nineteenth century would have claimed that sport was bad in itself, there were many who claimed that 'pleasure-seeking' had become a dangerously all-consuming pursuit, diverting the youth, in particular, from more serious concerns. The fact that sporting activity often took place on Sundays, or was associated with drinking or gambling, clearly meant that what might be good in principle was often bad in practice.[42] Meanwhile, enthusiasts for Sunday sport defended their position by alleging that sport had more beneficial effects than going to church, and sections of the sporting press made a habit of ridiculing the Churches and clergy.[43] This animus was particularly strong among enthusiasts for prize-fighting, because clergymen were so often the leaders in campaigns to suppress their sport. A history of pugilism written about 1880, soon after its demise, never missed an opportunity for a hit at the clergy. Noting, for instance, that Bendigo, one of the most famous fighters of the 1830s and 1840s, subsequently became a Methodist preacher, the author claimed that: 'There is a closer psychological connection between fighting and fanaticism, pugnacity and Puritanism, than saints and Stigginses can afford to admit . . . and the fatal step from preachee to flogee of parsons of all sects and times, needs no citations of history to prove.'[44]

Masculinist anticlericalism was directed most strongly at Anglo-Catholics. *Punch*, the favourite humorous magazine of the middle class, poured constant scorn on the ritualists' taste for fancy vestments, strange scents and tinkling bells, with the clear implication that they were not 'real men'. 'Parsons in Petticoats' was the title of an article published in 1865, and their cartoonists were fascinated by everything that was 'feminine' about the Anglo-Catholic priest – from his passion for new clothes to his lack of facial hair. From the time of the Oxford Movement onwards, accusations of 'effeminacy' were constantly levelled at the Tractarians and their successors. Sometimes this merely implied a lack of 'masculinity', with no further message being intended. But at other times the references to the large numbers of 'young men' attending Anglo-Catholic churches were clearly intended to imply that they and their priests were homosexual.[45] When not accused of homosexuality, the latter might find themselves equally under attack for a crime almost equally heinous in masculinist eyes – celibacy.

However, this was only an extreme form of a kind of prejudice to which most clergymen were vulnerable, although many, from the time of Charles Kingsley and Thomas Hughes onwards, tried to counter it by a cult of physical strength and fitness.[46] In the eyes of many men, churches were 'women's space'.[47] Clergymen, if they practised the Christian virtues of forbearance and forgiveness, were said to be lacking in the 'masculine' virtues of pride and courage. The heavy drinking, gambling and illicit sex which were sources of status in many male sub-cultures were none of them permitted to the clergyman: if he abstained from these things his masculinity was in question, and if he indulged he could be accused of hypocrisy. As so often, the parson found that he was 'damned if he did, and damned if he didn't'. The clergyman was also in some respects a double outsider. He was excluded by working-class definitions of masculinity in terms of physical strength and manual skill, and generally excluded by middle-class definitions which stressed business acumen and ability to make money.

The masculinist perception of the Anglican clergy was brilliantly conveyed by a *Punch* cartoon of the 1850s entitled 'An Attempt at Converting the Natives' (Figure 1),[48] which shows a sleek young curate confronting two very rough-looking miners who are leaning against a wall and smoking. The joke is that there is a misunderstanding. The curate says, 'Well then, I do hope I shall have the pleasure of seeing you both next Sunday!' meaning that he hopes to see them at church, whereas the two miners think that the curate wants to come to the cock-fight which they have planned for Sunday. But the joke is clearly at several different levels. It is a joke about class, and the different ways of thinking and speaking that go with class. (The miners speak a broad north-eastern dialect, which is likely to be semi-incomprehensible to the curate.) And it is also a joke about gender. The miners, with their working clothes, their pipes and their beards, are unmistakably masculine, and their proposed manner of spending Sunday drinking beer and watching a cock-fight is also clearly masculine. But the sexual status of the curate is much more ambiguous: he has no facial hair, he wears gloves and carries an umbrella, his nervously erect stance contrasts with the slough of his interlocutors, and he is proposing to spend Sunday in what is likely to be predominantly female company in church.

Finally, the *realist* critique of the clergy is encountered throughout this period, and remains with us to the present day. There were many people who regularly went to church and were maybe quite devout, who none the less wanted to separate out a sphere into which religion should not be allowed to intrude, whether it were business, politics, the family or whatever. They were like the Nottinghamshire farmers described by Samuel Butler in his autobiographical novel *The Way of all Flesh*, who 'would have been equally horrified at hearing the Christian religion doubted, and at seeing it practised'.[49] Clergymen naturally wished to assert the principle that religion should influence every area of life. They were consequently accused of 'meddling', of 'ignorance', of 'foolishness' and of a lack of practical

Figure 1: 'From the mining districts: an attempt at converting the natives.'

Assiduous Young Curate: 'Well then, I do hope I shall have the pleasure of seeing both of you next Sunday!'

Miner: 'Oh! Thee may'st coam if 'e wull. We foight on the Croft, and Old Joe Tanner brings th' beer.'

sense. Again, this view occurs frequently in the notebooks compiled in London during the 1890s by Charles Booth and his assistants. In spite of their own Anglican antecedents, Arthur Baxter often got on well with Nonconformist ministers, while Ernest Aves had some successful encounters with Roman Catholic priests. But in the case of the Anglican clergy, familiarity seemed to have bred contempt. Baxter liked to refer to the men he interviewed as 'poor creatures' or 'one of the large class who are fit for no career but the church'.[50] Criticisms of this kind were even made by some of the clergy themselves. In Deptford Baxter interviewed two Anglicans who had pursued other careers for some years before their ordination. Both said that all clergymen should be required to do the same. One complained that because of the narrowness of their experience, the clergy were 'such fools', and the other refused to attend clerical conferences, claiming that his colleagues were 'so bigoted' and 'amazingly unwise'.[51]

We have already referred to examples of the numerous *Punch* cartoons subjecting clergymen to humorous comment, often gently mocking, but sometimes more openly hostile. Looking across the whole period from the middle of the nineteenth century until the eve of the First World War, one must be struck by the frequency with which their artists drew upon the Church (usually the Church of England, but occasionally other denominations) for their material. The year 1866 saw eleven such cartoons; in 1880 the number was up to eighteen, while in 1910 it was still seventeen. There were fluctuations from year to year, but over the whole period the liking for ecclesiastical subjects remained more or less constant. There were several standard jokes, each of which had numerous variations. As the chief upholders of moral as well as religious orthodoxy, the clergy were expected to adhere to levels of propriety and respectability which would be demanded of no one else. They could thus be lampooned for observing these standards, and perhaps taking them to ridiculous extremes, or alternatively for trying to get away, perhaps by rather devious means, with a less strict observance (Figure 2).[52] Furthermore, this role of defender of propriety, combined with their distinctive and, in many people's eyes, somewhat absurd garb, led to jokes which depended on juxtaposing clergymen with their opposites – with women, with members of the lower social classes, or with those lacking in any sense of tact or convention, such as children, bohemians or drunks. Another standard focus was the clergyman's sexuality: in the eyes of some humorists, this was ambiguous – there was, as George Eliot once put it, a third 'clerical sex';[53] but in the eyes of others the masculinity of the clergy was all too evident, and the joke was at the expense of the women of the parish, young or not so young, and their transparent stratagems to win the favour of the curate.[54] But while some jokes never seem to have worn thin, clerical stereotypes were nevertheless evolving, and the kinds of criticism which were being levelled at the clergy also changed.

Around 1860 criticism was directed mainly at 'extremists' and 'fanatics'. In terms of the typology adopted in this chapter, the 'Protestant' and 'masculinist'

Figure 2: 'The churchman armed against the errors of the time.'
Reverend and jolly old Mr Hoodwink, our country rector, has (of course) come up for the
May meetings; but he managed to run down to the Derby (in a black tie), and here he
finishes the week by winning honours with his clever cob, at the horse show, where
he passes for, at least, a swell stud-groom.

critiques predominated. For instance, a cartoon of 1866 showed a tall, over-refined
Anglo-Catholic in priestly vestments, exuding arrogance, fighting over the Prayer
Book with a shorter, coarser-looking and highly pugnacious, gowned Protestant
preacher, while a genial and sensible-looking archbishop reproved them with the
words, 'My friends! My friends! You'll destroy that good old book of prayer
between you' (Figure 3).[55] Most often, the victims of *Punch*'s satire were Anglo-
Catholics, and the hierarchy were sometimes criticised for lack of vigilance. In the
same year John Bull was shown berating a group of bishops, who were standing by
while an absurd-looking Anglo-Catholic priest was parading around amidst a
cloud of incense (Figure 4).[56] Besides the charge that they were a treacherous,
Romanising fifth column within the national Protestant Church, Ritualists were
repeatedly ridiculed for their unmasculine appearance and their love of dressing
up. In 1866 a cartoon depicting a group of clergyman trying on new vestments
was clearly intended to evoke comparisons with women in a dress shop.[57] At the

Figure 3: 'The Battle of the Rubric.'

Archbishop of Canterbury: 'My friends! My friends! You'll destroy that good old book of prayer between you.'

Figure 4: 'Pernicious nonsense'.
Mr Bull: 'I'll pay your reverences to look after my establishment, and if you neglect your
duty, I shall see to it myself'.

same time there was also an anti-puritan current in some of *Punch*'s humour,
directed mainly at ultra-Protestants. For instance, an article in 1860 defended
dancing against a 'fanatic' and 'morbid' writer in the Evangelical *Record*.[58]

By 1880 distinctions between Church parties no longer seemed so important to
the cartoonists. Their tendency now was to present a homogenised clergy as the
chief upholders of propriety – to outward appearance formidable figures, yet
vulnerable because so easily shocked. For instance, an 'English Church Dignitary'
on a visit to Paris with his family was depicted trying, in laboured French, to order
a book, and gasping with horror as the blasé young saleswoman presented him
with a novel by Zola (Figure 5).[59] Meanwhile, in a Lancashire slum, a 'zealous
curate', top-hatted and dressed all in black, was shown equally disconcerted by the
outspokenness of a sexy young widow.[60] Although ritualist tastes in 'ecclesiastical
millinery' still came under occasional attack, the main form of implied critique
was now the 'anti-puritan', and the principal targets were sabbatarians.[61]

Figure 5: 'An affair of taste.'

English Church Dignitary: 'Oh – er – j'ai beswang d'oon livre ou deux, pour lire à ma fameel, vous savvy. Quelque chose de moderne, et pas difficile à comprendre! Avvy vous?'

Fair Parisian Bookseller: 'Oui, Monsieur, nous avons ça! Voici *L'assommoir*, par Zola. C'est très gentil. Ou préférez-vous *Nana*, par le même auteur – édition illustrée?'

His Reverence (aghast): '*Oh* nong, Mademoiselle!'

Fair Parisian Bookseller: 'Non? C'est pourtant *bien joli*, Monsieur!'

By 1910 the most readily visible changes were that the clergy had lost a lot of weight, and that most of them had taken to wearing glasses. Admittedly, there had been slim, even thin, clerics in 1860 or 1880 – including most Anglo-Catholics. But there were also many who were well-built, or even portly, as well as some sporting parsons of the old school who were positively rotund (see Figure 2). By 1910 the preferred stereotype was the slight, rather weedy-looking, nervous curate or bumbling vicar (Figure 6).[62] If there was a figure to be reckoned with in the vicarage, it was now more likely to be the vicar's wife – sometimes portrayed as an elderly battle-axe, and sometimes as young and glamorous.[63] It may also be significant that at a time when over 80 per cent of the population of England and Wales was living in urban areas, cartoonists persisted in depicting country vicars in conversation with semi-literate and/or drunken village yokels. The prevailing critique was now of the 'realist' kind – the clergy being presented as well meaning but ineffectual, standing at a distance from the centres of modern life.[64]

So Eric Evans is probably correct in pointing to a decline in the status and perceived influence of the clergy during the second half of the nineteenth century, though, if the cartoonists' observations are to be trusted, this happened considerably later than Evans suggests. Also, if the argument of this chapter is correct, this did not necessarily lead to a decline in the extent of anticlericalism, but rather to a change in the forms which it took.

In conclusion, it should be noted that many of the potential sources of anticlericalism were doubled-edged, since they were also potential sources of devotion to the clergy. For instance, celibacy could be a source of suspicion, but it was also an important aspect of the charisma of some Roman Catholic or Anglo-Catholic saints; similarly the political leadership provided by the clergy was a major source of both the hostility of some and the attachment of others. By comparison with, for instance, France, it is the relatively low-key nature of relations between clergy and people in England that is most striking. Neither the furious anticlerical invective nor the intense loyalty to the clergy, both of which were common in France during this period,[65] were typical of England. It remains true, however, that in the period 1870–1914, ministers of religion remained, in spite of some decline, a numerous, familiar and in many respects powerful group in English society, who exercised a wide-ranging influence, and evoked reactions of many different kinds. Eric Evans goes much too far in his emphasis on the spread of 'apathy' or 'indifference'.[66] A more fully nuanced account of relations between clergy and laity during this period would have to take account of class and gender differences, of the factors that could make one clergyman 'popular' and his successor 'unpopular', and also of the ambivalence and complexity in the attitudes of many individuals.[67] Most historical accounts are still lacking in such nuances. Even in a country like England, which has been largely spared the extremes of clericalism and anticlericalism, the history of the clergy remains an emotive subject which few historians can approach with detachment.

Figure 6:

Country Vicar (visiting a family where a child has scarlet fever): 'I suppose you keep him well isolated?'

'Lor' bless you, Sir, yes. He keeps behind that clothes-horse, and don't come among us but for meals.'

Notes

1   *European Studies Review*, vol. 13, no. 2 (1983) was a special issue devoted to 'Anti-clericalism', including an overview and articles on specific countries.

2.   E.J. Hobsbawm and George Rudé, *Captain Swing* (London, 1969), pp. 112–13, 120, 153–4, 158, 164 and 229–32.

3.   Eric J. Evans, 'The Church in Danger? Anticlericalism in Nineteenth-century England', *European Studies Review* 13 (1983), pp. 201–23.

4   See, for instance, two of the most recent additions to the literature: S.J.D. Green, *Religion in the Age of Decline: Organisation and Experience in Industrial Yorkshire 1870–1920* (Cambridge, 1996); S.C. Williams, *Religious Belief and Popular Culture in Southwark* c. *1880–1939* (Oxford, 1999).

5   Brian Heeney, *A Different Kind of Gentleman* (Hamden, CT, 1976); Anthony Russell, *The Clerical Profession* (London, 1980); Alan Haig, *The Victorian Clergy* (Beckenham, 1984); Rosemary O'Day, 'The Victorian Clerical Renaissance', in Gerald Parsons, James R. Moore and John Wolffe (eds), *Religion in Victorian Britain*, 5 vols (Manchester, 1988–96), vol. I, pp. 184–212; Rosemary O'Day, 'The men from the Ministry,' in ibid., vol. II, pp. 258–79.

6   Eugenio F. Biagini, *Liberty, Retrenchment and Reform: Popular Liberalism in the Age of Gladstone 1860–1880* (Cambridge, 1992), pp. 192–253.

7   Charles Booth (ed.), *Life and Labour of the People in London*, 17 vols (London, 1902–3); see also Rosemary O'Day and David Englander, *Mr Charles Booth's Inquiry: Life and Labour of the People in London Reconsidered* (London, 1993).

8   Booth Collection, A33, pp. 35–6 (London School of Economics Library).

9   Ibid., A40.7, pp. 40–1.

10   Stan Shipley, *Club Life and Socialism in Mid-Victorian London* (Oxford, 1972), p. 30; see also Paul Thompson, *Socialists, Liberals and Labour: The Struggle for London 1885–1914* (London, 1967).

11   See, for example: John Wolffe, *The Protestant Crusade in Britain 1829–1860* (Oxford, 1992); D.G. Paz, *Popular Anti-Catholicism in Mid-Victorian England* (Stanford, CA, 1993).

12   Biagini, *Liberty, Retrenchment and Reform*, pp. 231–3.

13   Evans, 'The Church in Danger?', p. 213.

14   Paul Thompson and Thea Vigne, 'Interviews on Family Life and Work Experience before 1918', University of Essex Oral History Archive (hereafter cited as 'Essex Interviews'), no. 359, p. 59.

15   Ibid., no. 22, pp. 24–5 and 204.

16   Hugh McLeod, *Religion and Society in England 1850–1914* (Basingstoke, 1996), pp. 13–27.

17   See, for example, Owen Chadwick, *The Victorian Church*, 2 vols (London, 1966–70), vol. II, pp. 269–86. For the local importance of radical clergymen in various areas of London, see Thompson, *Socialists, Liberals and Labour*, pp. 22–5.

18   Robert Moore, *Pit-men, Preachers and Politics* (London, 1974); Leonard Smith, *Religion and the Rise of Labour* (Keele, 1993).

19   Robert Tressell, *The Ragged Trousered Philanthropist* (London, 1955), p. 186.

20   Gillian Rose, 'Locality, Politics and Culture: Poplar in the 1920s' (University of London, PhD thesis, 1989), pp. 272–7.

21   Hugo Young, *One of Us: A Biography of Margaret Thatcher* (revised edn, London, 1993), devotes a chapter to Thatcher's disputes with the Churches.

22   Alan Bartlett, 'The Churches in Bermondsey 1880–1939' (University of Birmingham, PhD thesis, 1987), pp. 125–9.

23   Kenneth D. Brown, *A Social History of the Nonconformist Ministry in England and Wales 1800–1930* (Oxford, 1988), pp. 147–61.

24.   Hugh McLeod, *Piety and Poverty: Working Class Religion in Berlin, London and New York 1870–1914* (New York, 1996), pp. 194–5.

25   Essex Interviews, no. 155, pp. 47–8.

26   While the author would agree with Biagini (p. 218) that anticlericalism was directed primarily against the Anglican clergy, he would not accept that 'the Nonconformist churches were . . . virtually invulnerable to anti-clerical hostility'.

27   For examples, see Nigel Yates, *Leeds and the Oxford Movement 1836–1934* (Leeds, 1975). In 1899 the High Church Vicar of All Saints, Surrey Square, interviewed by Charles Booth's team, reported that doors were slammed in his face when he visited the homes of militant Protestants in his parish: Booth Collection B276, p. 71.

28   For Methodist internal conflict, see Robert Currie, *Methodism Divided* (London, 1968).

29   See the discussion of these issues in Hugh McLeod, 'Protestantism and British National Identity, 1815–1945', in Peter van der Veer (ed.), *Nation and Religion: Perspectives on Europe and Asia* (Princeton, NJ, 1999), pp. 44–70.

30   See, for example, Clyde Binfield, '"We claim our part in this great inheritance": the Message of Four Congregational Buildings', in Keith Robbins (ed.), *Protestant Evangelicalism: Britain, Ireland, Germany and America* c. *1750*–c. *1950* (Oxford, 1990), pp. 201–23.

31   Chadwick, *The Victorian Church*, vol. II, p. 444.

32   See the essay on 'The Victorian Conflict between Science and Religion: a Professional Dimension', in Frank M. Turner, *Contesting Cultural Authority: Essays in Victorian Intellectual Life* (Cambridge, 1993).

33   Sheridan Gilley and Ann Loades, 'Thomas Henry Huxley: the War between Science and Religion,' *Journal of Religion* 61 (1981), pp. 285–308; Adrian Desmond, *Huxley: From Devil's Disciple to Evolution's High Priest* (London, 1998), pp. 276–81.

34   Turner, *Contesting Cultural Authority*, p. 170.

35   Ibid., pp. 201–28.

36   See Standish Meacham, *Toynbee Hall* (London, 1987).

37   Hugh McLeod, *Class and Religion in the Late Victorian City* (London, 1974), pp. 252–3.

38   Ibid., pp. 239–42.

39   Raphael Samuel, 'The Discovery of Puritanism, 1820–1914', in Jane Garnett and Colin Matthew (eds), *Revival and Religion Since 1700* (London, 1993), pp. 201–47.

40   See Jeffrey Cox, *English Churches in a Secular Society: Lambeth 1870–1930* (Oxford, 1982), pp. 230–40; McLeod, *Class and Religion*, pp. 239–42 and 254–5.

41   McLeod, *Religion and Society*, pp. 150–5.

42   Peter Bailey, '"A mingled mass of perfectly legitimate pleasures": the Victorian Middle Class and the Problem of Leisure', *Victorian Studies* 21 (1977–8), pp. 7–28.

43   John Lowerson, *Sport and the English Middle Classes 1870–1914* (Manchester, 1993), pp. 271–2.

44   Henry Downes Miles, *Pugilistica: The History of British Boxing*, vol. 3 (Edinburgh, 1906), p. 4.

45　David Hilliard, 'Unenglish and Unmanly: Anglo-Catholicism and Homosexuality,' *Victorian Studies* 25 (1981–2), pp. 181–210.

46　Norman Vance, *The Sinews of the Spirit* (Cambridge, 1985).

47　Rose, 'Locality, Politics and Culture', pp. 266–9; see also McLeod, *Piety and Poverty*, Chapter 7.

48　*Punch*, 3 March 1855.

49　Samuel Butler, *The Way of all Flesh* (Harmondsworth, 1966) (first published 1903), p. 94.

50　Booth Collection, B231, pp. 63–5; B221, p. 195.

51　Ibid., B284, pp. 19–21, 43.

52　*Punch*, 26 March 1870.

53　George Eliot, *Scenes from Clerical Life* (Harmondsworth, 1973) (first published 1858), p. 275.

54　This was one of the themes of George Eliot's story 'Janet's Repentance' in ibid. It was also one of the favoured themes of *Punch* cartoonists: see, for example, *Punch*, 10 November 1866 and 6 November 1880.

55　Ibid., 24 February 1866.

56　Ibid., 3 November 1866.

57　Ibid., 22 December 1866.

58　Ibid., 22 December 1860.

59　Ibid., 3 April 1880.

60　Ibid., 1 May 1880.

61　Ibid., 17 January and 26 June 1880.

62　Ibid., 25 May 1910. See also two cartoons on 8 June 1910.

63　For different versions of the vicar's wife, see ibid., 12 and 26 October 1910.

64　For example, 19 October, 16 November and 21 December 1910.

65　For French anticlerical invective, see Jacqueline Lalouette, *La Libre Pensée en France 1848–1940* (Paris, 1997), pp. 245–50; René Rémond, *L'anti-cléricalisme en France de 1815 à nos jours* (Paris, 1976), pp. 190–1. For an overview of the French clergy in this period, see Ralph Gibson, *A Social History of French Catholicism 1789–1914* (London, 1989), Chapters 3–4. An excellent local study is Philippe Boutry, *Prêtres et paroisses au pays du curé d'Ars* (Paris, 1986).

66　Evans 'The Church in Danger?', pp. 219–20.

67　One of the best-balanced discussions of these themes is Bartlett, 'The Churches in Bermondsey'; Frances Knight, *The Nineteenth-century Church and English Society* (Cambridge 1995), is good on both laity and clergy, but has less discussion of the relationship between them; see also Williams, *Religious Belief and Popular Culture in Southwark*, which provides interesting new perspectives on working-class attitudes, using oral history.

FURTHER READING

Cox, Jeffrey, *English Churches in a Secular Society: Lambeth 1870–1930* (Oxford, 1982).

McLeod, Hugh, *Class and Religion in the late Victorian City* (London, 1974).

Piety and Poverty: Working Class Religion in Berlin, London and New York, 1870–1914 (New York, 1996).

Religion and Society in England, 1850–1914 (Basingstoke, 1996).

Russell, Anthony, *The Clerical Profession* (London, 1980).

INDEX

Act of Toleration, 68–9

Act of Uniformity, 61

agnosticism, 207

alcohol, 176 n.34, 196 n.54, 209

America, 68, 80–5, 86, 99, 105, 120

Annals of the Parish (1821), 146

anticlericalism:

    and friars, 3–4

    aristocratic, 128, 172–3

    Conservative, 185–8, 203

    definitions, xi–xx, 1–2, 49, 67, 93, 109, 201

    dissenting, 68–92, 181–4, 204–6

    in rural areas, xiii–xiv, 159–78, 201–2,
        209–11

    in urban areas, xiv, 167–8, 202

    liberal, 206

    priestcraft, 69, 77, 93, 96, 127

    radical, 50, 68–92, 129, 181–4, 202–4

    Whig, 46, 55–6, 63, 70, 97, 99–100, 107,
        118–21, 125

Aston, Nigel, xv–xvi

Atterbury, Francis, 54–5, 62

Aves, Ernest, 207, 211

Bangorian Controversy, 45

Baptists, 68, 99, 180, 191, 205

Barrie, J.M., 152–3

Baxter, Arthur, 199–200, 211

Baxter, Richard, 86

Bennett, Gary, 52–3

Biagini, E., 199, 219 n.26

biblical authority, 9, 12, 77, 84–6, 98

Black, Jeremy, 79

Blackburne, Francis, 81, 94, 96, 98, 100–1, 104,
    117

Booth, Charles, 199, 207, 211

Bourn, Samuel, 78–9

boxing, 208

Bradbury, Thomas, 73–8, 81–3

Bradley, James, xii, 109, 119–20

Bridenbaugh, Carl, 81, 91 n.85

Bright, John, ix

British Association for the Advancement of
    Science, 206–7

Brown, Callum, xiv–xv, xix

burials, 171–2, 189, 190

Butler, Samuel, 209

Cambridge University, 58, 72, 95, 98

Carlile, Richard, xiv, 167–8

Carmarthen, 191–2

Census, religious (1851), 163, 179, 202

Chalmers, Thomas, 154

Champion, Justin, xvii, 85, 87, 94, 116

charities, 7

church rate, 167–8, 182, 190–3

Church of England, 45, 48

    and government, 50, 99–100, 132

    and Monarchy, 105

    and Restoration, 52

    and Rural England, 159–78, 198, 201–2

    and urban areas, 202

    Anglo-Catholics, 205–6, 208–9, 212–14,
        216

    associations with popery, 74–9, 123–4

    authority within, 82, 123

    Book of Common Prayer, 48

    character of, 122

    disestablishment, 86, 168, 187

    hostility towards, 74, 169

    pastoral effectiveness, 130–1

    Ritualism, 205

Sacraments, 9, 74
Thirty-Nine articles of, 48, 71, 98, 100–1,
    117, 124, 126
wealth, 6, 116
Civil War, 78
Clark, J.C.D., xii, 48, 62
clergy:
bishops and, 118, 127
celibacy, 4–5, 19–22, 168, 209, 216
character of clerical office, 11, 29, 36–7,
    43–4, 46–7, 52, 57, 97–8, 126–7
curates, 24, 136 n.71, 177 n.64, 188
effigies of, 176 n.46, 193
incompetence of, 10, 50, 74, 183–4
intellectual pre-eminence of, 21, 23, 122,
    206–7
Ireland, 132
Jacobitism and, 97, 118, 120
Magistrates, 34–5, 69, 107, 127–8, 162, 166,
    180, 201
manliness, 144, 153, 208–10, 214
monarchy and, 43–4
Nonjurors, 117
parishioners and, xvii, 2, 5, 18–37, 44, 116,
    128–30, 139–43, 179, 188–93, 219 n.27
politics, 42–3, 48, 53–4, 60–1, 180, 184–8,
    216
profession, 46–7, 126, 159, 206
relations with dissent, 108, 183
science and, 206–7
Scotland, 120
social status, xiii, 6, 18–19, 23, 27–30, 34, 60,
    103, 159–60, 168, 203–4, 216
superstition and, 196 n.32
training, 12, 205
tyranny of, 59–60, 69, 183–4, 191, 205
violence against, 19, 163–7, 188
Wales, 20, 180–4, 188–9, 192–4
wealth, xv, 5, 19, 49–50, 103, 108, 128–30,
    140–1, 168, 170–1
wives and, 28, 35
Cobbett, William, 168–9

Commonwealth, 87
Congregationalists, 68, 73, 114 n.82, 180,
    205
Convocation, 45, 54–5, 62, 97, 122
Canterbury, 45, 69, 115
York, 115
Conybeare, W.J., 170
Cragoe, Matthew, xiv–xv, xix
Crockett, S.R., 150–1

Dale, R.W., 205
Darwinism, 207
Defoe, 54, 69, 73, 76
Deists, 51, 87
Denning, Revd James (Brecon), 181
Dickens, A.G., 49
Ditchfield, Grayson, xii, xvii, xix
Duffy, Eamonn, xviii
Dunbabin, J.P. (historian), 193

education, 6–7
clergy and, 109, 174 n.1
Dissenting Academies, 69, 72–3, 188
elementary, 147, 189, 190
higher, 206
in Scotland, 147, 151
Eliot, George, 211
enclosure, 128, 159, 162, 165, 180
Enlightenment, 51, 115, 206
Evans, Eric, xiv, 107, 109, 160–7, 73–4, 180,
    198–9, 216
Evans Judgement (1767), 103

Feathers Tavern petition, 99, 101, 114
Fitzpatrick, Martin, 96, 98
Foucault, M., 143
Fox, Charles James, 100
Foxe, John, 4
France, x, xi, 93, 214–15
Gallican Church, 105, 115–16, 130
revolution, xvi, 86, 93, 101, 107, 121, 130
Frend, William, 96, 101, 105

Galt, John, 146
Galton, Francis, 207
George III, 105, 120, 122
Glorious Revolution, 43, 45, 68
Goldie, Mark, 118
Griffiths, Revd John, 181–2
Gwynedd, Ieuan, 181

Haigh, Christopher, xvi, xviii, 1–2, 5, 8, 49
Hampden, John, 43
Harling, Philip, 169
Harvey, Sir George, 154
Haydon, Colin, 104
Henry VIII, 11–14
heresy, 8
Higgins, Ian, 118
Hill, Christopher, 50
Hoadly, Bishop Benjamin, xvii, 44–7, 60, 63, 71,
     74, 95–6, 98, 120
Hobbes, Thomas, 46, 49–50
Hollis, Thomas, 94–5, 99, 102, 104
Holmes, Geoffrey, 70
Horne Revd George, Dean of Canterbury, 121
Horsley, Bishop Samuel, 121–2
Hughes Hugh, artist, 181
Hughes, Thomas, 209
Huxley, Thomas, 206

Independent Labour Party, 203
Ireland, xi, xv, 107, 121, 130, 132, 184–8

Jacobites, 56, 62, 69, 73
Johnson, Samuel, 42–3, 46–7
Joyce, Patrick, 144

Kingsley, Charles, 209
Knight, Frances, xiii–xv, xvii, xviii

Latitudinarianism, 97–8
literature 69, 123
  biographies, 146–50
  'Honest Whigs', 99

in Scotland, 143–54
  novels, 150
Loades, David, xii–iii, xviii, xix
Lollards, 7–8
London, 1, 8, 43, 56, 58, 61, 70, 79, 83, 144,
     168, 184, 190, 199–200, 207, 211–13

McCalman, Iain, 107
Macgowan, John, 83–4
Maclaren, Iain, 150–2
McLeod, Hugh, xiv, xvii
Methodists, 109, 161, 205
  Calvinistic, 186–8
  Independent, 204
monarchy, 2, 45, 89 n.44
  Restoration, 51
monasteries, 2–4, 6, 12–13, 15 n.13, 116
Montagu, Richard, 31–2
Morgan, George Osborne, 189–90
Morrill, J., 50
Murray, James, 82

Nelson, Robert, 47–8
Newcastle, Duke of, 97, 119
New Poor Law (1834), 167, 189
Nonconformist ministers:
  and alcohol, 208
  and politics, 184–8
  threats of coercion, 186–8
Nonconformity, 67–92, 180–4
Nottinghamshire, 209

Obelkevich, James, 172
Occasional Conformity, 55, 69–70, 73, 118
Oldham, 163
Owen, Charles, 78
Oxford Movement, 121, 131, 173, 205
Oxford University, 55, 58, 72, 83, 97, 118,
     125–6, 206, 208

Paine, Thomas, 106
painting, 154

caricatures, 132
cartoons, 181–2
prints, 46, 53
Paley, William, 101
Palmer, Samuel, 72
parish, 139–43
Pestell, Thomas, 36–7
pew rents, 141
Phillips, John, historian, 108
Phillips, Revd John (Bangor), 189
Porteus, Bishop Beilby, 131
Presbyterian Ministers, 138–55
Presbyterians, 68, 115, 139
Priestley, Joseph, 84, 94, 102, 107, 120–1
print, 7, 139, 167–70
Pugh, Revd J., 181–2
Punch, 208

Quakers, 76, 80, 107, 115, 136 n.61, 204

Rational Dissent, 102–7
Rees, Revd Henry, 189–90
Rees, Revd Thomas, 179, 182–3, 189
Reformation, xviii, 1–2, 8, 12–13, 10
Reform Bill, 162, 166, 176 n.46, 180,
    198
Republicanism, 44, 46, 87, 104–6, 168
Richard, Henry, 182–4, 193
Riots:
    Gordon Riots, 63
    Littleport and Ely riots, 163–4
    Rebecca Riots, 188
    Sacheverell, 58, 66 n.84
    Swing Riots, 166
Robbins, Caroline, 98, 101
Roman Catholicism, xv, 11, 53, 79–80, 109, 118,
    121, 206
    anti-Catholicism, 67–92, 96, 104, 200–1
    clergy, 194, 201, 211
Root and Branch Petition (1640), 35
Royal Commission on Education (1847), 180–4,
    186

Sacheverell, Henry, 44, 54, 55–63, 69–70, 72–3,
    84, 103, 119, 123
Salvation Army, 204–5
Scotland, xvi, 85, 99, 115, 120–1, 138–58
    Church of Scotland, xv, 99, 103, 127, 130,
        142–3
    Relief Church, 143–5
    Secession Church, 143–5
Secker, Archbishop Thomas, 102, 122–3
Selden, John, 31–2, 35
Sharp, Richard, 120
Sherlock, Bishop Thomas, 120, 126–7
Shipley, Stan, 200
Smith, Mark, xv, 163
Socialism, 202–3
song, 193–4
SPCK, 125
sport, 208
Spurr, John, 52
Statistical Account, The (1790–8), 145
Stuarts, 118
Sullivan, Robert E., 125
superstition, 9, 77, 196 n.32
Swift, Jonathan, 58, 124

Taylor, Stephen, 98, 110 n.18
Test & Corporation Acts, 61, 85–6, 100, 103,
    105, 107–8
Thatcher, Margaret, 203
Thompson, Paul, 200
Tindal, Matthew, 58
tithes, xiii, xv–xvii, 5, 25, 27, 30–6, 48–50, 100,
    107–8, 115, 119, 128, 159, 161–2, 166–9,
    193–4
    teinds, 140–1
Toland, John, 51–2, 58–61
Tories, 53, 69
    and Jacobitism 69
Towgood, Micaiah, 84–5
Toynbee Hall, 207
Trenchard, John, 51, 71, 81
Tressell, Robert, 203

Turner, Frank, 207
Tyneside, 204

Unitarians, 84, 94–5, 101–3, 107, 120–1, 205

Victoria, Queen, ix
Virgin, Peter, 162, 170
Voltaire, 116

Wade, John, 169–70
Wakefield, Gilbert, 96, 106

Wales, xii, xiv–xvii, xix, 179–97
Walkowitz, Judith, 144
Walpole, Horace, 104, 119, 126
Walpole, Sir Robert, 56–7, 63, 119
Warburton, Bishop William, of Gloucester, 82–3
Wells, Roger, 166–7
Wesley, Samuel, 72–3, 132
Wilberforce, Samuel, 207
Wycliffe, John, 7–8
Wyvill, Christopher, 104, 107